MEXICO 1994
ANATOMY OF AN EMERGING-MARKET CRASH

SEBASTIAN EDWARDS AND MOISÉS NAÍM, EDITORS

ROBERT L. BARTLEY, NANCY BIRDSALL,
SHAHID JAVED BURKI, AGUSTÍN CARSTENS,
RUDI DORNBUSCH, DENISE DRESSER,
JEFFRY A. FRIEDEN, MICHAEL GAVIN,
FRANCISCO GIL-DÍAZ, DAVID D. HALE,
RICARDO HAUSMANN, CLAUDIO M. LOSER,
PETER H. SMITH, AND EWART S. WILLIAMS

CARNEGIE ENDOWMENT FOR INTERNATIONAL PEACE

Mexico 1994: Anatomy of an Emerging-Market Crash
may be ordered ($22.95) from Carnegie's distributor,
Brookings Institution Press, Department 029,
Washington, D.C. 20042-0029, USA.
Tel. 1-800-275-1447 or 202-797-6258.
Fax. 202-797-6004. E-mail: bibooks@brook.edu

Design by Paddy McLaughlin Concepts & Design.
Printed by Automated Graphic Systems.

Library of Congress Cataloging-in-Publication Data

Mexico 1994: anatomy of an emerging-market crash / Sebastian Edwards
and Moisés Naím, editors.
p.   cm.
Carnegie Endowment for International Peace.
Includes bibliographical references.
ISBN 0-87003-154-6
1. Financial Crises—Mexico.   2. Mexico—Economic policy—1994-
3. Mexico—Economic conditions—1994-   4. Monetary policy—Mexico.
5. Devaluation of currency—Mexico.   I. Edwards, Sebastian   II. Naím,
Moisés, 1953-
HC135.M52787   1998   97-51274
332'.0972'09049—dc21   CIP

CONTENTS

Acknowledgments   v

INTRODUCTION: ANATOMY AND LESSONS OF MEXICO 1994   1
Sebastian Edwards and Moisés Naím

1. POLITICAL DIMENSIONS OF THE PESO CRISIS   31
Peter H. Smith

2. FALLING FROM THE TIGHTROPE: THE POLITICAL
ECONOMY OF THE MEXICAN CRISIS   55
Denise Dresser

3. THE POLITICS OF EXCHANGE RATES   81
Jeffry A. Frieden

4. BAD LUCK OR BAD POLICIES?
AN ECONOMIC ANALYSIS OF THE CRISIS   95
Sebastian Edwards

5. THE FOLLY, THE CRASH, AND BEYOND:
ECONOMIC POLICIES AND THE CRISIS   125
Rudi Dornbusch

6. THE PESO FOLKLÓRICO: DANCING AWAY
FROM MONETARY STABILITY   141
Robert L. Bartley

7. PRIDE AND PREJUDICE: THE ECONOMICS
PROFESSION AND MEXICO'S FINANCIAL CRISIS   165
Francisco Gil-Díaz and Agustín Carstens

8. THE MARKETS AND MEXICO: THE SUPPLY-SIDE STORY   201
David D. Hale

9. A FATE FORETOLD: THE WORLD BANK
AND THE MEXICAN CRISIS   247
Shahid Javed Burki

10. **THE MEXICAN CRISIS AND ITS AFTERMATH:**
    AN IMF PERSPECTIVE   **259**
    Claudio M. Loser and Ewart S. Williams

11. **GETTING THE LESSONS RIGHT: A VIEW FROM**
    THE INTER-AMERICAN DEVELOPMENT BANK   **275**
    Nancy Birdsall, Michael Gavin, and Ricardo Hausmann

12. **MEXICO'S LARGER STORY**   **295**
    Moisés Naím

APPENDIX. MEXICO: A CHRONOLOGY OF FINANCIAL,
           ECONOMIC, AND POLITICAL EVENTS   **313**

About the Authors   321

Carnegie Endowment for International Peace   325

ACKNOWLEDGMENTS

An edited book is, by definition, a collective enterprise, and this one is no exception. The distinguished group of authors that accepted our invitation to participate in the book contributed much more than their chapters. They also displayed an uncommonly generous tolerance for the changes we suggested and the delays the project experienced.

This book would not have been possible without the material support of the World Bank and the Carnegie Endowment for International Peace. At the World Bank, Shahid Javed Burki, the Vice-President for Latin America and the Caribbean, imagined this book together with us, and, throughout its preparation, supported us with the sound advice and guidance for which he is so well known among his friends and colleagues. The enthusiasm shown by Morton Abramowitz, the President of the Carnegie Endowment at the time the project was launched, was an important pillar on which we rested. We were fortunate that Jessica Mathews, who succeeded Abramowitz as President of the Endowment, not only shared his enthusiasm but also provided much-needed support during the critical last stages.

Many talented individuals helped us in the coordination and production of this book. Without Valeriana Kallab's professional and effective guidance through the final editorial and production stages, the book would have taken much longer to get published. We are especially grateful to Anthony Ody for his invaluable role, and to Judith Evans, who also worked very hard to make this book happen. Jennifer Abner was able to keep a clear perspective about the flow of papers, diskettes, graphs, and charts across countries, cities, and institutions. Jennifer Stanley, Maria Sherzad, and Sherry Pettie patiently and attentively handled the copy editing and manuscript production. To all of them our lasting gratitude.

Sebastian Edwards and Moisés Naím
December 1997

MEXICO 1994
ANATOMY OF AN EMERGING-MARKET CRASH

INTRODUCTION: ANATOMY AND LESSONS OF MEXICO 1994

SEBASTIAN EDWARDS AND MOISÉS NAÍM*

The late Chinese premier, Zhou Enlai, was reportedly once asked what he considered the most important consequences of the French Revolution. "Too soon to tell" was the reply. Zhou's comment has sometimes been quoted as if it provided a paradoxical example of supposed Chinese inscrutability. However, to anyone who recognizes communism itself as one of the children of 1789, Zhou's comment seems almost eerily prescient: an informed answer to the question Zhou faced would indeed be significantly different today from the response that would have been given ten or twenty years ago.

Writing in the closing days of 1997, it is tempting to answer questions about the interpretation of the Mexican financial, economic, and political crisis of 1994-95 with the same words that were used by Zhou Enlai. At one level, it is indeed too soon. Developments in Mexico and elsewhere that were set in train or influenced by the crisis are still unfolding; dilemmas that the crisis posed are still unresolved. On the domestic political side, for example, the ongoing process of change in Mexico has produced for the first time in living memory both a Mexican Congress no longer controlled by the governing party (that generated unprecedented debate over the administration's proposed budget) and the first elected mayor of Mexico City (who happens to be the ruling party's most celebrated critic on the Left). On the economic and financial side as well, Mexico is still digesting changes put into motion as a consequence of the events of 1994-95, including, for example, attempts to fundamentally transform the country's previously sheltered and opaque banking industry. Further south, the political system of Argentina is

* We are extremely grateful to Anthony Ody for his assistance in preparing this introduction. If it weren't for his legendary modesty, his name would be with ours as a co-author.

1

wrestling with proposals for the reform of labor markets that might not be so high on the agenda (or might not have taken the same form) had the Argentine peso not come under attack as a result of "contagion" from Mexico—an attack resisted successfully, but at the cost of an upsurge in open unemployment that the authorities are still seeking to address effectively.

The catalog of open issues could be expanded. Who can say with confidence, for example, how lasting a role the peso crisis may have played in fanning doubts within the United States concerning not only NAFTA specifically but even the broader processes of trade liberalization and integration—doubts that have crippled the Clinton administration's efforts to renew the President's trade negotiating authority? On another front, the rescue package for Mexico, which was hurriedly improvised by U.S. and international officials in the early days of 1995, broke or at least stretched a number of the rules and conventions previously thought to govern international financial dealings and institutions, thereby casting doubt on the adequacy of the old arrangements. Yet as we watch another major crisis unfolding today in East Asia, we see the same frantic signs that the rules are being made up from day to day, and that the world economic community has yet to address systematically the dilemmas that new-style crises pose for its systems of governance.

For one of the things that does already seem clear is that Mexico was the first of a new style of crisis. This recognition has been expressed in different ways. The Managing Director of the International Monetary Fund, Michel Camdessus, reportedly described Mexico as "the first crisis of the twenty-first century." David D. Hale, commenting in this volume on the role that unprecedented private capital mobility played in the origins and unfolding of the events in Mexico, writes of "the first crisis of the post–Cold War boom in securitized capital flows." In launching the present exercise, we were ourselves convinced that Camdessus and Hale were right in singling out Mexico as a unique event that also serves as a harbinger of larger changes—and that, as such, deserves the effort at understanding implied by a book-length analysis. We were also convinced (in spite of Zhou Enlai's implied warning) that, even if it is too soon for a *definitive* account of the Mexican crisis, there is value in attempting a review—based on the considered perspectives and insights of a diverse range of well-informed observers and participants—focusing primarily on distilling immediate lessons for policy design and implementation. Our objective has been to write a book about Mexico, yet not only about Mexico. The book may be regarded as a case study of how, in contemporary circumstances, national policy-making can become intimately interwoven not only with domestic political considerations but also with the pressures and mandates of capital markets operating on a global scale.

Understanding the way events unfolded in Mexico during the early 1990s continues to be fundamentally important to assessing the mechanics of currency crises. More important, perhaps, the eruption of the East Asian currency crises in the summer and fall of 1997 has raised the question of whether the lessons from Mexico have indeed been learned by policy-makers, private-sector analysts, and international civil servants. More specifically, as a result of the recent events in East Asia, many observers have argued that the international financial organizations—the IMF and the World Bank—and the governments of the advanced countries have failed to revamp the early warning system that was supposed to prevent a repetition of a Mexico-style crisis.[1]

Despite the proliferation of post mortems on the Mexican crisis, there are still a number of unresolved issues. These include: Should perceptive Wall Street analysts have known that things were getting out of hand? And if they did, why didn't they alert their clients? How much did officials at the U.S. Treasury know about the depth of the Mexican problems? What was the role of the media? Did Mexico's unique political system influence the way in which economic policy was handled in the months preceding the crisis?

The present volume had its genesis in a meeting held at the Carnegie Endowment for International Peace in Washington, D.C., a year and a half after the peso collapse, at which earlier drafts of the papers now included as chapters in the book were presented and debated. Our authors come, as their biographies indicate (see pp. 321-24), from a range of different disciplines and backgrounds. As individuals, they all bring credentials to the table that entitle them to be heard on this subject; as a group, we hope that the diversity of their training and experience, not to mention their sometimes strong differences in beliefs and interpretations, will be recognized as making the whole greater than the sum of its parts. We ourselves have expressed some of our views in the chapters that appear under our names. As editors, we have not attempted to impose any artificial unity of interpretation on our contributors. In this Introduction, we have two purposes. We endeavor to provide the reader with a roadmap to the main ideas expressed in each of the chapters in the book. We then outline—solely from our own perspective—a view of

---

[1] See, for example, the article by Robert Chote in the *Financial Times*, September 19, 1997.

the key lessons that we believe analysis of the Mexican crisis can offer to other countries around the world, including but not limited to those economies in East Asia that today find themselves occupying Mexico's earlier uncomfortable place on the front pages of the world's newspapers.

A GUIDE TO THE BOOK

The book opens with three chapters that examine the Mexican crisis primarily from a *political* perspective.

1. In the first chapter, American political scientist **Peter H. Smith** argues that the policy course of the Mexican leadership that culminated in the peso crisis—although possibly easy to label as irrational from the economist's perspective—for the most part followed a logic of its own when seen from the viewpoint of the political interests of the key players. Smith sees the longer-term political context for the crisis in the gradual fraying of Mexico's authoritarian and corporatist "perfect dictatorship"—as the coalition around the ruling Institutional Revolutionary Party (PRI) fragmented, electoral competition from the two opposition parties increased, and feuds within the political elite intensified. For Smith, political logic explains such otherwise problematic decisions during 1993-94 as forswearing devaluation, easing domestic monetary policy, and rolling over much of Mexico's public debt via the issue of massive quantities of *tesobonos* (Mexican government bonds indexed not to the peso but to the U.S. dollar). While minimizing the likelihood that the PRI might actually have lost the 1994 presidential election to its deeply divided opposition, Smith emphasizes that stability served the goals of: first (during 1993), ensuring the consummation of Mexico's membership in NAFTA; and subsequently, securing for then President Carlos Salinas de Gortari a place in Mexican history (and a hoped-for future as the first Director General of the World Trade Organization), as well as protecting the PRI's overall domination of the domestic political scene and the sources of patronage. The one departure from the logic of political rationality that Smith highlights is the clumsy initial handling by the incoming Zedillo administration of the December 1994 devaluation; and this he ascribes largely to the new team's inexperience in working with the financial markets.

While cautious in attributing longer-term political consequences directly to the peso crisis, Smith does emphasize that the process of internal political change in Mexico is an ongoing one, whose end-point is by no means predetermined. Though further democratization and liberalization constitute one possible path, plausible alternatives could involve a resurgence of authoritarianism, or a process of fragmentation and dispersion of power. If there is a broader political lesson to be learned from his analysis of the Mexican crisis, Smith suggests, it may be that better economic management ultimately requires not just better analysis but changing the political incentives facing policy-makers. Achieving this means further movement in the direction of political opening, electoral competition, and public accountability.

2. For **Denise Dresser**, a Mexican political scientist, the crisis was rooted in "the conflicting imperatives of economic adjustment and political survival." Dresser sees the Salinas administration as presenting two contrasting identities to the world. The first persona stressed the government's commitment to economic liberalization, deregulation, and privatization. In Dresser's view, marketing the Salinas Mexico to external audiences, including both private investors and the Washington establishment, was very successful. The second (contrasting and more inward) incarnation of the regime deployed multiple instruments of patronage and discretionary intervention in seeking political support through the compensation of strategic domestic interest groups, including those that might see themselves as losing out as a result of liberalization. The glue that was designed to hold the two ill-matched twins together was Salinas's own highly personalized style of "hyper-presidentialism." Dresser presents the political rationale that underlay the administration's dualistic approach, which she sees as the need to broaden the base of support for policies of economic liberalization that might, especially in their earlier stages, directly benefit only a quite narrow set of groups in the country (such as export-oriented businesses); from this perspective, the apparent schizophrenia may be interpreted as reflecting the demands of a transition to a hoped-for new political equilibrium.

Yet Dresser places more emphasis on the contradictions between the two policy imperatives. The need to assuage domestic interests, her discussion suggests, compromised the integrity of market reform objectives in such areas as privatization of public monopolies and regulation of the newly privatized banking sector, and it scared the Salinas government away from any serious attempt to reform social security. Inherent stresses within the model were accentuated by its failure to deliver the goods in the shape of significant economic growth. This helped expose the superficiality of the Salinas model's coalition-building potential, which relied more on pay-offs than on the development of mechanisms for dialogue that might have helped construct a more resilient political consensus. In the run-up to the 1994 election, the administration's need to cultivate support resulted in its following the mutually contradictory policies of monetary and fiscal expansion on the one hand, and a fixed exchange rate on the other. Even after the election, the government resisted adjustment, in Dresser's view, primarily out of concern for the vulnerabilities of the domestic banking sector, a key element in the PRI's political coalition.

Looking beyond the crisis, Dresser sees the Zedillo administration as facing a fresh constellation of challenges and contradictions. If Salinas over-politicized adjustment, she argues, what she sees as Zedillo's attempts to de-politicize policy may create risks of their own. With any "trickle-down" benefits for the mass of the population from further economic liberalization still likely to be slow to materialize, at best, it remains an open question whether Zedillo's forswearing of patronage and his more aggressive pursuit of democratic political reforms will represent a sustainable mix or not.

3. Political scientist **Jeffry A. Frieden** focuses on the "domestic politics of exchange rates." He argues at the level of general principle that the exchange rate is a policy variable that is determined *politically*. It is misleading, in this view, to speak of any specific exchange rate as *technically* unsustainable, for at the technical level governments always have alternatives (interest rate hikes, deflation) to devaluation. Thus exchange rate sustainability is more usefully seen as a *political* rather than an economic concept. Both special interests and the broader public can be expected to have a political stake in the level (as well as, separately, the stability or lack thereof) of the exchange rate. Typically, for example, producers of internationally tradable goods (such as exporters) can be expected to favor exchange rate depreciation as being in their own interest. International investors or traders are obviously likely to have a strong preference for a stable exchange rate. The preferences of the population as a whole may be somewhat harder to predict *a priori*. If unemployment and slow growth are viewed as the alternatives to devaluation, then public sentiment may be expected to prefer depreciation, with its assumed accompaniment of growth. On the other hand, public opinion may also attach importance to the price stability associated with adhering to a stable exchange rate as well as to the inexpensive imported consumer goods that result from an overvalued domestic currency.

In his application of this approach to Mexico, Frieden presents the PRI as unable, in an election year, to afford the political costs of a devaluation, primarily due to its likely adverse impact on politically crucial middle-class and lower-middle-class consumers. The government's hands were further tied by its own prior actions in linking its policy credibility to nominal exchange rate stability. However, the option of engineering a gradual and relatively mild deflationary adjustment became compromised by the political shocks of 1994, including the March assassination of PRI presidential candidate Luis Donaldo Colosio and the September murder of José Francisco Ruíz Massieu, the Secretary General of the PRI. The evidence that the shocks and associated elite infighting provided of leadership divisions sapped the PRI's credibility with key constituencies—and hence sabotaged the party's capacity to broker an orderly adjustment process.

With the next chapter, the book's focus shifts from the insights of political science to those of the economics profession.

4. At the heart of **Sebastian Edwards**'s analysis is an exploration of the Mexican experience as a case study in the management of an exchange rate–based stabilization program (that is, a plan under which a country chooses to use a more or less fixed nominal exchange rate as an anchor designed to force domestic inflation down to international levels). Edwards sees such programs as inherently liable to induce currency overvaluation, in part because of inertial momentum in domestic inflation after the exchange rate is fixed. He takes the analysis further by relating Mexico to debates on the optimal sequencing of different economic reforms. Most economists, he indicates, have counseled reforming countries to proceed cautiously in liberalizing capital flows into (and out of) the country, introducing this change only gradually and toward the end of their overall reform program. This advice on sequencing (which Mexico departed from, largely completing capital account liberalization as early as 1989) partly reflects concern over the potentially disruptive effect of sudden, large inflows of capital.

Any significant inflow on the capital side must logically be matched, if the overall external accounts are to stay roughly in balance, by a deficit of comparable size on the current account (which mainly reflects trade transactions). To accomplish this current-account gap, in turn, an appreciation of the "real" exchange rate (i.e., the exchange rate adjusted for international differences in inflation) is a logical necessity. The appreciation of the real exchange rate can prove excessive and disruptive if there is, temporarily, significant overshooting in the volume of capital inflows relative to their sustainable, longer-term level. Should overshooting occur, then the trend in the real exchange rate will at some stage have to be put into reverse—meaning a real exchange rate depreciation—in order to engineer the rebound on the current account required to offset the slowdown in capital inflows. Edwards's analysis implies that a real depreciation was bound to come sooner or later: however, the Mexican authorities, with their insistence on sticking to a nominal exchange rate anchor, deprived themselves of the preferred policy instrument for implementing real depreciation in an orderly manner.

Against this stylized background, Edwards examines some of the missteps and misunderstandings that led to the crisis. In defending their policy approach at the time, the Mexican authorities emphasized the safety margin afforded by an initial undervaluation of the currency, a degree of flexibility in the exchange rate anchor, and a large cushion of foreign exchange reserves. Crucially, they seem to have remained convinced that a surge in productivity—in response to their reforms and Mexico's 1993 entry into NAFTA—was imminent, and that the resulting boost for competitiveness would take care of any problems on the external side. Relatively few outside observers challenged the prevailing optimism at the time—a rare exception being Dornbusch, who in early 1994 pointed to the dangers posed by a peso overvaluation that he estimated at about 30 percent. Edwards traces the succession of political shocks and policy improvisations of the election year itself, including the relaxation of previously tight monetary and fiscal policies and the government's decision to refinance its own debt largely through the dollar-indexed *tesobonos*. The account continues with the Salinas administration's refusal to devalue the peso after the election (which Edwards, like Dresser, attributes primarily to concerns over the fragility of the domestic banking system), the initially mis-handled devaluation, the rescue package, and the road back to the restoration of confidence. Summing up, the key lesson of the crisis for Edwards is that exchange rate rigidity is no shortcut—either to price stability or to healthy economic growth.

5. Economist **Rudi Dornbusch** presents the 1994 crisis as the latest in a long line of financial bubbles in which overeager investors have fed the appetites of irresponsible borrowers. Like Edwards, he sees the increasing overvaluation of the peso in the pre-crisis period as the key to the story, together with what he considers the Salinas administration's "obsessive preoccupation" with inflation (and hence with nominal exchange rate stability). Comparing U.S. and Mexican inflation at the wholesale price level (to avoid distortionary effects at the consumer price level), Dornbusch detects a pre-crisis real exchange rate appreciation of over 45 percent, which he suggests implies an overvaluation of at least 25 percent. Arguing that, in the early 1990s, aggregate Mexican output could hardly keep up with labor force growth, Dornbusch challenges the reliability of Mexican estimates of manufacturing productivity and labor competitiveness, which have been used (by, among others, Gil-Díaz and Carstens in the present volume) to minimize the extent and significance of exchange rate appreciation in the pre-crisis period. The point is not, Dornbusch emphasizes, that the Salinas reforms as a whole had no substance or merit, but instead that the central error in exchange rate policy constrained the realization of the benefits from generally sound reforms. Once the chance had been missed to devalue in an orderly manner well ahead of the election, the authorities found themselves in a desperate game to buy time, resorting to such expedients as the *tesobono* bonanza and a domestic credit boom.

For Dornbusch, Argentina and Chile hold up revealing mirrors to the Mexican experience. He sees Argentina's high unemployment rates since 1994 as additional confirmation of the difficulty of achieving real depreciation under a fixed exchange rate, especially when domestic labor markets are comparatively rigid. In Chile's extended period of real income growth, by contrast, he sees benefits to be gained from a more gradualist approach to reducing already moderate inflation rates, accompanied by the flexibility he advocates in nominal exchange rate policy.

6. In his chapter, *Wall Street Journal* editor **Robert L. Bartley** takes issue with the Edwards-Dornbusch view of the crisis from the vantage point of a confirmed skeptic of the merits of exchange rate flexibility. For those like himself who believe that the world economy is consummately integrated, he writes, devaluations are not merely folly but themselves shocks likely to disrupt real growth. Part of the promise of the Salinas administration, in Bartley's view, lay precisely in the possibility it seemed to offer of escaping the almost choreographed cycle of boom, bust, and devaluation that had characterized the previous three presidential terms. Even well into the final year of Salinas's administration, Bartley argues, Mexico did not look like a country doomed to devalue: inflation was down to 8 percent, external debt had been halved and was moderate by OECD standards, the fiscal accounts were in balance, and exports were growing rapidly. The current-account deficit that causes Dornbusch and Edwards so much concern seems to Bartley plausibly interpreted as the logical obverse to an inward investment boom sparked by enthusiasm over Mexico's post-NAFTA prospects. Over the course of 1994, however, serious errors were made in monetary policy. If Mexico was serious in defending its fixed exchange rate with the U.S. dollar, its policy-makers needed sooner or later to recognize that their monetary policy would have to follow that of the U.S. Federal Reserve Bank. Instead, the Bank of Mexico followed a policy of sterilization of reserve losses that, in Bartley's words, lay "at the heart of the crisis"—while the government upped the ante by converting much of its own debt into dollar-indexed *tesobonos*.

Bartley differs with other commentators in this volume on the eventual inevitability of the devaluation. As late as December 19, 1994, he argues, the authorities could still have chosen the alternative of a sharp tightening of monetary policy to defend the parity (the ensuing high interest rates would of course have put pressure on the domestic economy, but it is not self-evident that the pain would have been any worse than what followed the devaluation anyway). Better still, for Bartley, would have been the institutionalization of the exchange rate anchor through a currency board arrangement, such as Argentina's Convertibility Plan, which guarantees the convertibility of the domestic currency into U.S. dollars at a fixed rate, and which Bartley presents as producing better results in terms of growth, stability, and political acceptance than the Mexican alternative of devaluation.

7. **Francisco Gil-Díaz** and **Agustín Carstens**, writing from their perspective at the Bank of Mexico, subject the analyses of the crisis published by many economists outside Mexico, including some of those in the present volume, to critical scrutiny. Questioning the thesis of peso overvaluation in the pre-crisis period, they point out that—if consumer prices are employed as the indicators of differential inflation—real currency appreciation over the period 1987-94 was only in the 34-39 percent range, which they consider neither unnatural nor excessive, given the efficiency-increasing reforms under way during this period. If relative labor costs are taken as the inflation indicator, which Gil-Díaz and Carstens argue is more meaningful, the real appreciation becomes almost insignificant. As further evidence, they describe Mexico's export growth as "without parallel even among the legendary Asian tigers" and point to overall export growth of more than 17 percent during 1994, when overvaluation should presumably have been at its peak. Gil-Díaz and Carstens would, in addition, modify the picture some authors have painted of sluggish growth in GDP and productivity in Mexico during the early 1990s. A recent updating of sectoral weights in the calculation of GDP, they report, has raised estimated GDP growth for 1989-94 to over 3.9 percent a year; they suggest the expansion would have been still stronger had not uncertainties over NAFTA ratification during 1993 led many in the private sector to postpone planned investments in Mexico.

Gil-Díaz and Carstens also take issue with claims that monetary policy was unduly lax during the pre-crisis period. They point out that the average expansion in the money supply during 1994 (as measured by M1) was only 12 percent, identical to growth in nominal GDP, while the average inter-bank interest rate never fell, after April 1994, below 10 percentage points above LIBOR. Defending the central bank's policy of sterilizing losses in foreign exchange reserves during 1994, the authors contend that the policy's critics are themselves divided over whether a more aggressively restrictive policy would have averted the crisis or sparked economic collapse. In any case, they argue, Mexico's monetary institutions allowed little choice in this regard, as they "were not designed to fight off a speculative attack through sudden quantitative adjustments in credit, nor could they have been adapted overnight." Gil-Díaz and Carstens minimize the extent of any pre-crisis stimulus to the economy from the fiscal accounts, which in the period under review never recorded a deficit of any consequence. They challenge published suggestions that the absolute *level* of Mexican savings rates in the early 1990s was unusually low by international standards. They also raise questions about the extent (as well as the interpretation) of the *decline* in savings rates, which some analysts have portrayed as an important pre-crisis source of vulnerability. The authors deny claims that the publication of data on foreign exchange reserves was arbitrarily delayed during 1994, and they challenge assertions that Mexican nationals benefited from preferential access to information to bail out of pesos ahead of the devaluation.

The authors' own interpretation of the crisis presents Mexico in 1994 as a country that was pursuing an essentially sound reform program but was knocked off course by speculative attacks prompted by the year's remarkable series of political shocks. Given the volume of funds now at play in international markets, they maintain, no government has the resources to resist such a full-blown speculative attack on a fixed exchange rate. At the same time, Gil-Díaz and Carstens do accept that certain aspects of Mexico's policy design may have accentuated the country's vulnerability. They point in particular to serious defects in the financial sector regulatory framework within which many of the Mexican banks had been privatized, including weak supervisory capacity, inadequate accounting standards, failure to enforce appropriate levels of capital adequacy, and problems of "moral hazard" created by indiscriminate government guarantees of bank deposits. Alongside the fragile private banking sector, development banks still in public ownership were responsible for an increasing volume of credit (rising over 1990-94 from 1.0 percent of GDP to 3.7 percent). Changes in accounting conventions removed these flows from the published fiscal deficit, the authors report, and at least half of the development banks' loans could have been considered unsound even in the absence of the subsequent crisis.

8. **David D. Hale,** writing from the perspective of a senior advisor to international money managers, characterizes the Mexican debacle as the first major crisis of the post–Cold War surge in securitized capital flows to the developing countries now known as "emerging markets." No developing country, he writes, had depended so heavily on securitized flows to finance a large external deficit since before World War I. Hale illustrates the growth—in the United States and other industrial nations—in the volume of private savings managed by institutions such as pension plans and mutual funds. Institutional and personal investors' appetite for returns makes them potentially receptive to new sources of high-yielding investments such as "junk bonds" and, subsequently, emerging markets—a tendency probably encouraged by the drop in U.S. domestic interest rates in the early 1990s. Mexico was able to capitalize to an exceptional degree on the post–Cold War enthusiasm for emerging markets. This partly reflected adroit marketing of the "Mexican miracle" by President Salinas and his Secretary of Finance, Pedro Aspe, who helped lull most market observers into complacency, but was reinforced by the sales efforts of many Wall Street institutions, which moved Mexican paper (both government and corporate) from a specialized, high-risk market niche toward mainstream investors. The collapse of confidence, when it came, was the more violent for being so largely unexpected. However, though the flow of new foreign money stopped almost instantly, available data do not point to a massive selling of Mexican assets by overseas investors—indeed, several studies identify capital flight by Mexican nationals as responsible for draining the reserves.

Hale considers it possible that the inevitable adjustment could have been engineered with less disruption if Secretary of Finance Aspe had been retained in office by incoming President Ernesto Zedillo rather than replaced by Jaime Serra Puche, who—though prominent as Mexico's chief NAFTA negotiator—was an unknown quantity to most market participants. Hale views the unprecedented post-crisis rescue package for Mexico assembled by the United States and multilateral agencies as defensible *ex ante* and a success *ex post*; the alternative of a default could have interrupted reform and liberalization not only in Mexico but also, via contagion effects, among developing countries more broadly. As it is, Mexico regained access to voluntary financing within a matter of months, and no evidence of reform back-tracking has emerged.

Hale then examines how the global economy can be expected to protect itself against future Mexico 1994–style crises. He takes note of discussions on the possible strengthening of official multilateral defense systems, such as expanding the resources available to the IMF. However, he also indicates the importance of private investors protecting themselves better by a more sophisticated awareness of the risk factors in different emerging markets, including the structure of foreign financial flows, the robustness of the domestic banking sector, and the particular country's approach to monetary and exchange rate policy. Aware foreign investors will also consider the external support likely to be available should a country get into difficulties and will keep an eye open for danger signals raised by the behavior of the (often better informed) *domestic* investor community.

The book continues with a group of chapters presenting the perspectives of senior officials from three multilateral financial organizations closely associated with Mexico before, during, and since the crisis.

9. The chapter contributed by **Shahid Javed Burki**, World Bank Vice President for Latin America and the Caribbean, concentrates primarily on the policy dialogue between the World Bank and the Mexican authorities in the three years preceding the peso's fall. Burki's central thesis concerns the dilemma faced by official multilateral agencies like the World Bank when they perceive a member country following a high-risk or unsustainable strategy, but are unable through quiet diplomacy to persuade the authorities concerned to change course. Burki argues that World Bank analysts appropriately identified the key issues for Mexican macroeconomic policy over the period 1992-94, including overdependence on potentially volatile capital flows, a sharp decline in domestic savings, mounting risks in the banking sector, and the central need for a change in exchange rate policy (though he concedes the institution was slow to recognize the significance of some of the policy shifts that occurred during 1994, including the *tesobono* explosion). The Bank presented its analysis and concerns to the Mexican authorities on multiple occasions, and at the highest levels, but while the government accepted some of the less controversial points (such as the need to strengthen supervision in the financial sector), the Bank's message on the exchange rate was firmly rejected.

What should be the public stance of an agency like the World Bank in such a situation? asks Burki. Bank officials know that, if they go public with the full extent of their concerns, they may themselves precipitate an immediate crisis. Yet an excessively uncritical show of public support can be criticized as potentially misleading to private investors. As it was, Burki reports, the World Bank followed a compromise course in which many of its public statements, while emphasizing Mexico's genuine achievements, alluded to the agency's concerns only in more guarded tones than those used in private with government leaders. Burki sees no obvious alternative to this approach of "speaking with two voices." He argues that agencies like the World Bank are accountable for the quality of the advice they provide to their members (and their public statements should not mislead), but that the multilaterals cannot realistically be expected to ensure that their clients will always accept the advice they give.

10. Complementing Burki's account, the chapter by **Claudio M. Loser** and **Ewart S. Williams** of the IMF's Western Hemisphere Department concentrates primarily on the response to and aftermath of the crisis. When the crisis broke, the authors report, some commentators advocated a unilateral suspension of debt payments, which could have been highly disruptive. To their credit, the Mexicans rejected this advice and instead adopted a tough, market-based stabilization program designed in close consultation with the IMF and supported by a large-scale international financial rescue package in which the Fund also played a major role. The adjustment program included a substantial tightening of fiscal and monetary policies, consistent with slashing the current-account deficit to around 1 percent of GDP in 1995. Special safeguards were adopted to allow the banking system time to restructure in an orderly manner and to mitigate the effects of the austerity program on the poor (including protection of basic education and health spending, and emergency employment schemes). In parallel, structural reforms like deregulation and privatization were to be advanced further. The authors discuss the international efforts that assembled an unprecedented financing package of over $40 billion to support Mexico's adjustment. The IMF's own contribution to the package, close to $18 billion, constituted the largest such arrangement in the agency's history. The authors contend that the Fund's action, though not without its critics at the time, was consistent with its Articles of Agreement and played an essential role in helping avoid the disruption that a moratorium could have caused.

Loser and Williams argue that the post-crisis package has achieved remarkable success. The current-account deficit was almost eliminated during 1995; domestic savings shot up; and access to voluntary external financing was rapidly resumed. Though output slumped and inflation surged in the first year of the program, by 1996 and 1997 GDP growth was running at healthy levels of 5-6 percent, and inflation was coming down as planned. The authors see the lessons of the crisis for policy-makers as centering on the necessity of combining economic openness with policy discipline, including avoiding large current-account deficits. The IMF itself, they add, has absorbed the need to intensify its monitoring of member countries' economies and to develop better early warning systems. This includes insisting on timely and accurate data on key variables like reserves and external debt. The chapter outlines recent discussions aimed—in view of the larger scale of capital flows in recent years—at expanding the resources available to the Fund.

11. Writing from the Inter-American Development Bank (IDB), **Nancy Birdsall**, **Michael Gavin**, and **Ricardo Hausmann** depict Mexico as following, in somewhat accentuated form, a pattern they have identified in almost twenty episodes of stabilization and reform in Latin America in recent years. At the start of the sequence, adoption of a major stabilization and reform program stimulates an economic scenario characterized by surging investment and consumption. External capital flows in; improved confidence stimulates remonetization of the economy, thereby enabling domestic banks to launch a lending spree; and even the government's fiscal receipts respond to the general increase in prosperity. The boom cannot continue indefinitely, however, and the economy enters a period of stress that can be expected to culminate in a crisis unless a correction is engineered with some skill. The authors emphasize two particular sources of vulnerability that tend to develop in the course of the upswing. First, governments treat their new revenues as if they were permanent, and they expand their spending *pari passu* (instead of following a more prudent counter-cyclical policy of accumulating surpluses during the good years to help them get through the bad). Second, banks find it hard during a boom to sort out good loans from bad, and thus accumulate a fair proportion of the latter on their books, which will come home to roost once the boom starts to sputter. Additional imbalances also build up, for example on the external account.

Birdsall, Gavin, and Hausmann believe that the above model captures the essential features of the Mexican experience better than accounts that give a starring role to the real exchange rate (which they see as a symptom of problems more than a cause) or to low savings (cross-country studies, they report, have thus far detected no correlation between savings levels and instability). Several actions by the Mexican authorities may well have accentuated the normal sources of financial-sector vulnerability: (a) privatizing and liberalizing domestic banks in advance of strengthening the regulatory and supervisory framework; (b) failing to establish reserve requirements for commercial bank deposits; and (c) using the government's privatization receipts largely to retire debt held by the domestic banks, further fueling the lending boom. On a separate front, countries should keep social protection programs in good repair, in preparation for sudden crises when large numbers of people may temporarily lose employment or suffer serious declines in income. Summing up, the key lessons in the perspective of these authors involve the merits of counter-cyclical fiscal policy and the need for greater awareness of the inherent dangers created by letting lending booms run their course.

12. In the book's closing chapter, **Moisés Naím** places the crisis in its broader international context. Naím's contribution examines the interaction between external forces—including massive capital flows—on the one hand, and the Mexican government's market reforms and domestic political goals and constraints on the other. "The nature of Mexico's disaster," Naím writes, "clearly indicates that national financial crises are no longer what they used to be. The actors, the volumes of money involved, the nature of the crisis, and the dizzying speed of the financial markets' reaction were unprecedented." Fund managers today control sums of money that dwarf the resources now available to institutions such as the IMF and the World Bank. This makes assuaging such managers' concerns a dominant priority for contemporary finance ministers. Pointing to pressure by fund managers on the Mexican authorities to put the interests of foreign investors first, Naím writes that "the conditionalities of the IMF and the World Bank look enlightened and flexible—even benevolent—by comparison." Unlike foreign direct investors, who make a relatively long-term commitment to the host country, today's money managers can bail out of their positions in a country at the flick of a switch. This facility makes the markets extremely unforgiving of policy-makers' mistakes, which can bring massive and instantaneous punishment. Beyond this, the markets' herd instinct can set up "neighborhood effects," whereby economies showing any sign of vulnerability can be caught in the wake of a crisis originating elsewhere, as the East Asian crisis has highlighted.

At the national level, Naím agrees, the crisis reinforces the premium attached to prudent management of the broad macroeconomic variables (current- and capital-account balances, the exchange rate, fiscal and quasi-fiscal policy, etc.). In Naím's view as in Peter H. Smith's, better economic management is not just a technical question but one that bears on the political context within which decision-makers operate. The broader interest of the crisis, Naím argues, lies not so much in providing major new insights into the content of prudent macroeconomic policy as in showing the difficulty that even highly qualified officials may experience in actually applying economic best-practice when political pressures point in the other direction. "The intersection of market reforms, domestic politics, and international conditions," he writes, "did not leave the government much room to maneuver." In such a situation, Naím suggests, even "smart guys" may make what (with the benefit of hindsight) look like "dumb mistakes." As the East Asian crisis now also shows, the problem was not the government's lack of information or technical skills. Rather, their incapacity to act on lessons well learned everywhere else was a reflection of what Naím calls "politically induced learning disabilities."

At the international level, the crisis shows that "existing mechanisms of global monetary governance are no longer adequate to deal with a world of integrated, securitized, electronically linked capital markets." With the IMF's resources inadequate to mount a credible rescue for Mexico, Naím reminds the reader, a special *ad hoc* package had to be improvised; and although the Clinton administration and the Republican leadership in Congress both argued the importance of the issue for wider U.S. interests, the Congress as a whole declined to back U.S. involvement in the rescue, obliging the executive branch to take action on its own responsibility. It is unclear what precedents the international rescue package for Mexico should be seen as setting. Which other countries would be considered sufficiently "strategic" to warrant a similarly tailor-made coalition of rescuers? There are also "moral hazard" issues to be considered: Do rescues of this nature absolve foreign investors of responsibility for indiscriminate lending, thereby encouraging further irresponsibility in the future? Reforming the way the international financial system is governed will take time, Naím concludes. The experts disagree on what can be done, and the difficulties are enormous. Failure to achieve reform, however, will ensure many unhappy surprises in the future.

LESSONS FROM MEXICO

Tolstoy observed, in the opening to *Anna Karenina*, that while all happy families are alike, every unhappy family is unhappy in its own unique way. A similar comment might usefully be made about countries in deep economic crisis. In preparing this book for publication, we have periodically needed to remind ourselves that Thailand in 1997 is not Mexico 1994, and that Korea 1997 is different from both. It would indeed be facile to suppose that one can derive from the present volume's analysis of the Mexican case (or from any other source) a cookie-cutter diagnosis that will fit all the details of each of these recent crises—let alone a uniform prescription for their resolution. On the contrary, the world is still learning the variety of shapes and sizes that contemporary crises can take.

This said, we do believe that this book's relatively exhaustive examination of the Mexican experience has a relevance that goes beyond the specific historical episode reviewed. And though the East Asian countries currently caught up in economic turmoil certainly exhibit some major differences from Mexico in 1994—the famously high domestic savings rates in many of the Asian economies, for example—there also seem to be sufficient parallels to make it worthwhile to start thinking about comparative analysis.

Certainly it does not seem to us to stretch the facts to classify Mexico 1994 and East Asia 1997 as, respectively, the first and second of what David D. Hale labeled the "post–Cold War" crises—namely, crises whose evolution is heavily influenced by huge and potentially volatile private capital flows. There are family resemblances. Moisés Naím's observations in this volume, first written well before East Asia started to rumble, seem worth repeating: first, we live in a world where mobile capital flows are capable of punishing policy-makers' mistakes massively and almost instantly, and, second, once the markets' herd instinct is aroused, those living in the "neighborhood" of the initial crisis can be exposed to heightened vulnerability. The

Asian outbreak encourages us to make more explicit a point that we consider to be at least implied by some of the present book's discussion: *There are different patterns of "mistake" that countries can be punished for.* A warning, based on Mexico's experience, about the perils of extended large current-account deficits relative to GDP could usefully have received closer attention over recent years from the authorities in Bangkok. Equally clearly, this particular injunction does not fit the stylized facts of the Korean situation. On the other hand, the lessons several of our contributors offer on the vulnerabilities inherent in sheltered and opaque domestic banking sectors, and in a build-up of short-term international debt, appear to us to catch essential aspects of the Korean experience as we understand it. Like Tolstoy's families, in short, countries have more than one way of being unhappy.

Bearing our own caveat firmly in mind—that it may not be necessary to make all the mistakes the Mexicans made for a country to risk punishment (and, conversely, that there are mistakes Mexico more or less avoided that, if committed, could land a country in trouble)—we want to propose here a reasonably compact list of lessons of general validity (even though not all will necessarily be relevant to all countries at all times) that we consider can fairly be derived from the analysis in this book. We should also make it clear that, while our list of lessons certainly reflects the influence of our fellow contributors to the book, we do not mean to imply that all of them would necessarily subscribe to all of the lessons we are distilling here.

1. Policy-makers need to develop a new respect for the power of global financial markets. This is the most fundamental lesson of the past three years, and it underlies almost everything else we have to say. The level of net capital flows to developing countries, according to World Bank estimates, increased sixfold during 1990-96 (to reach $265 billion in the latter year) and is now approximately four times higher than at the peak of the 1978-82 commercial-bank lending boom. For countries that are favored by the markets (and these flows are concentrated, with just a dozen countries accounting for 80 percent of the total), the benefits can be very sizable, particularly in what is often a strong initial surge. Wisely used, capital imports can powerfully supplement domestic savings and stimulate growth, as well as help to introduce new technologies and management techniques and increase competition in domestic markets.

Recent crises suggest that host governments have shown a tendency to take the benefits of large capital inflows almost for granted, while giving little thought to (or planning for) the dangers and vulnerabilities which, under certain circumstances, dependence on such flows can entail. We have seen in Mexico, and again in East Asia, the potential for rapid reversals in market sentiment that can put intense pressure on currency parities and, in the short term, shut off a country's access to financial markets almost totally and at any price. Few countries, however, have given sufficiently serious attention to preventive and precautionary measures designed to avoid or mitigate the downside risks.

2. A fixed exchange rate is a hard act to sustain. The sheer volumes of finance now involved in global markets, and the speed with which they can move, make a good deal of earlier thinking about exchange rate management obsolete. To begin with a rather obvious point, as one commentator observed, "reserves aren't what they used to be." In earlier periods, when current-account transactions dominated total foreign exchange trading, it made sense to measure a comfortable safety margin in terms of "months of imports." Nowadays, though, a large developing country can lose $10 billion of reserves in a single day's trading. But the point goes deeper than this. Mexico and East Asia (as well as other recent cases, for example in Eastern Europe) have shown the strong tendency for the adoption of fixed parities to be followed by real appreciation leading eventually to overvaluation. As one of us (Edwards) demonstrates in his chapter in this volume, a significant portfolio adjustment in foreign investors' desired holdings of a specific country's securities will require, first, a real appreciation in the country's exchange rate, followed later by a real depreciation. Adjustments of this kind are far more easily engineered within a flexible nominal exchange rate policy. An additional concern is the pattern of risks that is set up when private parties (and possibly the government itself) assume that the exchange rate is immutable and proceed to contract debt denominated in foreign currency while investing in domestic assets.

This suggests that, in a reforming economy with a high rate of inflation, a reasonable strategy is to use a fixed exchange rate as a *temporary* tool to guide expectations and impose discipline during the early phases of the program. After these initial objectives are achieved, and once the fiscal and monetary sides are under control, a switch of anchor will be called for, and a more flexible system— either a managed float or a crawling peg—should be adopted. This was indeed the approach followed with great success by Israel in the late 1980s and Poland during the 1990s. This policy could imply that inflation will decline more slowly; however, this will be more than offset by the growth, employment, and export expansion benefits of a competitive real exchange rate.

The Mexican authorities considered at several points between 1992 and 1994 switching anchors. However, the notion that a more flexible exchange rate regime would result in slower decline in inflation was considered, in the final analysis, to be unacceptable. In hindsight, we can see the problems with this position: Although inflation could have turned out to be somewhat higher, the flexible rate would have allowed the country to accommodate the external shocks and macroeconomic imbalances of 1993 and 1994 without traumatic consequences. This has, indeed, been a fundamental lesson of recent history in a number of more advanced countries. Several nations that went from a rigid to a flexible exchange rate regime during the 1980s were able to achieve very drastic depreciations— recall the peseta, the escudo, the lira, and the pound—without negative effects on their real side.

Our point is not that it is absolutely impossible to sustain a fixed exchange rate policy. In post-1994 Latin America, Argentina provides an obvious counter-example. It is still possible to debate, as some of our contributors do in this volume, the relative achievements of the Argentine and Mexican models over the post-crisis period. Indeed, if growth is taken as the comparator, the only fair answer may be that the jury is still out.

Real GDP Growth Rate
(percent)

Year	Argentina	Mexico
1995	-4.6	-6.2
1996	4.4	5.1
1997 (est)	7.8	7.0

Source: World Bank.

What these numbers do not fully reflect, however, is the determination that is needed to sustain a fixed exchange rate policy not during the periods of smooth sailing, but during times of acute financial, economic, and political pressure. In this respect, we consider that Argentina in these three years since 1994—with a self-confident president and strong economic teams prepared to take the heat for austerity and high unemployment (17.5 percent in 1995, 16.1 percent as of mid-1997) even during an election year—has been a rare exception rather than a model we would advocate for general adoption. The more common pattern, in which a fixed exchange rate is first adopted, then clung to, and finally abandoned, is one that seems to us to have very little to recommend it.

3. Large, sustained current-account deficits should not be shrugged off. An argument that was heard quite often before the Mexico crisis was that current-account deficits need not concern policy-makers as long as they are the result of decisions by private parties (i.e., as long as they are not the counterpart to a significant fiscal deficit). Both Mexico 1994 and East Asia 1997 have exploded this argument. It is now clear that fiscal deficits are only one of several possible ways for countries to get into trouble. As one of us (Edwards) argues in his chapter, private flows may reach unsustainable levels in relation to GDP, and both Mexico before 1994 and Thailand subsequently were clearly in the danger range.

When capital surges occur, one important question concerns the macroeconomic management of a "soft landing." On this point, we have argued above for the merits of flexible over fixed exchange rate regimes, and we pick up later the arguments for counter-cyclical fiscal and monetary policies, to help avoid the scenario where foreign savings substitute for domestic savings and in essence fund a consumption boom. Of course, it also makes a difference what types of investment the foreign savings end up financing: whether domestic market signals and institutions channel them mainly to productive purposes or, alternatively, to real-estate speculation or politically inspired white-elephant projects.

4. In the presence of volatile capital flows, fiscal and monetary policies must sometimes lean against the wind. Some of the keenest debates among our contributors concern the appropriateness of the fiscal and monetary stance adopted by the Mexican authorities in the pre-crisis period. In brief, the case for the defense is that fiscal policy was basically in balance (apart from possible concern over quasi-fiscal lending by development banks), and that, on the monetary side, there was no practical alternative to the central bank's policy of sterilization. The critics counter that, in a period characterized by heavy capital flows, aiming for fiscal balance may not be enough: In short, the authorities should have followed a counter-cyclical fiscal policy. Also on the monetary side, critics such as Birdsall, Gavin, and Hausmann have been able to point to several specific government actions that fueled rather than restrained the pre-crisis domestic lending boom. Critics also argue that, to the extent that it is true that Mexico approached the crisis with limited alternatives to sterilization of outflows (itself a contested point), this was *per se* an indictment of the longer-term conduct of monetary policies. We find the critics' case broadly persuasive and consider this to be among the more important of the lessons the Mexico crisis has helped to clarify.

5. Sheltered and opaque domestic financial systems are time bombs waiting to explode. Recent crises have brought home the truth that weak, protected banking sectors involve not merely efficiency losses, but major sources of country risk. Several of our contributors have emphasized the extent to which policy-makers' awareness of the fragility of Mexico's domestic banks constrained domestic macro policies in the months up to and including the peso crisis; both devaluation and further tightening of monetary policy were, reportedly, put off at least partly for this reason. More fundamentally, we can now recognize more readily some of the ways in which banks that are poorly capitalized and supervised (and possibly controlled by groups that either lack banking experience or are compromised by outside interests) can be tempted—especially in the presence of implicit or explicit public-sector guarantees—to take risks of various kinds that may end up *de facto* being socialized.

Mexico found out that it was not easy to create a solid regulatory framework effectively and rapidly. The lack of trained personnel—including inspectors and accountants—in many cases slowed down the process, as did the rivalry among different government institutions with overlapping responsibilities. When the peso crisis erupted in December 1994, the supervisory system was still seriously underdeveloped, and Mexico's financial sector was in a rather weak position. The types of policies that could have averted the exchange rate crisis—for example, the tightening of monetary and fiscal policy in 1994—conceivably would have made the situation more pressing on financial institutions. In fact, concerns regarding the strength of the financial system probably influenced—though they certainly do not justify—the decision to strive for a policy of low interest rates in spite of the pressure against the domestic currency. In the end, macroeconomic problems and financial sector weaknesses fed into each other, making a bad situation even worse.

The types of measures that need to be taken to reform and open up diseased financial sectors of this kind are by now reasonably well understood among professionals working in the field internationally. They include enforcing recognized standards of capital adequacy and accounting for problem loans, as well as prudential standards for risk assumption more generally; improving transparency and protection against conflicts of interest; and strengthening regulatory and supervisory capacity. Undoubtedly one of the most effective and timely ways that countries can reinforce fragile financial sectors is to relax or remove earlier restrictions on the participation of foreign banking institutions (in Mexico itself, in the three years since the peso crisis, such measures have raised the share of banking assets in foreign-controlled banks from zero to around a quarter of the total). The barriers to fundamental change all too often lie not at the technical but at the political level, where the opposition of vested interests can conveniently camouflage itself under a veil of nationalism. It is sad that it seems so often to require a major crisis before the obstacles to reform can be overcome; it is all the more important that the crisis, when it does come, be used to take decisive action in this area.

6. Policy-makers need to be concerned not only with the aggregate volume of debt but also, crucially, with its term structure and currency profile. In the Mexican case, the period before the crisis saw, in effect, the conversion of internal to external debt on a large scale. The adoption of the *tesobono* strategy involved the government itself assuming the exchange rate risk on a major portion of the public debt. In addition, as Birdsall, Gavin, and Hausmann point out, the debt came to be concentrated heavily in short-term instruments. As happened in Mexico, and more recently in Korea, a situation of heavy short-term debt requiring to be turned over in apprehensive markets can spark fears of default and thus help precipitate the eventual crisis.

Governments of course find it tempting, particularly in election years, to buy time by shortening maturities and/or socializing currency risk in their own borrowings rather than to pay the insurance premium associated with longer maturities (or take timely policy measures to allay market apprehensions). But public debt is not the only concern here. Leaving aside the element of "private" borrowing that is in effect disguised public-sector debt (such as borrowing through publicly controlled development banks), once a currency comes under pressure, the demand for foreign exchange from private borrowers needing to service their short-term borrowings is highly inelastic with respect to price. There are no easy answers to this part of the equation. Regulation of the assets and liabilities of financial-sector institutions could constitute one line of defense but would not address the positions of non-financial corporations. Our own preference for exchange rate flexibility is also influenced in part by concern over the incentives that a fixed rate policy gives to domestic borrowers to borrow heavily in foreign exchange.

7. Providing accurate and timely data on key variables should be considered non-negotiable. One of the central lessons the international community rightly drew from the Mexican crisis concerned the need for data transparency (Loser and Williams discuss in their chapter in this volume some of the initiatives promoted by the IMF after the crisis in an effort to improve data standards). The "tradition" whereby Mexico published official reserve data only three times a year (and on somewhat flexible dates) is one that lenders would no longer be prepared to accept. Indeed, given the day-to-day volatility we noted earlier, it is clear that certain data (including reserves and short-term liabilities) are in times of pressure only meaningful on a virtually "real time" basis. Some consternation was caused (in early December 1997) when it was revealed that data provided to the international community on Korean short-term debt were seriously incomplete. Many market participants have indicated that part of the reason for the sudden and precipitate collapse of confidence in Mexico in December 1994 was the conviction of investors and fund managers that they had been manipulated and misled by the Mexican authorities in their handling of key data. Any short-term gain from data manipulation, we would argue, is liable to be more than wiped out by the subsequent loss of credibility.

Whereas transparency in the publication of official data (such as official reserves and debt) is usually more a matter of political will than of technical capacity, different issues may arise concerning information on the health of the domestic banking sector. This is a particularly difficult case of "asymmetric information," in which those best able to judge the true state of a bank's loan portfolio are insiders, who may have strong incentives to conceal the scale of any problems. This emphasizes the importance of the financial sector reforms discussed in section 5 above.

8. The credibility of policy-makers is fundamentally important. Since credible policy commitments are very difficult to enact and enforce, several countries have endowed their central banks with independence from the government. From a practical point of view, independence means that central bank authorities are appointed for long periods of time that generally do not coincide with those of the elected government. The idea is that an independent central bank will not be subject to the pressures of the political cycle and, thus, will not be tempted to abuse its power to print money and inflate. As with justices to the higher courts, independent central bank directors, once appointed, cannot be removed by the government.

This institutional arrangement has been credited with facilitating the process by which central banks have established policies that strive for long-term stability and not for short-term, ephemeral gains. After all, whereas a government that is about to leave office may be tempted to perform expansionary policies that will, while producing short-term economic stimulus, eventually translate into higher inflation, an independent central bank should attach significant importance to enhancing its reputation. While an elected government is here today but not tomorrow, an independent central bank is here to stay. Given its long-term appointment and the fact that it values its reputation, an independent central bank can commit itself in a credible manner, thereby delivering policies that are welfare-enhancing when compared with alternative discretionary policies.

Although there is evidence that countries with truly independent central banks have lower inflation rates, a complex causality issue is involved. After all, even though in principle an independent bank should deliver a lower rate of inflation, from a practical point of view it might well be the case that countries with a long tradition of stability are the most likely to grant independence to their central banks. Tradition can be so important that in some societies intolerance toward inflation is so widely held that price stability is always high on the policy agenda of the government, reducing the importance of central bank independence. It seems fair to say that, while independent central banks are not a sufficient condition to achieve macroeconomic stability, in most cases they might well be necessary.

Some countries have gone even further in reforming their central bank charters to include price stability as the only goal for which the central bank should strive. Achieving price stability should be understood as a long-term goal, attainable through sustainable monetary, fiscal, and exchange rate policies. Significant short-lived reductions in inflation—attained by overvaluing the currency or engineering a spectacular recession—are rather easy to obtain, but are intrinsically vulnerable to being undone by future policy reversals.

Following the trend that started in Chile in 1989, the Bank of Mexico was granted independence in April 1994. It is by now quite clear that there were several problems with the design of monetary policy during 1994—in particular, the decision to sterilize the decline in reserves after March, in spite of having (for all practical purposes) a fixed exchange rate, is rather puzzling. The alternative policies were either to allow early on—that is in March or April—for greater flexibility of the exchange rate system, accompanied by a tighter macro stance, or to defend the fixed exchange rate with a more restrictive monetary policy. The latter policy would have implied a significant reduction in growth, while the former would have had an impact on prices. As many of our authors have emphasized, the increasingly precarious condition of the banking system complicated policy decisions considerably. The implementation of a restrictive monetary policy would have affected not only economic activity but also the financial health of the banks. Both outcomes spelled trouble for the government, especially given that it was an election year. The central bank finally acted rather as one might expect of an elected government about to leave office: It sold reserves and delayed the much needed adjustment.

If anything, events in Mexico reinforce the importance of having truly independent central banks. They also remind us that institutional changes are much more easily done on paper than in practice. Mexico in 1994 is not an example of the irrelevance of independent central banks. Quite the contrary: It testifies to the fact that meaningful institutional changes ought to be an important element of the broad process of economic reform.

9. Mexico's experience encourages the belief that strong policy measures, well supported, can provide the basis for an early recovery. Mexico's experience after the peso crisis was not painless. Reported urban unemployment levels (which many observers consider incomplete) surged from 3.6 percent in 1994 to 6.3 percent in 1995 (subsequently easing to 5.6 percent in 1996 and 4.1 percent by mid-1997). Not only the poor suffered: Articulate lobbies drew attention to the impact of interest-rate hikes on middle-class debtors and succeeded in winning relief from the authorities. At the same time, as Loser and Williams point out in their chapter, the package that, after a couple of false starts, was adopted and implemented by the Zedillo government—and supported with large, short-term financing from the international community—must in the circumstances be considered a striking success. Mexico's access to voluntary international financing was restored within months of the crisis, growth has resumed at healthy rates, and the country has, as of the time of writing, escaped speculative pressures during the current East Asian crisis. Meanwhile, fundamental policy changes were initiated that have laid the way for the restructuring of the financial sector.

As we write, we are aware of some of the public controversies presently being aired about the detailed design of some of the East

Asian rescue packages. Our own review of the lessons from Mexico does not substitute for the detailed knowledge of Asian conditions that would be needed to enter this public debate. However, we do take from the Mexican experience the lesson that successful crisis management calls for a combination of decisive leadership to restore confidence and the willingness to take strong measures to start addressing serious structural problems, including those in the domestic financial sector. If that combination can be put in place, Mexico provides grounds for hoping that a rebound can come about sooner rather than later.

OPEN QUESTIONS

Our contributors' discussion of the lessons from Mexico has also left us with a number of still very open questions in our own minds. The first of these concerns the implications for the international community's crisis-response capacity. The scale of the Mexican crisis, as this book shows, strained all earlier precedents within the IMF on the volume of funds required for the bailout, and it required creativity on the part of both U.S. and international officials in fashioning a tailor-made response. Over the subsequent three years, the international community has provided a somewhat qualified vote of confidence on the IMF's central role in crisis response: On the one hand, the Fund has been able to fight off potential rivals, such as the Asian Fund in some of its earlier incarnations; on the other, its management has not been able to achieve the expansion in permanent Fund resources it considers necessary. Thus the Asian crisis has inspired the creation of similar *ad hoc* coalitions. Commentators increasingly worry about the "moral hazard" dangers that repeated bailouts will pose, but few alternative proposals simultaneously recognize the genuine externalities that a major moratorium might unleash. Further intensification of international "surveillance" will surely emerge from the present crisis, but Burki's question of how to attract the attention of recalcitrant governments has no easy answer.

The second set of questions provoked by this book's discussion of Mexico concerns the political context and consequences of major economic crises. Peter H. Smith argues that the avoidance of economic mismanagement in the future may require not merely better technical advice, but changing the political incentives facing decision-makers. Some years ago, A. K. Sen made the striking observation that no democracy had ever experienced a major famine. Sen's own explanation for this is that democracies are better than other political systems at surfacing information, flashing warning signs, and ensuring that grave suffering is addressed. One cannot make as strong an observation about economic crises, but Smith at least challenges us to consider whether, for similar reasons, we may not expect functioning democracies to do a better job at steering clear of the rocks than more closed political systems. Several of our commentators also connect the crisis of 1994 to the further political liberalization that we have seen subsequently in Mexico. This possibility—that a profound economic crisis may help to open up previously authoritarian domestic political systems—is also of obvious relevance for a number of the countries in East Asia that are currently experiencing financial and economic pressure. The thesis is provocative, but for now we feel obliged to take refuge in the quotation with which we opened: "Too soon to tell."

1. POLITICAL DIMENSIONS OF THE PESO CRISIS

PETER H. SMITH*

t seemed like such a promising affair. Laden with pageantry, the inauguration of Ernesto Zedillo Ponce de León as president of Mexico on December 1, 1994, attracted throngs of dignitaries from home and abroad. Outgoing President Carlos Salinas de Gortari received a thunderous ovation in honor of his remarkable *sexenio* and, in transfering the sash, conferred upon his hand-picked successor not only a symbol of the nation's highest office but also a public gesture of political endorsement. A sympathetic audience listened to the earnest but untested new president offer pledges of honesty, reform, and expanded political opening. Observers noted the conspicuous absence from the incoming cabinet of Pedro Aspe Armella, the much-admired Secretary of Finance under Salinas, but they found consolation in the presence of several holdovers. At luncheon the following day, a glittering assemblage of business people took heart from Zedillo's repeated insistence that the economic watchword of his new administration would be "stability, stability, stability."

The chorus of praise then moved to Miami, where President Bill Clinton on December 9-11 hosted a resplendent gathering of Hemispheric heads of state (except Fidel Castro) known as the "Summit of the Americas." Characteristically effusive about prospects for democracy and prosperity throughout Latin America, Clinton repeatedly extolled the North American Free Trade Agreement (NAFTA) as an exemplary case of economic integration and praised Mexico for its performance as a strong and dependable partner. There could be no doubt about it: Mexico was still on its roll.

Suddenly the wheels came off. On December 19, as foreign reserves were rapidly dwindling, the Zedillo administration unexpectedly widened the band for trading pesos with dollars from 3.47

* The author wishes to acknowledge the superb research assistance and analytical insight of Antonio Ortiz Mena L.N., a graduate student in political science at the University of California, San Diego.

31

to 4.00—in effect permitting a 15 percent devaluation of the peso—violating Zedillo's heartfelt December 2 pledge. This prompted a speculative run against the peso; within two days, the government was obliged to abandon its position, letting the peso float freely against the dollar. Unable to persuade foreign investors of Mexico's trustworthiness, the newly installed Secretary of Finance—Jaime Serra Puche, who had been Secretary of Commerce under Salinas and had played a key role in the NAFTA negotiations—submitted his resignation after merely three weeks on the job. By late January, the Clinton administration managed to put together a multilateral package of nearly $50 billion, including $20 billion from the U.S. government, but the peso continued to slide. One of the most judicious and knowledgeable U.S. experts on Mexico, Sidney Weintraub, arrived at a gloomy conclusion: "Ernesto Zedillo is off to a horrible start as president of Mexico."[1]

What could have gone wrong? Calamity struck unexpectedly in a country that in recent years had undertaken major economic reform, entered NAFTA with Canada and the United States, acceded to the prestigious Asia-Pacific Economic Cooperation forum (APEC), and gained full membership in the Organisation for Economic Co-operation and Development (OECD). Moreover, the nation could boast exceptionally talented, energetic, and intelligent leadership, as symbolized by the transmission of presidential power from one accomplished student of economic policy (Ph.D., Harvard University) to another (Ph.D., Yale University.) As Moisés Naím would later ask of the December debacle, "How can such smart guys make such dumb mistakes?"[2]

My purpose in this chapter is to explore political dimensions of this question. First, I establish the long-term political context for the peso crisis. Second, I trace specific events and decisions leading up to the peso debacle, with special emphasis on the period from mid-1993 to end-1994. Instead of arguing that key actors in Mexico were making stupid decisions for irrational reasons—as a rigid application of economic criteria might suggest—I here maintain that they were responding in rational and self-interested ways to existing political incentives and constraints (as will be shown, however, they could also make mistakes within this context). My argument is that political logic prevailed over economic logic throughout this period.

---

[1] Weintraub (1995), p. 1. For additional analysis, see Lustig (1995), pp. 374-382; Ros (1995), pp. 43-49; and Schettino (1995).

[2] Naím (1995), p. 115.

Third, I offer speculation about long-term consequences of the peso crisis for the Mexican political system, now in the process of fundamental transformation. It must be recognized, of course, that most tendencies toward political change stemmed from factors other than the peso crisis, but virtually all of them were affected by it in one way or another. My opinion is that the unintentional (and unforeseeable) implications of the crisis will continue to unfold over time, and that a comprehensive analysis of the political effects of December 1994 may not prove possible for many years.

Finally, I conclude with modest observations about the relationship between political change and economic reform. As this chapter indicates, political factors are more than just unwelcome "nuisances" that stand in the way of coherent policy-making. Ultimately, political change must become part and parcel of successful economic transformation.

POLITICAL CONTEXT FOR CRISIS

The framework for the 1994-95 crisis derived not from short-term events but from the long-term evolution of the Mexican political system. From the late 1920s to the 1980s, an authoritarian regime marked by a close alliance between technocrats, politicians, and leaders of key groups—especially labor and the peasantry—successfully imposed social and political stability. These coalitions were frequently sealed in explicit compacts, or *pactos*, that achieved and implemented consensus on economic policy. Key decisions were made at the top, behind closed doors, as an official party (the Partido Revolucionario Institucional, or PRI) routinely and regularly triumphed in not-very-contested elections. Opposition voices were muted, the media conspired openly with the ruling establishment, and instances of rebellion and protest were sparse. From the 1940s on, even the armed forces accepted a civilian monopoly on the presidential office. Turbulent Mexico, land of the first major social revolution in the twentieth century, thus succumbed to forces of political domination. With traces of envy and admiration, the Peruvian novelist-politician Mario Vargas Llosa christened Mexico's system "the perfect dictatorship."

A defining feature of the regime stemmed from its tradition of presidential succession. In keeping with a key tenet of the Revolution, re-election to high office was strictly prohibited. Within the course of each *sexenio*, however, the ruling president exerted supreme control over the nation's political life. Effective power flowed directly from the executive office and, as part of this arrangement, the outgoing president exercised a time-honored right to select his own successor. Indeed, this process of *dedazo,* or *destape,* was the culminating expression of presidential power. The inevitable triumph of this "chosen one" in the subsequent election constituted not a competitive victory but a ritual of confirmation, an acceptance of decisions from above by a pliant people.

Hyper-presidentialism permeated the Mexican system with an exaggerated form of what has come to be known as "temporal rigidity," a source of inflexibility for the transmission of political power. The outgoing president exercised supreme authority right up to the final moment of the *sexenio,* at which point the successor instantly assumed full command. Traditionally, too, relatively high rates of turnover in top-level positions heightened both the level and the perception of change.[3] The presidential inauguration thus signified an instantaneous, complete, and profound interruption and transfer of power. In Mexico, the process of executive transition was as brittle in substance as it was smooth in appearance.

INSTITUTIONAL TRANSFORMATION

Starting as far back as the 1970s, the dominant-party system began to undergo fundamental rearrangements in its power structure. First, the historic coalition started to weaken: the peasantry no longer represented a significant resource; organized labor lost authority; and while small and medium business remained a fragile sector, large-scale business was accumulating power and independence from the government. Second, the party system shifted: though still strong, the PRI came to stand at the center of a three-party system, with the Partido Revolucionario Democrático (PRD) on the left and the Partido de Acción Nacional (PAN) on the right, both of which were attracting considerable support from the urban middle class. At the same time, traditional fiefdoms re-emerged: old-time politicians (*dinosaurios*) found refuge in state governorships, for instance, and in niches within the party apparatus of the PRI.

During the 1980s and 1990s, international drug cartels began to pose a serious challenge to legal authority. Soon after taking office, President Zedillo received an official report warning that "the power of the drug-trafficking organizations could lead to situations of ungovernability." The most dangerous of these cartels were involved not so much in marijuana or heroin, traditional products of Mexico, but in the trans-shipment of cocaine from Colombia. With an estimated $7 billion in annual profits, these groups could spend

---

[3] See Smith (1979), especially chapter 6.

as much as $500 million per year on bribery—more than twice the total budget of the attorney general's office. By the mid-1990s, Mexico had about a half-dozen drug organizations of truly international scope (in Tijuana, Sinaloa, Ciudad Juárez, Guadalajara, and in the state of Tamaulipas, where traffickers operated a flourishing cocaine pipeline along the Gulf of Mexico). Drug cartels were implicated in a wave of violence that swept through Mexico, including the assassination of a Roman Catholic cardinal in 1993. Former prosecutor Eduardo Valle Espinosa proclaimed that the country had fallen under the heel of drug traffickers and, like Colombia, had become a "narco-democracy."[4] Violence and disorder were climbing to unprecedented levels.

In summary, Mexico was undergoing a significant erosion of institutional authority. There was less power at the center, even in the presidency, than there used to be. To be sure, Salinas was able to exert authority in an exceptional way, partly through personal guile and partly as a result of his lifelong immersion in the system, but Zedillo had neither the resources nor the opportunity to wield comparable strength. Power was no longer as concentrated or extensive as it had been for many years: forever resistant to facile nomenclature, Mexico's political regime might now be thought of as "neo-authoritarian."[5]

One corollary of this process of institutional deterioration was the increasing prominence of individual actors. It was Carlos Salinas, not the PRI, who represented and personified the regime as a whole. And it was Pedro Aspe, not the government or the economic team, who came to be seen as the guarantor of macroeconomic stability. Throughout 1994, foreign and local investors became increasingly preoccupied, and sometimes obsessed, with speculation about whether or not Aspe would remain as Secretary of Finance in the post-Salinas administration. Such fixation upon one individual should have been a warning in itself.

THE FAMILIAL CRISIS

Adding to this dissipation of institutional power was what might be called a "familial" crisis—the emergence of profound schisms within Mexico's political elite, once regarded as the "revolutionary family." For decades, the coherence (and internal discipline) of this ruling elite had comprised a central foundation for the persistence of

---

[4] Valle (1995) and Paternostro (1995), pp. 41-47.
[5] See Dresser (1996); Zaid (1995); and González Sandoval and González Graf (1995).

political stability.[6] While there had been stresses and strains from the 1940s through the 1980s, and occasional cracks in the edifice of power (including the split-off of the *corriente democrática* against the PRI in 1986), there had been nothing that would compare with the fissures of the 1990s. Overt symptoms of these new tensions would not appear until 1994, but they pointed clearly to subterranean pressures and trends that were unfolding throughout the Salinas *sexenio*.

A central and spectacular scene in this drama revolved around two pairs of brothers: Carlos Salinas de Gortari and his older brother, Raúl; and José Francisco Ruíz Massieu and his younger brother, Mario. Both families had long been pillars of the Mexican establishment. José Francisco Ruíz Massieu had also married (and divorced) a sister of the Salinas brothers and was serving as Secretary General of the PRI in late 1994. There was said to be affection, rivalry, and tension among all four of these men.

As he left a political gathering, José Francisco Ruíz Massieu was assassinated in downtown Mexico City on September 28, 1994.[7] His brother Mario, the Assistant Attorney General, was placed in charge of the investigation. Within a month, Mario Ruíz Massieu issued a statement suggesting that drug traffickers might have ordered the murder and that high-level politicians were in league with *narcotraficantes*. In late November, about a week before Salinas was to step down from the presidency, Mario Ruíz Massieu publicly resigned from both his position and the PRI, accusing party leaders (but not Salinas) of conspiring to cover up the assassination.

On February 28, 1995, governmental authorities (presumably with Zedillo's permission) arrested Raúl Salinas de Gortari in connection with the Ruíz Massieu assassination. Rumors immediately began to circulate that Carlos Salinas must have been involved in the plot, on the ground that Raúl would never have undertaken such a brazen scheme without his brother's approval. On March 1 the Deputy Attorney General, Pablo Chapa Bezanilla, accused Mario Ruíz Massieu of obstructing justice during the investigation of his brother's assassination. The next day, Carlos Salinas de Gortari began a hunger strike in order to clear his reputation; Mario Ruíz Massieu left Mexico for the United States, where he was soon arrested (for carrying large amounts of undisclosed cash) while boarding a plane for Madrid. Carlos Salinas ended his fast on March 4, after

---

[6] See Smith (1979); Centeno (1994); and Ai Camp (1995).

[7] See Aguirre, et al. (1995).

the Zedillo government released a mollifying statement, but soon left the country in disgrace.

The Salinas–Ruíz Massieu intrigues evoked images of six-teenth-century Italy under the Borgias rather than a modernizing country of the late twentieth century, and they contained profound political significance. First, they revealed a split within the ruling elite that became more public and irreversible than at any time since the mid-1930s. Second, they indicated a breakdown in rules of civility that had long prevailed within the national elite. Even at the highest levels of the political establishment, violence and murder were coming to replace the once-prized arts of bargaining, negotiation, and co-optation.

Moreover, these developments left Ernesto Zedillo with an ambiguous claim to political legitimacy. It is to be remembered that Zedillo, the substitute candidate who was *destapado* by Salinas after the assassination of presidential candidate Luis Donaldo Colosio, had a minuscule political base of his own. He ran for president on a platform stressing continuity with Salinas and his policies. To a very considerable extent, people who voted for him in August 1994 were voting for Salinas. The public rupture with Salinas in early 1995 thus left Zedillo to his own devices. While many angry Mexicans applauded Zedillo's actions, including his approval for the arrest of Raúl Salinas, the Salinas issue was far from resolved. In the meantime, the new president was facing the challenge of constructing his own political base.

Another stunning indication of intra-elite discord emerged in December 1995, when Carlos Salinas (in Canada at the time) dispatched a late-night fax to Mexico City newspapers in which he denounced "the political offensive against me" by Luis Echeverría, who had been president of Mexico from 1970 to 1976. In a system where former presidents were accustomed to maintaining complete solidarity (and a good deal of silence), this was an extraordinary breach of political etiquette. To be sure, Echeverría had criticized Salinas's management of economic policy in prior months, but he stoutly denied participation in any kind of coordinated campaign.[8] Even so, the *salinista* broadside offered further confirmation of the depth and rancor of cleavages within the national ruling elite.

In effect, Mexico was witnessing political disintegration at two distinct levels—among its uppermost institutions and within the political class. These developments intersected with each other and

---

[8] *Reforma*, December 4-5, 1995.

multiplied their mutual effects. Together, they set the stage for economic crisis.

PRESIDENTIAL SUCCESSION AND THE PESO CRISIS

The peso crisis of December 1994 resulted from a series of decisions and events that unfolded over the course of more than a year. Different political constraints were exerting themselves at different moments on different decisions. The central question is: What political factors prevented Mexican authorities from implementing orthodox economic policy? What prevented them from responding effectively to market signals and repeated warnings?

Vulnerabilities in the Mexican economic strategy were self-evident, especially in retrospect. The country was running a massive current-account deficit, as imports steadily exceeded exports; during the early 1990s, the deficit was being covered by inflows of foreign capital. The problem was that most of this capital came in the form of short-term portfolio investment rather than longer-term foreign direct investment (FDI), with the result that it could be withdrawn from the country at the touch of an electronic button. As shown in Table 1, portfolio investment vastly exceeded FDI from 1991 through 1993, by which time the ratio had climbed to more than 6:1. And just as quickly, the inflow of portfolio capital dropped to $8.2 billion in 1994. Here was one key to the crisis.

Confronted by this situation, Mexico's economic managers chose to rely on two hopes: first, that improvements in productivity would increase export competitiveness and close the trade gap; second, that the implementation of NAFTA would attract capital, especially FDI, and thus provide some breathing room. These were, however, long-term aspirations. In the meantime, short-term pressures were evident and mounting.

Table 1. Capital Flows into Mexico, 1991-94

	1991	1992	1993	1994
	(U.S. $ billions, year-end)			
Portfolio Investment	12.1	18.0	28.4	8.2
Foreign Direct Investment	4.7	4.4	4.9	8.0

Source: Adapted from data in *Lessons of the Mexican Peso Crisis: Report of an Independent Task Force* (New York: Council on Foreign Relations, 1996), p. 9.

The reaction of the Salinas team was to finance the current-account deficit by draining the country's international reserves, which dropped from around $30 billion in February 1994 to $5 billion by late December. The government thus squandered the nation's resources in an ultimately unsuccessful effort to sustain the value of the currency. Especially in retrospect, according to most experts, an earlier and large-scale devaluation would have been a much wiser course.

WHY NOT DEVALUE?

The key political fact was that, for almost all of 1994, Carlos Salinas de Gortari was in the final year of his *sexenio*. To enshrine his place in history, and to promote his candidacy for the directorship of the World Trade Organization (WTO), he no doubt was eager to finish his term in a blaze of glory. This was not as simple as it might seem: as Jorge Castañeda has written, "Few things in the world are as persistent and disheartening as the impossibility for presidential terms to end well in Mexico."[9] With the partial exception of Miguel de la Madrid, every president over the previous quarter-century had left office in disrepute and/or disgrace. All had been relegated to ignominious retirement or to minor positions in the bureaucracy. Still young and ambitious, Salinas was determined to challenge this trend.

For symbolic, political, and economic reasons, devaluation of the peso had pealed a death knell for outgoing presidents of Mexico. As José López Portillo observed from his own experience in 1982, "the president who devalues is himself devalued." As long as he could forestall it, Salinas was not going to take that step. This meant that he would have to court additional foreign investment, whatever the cost; and this, in turn, required maintenance of a stable currency. Ironically enough, his efforts brought about precisely the result that he was seeking to avoid. Like his predecessors, Salinas would discover the fateful rhythm of presidential politics to be unsparing and merciless.

But it was not only a question of personal ambition. As of late 1993, Mexico was anxiously awaiting U.S. ratification of NAFTA. As Congress prepared to cast its vote, pro-NAFTA forces persistently argued that the treaty would stimulate American exports and create new jobs. This scenario presumed a strong peso. For precisely this reason, opponents of NAFTA, like Representative John LaFalce of New York, held hearings on the stability of the peso and accused the

---

[9] Castañeda (1995), p. 65.

Mexican government of withholding its intention to devalue. Since Salinas had bound his political destiny so closely to NAFTA, he had no choice in the matter. There could be no possibility of devaluation before, during, or just after ratification.

Implementation of NAFTA commenced on January 1, 1994, the same day that rebellion unexpectedly erupted in the southernmost state of Chiapas. Under the colorful leadership of Subcomandante Marcos, the Zapatista National Liberation Army (EZLN) rose up to challenge established authority, demand political reform, denounce NAFTA, and, for a time, capture popular imagination throughout Mexico. Despite extensive media coverage, however, the Chiapas rebellion never posed a serious threat to political or economic stability.

Even so, the Salinas government needed to allay the anxieties of foreign investors. The administration thus sought to minimize the importance of the EZLN and cast doubt upon its authenticity, while mobilizing the military and sustaining peso-dollar parity. Apparently mollified, investors continued to pour capital into the country during January-February 1994.

Ultimately, the Zapatista uprising contributed to the debilitation of Mexico's political system not by its military prowess or by the possibility that it might succeed. Rather, it was the prolongation of the conflict that accentuated a sense of uncertainty and erosion of power. The much-vaunted regime, and the president, began to look helpless and hapless in the face of what would otherwise have been a minor regional rebellion.

WHY THE TESOBONOS?

In April 1994, the Salinas administration began issuing a series of dollar-indexed bonds known as *tesobonos*. The goal was to attract foreign capital, of course, and in this sense, the idea paid off: before the end of the year, the Mexican government had issued approximately $30 billion in *tesobonos*. Because of its reliance on exchange rate stability, this strategy incurred monumental risk—and would help precipitate disaster in December.

The immediate political rationale for the *tesobonos* derived from the assassination of *priista* presidential candidate Luis Donaldo Colosio on March 23, 1994, after a political rally in the northern-border city of Tijuana. This utterly shocking event unleashed political uncertainty in Mexico, raised doubts about stability, and, within days, led Salinas to designate Ernesto Zedillo as the substitute PRI candidate for the presidency.

The Colosio assassination frightened investors as well. Within hours, according to one report, a youthful fund manager from Fidelity Investments was on the telephone seeking assurances from central bank officials that the peso would hold within its trading band. He was certainly not the only one. Within a couple of weeks, a consortium known as the Weston Forum approached the Salinas government with a series of "suggestions": that Mexico curb the speed of the peso's daily devaluation, insure foreign investors against currency-exchange losses on peso-denominated securities, issue long-term *tesobonos*, and, perhaps most important, back all these measures with central-bank peso purchases to bolster the currency.[10]

Confronted by this ultimatum, the Salinas government responded with a multi-part strategy: hiking interest rates, lifting the exchange rate to the top of the peso-dollar band (without changing the band itself), buying up pesos on the international market, and offering $10 billion in *tesobonos*. The effort was not entirely successful, as investors withdrew $10 billion from Mexico within six weeks of the Colosio assassination, but it may well have prevented even more capital flight.

It is difficult to measure the impact of the Weston Forum threats. "We have to listen to these guys," acknowledged Guillermo Ortiz Martínez, then Under Secretary of Finance. "But one thing is to listen and the other is to follow their policy recommendations. It is pretty obvious that we would be in deep trouble if we were to be following the advice of investors" about how to run the economy. But as the *Wall Street Journal* observed in June 1994,

> So far, the fund managers have reason to be pleased with Mexico's response. Soon after the Weston Forum meeting, Mexican officials launched a peso rescue operation. They issued longer-term *tesobonos* as the investor group asked, and cut back on the auctions of Mexican treasury bills, or *cetes*, to reduce short-term rates. Then, senior Mexican finance officials flew to Washington to announce a trilateral currency support program among the U.S., Canada, and Mexico. After these meetings, Mr. Aspe, the finance minister, visited with Fidelity's fund managers.[11]

Whether or not as a result of their efforts, foreign investors appeared to be getting their way.

Additional international influence came from a rise in U.S. interest rates, also beginning in April 1994. This had two consequences

---

[10] *Wall Street Journal*, June 14, 1994.
[11] Ibid., p. A6.

for Mexico: first and most important, it attracted capital away from Mexico (and other emerging markets); second, it exerted upward pressure on interest rates in Mexico. When U.S. Federal Reserve Chairman Alan Greenspan began lifting interest rates in early 1994, Mexico would feel direct effects. As Moisés Naím later observed, "The hike in U.S. interest rates to curb inflationary pressures in the United States caused the Mexican markets to drop much more than did the news of a revolt in Chiapas."[12]

WHY EXPAND THE MONEY SUPPLY?

Instead of raising interest rates in Mexico, however, the Salinas administration began easing restrictions on credit. Interest rates on 28-day *cetes* dropped from a peak of 18 percent in April to about 13.5 percent in November, even as the United States and other countries were raising interest rates. Although internal and external imbalances emerged, the government continued to run down reserves rather than raise interest rates. Autonomous in name but not in fact, the central bank expanded credit to the financial system by 400 percent from mid-1993 to mid-1994. During 1994, monetary expansion of more than 20 per cent and lax credit policies added to the economic instability created by the decline in foreign investment.

The conventional explanation for this policy tends to focus on the electoral cycle (which is also viewed by many as the reason for the refusal to devalue). The basic idea is that the government was seeking to stimulate economic growth in order to earn the support of voters and thus to secure a victory at the polls for the PRI and for Zedillo. This was especially necessary in 1994, it is often argued, since Zedillo was a second-choice candidate and an uncharismatic campaigner. By expanding the money supply, in other words, the Salinas administration was attempting to buy the election.

This interpretation contains a grain of truth, but tends toward exaggeration. It assumes that elections are competitive, that policymakers are shortsighted, and that voters are unable to ascertain chicanery (according to one deft formulation, the model suggests that a handful of rogues are conspiring to deceive a populace of dupes).

Elections did not affect political decisions the same way in Mexico as in many other countries. The PRI had won every national election since 1929. As of 1994, an opposition triumph in a presidential election remained unthinkable; and, though the opposition might have garnered more votes than the PRI in 1988, according to some accounts, the outcome was controlled by official fraud. So there

---

[12] Naím (1995), p. 113.

seemed little genuine prospect that the opposition could win the presidential contest of 1994. It was not until early May that *panista* candidate Diego Fernández de Cevallos routed both Zedillo and *perredista* Cuauhtémoc Cárdenas in a television debate and posed, for the first time in living memory, the possibility of an opposition victory; and at precisely that point, Fernández suddenly and mysteriously stopped campaigning. When the ballots were counted in August, Zedillo emerged with a clear and decisive triumph.

In this setting, the goal of economic policy toward the end of the *sexenio* was not to obtain an electoral victory for the incoming president, but to secure the legacy and popularity of the outgoing president. (In this particular instance, too, Salinas wanted to promote his candidacy for the WTO directorship.) Another traditional motivation was to maintain patronage and discipline within the PRI, among recalcitrant leaders as well as among the rank-and-file, and thus to perpetuate the dominance of the nation's political machine. In all such respects, government decisions had more to do with the dynamics of presidential succession in an authoritarian system than with competitive prospects in the electoral arena.

WHY THE DECEMBER DEBACLE?

In retrospect, it may appear that the period between the August elections and the December inauguration should have offered another opportunity for peso devaluation and macroeconomic readjustment. After all, there was historical precedent: both Echeverría and López Portillo had devalued the peso shortly before leaving office. According to many sources, Zedillo requested that Salinas do the same, but Salinas firmly refused. Here is precisely the point: Salinas was determined to avoid the fate of his predecessors, who had suffered vilification over the years. To preserve his political stature, to enhance his international image, and to strengthen his campaign for the WTO, Salinas was insistent on leaving office with an untarnished record.[13]

Characteristics of the Mexican political system shed additional light on the unfolding of the crisis in December 1994—what ex-President Salinas would caustically refer to as "the December mistake." As explained above, the process of presidential succession creates an extraordinary degree of uncertainty. Anxiety about the transmission of power and the incoming administration necessarily generates apprehension among investors, especially those who are knowledgeable about Mexico. (It is thus not coincidental that Mexican investors, not foreigners, were the first to begin removing funds

---

[13] See Dornbusch (1995), p. 20.

from the country early in December.) The existence of "temporal rigidity" in politics tends to create problems for economics.

Moreover, the pattern of presidential succession made it difficult (if not impossible) for the Salinas team to devalue the peso during the month of November in a coherent fashion. As Pedro Aspe has maintained, it would have been necessary to embed a devaluation within an overall economic package—which could be assembled only by the incoming Zedillo team. So at a fateful meeting on November 20, 1994, there were six people present: Salinas, Aspe, the head of the central bank, two other cabinet ministers, and a top Zedillo representative. This group considered and rejected the possibility of a devaluation.[14] Later in the day, spokesmen for the prevailing *Pacto* expressed support for this decision.

Upon taking office, Zedillo continued efforts to sustain the peso, spending all but $3 billion of foreign reserves in the process. And when the government decided to devalue, the Zedillo team committed a number of blunders—attempting a mini-devaluation instead of overshooting expectations, inadequately informing the international community, and failing to support the devaluation with an overall economic package. Why did this young government make so many errors?

In part, it may have been a matter of inexperience. Jaime Serra Puche had been an outstanding Secretary of Commerce, for instance, but he had relatively little preparation for the shift to Finance. Bad luck (such as the rise in U.S. interest rates) may have played a role. Moreover, there was the built-in rigidity of the system, which meant that the Zedillo administration would start anew on December 1, thus raising the specter of potential change in policy and personnel.

Here occurred a failure of political analysis. Given the tradition of cabinet-level turnover, it was utterly in keeping with past political practice for Zedillo not to reappoint Pedro Aspe as Secretary of Finance (although there was a precedent, as Antonio Ortiz Meña had served two successive terms at this post from 1958 to 1970). The problem apparently was that Zedillo and his associates did not understand the extent to which the investment community identified macroeconomic stability not with the system but with Aspe himself. To emphasize the point, Mexico's *Bolsa* promptly reacted to the unveiling of Zedillo's cabinet, *sans* Aspe, by dropping 50 points. In

---

[14] Accounts of this gathering appear in the *Wall Street Journal Americas*, July 6, 1995, with a response by Pedro Aspe in *Reforma*, July 14, 1995.

other words, the Zedillo team failed to comprehend the degree to which the deterioration of long-standing institutions was leading to the personalization of politics and policy.[15] Although they were operating according to rules of political logic, they made a serious miscalculation.

POLITICAL CONSEQUENCES OF CRISIS

Inevitably enough, the peso crisis of December 1994 had a long and painful aftermath. The economic solution was not, of course, just a matter of adjusting the rate of exchange. There proved to be structural problems as well. Draconian adjustment measures led to steep rises in interest rates (and in inflation), the liquidation of hundreds of small and medium-size businesses, sharp declines in purchasing power, the loss of perhaps one million jobs, and an estimated contraction in economic output for 1995 of approximately 7 percent (-10.4 percent for the first six months of the year). The peso crisis of 1994 precipitated a profound economic crisis lasting throughout 1995.

In the political realm, public reaction to the crisis exacerbated the nation's ongoing crisis of institutional authority. For the first time in decades, rumors began circulating that an elected PRI president might not be able to finish his term. One public opinion poll in early 1995 showed that 48 percent of the respondents believed a military coup was possible.[16] Voters in the state of Jalisco, long a bastion of the PRI, elected an opposition-party PAN candidate as governor. Even where the PRI claimed outright victories, as in Tabasco and Yucatán, the results were sharply contested.

The fallout was far-reaching. One immediate consequence of the peso/economic crisis was, of course, the utter ruination of Salinas and his reputation. In late 1993, as president, Carlos Salinas had enjoyed approval ratings of higher than 60 percent, and he had been widely revered as a national leader of historic proportions.[17] By early 1995, in the early months of the crisis, he was thoroughly reviled: a March survey showed that 83 percent of the Mexican people held "no confidence" in Salinas (compared with a 54 percent confidence rating for the still-struggling Zedillo). At this same time, nearly two-thirds of the populace—64 percent—expressed the conviction that

---

[15] Reliable reports indicate that Zedillo offered Aspe any cabinet-level post he might want, with the sole exception of Secretary of Finance.

[16] Encuesta Telefónica Nacional de MORI de México/*Este País*, March 1, 1995.

[17] *Este País*, September 1994, p. 19.

Carlos Salinas was somehow "implicated" in the assassination of José Francisco Ruíz Massieu.[18] Pundits routinely observed that Salinas had become so unpopular, and so widely detested, that it would be unsafe for him to appear in the streets of Mexico City. Forced to withdraw his candidacy for the directorship of the WTO, Salinas found his political fortune in tatters.

Second, the economic costs of the crisis produced a considerable backlash against NAFTA and, by implication, against the neoliberal model of economic reform. Early in 1995, 36 percent of respondents in a national survey declared the effects of NAFTA to be "bad" or "very bad," especially in view of its apparent impact on unemployment, while 30 percent judged it to be "good" or "very good."[19] The country was becoming polarized around this issue. Even more remarkably, barely one-third of business and finance executives (34 percent) agreed that the "neo-liberal" economic model should stay in place as it was; another third (32 percent) believed that it should stay intact, but with substantial modification; and nearly as many (29 percent) wanted it to be discarded altogether.[20] Whatever neo-liberal consensus existed in Mexico was coming apart at the seams.

There was little room for optimism. A March 1995 questionnaire sought to explore popular perceptions of national well-being both over the previous year and in anticipation of the year to come. The results, shown in Table 2, revealed a widespread picture of deterioration: 89 percent said that economic conditions were worse, 52 percent thought that political conditions were worse, 48 percent reported that social conditions were worse. Expectations for the future were a bit less gloomy (perhaps because some believed that conditions could only get better), but about one-third of the population expressed the view that conditions would continue to get worse in all three dimensions.

In sum, Mexican citizens were beginning to see themselves as engaged in a zero-sum game: if total resources were stagnating, one person's gain could come only at someone else's loss. In stark contrast with the optimism of the early 1990s, this must have been eerily (and sadly) reminiscent of the despair that gripped the country in the 1980s. It was an ominous trend, and it helped explain the palpable rise in crime and violence that the country experienced in 1994-95.

---

[18] *Reforma*, March 2, 1995.
[19] *Reforma*, January 9, 1995.
[20] *Reforma*, January 30, 1995.

Table 2. Perceptions of National Well-Being, March 1995

A. Reflections on Past Year
(responses, in %)

Situation	Better	Same	Worse	Don't Know
Economic	1	9	89	1
Political	16	26	52	6
Social	9	34	48	9

Text of Question: "Cómo siente las siguientes situaciones comparadas con hace un año?"

("How do you feel about the following situations in comparison with a year ago?")

B. Expectations for Coming Year

(responses, in %)

Situation	Better	Same	Worse	Don't Know
Economic	35	23	29	13
Political	37	27	21	15
Social	35	29	21	15

Text of question: "Cómo cree que serán las siguientes situaciones para el próximo año?"

("How do you think the following situations will be next year?")

Source: *Reforma*, March 10, 1995.

Finally, the economic crisis led to prolonged disenchantment with Ernesto Zedillo as president. While many people appreciated his personal honesty and modesty and admired his willingness to stand up to the Salinas family, they did not regard him as an effective leader. As shown in Table 3, his approval ratings dropped from 53 percent in March 1995 (after the arrest of Raúl Salinas) to just 31 percent in June (as inflation and unemployment were on the rise);

similarly, his disapproval ratings jumped from 34 percent in March to 61 percent in June and remained around that level through November.[21]

Table 3. Approval/Disapproval Ratings for Ernesto Zedillo, 1995
(responses, in %)

	March	June	August	November
Approve	53	31	34	31
Disapprove	34	61	56	60
Don't Know	13	8	10	9

Text of question: "Aprueba o desaprueba la forma como el Presidente Ernesto Zedillo está manejando el país?"

("Do you approve or disapprove of the way that President Ernesto Zedillo is running the country?")

Sources: *Reforma* March 10, April 27, June 11, July 11, September 1, December 1, 1995.

As Zedillo completed his first year in office, Miguel Pérez offered a retrospective assessment in the respected newspaper *Reforma*:

> With an unprecedented economic crisis, with inflation about to surpass official estimates, with a high rate of unemployment, without any progress [*claridad*] on investigations of the assassinations of Luis Donaldo Colosio and José Francisco Ruíz Massieu, and with the sewer of official corruption wide open, President Ernesto Zedillo today completes one year at the head of the government of Mexico.
>
> In merely 365 days, the country's GDP fell by more than 7 percent; inflation rose from 7 to 49 percent; and the rate of [open] unemployment climbed to more than 6 percent, which means that there are 2.5 million people without work.[22]

It was a devastating summation of a devastating year.

---

[21] As measured on a ten-point scale, Zedillo's ratings among the general public also dropped steadily throughout the year. See *Reforma*, March 10, April 27, June 11, July 11, September 1, and December 1, 1995.

[22] Pérez (1995).

Ultimately, the harshness of such judgments on Zedillo implied that Mexicans were becoming disenchanted with the nation's entire political elite, including its technocratic cadres. Personal vilification of Salinas was in some ways understandable. Denunciations of Zedillo appeared to represent a more deep-seated malaise; they suggested that, in the eyes of many Mexicans, there could be little hope for honest and effective leadership. There were no good guys any more.

FUTURE PROSPECTS

Relegitimation of the regime and the restoration of presidential authority would depend not only on the resumption of economic growth but also on the effectiveness of responses to structural challenges to economic development, especially the persistence of poverty and inequality. Between 1963 and 1981, the proportion of Mexicans below the poverty line dropped from 77.5 percent to 48.5 percent; but from 1982 to 1992, under the pro-market reforms, it rose again to 66 percent. And despite the government's cooperation with international creditors, Mexico still confronted a massive external debt of more than $120 billion, with annual interest payments consuming about 12-14 percent of export earnings, not to mention the urgency of ever-present *tesobonos*.

Over the long term, three potential resolutions of political uncertainty in Mexico loomed large:

- First, and most favorable: *an acceleration of the processes of liberalization and democratization.* The crisis of authority could lead to replacement of the long-standing system by truly democratic politics. Opposition advances in the mid-term elections of July 1997 gave substantial impetus to this scenario. The ultimate test for such a transition could not come until the elections of 2000, however, at which point it would have to be genuinely possible for an opposition candidate to win the presidency. (One difficulty inherent in this criterion is that the only credible proof of such a possibility would be an opposition victory.)

- Second: *an authoritarian throwback—a return to populist and nationalist politics* engineered by, perhaps, an alliance of old-line *priísta* dinosaurs with segments of the Mexican military. This could occur in response to mass protest, social disorder, and continued evidence of the disintegration of power.

- Third: *a fragmentation and dispersion of power—a redistribution of power among a congeries of regional and bureaucratic fiefdoms.* According to this scenario, processes of disintegration would continue apace. Power would reside in pockets: some might

49

follow democratic practices, others would be blatantly authoritarian. Contests among these fiefdoms would be chronic, continuing, and probably brutal. The future of Mexico might lie in contemporary Russia and the former Soviet Union.

All in all, the long-term political consequence of the economic crisis was to generate uncertainty and instability. While the traditional system appeared to be on the way out, it was by no means clear where Mexico was heading.

LESSONS FOR GIVING LESSONS

Not surprisingly, the Mexican peso crisis precipitated a nearly instantaneous and multifaceted quest for "lessons" that it might convey. Journalists have written widely on the subject. The Council on Foreign Relations in New York mounted an "independent task force" for just this very purpose.[23] In one of the most thoughtful of these efforts, Sebastian Edwards has emphasized the importance of the current account, the dangers of portfolio investment, the need for productivity gains, the rigidities inherent in fixed exchange rates, and the structure and maturation of public debt.[24]

In many of these analyses, politics emerges as something of a nuisance—as a series of unpredictable and unwelcome intrusions on the policy process. In discussing the peso-dollar exchange rate, for example, the Council on Foreign Relations group observed that international confidence was holding steady over time: "However, political turmoil—events in Chiapas, the assassination of José Francisco Ruíz Massieu, and a series of political kidnappings—continued to erode confidence in Mexico's polity. The peso came under renewed pressure when the tensions between the government and the Zapatista insurgents intensified in December [1994]."[25] But for these unseemly intrusions, economic rationality might have prevailed.

But politics consists of more than random happenings and nettlesome events. It embraces the nature of the prevailing regime, the rules for allocation of power, and the incentives for political actors. To understand the behavior of policy-makers in Mexico, from Salinas to Zedillo, it is necessary to comprehend the nature of the country's authoritarian system. As I have attempted to demonstrate

---

[23] Council on Foreign Relations (1996). See also Sachs, Tornell, and Velasco (1995).

[24] Edwards (1995), pp. 301-302.

[25] Council on Foreign Relations (1996), p. 11.

throughout this chapter, policy-makers were acting in accordance with a long-standing (if not especially laudable) political logic.

Altering behavior in Mexico will necessitate change in the structure of incentives—which means reshaping the political system as a whole. Piecemeal institutional reform has no hope of succeeding within the prevailing regime. It will be impossible to achieve true autonomy for the central bank, as many have urged, as long as the president remains in command of supreme power. It will be senseless to insist on a transparent budgetary process with full legislative review, as others have suggested, as long as the Congress has no significant power or role of its own.[26]

What needs to be understood is that, despite their modest appearance, such institutional prescriptions require radical political surgery. They amount to a call for nothing less than the full democratization of Mexico. There is no other way for economic reforms to acquire popular support.[27] There is no other way that government can be held accountable. There is no other way for public institutions and branches of government, including the central bank, to achieve genuine autonomy. It may well be that the ultimate lesson of the Mexican peso crisis is that authoritarianism might be effective for initiating economic reform, but only democracy can achieve consolidation and perpetuation.

Finally, the peso crisis of 1994-95 suggests the need for preparedness, for a willingness to broaden horizons about the possible course of future events in Mexico, and for tolerating the unexpected. Policy-makers in the United States and elsewhere need to realize that although Mexico has embarked on a path of irreversible transition, setbacks and shifts in direction are almost certain to occur. There has been a tendency, in general, to place too much faith in the capacity to settle Mexico's short-term financial crises—and to assume that all will then be well.[28] This smacks of hubris and shortsightedness. A more effective way to facilitate and foster orderly change in Mexico would be to make ample allowance for less-than-optimal scenarios. The best way to avert future crisis may well be to expect it.

---

[26] These prescriptions appear in Edwards (1995), pp. 303-309.

[27] See Haggard and Webb (1994).

[28] See, for example, the ebullient remarks about the Mexican rescue by Lawrence H. Summers, Deputy Secretary of the U.S. Treasury, *New York Times*, June 19, 1996. For a more measured interpretation see De Long, De Long, and Robinson (1996), pp. 8-14; and, for a skeptical view, Castañeda (1996), pp. 92-105.

REFERENCES AND BIBLIOGRAPHY

Aguirre, Eugenio, et al. (1995). *Ruíz Massieu: el mejor enemigo*. Mexico: Espasa-Hoy.

Ai Camp, Roderic (1995). *Political Recruitment Across Two Centuries: Mexico, 1884-1991*. Austin: University of Texas Press.

Castañeda, Jorge G. (1996). "Mexico's Circle of Misery," *Foreign Affairs* 75, no. 4.

————— (1995). *The Mexican Shock: Its Meaning for the United States*. New York: The New Press.

Centeno, Miguel Angel (1994). *Democracy within Reason: Technocratic Revolution in Mexico*. University Park, Penn.: Pennsylvania State University Press.

Council on Foreign Relations (1996). *Lessons of the Mexican Peso Crisis: Report of an Independent Task Force*. New York: CFR.

De Long, Bradford, Christopher De Long, and Sherman Robinson (1996). "The Case for Mexico's Rescue," *Foreign Affairs* 75, no. 3.

Dornbusch, Rudiger (1995). "We Have Salinas to Thank for the Peso Debacle," *Business Week*. January 16.

Dresser, Denise (1996). "Mexico: The Decline of Dominant-Party Rule" in Jorge I. Domínquez and Abraham F. Lowenthal, eds., *Constructing Democratic Governance: Latin America and the Caribbean in the 1990s*. Baltimore: The Johns Hopkins University Press.

Edwards, Sebastian (1995). *Crisis and Reform in Latin America: From Despair to Hope*. New York: World Bank/Oxford University Press.

González Sandoval, Juan Pablo, and Jaime González Graf, eds. (1995). *Los límites rotos: anuario político*. Mexico: Oceano.

Haggard, Stephan, and Steven B. Webb, eds. (1994). *Voting for Reform: Democracy, Political Liberalization, and Economic Adjustment*. New York: World Bank/Oxford University Press.

Lustig, Nora (1995). "Mexico y la crisis del peso: lo previsible y la sorpresa," *Comercio Exterior* 45, no. 5. May.

Naím, Moisés (1995). "Mexico's Larger Story," *Foreign Policy* 99. Summer.

Paternostro, Silvana (1995). "Mexico as a Narco-Democracy," *World Policy Journal*. Spring.

Pérez, Miguel (1995). "El Presidente y sus 365 días," *Reforma*. December 1.

Ros, Jaime (1995). "La crisis mexicana: causas, perspectivas, lecciones," *Nexos* 209. May.

Sachs, Jeffrey, Aaron Tornell, and Andrés Velasco (1995). "The Collapse of the Mexican Peso: What Have We Learned?" Working Paper Series no. 95-7.

Cambridge, Mass.: Center for International Affairs, Harvard University. July.

Schettino, Macario (1995). *El costo del miedo: la devaluación de 1994/1995.* Mexico: Grupo Editorial Iberoamérica.

Smith, Peter H. (1979). *Labyrinths of Power: Political Recruitment in Twentieth-Century Mexico.* Princeton, NJ: Princeton University Press.

Valle, Eduardo (1995). *El segundo disparo: la narcodemocracia mexicana.* Mexico: Oceano.

Weintraub, Sidney (1995). "Mexico: Honeymoon from Hell," *Hemisfile* 6, no. 1. January/February.

Zaid, Gabriel (1995). *Adiós al PRI.* Mexico: Oceano.

2. FALLING FROM THE TIGHTROPE: THE POLITICAL ECONOMY OF THE MEXICAN CRISIS

DENISE DRESSER

I nterpretations of Mexico's 1994 financial crisis tend to reproduce the cacophony of voices in Akira Kurosawa's film *Rashomon*, where each one of the participants has a different and conflicting view of what is really happening. Economists stress specific poli-cy-making mistakes; political scientists view the crash as an inevitable byproduct of decades of dominant-party rule; Mexican politicians blame each other or former President Carlos Salinas de Gortari. In an effort to clarify the interpretive maelstrom, this chapter analyzes the political and institutional constraints that provided the context in which economic decisions were made during the Salinas years and that limited policy options. The Mexican "meltdown" was not caused exclusively by short-term policy mistakes, electoral cycles, or unbri-dled personal ambitions. The crisis was rooted in the conflicting imperatives of economic adjustment and political survival. Intent on liberalizing the economy without loosening its reins over the politi-cal system, the ruling technocracy designed a set of constantly con-tradictory policies.

Mexico's modernizing technocrats of the 1980s did not encounter a *tabula rasa* when they decided to reform the economy. The liberalization effort during the Salinas period (1988-1994) was rooted in and mediated by pre-existing institutional arrangements. In the Mexican case, policies geared toward expanding market forces were forced to coexist with a historical legacy of statism, clien-telism, presidentialism, and patronage. Consequently, the country's adjustment effort under Salinas presented distinct anomalies. The result was a hybrid policy package that combined technocratic and market guidance with extensive compensation of domestic interests for losses suffered through liberalization. The state promoted trans-parency in economic transactions, liberalization, and deregulation in support of the "winners" of the new economic model *and* increased the scope of compensatory allocations for the "losers." It promoted survival of the fittest in numerous sectors *and* offered compensation elsewhere. While state elites unleashed market forces, they also established strong barriers to democratic evolution. This uncomfortable and unstable mix of neoliberal and neopopulist policies—carried out in a context of tightly controlled political liberalization—created the conditions that led to the financial chaos of December 1994.

The market-oriented reforms implemented under Salinas were geared toward enlarging the scope of market forces, promoting transparency in economic policy-making, and ending discretionary entitlements for privileged members of the traditional populist-distributive coalition. However, the need to channel public funds for compensatory payments and pre-election patronage dictated continued state intervention, large doses of presidentialism and discretionality, the expansion of domestic credit, and postponement of the devaluation. The Salinas model of economic adjustment created a scenario of extreme vulnerability in which the country's entire financial stability became dependent on the *virtú* (or lack thereof) of specific individuals—whether the incumbent President Carlos Salinas, or his successor Ernesto Zedillo, or outgoing Secretary of Finance Pedro Aspe, or incoming Secretary of Finance Jaime Serra.

This chapter, divided into four sections, first focuses on the policy dynamics of the Salinas term, explains how efforts to construct a center-right coalition of support for economic reform were pursued, and analyzes the contradictions that those efforts created and the limitations they encountered. The chapter next discusses the problems that the hybrid model of economic adjustment left in its wake. It then presents current dilemmas, namely how renewed commitment to economic reform without the political concessions of the past may make a third round of market-oriented reforms more difficult to undertake or even unsustainable. A final section draws some conclusions and looks to the future.

1. THE SALINAS COALITION-BUILDING MODEL

E conomic policy under Carlos Salinas de Gortari can be interpreted as an effort to replace the populist-distributive coalition of inward-looking development with a new, center-right coalition geared toward export-led growth.[1] According to the architects

---

[1] Olson defines distributional coalitions as alliances of special interest groups that can reduce the rate of economic growth by taking for their own consumption resources that would otherwise be used for investment purposes. See Olson (1982.)

of Mexico's great leap forward, in order to surmount the lost decade, the country would have to rely on the magic of the market and the energy of private initiative. For economic liberalization policies to flourish, traditional bases of government support—the state bureaucracy, the organized working class—would have to be replaced by new, organized interests in the private sector and the middle class and by international investors.

The construction of a center-right coalition in Mexico presented two economic faces. As John Waterbury's work on Turkey[2] suggests, a center-right coalition in a developmental context tends to pursue liberalization, privatization, free trade, and private-sector expansion in key export sectors while using selective resources, through public spending programs, to compensate the losers in the new development model. In Mexico, state leaders intended to increase economic efficiency, promote deregulation, and reduce state intervention in many areas of the economy. However, this efficiency-oriented strategy was combined with strategic quantities of "political slush" and inefficient disbursements with compensatory objectives to assure political consensus.

The measures in Table 1 were the features of the face the Mexican government showed the international financial institutions, the negotiating team for the free trade agreement with the United States, and domestic and international business groups. It was the face applauded by the "Washington consensus" and portrayed in the *Economist*, the *Wall Street Journal*, and the *Financial Times*. It was a policy area managed by macro-strategy managers and technocrats in charge of designing and marketing an internationalist development project that could be presented at home and abroad as the most appropriate response to domestic and international challenges. This aspect of the Mexican adjustment model was rooted in what Paul Krugman has defined as the prevailing international paradigm, namely the belief that "Victorian virtue in economic policy—free markets and sound money—is the key to economic development."[3]

The measures encompassed in Table 1 accomplished several simultaneous objectives. The prospect of free trade with the United States became more palatable to domestic business groups because it was linked to financial and macroeconomic benefits. The North

---

The distributional coalitions associated with inward-looking development are usually composed of urban wage earners, organized labor, public-sector employees, manufacturing business, the intelligentsia, and the army.

[2] Waterbury (1992).

[3] Krugman (1995).

Table 1. Enhance Economic Efficiency and Attract Foreign Investment

- Debt renegotiation in 1989
- Liberalization, deregulation, privatization
- Public-sector reform
- Agricultural reform
- NAFTA
- Exchange rate policy

American Free Trade Agreement (NAFTA) was sold at home and abroad as synonymous with economic stabilization and growth. By "getting the policies right," Mexican modernizers were able to attract an unprecedented flow of foreign investment. Between 1990 and 1993, Mexico received an influx of $52.8 billion—a larger foreign flow than any other developing country.[4] A sophisticated government propaganda and public relations campaign focused international attention on the virtues of Mexico's neoliberal policy thrust. The approach summarized in Table 1 created and was the product of a unique convergence of interests among key players: the Mexican government, domestic business groups, foreign investors, and international financial institutions.[5]

Mexico's shift toward market-oriented reforms responded to the need to secure access to investments that would reignite growth. Under the Salinas strategy, government elites began to heed the voice of capital above the demands of other sectors. As economic liberalization progressed, Mexico's financial markets became increasingly internationalized, making it more difficult to induce domestic and foreign investors to make long-term fixed investments. Investors with liquid assets could easily "exit" to more lucrative foreign markets. The threat of exit induced Mexican policy-makers to strive to gain the loyalty of domestic and international business groups by promoting policies that would inspire confidence. The new neoliberal policy network defined by the measures in Table 1 was designed to satisfy the needs and interests of potential investors, international financial institutions such as the International Monetary Fund (IMF) and the World Bank, and credit-rating agencies.

---

[4] Elizondo Mayer-Serra (1995), p. 1.
[5] Naím (1995b).

Table 2. Coalition Maintenance Through State Intervention and Patronage

- Neutralize organized labor
- Control discretionary credit to private-sector groups
- Obtain the support of (or demobilize) popular groups: National Solidarity Program (Pronasol)
- Elicit middle-class support through consumption of imports
- Monetary and fiscal policy (in 1994)
- The Pact for Economic Growth and Stability (PECE)

Table 2 encompasses the features of the face Salinas turned toward his domestic political allies and outlines a parallel restructuring program that was managed by so-called "technobureaucrats": a new hybrid elite that combined technical expertise, negotiating skills, and political savvy.[6] It included policies such as export credits, tax incentives, financing for small and medium business, price controls, and poverty-alleviation programs, including the National Solidarity Program (Pronasol).[7] This discretionary and subsidizing face reflected the *political* imperatives that the Mexican government confronted under structural adjustment. The policies listed in Table 2 allowed the government to reach out to the informal sectors, attend to the needs of select businessmen, and maintain the acquiescence of recalcitrant labor groups.

During the Salinas period, the strategy of seeking political support through systematic compensation of strategic interest groups became a consolidated facet of the country's political economy. Government leaders aggressively bestowed benefits on pivotal prospective supporters in an effort to assure political peace, while business groups condoned this uneconomic behavior in the interest of broader stability. Given the broad divide between the "winners" and "losers" of the new model, government elites were forced to accommodate the political world, intensifying the importance of discretionary and distributive policies in certain sectors. The efficiency-

---

[6] The term "technobureaucrats" was coined by Miguel Centeno (1994).

[7] Pronasol was an umbrella organization aimed at developing health, education, nutrition, housing, employment, infrastructure, and other productive projects to benefit the extreme poor. See Cornelius, Craig, and Fox (1994).

oriented patterns that characterized the policy areas mapped out in Table 1 were intermittently compromised elsewhere in the Mexican political economy by the compensatory flows in Table 2.[8]

Under Salinas, Mexico witnessed not the retreat of the state but a new form of "statism." The Salinas team fervently declared that it did not want the big, overweight, subsidizing state of the 1970s, but rather the small, lean, administratively modern state of the 1980s and 1990s: "*un Estado rector*" that would not intervene or nationalize but would promote.[9] However, this rhetorical emphasis on state-shrinking obscured the new character of the Mexican state. In terms of its intervention in the economy and its use and channeling of resources, the state in Mexico during the Salinas period did not shrink except in the realm of public-sector employment. In a context of scarce resources and economic restructuring, the political elite sought to promote growth, maximize the discretionary allocation of resources, and keep a disparate coalition of economic actors together by keeping all of them guessing as to who would be the next beneficiary of state largesse. The need to promote foreign investment and generate private-sector support required state-streamlining policies. Yet at the same time the need to compensate required a state with broad discretionary authority.

The genealogy of the policies contained in Table 2 was rooted in politics. The turbulent July 1988 election—which Salinas almost lost—revealed that top-down, market-geared change could probably not be sustained without the support of organized constituencies. Coalitions of support for the neoliberal experiment would have to be created. One effort in that direction was to maintain as much power concentrated in the hands of the executive as possible, in order to be able to direct resources to trouble spots or disaffected groups in a speedy and targeted fashion.

Central to the dynamic of Mexico's new statism was the notion of "circles of compensation." Since the inception of the ruling Partido Revolucionario Institucional (PRI) in 1929, Mexican politics had operated largely in terms of institutionalized networks of players engaged in special, behind-the-scenes, reciprocal relationships of obligation and reward with the government. In return for consistent political support, the government provided constant benefits to key

---

[8] John Waterbury defines "compensatory flows" as state resources that support groups negatively affected by structural adjustment. Among the most common are wage increases, temporary subsidies, and public investment in infrastructure and services. See Waterbury (1989).

[9] Aguilar Camín and Meyer (1989), p. 289.

constituencies. The Salinas team built upon this ingrained practice: key to the initial success of Mexico's economic adjustment package was the process of creating circles of compensation among those most negatively affected by the new developmental course. Government officials succeeded at maintaining political stability through a range of policies directed at maintaining and expanding the PRI's electoral base.

According to the logic of technocratic state elites, over time, the policies in Table 1 would create new organized interests in the private sector—particularly internationally competitive consortia—that could sustain the center-right coalition by fueling economic growth via NAFTA. Salinas or any successor could then reduce the flow of compensatory resources channeled through the policies in Table 2. However, until the growth objective was achieved, the Salinas government had to channel resources to inefficient travel companions, including the urban and rural poor, labor organizations, and small and medium-size businesses.

The glue that kept these two disparate faces together was Salinas's "hyper-presidentialism": swift, decisive, presidential action on the fronts listed in Table 3. Tainted by claims of illegitimacy, Salinas from the beginning of his term sought to revive waning support by what could be called a strategy of refurbished presidentialism. The essence of presidential power in Mexico had always been the ruling party and its corporatist sectors. However, the dramatic results of the 1988 election indicated that traditional legitimizing mechanisms were under severe strain as a result of economic decline. Unable to meet the demands of corporatist sectors accustomed to a flow of material benefits, the PRI lost representativeness among its bases. Displaced by a technocratic team intent on implementing economic reform, and wracked by internal factionalism, the party was marginalized from the decision-making process. Incapable of guaranteeing mass support via uncontested electoral victories, the party began to fail as a legitimator of the regime.[10] Given that the PRI seemed incapable of fulfilling its traditional roles, Salinas placed the burden of legitimizing the political system on the institution of the presidency itself.[11]

---

[10] For further elaboration of this argument, see Dresser (1994).

[11] Under the 1917 Constitution, the Mexican president enjoys tremendous power. Among other things, he initiates legislation, can issue regulations without congressional approval, controls the budgetary process, is empowered to intervene in industrial and commercial activities, and sets domestic and foreign economic policy. The president has wide latitude to shift direction and operate on a case-by-case basis. He also has extensive powers of appointment, which he uses to place loyal supporters in key posts.

Table 3. Political Survival Through Presidentialism and Reform From Above

- Enhance presidential image
- Appeal to middle-class and lower middle-class
- Assure PRI hegemony
- Maintain the cohesion of the political elite
- Isolate the left-wing opposition
- Promote a new developmentalist ideology

Throughout the decade of structural adjustment, Latin American presidents extended the powers of their office far beyond their formal attributes. Alberto Fujimori, for example, temporarily suspended the legislature in Peru, and Carlos Saul Menem ruled in Argentina through *"decretismo."* Both presidents justified their actions by arguing that the severity of the economic crisis demanded prompt responses. The 1980s witnessed the birth of a fundamentally new style of politics in the region, wherein executives pursued their objectives in a relatively unconstrained fashion. Presidents captured and molded state institutions to maximize their interests, using whatever power resources they had at their command. The concentration of power in the presidency throughout the continent was the result of efforts to increase economic and political efficacy, allegedly to assure governability.

Mexico was no exception to this trend. From the beginning of his term, Salinas resorted to swift, unilateral presidential action as a means of furthering the reform agenda. Through the image of a strong and populist president, he sought to mobilize the energies and to capture the imagination of the population for the modernization effort. Throughout his presidency, Salinas strove to present the image of an informal president in touch with popular sectors: sitting under trees talking to peasants, participating in rallies without the use of a spectacular podium, descending from the presidential car to talk with workers. His presence compensated in a way for the drastic reduction in income that accompanied the stabilization policies of his predecessor, Miguel de la Madrid. The active presidential presence in the countryside became a kind of great national palliative that preempted social conflict—at least until the Chiapas uprising of January 1994.

The centralization of the policy-making process around the presidency and the authoritarian character of political life undoubtedly facilitated the government's ability to implement market reforms. By metamorphosing into a *neo-caudillo*, Salinas was able to take decisive action to undermine his opponents. By taking the initiative on human rights and the reform of the PRI, the President scored points among constituencies opposed to clientelism and corruption, and in favor of change. Salinas was perceived as a president *"con iniciativa"* waging a war of modernity against the old Mexico.

Salinas's political energies were devoted to the task of building a durable and long-term political base for the project of economic restructuring. Throughout his term, Salinas's attention centered on six issue areas: mending the rifts among the political elite, reforming the PRI to assure its hegemony, maintaining the mechanisms of *"concertación"* with the business sector, pushing through an electoral reform in alliance with the National Action Party (PAN), isolating the left-wing opposition, and promoting a new developmentalist ideology. The immediate goal of these strategic maneuvers appeared to be a clean electoral victory of the PRI in the 1994 presidential election. The long-term goal, however, was to dismantle the political constraints and at the same time construct the bases of consensus that would allow the continuation and deepening of the economic restructuring program. Thus, the importance of political management suggests the need to incorporate a third dimension—set out in Table 3—into the cluster of strategies linked to coalition construction and maintenance.

Given the constant interplay among the measures outlined in Tables 1, 2, and 3, the Salinas administration offered apparently contradictory images. The international financial community hailed Salinas as the champion of the market in the Mexican economy, a friend of domestic and foreign capital, and an enemy of state intervention in economic life. Others, mainly Mexicans, saw him as at best a pragmatist who used whatever economic and political instruments necessary to keep himself, his team, and the PRI in power, and at worst a closet authoritarian with little commitment to democratic politics. Ultimately, the contradictions generated by the contending imperatives of neoliberalism, neopopulism, and preservation of dominant-party rule unleashed the crisis of 1994.

Mexico's modernizing technobureaucrats were not immune to the political cycle, or to the *sexenio* cycle. Salinas's obsession with maintaining the PRI in power, assuring the political permanence of the ruling technocracy, and providing legitimacy for economic reform at the ballot box led to a hybrid adjustment model dependent on the use of "political slush" funds and on the enactment of inconsistent policies that ended up thwarting the stability of the economic reform program itself.

2. THE COSTS OF CONTRADICTION

The multifaceted neoliberal, compensatory, and presidentialist tactics outlined in the previous section proved to be politically and economically unsustainable. The triple-faced strategies involved in Mexico's coalition-building effort were a high-stakes gamble, and the attention devoted to the measures in Tables 2 and 3 undid those in Table 1 by altering the fragile equilibrium on which the country's stability was based. The three-pronged adjustment strategy became an economic and political tightrope walk whose success depended on the massive influx of foreign funding, the constant compensation of key groups to assure social peace, and the electoral victory of the ruling party. The erratic combination of policies shown in the three tables created conditions that jeopardized the long-term viability of the Salinas model.

To begin with, the model failed to deliver growth, and the little growth that did occur was unevenly distributed. Government elites were able to privatize, deregulate, liberalize, and attract foreign capital. However, although capital inflows reached over US$30 billion in 1993, the average annual rate of GDP growth between 1990 and 1994 was only 2.5 percent. The main policy concern among members of the Economic Cabinet was to tame inflation, and there was little focus on the growth issue until the 1994 presidential election began to loom large. When growth did occur, its benefits were unevenly distributed and concentrated in the export and financial sectors dominated by big business.

Second, compensation policies, although indispensable in a country with such broad income disparities, were rooted in the perception of politics as doling out funds to assure support. The lack of institutionalized mechanisms for generating consensus—a product of the postponement of political reform—rendered the regime vulnerable to political upheaval. Instead of opening up pressure valves by negotiating with the Left and implementing a thorough electoral reform, the Salinas government engaged in little more than piecemeal changes to the political system. The emergence of guerrilla warfare in the state of Chiapas in January 1994 revealed the weaknesses of an economic modernization strategy that attempted to buy social peace at the expense of democratization.

In addition, compensation through neopopulist strategies proved to be a double-edged sword. The need to finance the measures in Table 2 led to a pattern of surging imports, an overvalued currency, and over-reliance on capital flows. The capital inflow and the appreciation of the peso had a positive impact on key constituencies, including the lower and middle classes as well as business groups seeking to modernize and expand. Foreign financing permitted the government to maintain high levels of public expenditures on politically relevant allies and to attend selectively to the demands of labor and Pronasol beneficiaries.

However, although overvaluation helped build support among a middle class hungry for imports, it led to a burgeoning current-account deficit and to the growth of a savings-investment gap. The investment and consumption boom that Mexico experienced from 1989 to 1993 was generated not only by positive perceptions of Mexico's future economic performance but also by an unregulated expansion of credit. During the last two years of the Salinas *sexenio*, Mexico was trapped in a vicious cycle: the real exchange-rate appreciation created a growing imbalance in the current account that was financed by foreign capital flows. Capital flows fueled by the prospect of NAFTA, in turn, provoked even greater appreciation, thus worsening the current-account deficit. Although economic growth failed to occur, the government did not change course, due to the perception that the government's commitment to price stability was more important than the promotion of competitiveness through a currency devaluation.[12] Retaining the political support of urban voters and key business groups in an election year became one of the primary concerns of government policy.

During turbulent political times—after Chiapas and the assassination of Luis Donaldo Colosio, and before the presidential election—the temptation to pass from selective and fiscally responsible compensation to massive and expansive transfers became irresistible. The three-pronged, coalition-building model led to the enactment of contradictory policies, especially during 1994. Nora Lustig has argued that the devaluation was caused primarily by the fiscal and monetary policies adopted during that year.[13] To assure the continued influx of foreign capital, the government argued explicitly that its main objective was to maintain the existing exchange rate policy. Indeed, the exchange rate became a symbol of the government's overall policy credibility; any policy deviation

---

[12] Lustig (1995), p. 1.
[13] Ibid., pp. 7-9.

would have entailed a collapse in confidence.[14] But in clear opposition to that stated goal, fiscal and monetary policies during 1994 were more expansionary than they should have been, and therefore inconsistent with the exchange rate rule.[15] Lax credit of the development banks grew to an equivalent of 4.4 percent of GDP—1.9 percent of GDP more than in 1993.[16] Massive portfolio inflows ultimately discouraged good economic performance by allowing Mexican leaders to believe that hard economic choices such as devaluation or cuts in government spending could be delayed.[17]

The government's foreign investment imperative also led to another policy during that year that fueled the subsequent financial meltdown: the placement of almost all short-term government debt into dollar-denominated instruments (*tesobonos*) in order to keep foreign funds in the country. Confronted with an expanding current-account deficit—8 percent of GDP in 1994—and inconsistent fiscal and monetary policies, and aware of the Mexican government's abandonment at the end of every presidential term of its promise not to devalue, foreign and domestic investors began to flee. According to an IMF study undertaken after the devaluation, the first to flee were not fickle foreign investors but well-informed Mexican businessmen.[18]

The Mexican government's ability to adapt to the turbulent circumstances of 1994 was constrained by the symbiotic alliance it had established with the business community, especially with the banking sector. The government-business alliance constructed by the Salinas government, though crucial for the success of economic liberalization policies, included only the large firms and conglomerates that dominate substantial portions of the Mexican economy, especially the newly reprivatized banks. Mexican officials failed to adjust after the peaceful presidential election in August 1994, because they were concerned that a hike in interest rates would undermine the country's banking system. The government's imperative to protect a

---

[14] See Frieden chapter in this volume.

[15] According to Lustig, "The monetary authorities decided to 'sterilize' the fall in international reserves by increasing net domestic credit and so keep the monetary base constant. This led to a fall in domestic interest rates beginning in July [1994], a trend contrary to interest rates in the United States. The expansion of net credit exacerbated the pressures on the peso." On the fiscal side the public sector's borrowing requirement had risen by two percentage points due to the development banks' net lending. See Lustig (1995), pp. 14-15.

[16] Cited in Elizondo Mayer-Serra (1995), p. 23.

[17] A similar argument about how foreign flows masked deeper sources of Latin America's poor economic performance is made by Moisés Naím (1995a).

[18] Fuentes Beraín (1995).

highly vulnerable financial system saddled by a high ratio of non-performing loans lies at the center of the Mexican crisis.[19] Special interests—as Jeffry Frieden has argued in his chapter in this collection—contributed to establishing political constraints on exchange rate policy.[20]

The government's willingness and capacity to adjust the exchange rate was also constrained by the way in which economic bargaining with the private sector took place within the Pact for Economic Growth and Stability (PECE).[21] Designed as a concerted effort among productive sectors to curb rampant inflation and stabilize the economy, the *Pacto* became a political instrument for governance in the hands of the president. Salinas and his economic team mapped out goals (monthly inflation rates, exchange rates, etc.), negotiated their timing and implementation with representatives of business associations, and then used the bargaining forum provided by the *Pacto* to inform labor of previously agreed-upon decisions. Confronted with dwindling reserves in November 1994, the government believed that a renewal of the *Pacto* would be sufficient to shore up confidence in the incoming government's commitment to its exchange rate policy. Subsequently, the decision to devalue was debated within the context of the *Pacto*, thus providing key business groups with information that allowed them to "exit" the financial markets before the decision was announced.[22] The style of *concertación* embodied in the *Pacto* provided privileged groups with favorable conditions that ultimately exacerbated the financial crisis.

In hindsight, the Mexican government implemented economic liberalization measures in a half-hearted fashion, and as a result the impact of the financial crisis was harsher than it might have been. Political considerations prevailed and often thwarted the reform process. For example, the Salinas team did not bring about sufficient changes in the institutions that could have provided incentives for domestic savings, and it failed to wrest away the pension system from the control of the Mexican Social Security Institute (IMSS). Secretary of Finance Pedro Aspe was guided by the dual imperative of retaining union support for his potential presidential bid and

---

[19] Lustig (1995), p. 6

[20] Frieden (1995).

[21] In its first incarnation, the Economic Solidarity Pact was an agreement reached among the state, business leaders, and labor in December 1987 that called for combined efforts (*concertación*) to limit price and wage increases in order to combat spiralling inflation. The name changed in 1989, while substantive goals remained basically intact. See Kaufman, Bazdresch, and Heredia (1994), pp. 360-410.

[22] Fuentes Beraín, (1995).

keeping labor quiescent within the context of the *Pacto*. In addition, privatization frequently served to replace public monopolies with private ones, amid much scattering of lucrative favors. Financial reform was late and poorly regulated.

Another Achilles' heel of the Mexican coalition-building model under Salinas was its reliance on hyper-presidentialism. The trend toward concentration of power in the executive in Mexico resulted from an avowed effort to increase economic and political efficacy. Yet these objectives were accomplished at the expense of effective institutional checks on economic policy-makers. Salinas's personal style of governance instituted a form of decision-making that ran counter to institutionalization. No other institution within the Mexican government—not even the central bank—had the power or the autonomy to question the soundness of his judgment. The facade of stability and economic recovery had to be maintained in order to assure a successful presidential exit from office, and therefore the prospect of a controlled devaluation was unthinkable. Salinas placed economic policy at the service of his own political interests, and he was perhaps not fully aware of the deleterious economic implications of that decision.

Under Salinas, Mexican political authorities concentrated ample discretionary powers in their hands so as to be able to direct politically motivated flows where and when they wanted. Enhanced discretionary powers, however, contradicted Washington consensus arguments about the retreating state and macro reforms supposedly intended to promote transparency in economic policy-making. In addition, an insulated policy style produced an erroneous diagnosis of political problems and led economic authorities to perceive politically motivated financial instability as temporary and short-term. An unquestioned consensus prevailed: the instability of the financial markets was perceived as temporary, and markets were expected to return to normalcy once confidence was restored and the political turmoil subsided.[23] Dominant-party rule imbued the country's political economy with a rigidity that constrained an effective government response to changing circumstances, such as rising interest rates in the United States.

This opaque and discretionary policy style, built on the personalization of power[24] and on the withholding of critical economic information, was the product of decades of dominant-party rule. In

---

[23] Lustig (1995), p. 16.

[24] Foreign investors trusted their personal relationship with Finance Minister Pedro Aspe, not the institution of the presidency or the government itself. Investors resented the perceived arrogance of incoming Secretary of Finance Jaime Serra, who did not return their phone calls and had not been properly briefed by his predecessor.

effect, Mexico's financial crisis underscored the vices of a highly politicized economic system, in which the political predominance of the ruling party was critical. Given the imperatives of the electoral cycle, the economy was run for political—not economic—reasons. Key decisions were not made for their economic merit but rather for the perceived gain of the ruling party or the personal fate of key political players.

3. ADJUSTMENT WITHOUT COMPROMISE

The multiple crises of 1994—the Zapatista uprising, political cannibalism within the PRI, and the peso debacle—shattered the Salinas coalition-building model. Under Ernesto Zedillo, Mexico witnessed the unraveling of the process of tightly controlled political liberalization that had sustained previous adjustment efforts. The "deflation" of presidential authority created challenges of political and economic management. The president's lack of a strong base of support in the PRI (and outside it) hampered the government's capacity to construct stable coalitions to sustain a new round of economic adjustment. The Zedillo government demonstrated a strong commitment to Washington consensus policies geared toward enhancing economic efficiency and attracting foreign capital; however, the measures for coalition maintenance through compensation, and for political reform from above via hyper-presidentialism, were almost completely abandoned.

Mexico's political economy in the post-crisis era was characterized by the following trends:

- A decline in presidential authority and increasing decentralization of power to other political players;
- The growing importance of parties and elections as a determining force in the country's political life, coupled with the persistent presence of anti-institutional actors (the Zapatista army, organized crime, the narco-politicians, hard-line PRI governors from several southeastern states, and the debtors' movement *El Barzón*, among others);
- A growing polarization of income and a dramatic increase in poverty; and
- A foreseeable messiness and unpredictability in Mexico's political future that could hamper the government's efforts to promote further economic reform.

Zedillo's response to the political challenges created by the devaluation was to announce the modernization of the Mexican presidency and its transformation into a "politically neutral guarantor of the rule of law."[25] Zedillo offered to reduce discretionary policy-making, to promote a new federalist pact, and to decentralize power and bring an end to the symbiotic relationship between the presidency and the ruling party. As an accidental candidate and outsider to the PRI, Zedillo did not feel beholden to the clientelist networks in the party—and therefore believed that the costs of reform would be lower, given that he and his close-knit team of advisors were not previously tied to the beneficiaries of state largesse.

Zedillo became the first president from the ranks of the PRI who seemed willing to sacrifice his party for the sake of economic stabilization. The electoral ascent of the opposition and the twilight of the PRI became a price he was willing to pay. But beyond granting electoral victories to rival political parties, the Zedillo government was unable to develop a clear strategy for generating political consensus for economic adjustment. Zedillo's substantive preference was to achieve economic stabilization, and as a result he tended to neglect the political and economic needs of the unstable coalition on which his power was based. Zedillo and his top economic advisors routinely stressed that economic policy would not be modified, despite social pressures and criticisms voiced by members of the business class and the rank and file of the ruling party.

The initial lesson Mexican technocrats seemed to derive from the post-devaluation crisis was that economic adjustment should be implemented without compromise to social groups, electoral imperatives, or the ebbs and flows of politics. Whereas Salinas over-politicized economic reform, Zedillo sought to de-politicize it. The Zedillo team appeared unwilling to make the compromises or to face the delays associated with political bargaining. From the perspective of the Economic Cabinet, for economic recovery to set in, certain issues had to be removed from the political arena so that policies would not be perverted by short-term political considerations.

From the beginning of his term, Zedillo displayed a strong commitment to a restrictive monetary policy that sought to stabilize financial markets, normalize the influx of foreign capital, contain inflation, and generate a fiscal surplus. The government also announced long-awaited reforms to the social security system designed to enhance the country's capacity for domestic savings over the long term. The Zedillo stabilization strategy began to produce positive results, and, by 1996, Mexico returned successfully to inter-

---

[25] Kaufman and Trejo (1995).

national capital markets, raising US$6.5 billion. The Mexican government also repaid its obligations to the U.S. Treasury in a timely fashion—$7 billion in July 1996—leaving unpaid only a quarter of the bailout approved by the Clinton administration. Exports rose after the devaluation, growing 35 percent between 1994 and 1996.

However, the macroeconomic and financial success of the Zedillo strategy contrasted sharply with the perceptions of Mexicans. A poll undertaken by the Mexican newspaper *Reforma* in June 1996 revealed that 64 percent of Mexicans opposed the government's economic policy and did not think that their economic situation had improved.[26] Prior to the July 6, 1997, mid-term elections, President Zedillo proclaimed that economic recovery had set in. The results of the election, however, proved that a majority of Mexicans did not believe him, and the PRI was punished for a multiplicity of sins. The party lost 112 congressional seats and its relative majority in Congress, the governorships of two economically powerful states, and the mayoralty of Mexico City. Although the worst of the financial debacle of 1994 was over, the campaigns resurrected old grievances; people relived the hardships of the crisis and voted against the party that had produced them.

In its efforts to stabilize Mexico's macroeconomic indicators, the Zedillo team neglected socially beneficial microeconomic intervention by the state and dismantled many of the compensatory mechanisms Salinas had successfully implemented.[27] The crisis deepened the resource crunch faced by the regime and further undermined the remnants of Mexico's patronage system of politics. The Zedillo government decided to eliminate programs such as Pronasol, which provided an important social safety net to cushion the effects of austerity. However, it is at the micro level and among the poor—the followers of *El Barzón* (an increasingly popular organization of debtors) and the Zapatista National Liberation Army (EZLN)—that some of the greatest challenges to democratic governance were spawned.

The PRI has faced increasingly deep divisions, and as a result the ruling party's grip over organized sectors of civil society has steadily declined. Although in the electoral sphere Mexican politics is becoming more institutionalized, and more actors are willing to play by the rules of the game, several key groups and individuals continue to operate at the margins of established politics. Extra-

---

[26] *Reforma*, June 2, 1996, p. 4A
[27] Dresser (1995).

institutional actors—guerrilla organizations, narco-politicians—have been quick to fill the political void left by the perceived weakening of the dominant party.

The 1994 crisis and its aftermath contributed to undermining the coherence and capacity of the state. The cohesion of the ruling elite suffered from persistent internal conflict over the scope and speed of political and economic reform. Zedillo frequently underestimated the ferocity of PRI opposition to neoliberal policy initiatives and as a result lost battles to political enemies. Faced with mounting political opposition, the ruling technocracy was unable to undertake widespread privatization of the petrochemical and natural gas industries. Deregulation was halting and piecemeal at the micro level, and new regulatory schemes in the banking sector remained incomplete.

In his efforts to decentralize power and de-politicize and shrink the authority of the executive, Zedillo dismantled lines of control that had enabled the government to promote market-oriented reforms with little opposition. The regionalization of politics has created important challenges for economic policy coordination at the national level. Regional power brokers have gained significant leverage. As the power of the presidency waned, governors, mayors, and regional power brokers acquired an unprecedented degree of political autonomy and control over resources and social programs.[28] Political decentralization generated conservative political alignments among hard-line governors who opposed further economic adjustment and continually challenged presidential authority.[29] Members of traditional factions in the PRI took advantage of a perceived presidential weakness to strengthen their personal fiefdoms in states such as Guerrero, Tabasco, Yucatán, and Puebla. Hardliners at the helm of several PRI-controlled governorships constantly opposed economic and political liberalization and hence jeopardized governability.

The government's incapacity to translate incipient economic recovery into concrete benefits for the majority of the population heightened the risk of social frustration turning into violence—as growing instability in Chiapas underscrored—given that the arrival of electoral democracy has yet to improve the lot of poorer

---

[28] The Zedillo government has decentralized Pronasol's budget and personnel, and changed the name of the program. Approximately one-third of agencies were transfered to other ministries, municipal governments, and the Municipal Councils for Development.

[29] Kaufman and Trejo (1995), pp. 42-43.

Mexicans.[30] Under Zedillo, over 40 percent of the Mexican population continues to live in poverty, and real wages have declined to pre-1980 levels. Extreme inequalities in income and social well-being still prevail among states and regions, and between urban and rural areas. Between 1984 and 1992, the absolute number of Mexicans living in extreme poverty grew—along with the number of Mexican billionaires included in *Forbes* magazine's list of the world's richest persons. The richest 10 percent of Mexicans obtain more than 40 percent of total income, whereas the poorest 40 percent receive a mere 13 percent. These disparities were accentuated by increased inflation, a dramatic decline in GDP, and the loss of over 1 million jobs in the first six months after the devaluation.

In addition, the benefits of greater integration with the United States have been unevenly distributed within the country, deepening regional disparities between a prosperous North increasingly tied to the U.S. economy and a backward South (especially the states of Chiapas, Oaxaca, and Guerrero) plunged into agricultural stagnation. Mexico is increasingly becoming a dual society wherein a growing portion of the population is left without the bounties of free trade and economic reform.[31] Mexico has increasingly exemplified what Fernando Fajnzylber baptized as the "pathology of inequality" in Latin America. The past decade has accentuated the already disproportionate influence of the rich and reduced the political and economic power of labor unions, peasant movements, and middle-class associations.

Economic reform in Mexico since 1982 has entailed a transcendental process of coalition realignment, as well as a reshaping of the constituencies sustaining the government coalition in power. The "inclusionist" coalitions of import-substituting industrialization have gradually been replaced by the "exclusionist" coalitions of export-led growth. Under Salinas, the cement holding together this narrow coalition was the expectation of economic recovery, augured by NAFTA. Under Zedillo, a volatile economy has been unable to generate sufficient jobs for a labor force that grew at over 3 percent a year. For the neoliberal experiment to survive, Mexican leaders will need to broaden the coalition of beneficiaries of economic reform and lessen both economic and social polarization. How they will do so remains an open question.

---

[30] Chand (1995), p. 36.
[31] For an analysis of the uneven distribution of rewards in the Mexican economy, see Castañeda (1996).

In the age of what Paul Krugman calls "deflated expectations," markets will no longer channel vast amounts of capital into countries that fail to experience economic growth. The Mexican crisis heightened the risk-aversion of international investors regarding contexts of potential instability.[32] Although growth has begun to take place in Mexico, and certain sectors of the economy are reaping the benefits of an open economy, it will take a long time to translate those rewards into concrete improvements for the majority.[33] GDP grew at 7 percent between April and June 1996, but Zedillo himself recognized—given the magnitude of the crisis—that income levels that existed in early 1994 will only be achieved at the end of the century.[34] The government interpreted recovery as the reestablishment of financial stability and the reduction of inflation; however, this objective has been achieved by depressing consumer demand, maintaining low wages, and allowing dramatic increases in unemployment.

Mexico is currently saddled with increasingly messy politics and has lost its privileged status as a bastion of political stability. It has become "Latin Americanized," as Moisés Naím has argued. Increased political volatility raises the following questions: Is the deepening of economic reform possible in a country where modernizing technocrats do not control most of the political levers, and where change can no longer be induced from the top down or contained by the PRI? The technocracy's permanence, in Mexico as elsewhere, has been based on its capacity to deliver. As Miguel Centeno's work on technocratic politics has argued, the appeal to "efficient" solutions proposed by experts implies the exclusion of large parts of the population and requires acceptance of the inevitability of prescribed policies.[35] Is this scenario viable in a context of increasingly contested elections, diminished presidential power, and the decline of the PRI as a vehicle for the representation and organization of interests?

It seems that the only way the ruling technocracy can survive the current impasse is by providing institutional routes of political contestation, i.e., by channeling discontent through the ballot box and hoping that democracy becomes an effective containment policy. In coming years, Mexicans will continue to vote their pocket-

---

[32] Naím (1995b).

[33] Since exports account for less than 20 percent of GDP, they cannot generate a recovery on their own. A large percentage of the total is produced by a small number of firms, mostly in the North. "Wanted: growth," *Economist*, October 28, 1995.

[34] Zebadúa (1996).

[35] See Centeno (1993), pp. 307-35.

books, and the PRI will in all likelihood continue to lose a host of state elections. In the best-case scenario, the deepening of economic reform entails the inevitable unraveling of the PRI, the probable electoral ascent of the PAN or the PRD, and a benign transition to a reasonably stable two-party or maybe three-party system. In the worst case, electoral politics becomes insufficient to contain social disaffection.

Currently there is no wide social consensus regarding the objectives of state policy, and no clear willingness on the part of the population to endure individual sacrifices for the long-term good of the collective. As the results of the mid-term election revealed, Mexico is bearing the brunt of adjustment fatigue. The critical issue has become how to sustain prolonged confidence in the Zedillo team, given that there are no clear indications of the relatively quick success of economic policies. In addition, the birth of a truly democratic Congress will make painful economic reforms more difficult to market politically.[36]

As democratization proceeds apace, Mexico's leaders may need to do more than tout the resurrection of a macroeconomic miracle in order to maintain political stability. Mexico's 92 million people now have a lower average income than in 1980. Only 55 percent of Mexicans enroll in secondary school education, and only 14 percent go to college.[37] Democratization will make it more difficult to "muddle through" with long-standing social disparities.[38] Growing distributional conflict—Mexico's bane—makes the kind of class compromise associated with democracy in developed market societies difficult at best, and impossible at worst.[39] High levels of inequality may threaten the prospects for democratic stability. As Terry Karl has suggested, "It is hard to build or sustain democratic institutions in a society sharply divided by income and wealth, especially one that gives the impression of doing little to redress the situation or, worse, actively exacerbates it."[40] Until and unless structural inequality is lessened in Mexico, democracy will remain fragile and limited to certain political rights, namely the right to vote, at the expense of important civic and social rights of citizenship.[41]

---

[36] Krugman (1995), p. 40.
[37] The figures for South Koreans are 90 percent and 42 percent, respectively.
[38] Naím (1995a), pp. 61-62.
[39] Oxhorn and Ducatenzeiler (1996), p. 38.
[40] Karl (1996), p. 5.
[41] Oxhorn and Ducatenzeiler (1996), p. 43.

4. CONCLUSION

In the aftermath of the Mexican crisis, one question looms large: What could Mexico have done differently? An evaluation of the dynamics of the Salinas coalition-building model reveals three main flaws. First, dominant-party rule generated perverse incentives in policy-makers who avoided making painful short-term decisions, including whether to maintain a fixed or semi-fixed parity. The Mexican government grew too dependent on foreign capital flows and a cheap dollar, due to the political benefits that this combination offered.[42] An otherwise functional economic model (from the perspective of neoliberal reformers) was ultimately thwarted by over-politicization.

Second, the Mexican crisis was also fueled by the Salinas team's refusal to accept the possibility of transfering power to the opposition. Political reform would have defused the political crises of 1994 and their impact on the economy. The lack of political reform made the economic project extremely vulnerable to political upheaval, as the Chiapas uprising revealed. Also, had the ruling technocracy been willing to lose the presidential election, pre-electoral pump-priming via a lax monetary policy could have been avoided.

Third, the technocratic "dream team" severely underestimated the costs of the transition from the era of the state as Benevolent Leviathan to the era of market-led neoliberal reform. The compensatory, neopopulist component of the Salinas coalition-building project was unavoidable, and even desirable, in a country with such acute income disparities. However, targeted compensation through a high-profile antipoverty program proved to be insufficient to contain social disaffection, particularly when Pronasol was increasingly deployed to co-opt supporters of the opposition instead to alleviate the plight of the extremely poor. The Salinas policy style was based on the rejection of demands by broad sectors of the population and postponed satisfaction of perceived needs and wants. Had the Salinas regime broadened its social base, even at the expense of the scope and pace of economic reforms, the political instability of 1994 might have been deterred.

In the post-crisis era, reform from above has been replaced by two simultaneous processes: democratization and decentralization. As these trends accelerate, Mexico will face a growing and acute tension between the exclusionary nature of neoliberal economic reform

---

[42] Lujambio, Elizondo Mayer-Serra, and Blanco (1995), pp. 42-51.

and the inclusionary logic of democracy. Under Salinas, the lack of democracy hampered economic reform; under Zedillo, the uncertainty and the messiness of the country's unavoidable political transition may once again jeopardize the reform process. Mexico's current institutions are ill-suited for the tasks of governing politics and supporting further market reforms. However, deeper institutional changes are going to be harder to carry out, especially in the realm of social policy and welfare, and the Zedillo team seems unwilling (or unable) to reincorporate the compensatory dimension that was an essential ingredient of Mexico's early economic success under Salinas. The alternation of power among political parties may not be enough to buffer the costs of economic liberalization. To win elections in a more competitive environment, parties may have to pay closer attention to the voice of the people. This responsiveness may in turn create a scenario of weaker and more haphazard reform measures and, in due course, less impressive economic results. Thus, whereas in the past Mexicans were offered economic prosperity without democracy, in the future the reverse may be true.

REFERENCES AND BIBLIOGRAPHY

Aguilar Camín, Héctor, and Lorenzo Meyer (1989). *A la sombra de la Revolución*. Mexico: Cal y Arena.

Castañeda, Jorge (1996). "Mexico's Circle of Misery," *Foreign Affairs*. July/August.

Centeno, Miguel (1994). *Democracy Within Reason: Mexico's Technocratic Revolution*. University Park, Penn.: Pennsylvania State University Press.

——————— (1993). "The New Leviathan: The Dynamics and Limits of Technocracy," *Theory and Society* 22.

Chand, Vikram K. (1995). "Economic Crisis and Democratization: The Mexican Case." Paper presented at the conference "Financial Globalization and Emerging Markets: Policy Autonomy, Democratization, and the Lessons from Mexico." Providence, RI: Watson Institute of International Studies, Brown University. November.

Cornelius, Wayne A., Ann Craig, and Jonathan Fox, eds. (1994). *Transforming State-Society Relations in Mexico: The National Solidarity Strategy*. La Jolla: Center for U.S.–Mexican Studies.

Dresser, Denise (1995). "Dazed and Confused: Social Policy in Mexico Since the Chiapas Uprising." Paper presented at the XIX International Congress of the Latin American Studies Association. Washington D.C. September.

——————— (1994). "Embellishment, Empowerment, or Euthanasia of the PRI?: Economic Reform and Party Restructuring in Mexico," in Maria

77

Lorena Cook, Kevin J. Middlebrook, and Juan Molinar Horcasitas, eds., *The Politics of Economic Adjustment in Mexico*. La Jolla: Center for U.S.(Mexican Studies.

Elizondo Mayer-Serra, Carlos (1995). "Foreign Investment, Democracy and the 1994 Mexican Crisis." Paper prepared for the conference "Financial Globalization and Emerging Markets: Policy Autonomy, Democratization, and the Lessons from Mexico." Providence, RI: Watson Institute of International Studies, Brown University. November.

Fuentes Beraín, Rossana (1995). "Crónicas del peso," *Reforma*. May 18.

Karl, Terry (1996). "How Much Inequality can Democracy Stand? Or How much Democracy can Inequality Stand?" Paper presented at the workshop "Constructing Democracy and Markets: Comparing Latin America and East Asia," sponsored by the Pacific Council on International Policy and the International Forum for Democratic Studies. Los Angeles. January.

Kaufman, Robert R., and Guillermo Trejo (1995). "Regionalism, Regime Transformation and Pronasol: The Politics of the National Solidarity Program in Four Mexican States." Unpublished paper. New York: Columbia University. October.

——————, Carlos Bazdresch, and Blanca Heredia (1994). "Mexico: Radical Reforms in a Dominant Party System," in Stephan Haggard and Steven B. Webb, *Voting for Reform*. Oxford: Oxford University Press.

Krugman, Paul (1995). "Dutch Tulips and Emerging Markets," *Foreign Affairs*. July/August.

Lujambio, Alonso, Carlos Elizondo, and José Blanco (1995). "Las razones políticas de la crisis económica," *Enlace*. March-April.

Lustig, Nora (1995). "The Mexican Peso Crisis: The Foreseeable and the Surprise." Brookings Discussion Papers in International Economics. Washington, D.C.: Brookings Institution.

Naím, Moisés (1995a). "Latin America the Morning After," *Foreign Affairs*. July/August.

—————— (1995b). "Mexico's Larger Story," *Foreign Policy* 99. Summer. Reissued as chapter 12 is this volume.

Olson, Mancur (1982). *The Rise and Decline of Nations*. New Haven: Yale University Press.

Oxhorn, Philip, and Graciela Ducatenzeiler (1996). "The Problematic Relationship Between Economic and Political Liberalization: Some Theoretical Considerations." Unpublished paper.

Waterbury, John (1992). "Export-Led Growth and the Center-Right Coalition in Turkey," *Comparative Politics*. January.

—————— (1989). "The Political Management of Economic Adjustment and Reform." U.S.–Third World Policy Perspectives no. 12, *Fragile Coalitions:*

The Politics of Economic Adjustment, Joan Nelson, et al., eds. Washington D.C.: Overseas Development Council.

Zebadúa, Emilio (1996). "La recuperación inalcanzable," *La Jornada*. August 22.

3. THE POLITICS OF EXCHANGE RATES

JEFFRY A. FRIEDEN*

T here are many dimensions to the origins, trajectory, and aftermath of the Mexican crisis of 1994-95, and many of them are political. While much is written about international monetary events both in Mexico and generally, the politics of currency policy is rarely subjected to serious analysis. In this essay, I focus on the domestic politics of exchange rates and on what theory and experience tell us about Mexico's recent and continuing travails. I start with some general principles of the political economy of international monetary policy, then go on to the Mexican specifics. I state my case starkly, avoiding evenhandedness and contingent stipulations in the interests of time, space, and provocation.

FIRST PRINCIPLES

1. The exchange rate is a policy variable. It is set by policy-makers. The attention paid, for good reason, to the stringent demands and vagaries of currency markets has tended to obscure this fact. Certainly the foreign exchanges can bid currencies up and down with tremendous, virtually inexorable power. But "the markets" are usually responding to expectations about the relevant policies of monetary and other authorities.[1]

---

* The author thanks Sebastian Edwards, Judith Evans, Aldo Flores, and Moisés Naím for their useful comments and suggestions.

[1] I leave aside here the argument of some (see Obstfeld 1986, and, for an application, Eichengreen and Wyplosz 1993) that there may be (or, more strongly, are) rational and self-reinforcing runs on currencies that are not justified by any underlying factors other than the self-fulfilling expectations of currency traders. I am not convinced that these events are common, but to avoid controversy let me posit that such exchange-market attacks are not included in my discussion.

I also, perhaps more obviously, leave aside the insistence of some that nominal exchange rate movements are not relevant. Certainly in some (particularly high-inflation) environments, nominal currency movements have little real effect; but in the majority of cases there is clear evidence for a strong link between nominal and real exchange rates.

While politicians and observers often present international monetary events as though the markets were tossing and turning currencies at will, in fact governments are almost always capable of sufficiently affecting traders' incentives to drive currencies as they wish. Most trivially, a substantial increase in interest rates is generally capable of encouraging more domestic and foreign savers to buy local currency-denominated instruments.[2]

2. Policy variables are determined politically. Policy-makers respond to political pressures. No policy-maker, no matter how strong his or her personal convictions, can long undertake measures that will result in getting thrown out of office. Politics is the process by which governments are chosen and constrained by their constituents—whether those constituents are voters, powerful interest groups, or a cabal of military rulers and their supporters. By definition, then, the only policies that can be sustained are those that are politically sustainable.

So it may be that a government faced with large sales of its currency always has the option of raising interest rates to reverse this trend. But it may also be that a government that did this would soon cease to hold office and, therefore, that foresighted governments will not sacrifice the local economy in order to support a particular level of the exchange rate.

3. There is no such thing as a technically unsustainable exchange rate. There is no level of the exchange rate that cannot be maintained for purely economic reasons. It is common to see assertions that if, for example, a country with an inflation rate 20 percentage points higher than that of an anchor fixes its currency to that of the anchor, the rate will quickly become unsustainable. What is meant, of course, is that the real appreciation will begin to have substantial negative effects on the local economy. Eventually the exchange rate may be altered to accord with the country's macro-

---

[2] It might be objected that if markets do not believe government commitments even though they are "true," governments may be at the mercy of "irrational" trading. In this instance, it is true that incomplete and asymmetric information makes credibility a problem. But it is also true that governments can act on *their own* knowledge that they are serious to "counter-speculate," as it were. If indeed the government commitment to the exchange rate is rock solid and markets do not believe this, a defense of the currency can be fully successful. Problems might arise if the short-term cost of the currency defense is daunting, even given the certainty of earning it back. In any case, here I am dealing mostly with tendencies, not either/or certainties.

economic conditions. But the authorities always have the option of doing the opposite: forcing the country's macroeconomic conditions to accommodate the exchange rate. Prices, wages, and profits can be reduced so that, even if the *nominal* exchange rate appreciates, the *real* exchange rate does not. In other words, the local economy can be forced to fit the exchange rate rather than vice versa.

It is not simply an academic curiosity to insist that conflict between the nominal exchange rate and macroeconomic fundamentals does not necessarily end with the exchange rate adapting. For much of modern history, in fact, the contrary has been more common. Before World War II, price-level differentials among countries on specie standards were often eliminated by dramatic reductions in the overall price level of one or more of the countries. American prices more than doubled during the Civil War and were then forced back down to pre–Civil War levels—with great economic distress—in order to resume participation in the gold standard. This pattern was common, perhaps even the norm, until the 1930s. If we find it difficult to imagine countries actually reducing their price levels—not by 2-3 percent, but by 40-50 percent—it is not because the feat is not technically feasible but rather because it has become unthinkable for other reasons.

4. The sustainability of a nominal exchange rate is a purely political concept. Political conditions determine the range of policy options available to authorities. In some cases, it may be politically feasible to force wage and price reductions to bear the brunt of an appreciated exchange rate. In other instances, such a strategy would quickly be reversed by active opposition. Whether the national economy is forced into conformity with the exchange rate or vice versa depends on how intensely the government's constituents feel about the issue and the power of the relevant constituents. There may be active, broad, and influential support for a fixed exchange rate, even at the expense of national austerity; or there may be powerful lobbies for devaluation. In any case, *political* pressures circumscribe the range of action of monetary policy-makers.

This helps explain why we see so much variation in national currency-policy responses to similar conditions, both across countries and over time. Some members of the European Monetary System (EMS) were willing to undergo great hardship in order to maintain their currencies fixed against the deutsche mark; others never tried. These differences largely respond to differences in the national political lineups of the countries in question. Today, forcing severe deflation (not just disinflation) to protect a nominal exchange rate is very rare; it has been argued that this is largely due to the rise of the labor movement, which resists deflation.[3]

5. Pressures on the making of currency policy are both general and specific. They emanate both from very broad popular pressures and from more concentrated social groups. Those who care profoundly about the level or stability of the exchange rate can be sure to make their concerns known to politicians. In this sense, monetary policy is like other arenas in which "special interests" with large stakes have strong incentives to attempt to obtain favorable consideration. How successful such interest groups are varies widely among political systems, among groups, and over time. Views of how legitimate such interest-group pressures are also vary widely.[4] Nonetheless, particularistic groups can and do affect the political constraints on exchange rate policy; in this, it resembles other realms of the political economy.

Monetary policy is *unlike* most special-interest politics, however, in the great breadth of its impact. All policies affect everyone to some degree, but currency policy determines what is often regarded as the most important single price in any economy. Changes in the exchange rate can often affect growth, unemployment, inflation, and other aggregates. Even if these effects are relevant only in the short run, most of politics has to do with short-term pressures.[5] And while the macroeconomic aggregates are so diffuse that their direct impact on politicians is not always clear—after all, growth rates and Gini coefficients do not vote—they do often translate into politically meaningful public opinion. Policy-makers must of necessity attend to the wishes of the populace as a whole, although this may be only one of many of their concerns. A less contented populace can increase political, social, and economic instability in ways that even the most authoritarian regime must take into account.

---

[3] Eichengreen (1992).

[4] For the record, like most political scientists I regard these pressures as perfectly legitimate. I see no principled reason why those with strong preferences—and the willingness to take the time, energy, and money to express them—should not have a disproportionate impact on policy. A one-person, one-vote expression of preferences is not the only social choice mechanism used by societies, nor is it typically sufficient on its own to reach results that most of us would regard as normatively desirable (whether they satisfy Pareto criteria or not).

[5] This is not, in my view, because people have inherently shorter time horizons in the political arena than elsewhere. It is because elections have important characteristics of winner-take-all markets in which there are high levels of risk, especially for politicians. The price of losing an election six weeks off may be permanent political death, and the threat of political execution helps concentrate the mind, and raise the discount rate, of all involved. Analogous considerations apply to societal groups, for whom the identity of the policy-maker they will face in the future is always uncertain.

6. There are specific interest groups with currency policy preferences. Social groups are identifiable that might and do care about the exchange rate. Most analyses of national or international monetary policy emphasize broad electoral and related pressures, but like most economic policies, currency policy also has disproportionate effects on people in society. Investigations of exchange rate politics in historical and contemporary perspective provide us with some hints about the general characteristics of the potential interest-group lineup, although much depends on national particularities.[6]

Interest-group preferences on the exchange rate typically relate to two dimensions: its level and its stability. The level is relatively straightforward: Inasmuch as a depreciation helps tradables producers, they are its principal supporters and the principal opponents of a real appreciation. Currency stability is particularly important to those involved in cross-border economic activity, for whom uncertainty can be costly; internationally oriented investors and traders tend to value exchange rate predictability. On the other hand, those without international economic ties have little reason to want to sacrifice national monetary autonomy in the interests of currency stability.[7] Typically the most important specific pressures are from exporters and import competitors in opposition to a substantial real appreciation and from internationally oriented investors, financiers, and traders in opposition to substantial currency volatility. While these special-interest pressures can be very important at times, they are not a constant of currency politics but appear to be most prominent when either the real level or the volatility of an exchange rate is relatively extreme.

7. Broad political pressures are especially important for exchange rate policy. Policy-makers must worry about the wide-ranging political effects of their international monetary policies. While interest groups often care about currency values and movements, the general macroeconomic impact tends to be more politically pronounced. This includes popular concerns about growth and unemployment, which are often reflected in trends relevant to elected and unelected policy-makers alike. Such concerns are particularly important in the context of attempts to stabilize exchange rates; this is

---

[6] I present here my own undoubtedly biased views, summarized in Frieden (1994). Apart from the obvious reason for this, the modern literature on the politics of exchange rates is quite limited in this regard. For another example, see Henning (1994).

[7] A more detailed discussion would have to be much more careful and disaggregated. This is meant only to indicate broad lines of division.

because in many instances the policies required to sustain a currency's value imply austerity. If, as is typically the case, there is little popular enthusiasm for a fixed or even stable exchange rate *per se*, the sacrifices needed to obtain this are unlikely to be politically convenient.

Another common general concern regarding exchange rates has to do with their relationship to the anti-inflationary credibility of the authorities. Many contemporary stabilization programs, especially in high-inflation environments, have an external hard-currency component. Where the government has invested its expertise and reputation in an exchange rate peg as part of an inflation stabilization package, letting the exchange rate slide could so affect expectations that it would damage the government's ability to stick to a policy course it might otherwise like to maintain. Here again, policy-makers are subjected to broad political influences—both from those who want a relaxation of the exchange rate constraint to allow for more growth and from those who insist on sustaining the exchange rate to help fight inflation.

8. The exchange rate is not an inherent measure of a government's credibility. There is no intrinsic significance to the particular exchange rate stance of economic policy-makers. While exchange rates have been and can be linked to credibility, this is not innate but, rather, constructed. The exchange rate is typically an instrument, a means to achieve an end. Credibility, however, is about targets— about how serious the government is about hitting them, not what tools they use to do so.

There are plenty of instances in which governments have proved their general policy reliability without using the exchange rate. There are even plenty of instances in which monetary authorities have designed and implemented successful anti-inflation (or low-inflation) policies without any explicit link to the currency. Indeed, exchange rate policy is often seen first and foremost as a way of regulating the relationship between domestic and foreign prices, not as a way of stabilizing the price level. Cases in which the exchange rate is a symbol of anti-inflationary credentials are probably a minority.

9. Government policy can make the currency a repository of its credibility. The monetary authorities can choose to tie their integrity to a particular value or to the stability of the exchange rate. This complements what was said above: While the exchange rate says nothing in and of itself about government credibility, the government can make it speak this language. Should the authorities, for whatever reasons, imply or declare that the currency's value is itself a target, it would be perfectly reasonable for private agents to interpret exchange rate developments as direct indicators of the government's intentions and seriousness.

Use of the exchange rate to underpin stabilization programs has in fact become something of a trend. But it is worth remembering that there are many conditions for which exchange rates may be useful policy tools, and symbolizing the tenacity and honesty of the policy-makers is only one of them. It may in fact not be a very good symbol, in that a one-to-one link between the exchange rate and credibility effectively removes the exchange rate from the tool kit of monetary policy-makers. This may or may not be wise; it certainly runs the risk of unduly constraining policy.

10. Credibility cannot be "purchased" by technical measures. There is no cheap substitute for a government actually following through on its policy commitments. This flows from much of what has come before. If the exchange rate is used as a symbol of government seriousness, the government is compelled to retain it. This requires that the government force the national economy to conform to the exchange rate should there be pressure on one or the other. Inasmuch as carrying out the macroeconomic adjustments required for this purpose can be economically and politically difficult, the government will eventually be forced to earn its reputation rather than buy it with declarations about commitments to a hard currency.

A currency peg can serve to focus the attention of the markets on this indicator of government reliability. But this also means that any weakening of the exchange rate, for whatever reason, will call into question the government's seriousness. If the exchange rate as a symbol of credibility works on the upswing, it can also work on the downturn—in reverse.

These rudimentary points can be summarized. Whatever the underlying domestic and international economic conditions, the nominal exchange rate rests on the government's political ability to sustain it. Currency values are only sustained if governments have the political support necessary to sustain them. A wide variety of other factors are commonly adduced as the "true reasons" for a devaluation: the central bank ran out of reserves, there were adverse terms of trade shocks, confidence eroded. All of these can come to pass with no change in the nominal exchange rate if in the final analysis the government has the political ability to implement the domestic policies necessary to sustain the currency's value. This political ability depends on the domestic constellation of political forces and the government's position within it. Such political forces include broad popular desires for aggregate outcomes, and specific concerns of important social groups for more particularistic results. While this emphasis on the centrality of *political* constraints on exchange rate policy is unlikely to be particularly controversial, it is helpful to make the general point, and the constraints, explicit.

THE MEXICAN CURRENCY CRISIS

Insistence on the political underpinnings of the exchange rate implies that analysis of the Mexican crisis requires explicit attention to Mexican politics. The domestic politics of the currency crisis indeed has been neglected by scholars and other analysts. Nonetheless, the political dimensions of the crisis can be analyzed as systematically as the economic dimensions, at least in principle. In what follows, I present the bare bones of an analysis of the Mexican case. My goal is not to argue for one particular interpretation or another, but simply to highlight the kinds of issues worthy of attention both in this case and in others.

The Mexican events involve a chronology familiar to those who know modern Latin American monetary and financial history. The story typically begins with a very large capital inflow and a resumption of economic growth (leaving aside which may have caused which). The capital inflow is associated with a substantial increase in local demand, felt especially in the markets for non-tradable goods and services. The resulting real appreciation is experienced as some combination of rapid increases in non-tradables prices, downward pressure on (relative) tradables prices, and a widening gap in the trade balance. Eventually, the real appreciation gives rise to political pressures in two directions: some want a depreciation to provide relief for tradables producers and for the economy as a whole, while others want to stick to the existing exchange rate in order to maintain access to relatively inexpensive foreign goods and capital. Sooner or later, the pressures for depreciation gain strength, perhaps in tandem with a slowdown in the capital inflow, and the exchange rate is adjusted.

In Mexico, the substantial economic reforms of the late 1980s and ratification of the North American Free Trade Agreement (NAFTA) both led to a large flow of funds into (or back to) Mexico. Both long- and short-term investment in the country rose dramatically until in the early 1990s the net resource transfer was in the 5-6 percent of GDP range. This was associated with a resumption of economic growth and modernization, including a surge in imports even while exports grew rapidly. It was also associated with a real appreciation of the peso, as Mexican inflation (especially in non-traded goods and services) outpaced that of the United States by a wide margin.

Politically, this contributed to general satisfaction—especially among the urban middle and working classes crucial to the ability of the Partido Revolucionario Institucional (PRI) to maintain its pre-dominant position in the political system. Growth was politically popular, as it always is. The capital inflow and real appreciation had particularly favorable effects on some politically important segments of society. Middle-class (and some lower–middle class) consumers benefited from direct or indirect access to less expensive imported goods, which make up a far larger proportion of their consumption basket than that of the poor. The capital inflow provided for rela-tively cheap borrowing by businesses interested in expanding and modernizing. To the extent that they reduced the costs of borrowing and servicing existing debt, foreign funds allowed the government to maintain high levels of spending on politically influential sectors, such as small- and medium-size businesses, selected elements of the labor movement, and other beneficiaries of Pronasol (the govern-ment's "solidarity" program to ease economic adjustment).

But the real appreciation did not have unambiguously positive effects. It put competitive pressures on tradables producers, reflect-ed in a widening current-account deficit. Certainly many Mexican manufacturers were still able to tap North American markets, espe-cially with the expansion of closely held intra-industry trade (in auto parts, for example). Nonetheless, the real appreciation was taking its toll. In addition, the capital inflow began slowing, and during 1994 the government was forced to offer high interest rates and dollar-based instruments to keep money coming into the country. The for-mer affected domestic borrowers; the latter threatened public finances.

This provides us with a simple picture of the political pressures on policy-makers as of the first half of 1994. In principle, the gov-ernment had two choices: It could allow the peso to depreciate, or it could implement deflationary policies to sustain the peso. Both options had political pros and cons.

Depreciation. It can be argued in favor of this option that it would have reduced pressure on exporters and import-competers facing difficulties. It would also have permitted a lowering of domes-tic interest rates—a measure of interest to indebted and borrowing firms. On the other hand, depreciation would have reduced purchasing power, especially that of swing voters in the urban middle and working classes.

Deflation. This would have been popular with those (especially members of the business and financial community) who were worried about domestic inflation and wages. But it would certainly have weakened the government's broad political position—again especially in the cities, where deflationary measures are likely to have the most impact.

Either of these measures would have been difficult in the best of times. In 1994, the PRI faced a hotly contested presidential election, under international scrutiny. The government could not afford to alienate electorally important groups, such as the urban middle class. Adverse price pressures on manufacturers due to the real appreciation were less urgent, as was the longer-term concern about the fate of public finances.

Depreciation and its impact on middle-class purchasing power would threaten the PRI's base among urban consumers, crucial to winning the presidential election. Deflation would threaten relations with the PRI's allies in the business community and labor, both of which had generally cooperated in the policy developments of the previous years.

It is easy to understand why the Mexican government postponed adjustment, for adjustment would have threatened the PRI's presidential chances. But this was just a postponement; eventually, policy would have to tackle the issues. In this context, one potential strategy would be to maintain the exchange rate, at least until the election, while imposing moderate austerity measures with the cooperation of the labor-management "social partners." After the election, a modest depreciation and some continued austerity could be pursued.

The success of this strategy, which appears both reasonable and akin to what the government actually had in mind, depended heavily on the government's ability to convince participants in the *Pacto* to accept aspects of austerity. This had been a major contributor to policy success after 1987, and it would be needed again. The seasoned politicians who ran the PRI seemed capable of convincing labor and business, especially, that whatever measures were taken would be temporary and would be counterbalanced by favorable consideration once the course correction was complete. As long as the PRI could be expected to maintain its ability to balance the interests and maintain the loyalties of powerful social actors, especially labor and business, the situation seemed manageable.

To put it differently, business and labor were important to the government in their capacity to cooperate in the implementation of stabilization programs; the middle class was important as an electoral base of support. If the government and the PRI could sustain good relations with business and labor in carrying out a small adjustment without a devaluation, the middle class would not be too hard-hit, and the elections would be safe.

The situation was complicated, however, by the government's use of the exchange rate as a symbol of its overall policy credibility. This meant that any adjustment to the currency might cause a collapse of confidence in policy-makers. The impact would be manifold— including an erosion of trust between the government and members of the *Pacto* and an erosion of faith in government policy more generally. Tying the currency to overall credibility thus constrained policy-makers in their search for politically feasible alternatives.

In any case, all of this depended on the government's ability to manage and reconcile its various bases of support both within and outside the PRI. Labor and business leaders needed to be convinced that modest austerity was worth the cooperation and that they could expect eventually to be repaid for their support. Urban voters needed to be massaged into voting for the PRI—either indirectly, by continuing their access to inexpensive consumption goods, or directly, with the use of government spending (financed abroad). This was a delicate balancing act, but the PRI had managed more delicate ones in recent memory.

However, the March 1994 assassination of Luis Donaldo Colosio called into profound question the PRI's ability to broker this resolution, and the September 1994 assassination of José Francisco Ruíz Massieu made matters even worse. Evidence of serious divisions in the PRI raised questions about the reliability of any deals that might be struck. It was widely—and probably correctly—believed that Ernesto Zedillo's lack of an independent base of support in the PRI would hamstring his ability to hold together the disparate forces needed to sustain an orderly adjustment.

The erosion of confidence in the government's political strength was undoubtedly exacerbated by memories that two of the previous three transitions had been characterized by a cycle of capital inflows, real appreciations, large devaluations, and crises. The situation in 1994 was similar enough to that in 1976 and 1982 to raise concerns about the possibility of a major devaluation of the peso.

Most of the fears expressed after the Colosio assassination were indeed borne out. Factional conflict and a vulnerable presidential candidate caused serious doubts about the PRI's ability to hold together the *Pacto* and, more generally, the disparate component parts of its political support base. And in fact Zedillo, lacking as he did a base of his own or long-term ties with major political players, had difficulties establishing stable coalitions in support of the measures he tried to implement.

The political economy of the currency crisis thus seems straightforward. In an election year, the PRI could not afford a devaluation due to its impact on politically crucial middle-class and lower middle-class urban consumers. The association of monetary policy credibility with the nominal exchange rate tied the government's hands even further. The government could try to prevail upon its social allies in business and labor to help manage a mild adjustment, but this delicate balance was disturbed by the Colosio assassination and the infighting it revealed. The disturbance was aggravated by the perception that Zedillo's political weakness left him in a poor position to maintain the cooperation of essential business and labor leaders.

What might have been a simple currency crisis burgeoned into an all-encompassing economic and political crisis precisely because the government had insisted that it be judged on the basis of how well it maintained the peso fixed against the dollar. In this way, the administration's attempt to use the exchange rate as a commitment technology came back to haunt it. This was exacerbated by the fact that the incoming Zedillo administration inherited the previous government's insistence on tying the government's credibility to the peso. While it is arguable that the successful peg augmented the regime's credibility in the early 1990s, it is unquestionable that the peg's failure exacerbated the loss of confidence in the government. This helped put the government on a downward spiral from which it emerged at great economic and political cost.

POLITICAL ECONOMY LESSONS OF THE MEXICAN CRISIS

Without repeating too much of what has come before, several potential lessons of the Mexican experience (and of others like it) can be suggested. I restrict myself to the exchange rate and other closely related spheres, but many of these points could be made more generally.

1. A focus on macroeconomic fundamentals is insufficient and may be misleading. The fundamentals are crucially important, of course. But their impact on currency policy is and can only be mediated through national political and policy-making structures. In some countries, high levels of unemployment would translate directly and immediately into pressure on the exchange rate; in others, they would be irrelevant.

2. Explicit attention must be paid to the political constraints on policy. Economic and other technical features of policy and of the environment within which policy is made are important, and they typically get plenty of attention. But it is much less common for analysts, observers, and market operators to incorporate political considerations systematically into their evaluations of policy. This is a grave mistake and leads to poor understanding, bad explanations, and poorly devised forecasts.

3. Political constraints are both general and specific. In the monetary sphere, policy-makers have to balance the specific concerns of those most directly affected by currency policy against the policy's broad political (including electoral) implications. This is a difficult task to carry out, and a difficult one to analyze. But such factors as the role and influence of particularistic interest groups, the timing of elections, and features of the electoral system are crucially important to determining the range of maneuver available to policy-makers.

4. A policy without a political base of support will not long be policy. One often hears assertions to the effect that a particular strategy is likely to succeed because it is technically well designed, or because its authors are well trained, or because policy-makers have a good academic background in economics. Certainly all these are better than their opposites, but in the final analysis it is more important that policy-makers understand and be able to work with the political constraints on them than that they have particular expertise (which, after all, is readily available at a reasonable price). A good technician may well be able to design the socially optimal policy but have no chance of getting it adopted. A better result would be obtained by a seasoned politician willing and able to guide society toward a welfare improvement. Policy proposals, including those for optimal policies, are irrelevant unless they are politically feasible.

5. Politicians do have room for maneuver. Indeed, their job is largely to understand the constraints on them, to operate within these constraints, and to test their outer limits. Nothing discussed above should be understood to mean that politicians are impotent (just as new and improved theories of industrial organization do not make managers obsolete). Indeed, it leads to a healthy respect for politicians, who are pursuing their own comparative advantage in getting things done.

6. There is no magic source of credibility. While it may be fashionable to refer to an exchange rate peg as a commitment technology, this is misleading if it is meant to imply that one needs only to plug the technology in to have it work. A currency peg, like other commitment technologies, can help resolve some informational ambiguities. It cannot eliminate the requirements that policies find a base of political support and that underlying macroeconomic policies be coherent and consistent.

This insistence on the importance of politics to monetary policy may appear obvious. But it seems to bear repeating, for most analyses of international and domestic monetary affairs slide over political considerations quickly and haphazardly. Political constraints are decisive and unavoidable determinants of policies and outcomes, and they deserve to be incorporated systematically into our analyses.

REFERENCES AND BIBLIOGRAPHY

Eichengreen, Barry (1992). *Golden Fetters: The Gold Standard and the Great Depression 1919-1939.* New York: Oxford University Press.

——————— and Charles Wyplosz (1993). "The Unstable EMS." Brookings Papers on Economic Activity no. 1. Washington, D.C.: Brookings Institution.

Frieden, Jeffry (1994). "Exchange Rate Politics: Contemporary Lessons from American History," *Review of International Political Economy* 1, no. 1. Spring.

Henning, C. Randall (1994). *Currencies and Politics in the United States, Germany, and Japan.* Washington, D.C.: Institute for International Economics.

Obstfeld, Maurice (1986). "Rational and Self-Fulfilling Balance of Payments Crises," *American Economic Review* 76, no. 1. January.

4. BAD LUCK OR BAD POLICIES? AN ECONOMIC ANALYSIS OF THE CRISIS

SEBASTIAN EDWARDS*

INTRODUCTION

On October 28, 1993, Chile's Finance Minister Alejandro Foxley confidently entered the Waldorf Astoria Hotel in New York City. He was one of the keynote speakers at the Second *Wall Street Journal* Conference on the Americas, and he expected to be one of its stars. After all, under his watch, Chile had managed to make a remarkable transition to democratic rule—after almost twenty years of military government—while maintaining economic growth and deepening its renowned market-oriented reforms. In his view, Chile represented the type of emerging market on which investors should concentrate. The country had a new but solid democratic regime, a long record of rapid economic growth, healthy external accounts, rapidly growing productivity, and improving social conditions. Foxley rode the elevator with his small entourage. At 2:30 p.m., he entered the conference hall and was surprised to find it half empty. After waiting for a few minutes, he delivered his speech, which concentrated on the need for Latin America to continue to move toward global markets, on the importance of reducing industrial countries' protectionism, and on the need to tackle social problems while fostering investment and growth. When he finished, he invited the public to ask questions. A strange silence fell over the hall, and not a single question was asked. On the way out, Foxley expressed his frustration to his aides and to a small group of Chileans. What had happened? Why had the speech, so carefully prepared, gone wrong? Where were the rest of the people? As it happened, a large number of participants in the conference were still lingering in the dining room, where Mexico's Secretary of

* The author wishes to acknowledge that in the preparation of this paper, he benefited from discussions with Ed Leamer, Rudiger Dornbusch, Fernando Losada, Roberto Steiner, and Nora Lustig.

Commerce Jaime Serra Puche had delivered a luncheon address. The audience had been captivated by Serra's professional ways, by his command of the stage, and by his charm. The unmistakable sense among the participants—CEOs of large corporations, investment bankers, journalists, and pundits of various kinds—was that, in spite of Ross Perot's campaign against the North American Free Trade Agreement (NAFTA), Mexico was the brightest star in the Latin American firmament. The mood was one of euphoria and complacency; the calls for caution made by some of the speakers were brushed aside as signs of unjustifiable doom. The future looked brilliant, and after the enactment of NAFTA, Mexico would rapidly join the ranks of the more advanced countries with solid growth, stability, and prosperity. That evening, in a surprise visit to the conference, President Bill Clinton delivered a speech that basically supported this optimistic perspective.

Very few of the participants, if any, knew that as this conference was taking place in the venerable Waldorf Astoria, in Mexico's southern state of Chiapas hundreds of Indians and left-wing activists were going through the final stages of their military training in order to stage a major uprising that would shock the Mexican establishment, institutional investors, and the U.S. administration. Thus, a tale of two Mexicos was being forged: on the one hand that of a modern Mexico, on the verge of entering the first world; on the other, that of a quasi-feudal Mexico, with its sorrow and frustration. Throughout 1994, these two Mexicos coexisted and, while most international investors dismissed the Chiapas events as the effort of a handful of adventurers in the style of *El Zorro*, the fragilities of the Mexican road to the free market became more and more apparent to perceptive analysts. In December 1994, the international financial community had to face what most pundits had deemed impossible: for the third time in 18 years, Mexico's currency—the once strong and proud peso—collapsed.

The Mexican crisis raised, throughout the world, a number of questions regarding the sustainability—and even the merits—of the market-oriented reform process in Latin America and other regions. If Mexico was one of the best examples of a successful reformer, some observers asked, what could be expected of other cases? Although, contrary to some analysts' predictions, the Latin American countries have not suffered a meltdown in the aftermath of the Mexican crisis, understanding the way events unfolded in Mexico during the early 1990s continues to be fundamentally important. In particular, a careful analysis of this episode will allow policy-makers to draw valuable lessons that will help them avoid Mexico's fate.

In analyzing the Mexican crisis, it is useful to distinguish between two periods: 1990 to 1993, when the economy became increasingly vulnerable; and 1994, when external and political shocks precipitated the collapse of the peso. The crisis had a long period of gestation. Already during the early 1990s a series of developments suggested that Mexico was becoming susceptible to an external crisis. Among these, the most important were the real appreciation of the peso, the very large current-account deficit financed by massive (portfolio) capital inflows, the slow growth of productivity, and the declining trend in private savings. In spite of this vulnerability, by the end of 1993—and as illustrated by the euphoria with which Mexican officials were greeted in public event after public event—the market had high expectations for Mexico. The authorities, in turn, believed that the decline in savings was a temporary phenomenon, that the current-account deficit would be solved through productivity increases, and that—because of NAFTA—capital would continue to flow in at the rate of 1992-93, providing more time for adjusting the external accounts.

Despite the modest performance of the Mexican economy during 1990-93, many observers praised the experience as a major success. This optimism, coupled with important interest rate differentials, induced large volumes of capital into Mexico between 1990 and the first months of 1994. These flows helped generate a consumption boom and, in conjunction with a rigid nominal exchange rate policy, contributed to creating a significant overvaluation of the peso and a gigantic current-account deficit. Throughout most of 1994, Mexico had the opportunity to undertake a number of measures that would have allowed a smoother landing, but overoptimism and political considerations—including the fear of a major banking crisis—stood in the way of corrective actions.[1]

The Mexican crisis was of course the result of a combination of economic, financial, and political factors. At the center of it all, however, was the Salinas government's inability—and unwillingness—to implement severe adjustment measures in mid-1994, when external conditions turned drastically against Mexico. Instead of taking corrective measures consistent with these new external circumstances,

---

[1] There are by now a number of accounts of the Mexican crisis. See Lustig (1992); Leiderman and Thorne (1995); Sachs, et al. (1995); Calvo (1995); Naím (1995); the papers in the December 1996 special issue of the *Journal of International Economics;* and Calvo and Mendoza (1996a). Parts of this paper draw on Edwards, Steiner, and Losada (1996). See also Edwards (1995, 1996). A number of authors, however, began to point out some of the weaknesses of the Mexican economy as early as 1992. See, for example, Dornbusch and Werner (1994), Calvo (1994), and Edwards (1994).

the Mexican authorities tried to maintain the status quo by issuing large amounts of dollar-linked short-term debt—the infamous *tesobonos*—making the economic situation particularly vulnerable to a speculative attack.

This paper analyzes the causes behind the Mexican crisis and provides some discussion of the future prospects of the Mexican economy.

OVERVIEW: THE INVENTION OF THE "MEXICAN MIRACLE"

By now the main features of the Mexican reform program are well known. They include: (1) a fundamental opening of the economy to international competition; (2) a drastic privatization and deregulation process; (3) a stabilization program based on a predetermined nominal exchange rate anchor and supported by restrictive fiscal and monetary policies; and (4) a broad social and economic agreement between the government, the private sector, and labor unions—known as the *Pacto* and aimed at guiding price, exchange rate, and wage increases—that became an anchor of the program. The reliance on the *Pacto* was a key element of the program that distinguishes it from others that followed in, for example, Argentina and Chile. Because of this agreement, the authorities had limited scope for maneuver and had to tread cautiously in instituting changes. As time passed, the (yearly) renewal of the *Pacto* became a major political event, surrounded by anticipation and at times anxiety. The *Pacto* eventually became a fundamental institution in Mexico's political process, supposedly encompassing a major national project.[2]

Between 1988 and 1994, and despite the reforms, the performance of the economy was rather modest. Real growth averaged 2.8 percent—significantly lower than in Chile (7.1 percent) or Colombia (4.1 percent), for example; productivity growth was almost flat until 1993; export expansion was not impressive; real wages barely reached their 1980 level; the real exchange rate appreciated significantly; private savings experienced a major decline; and poverty and income distribution continued to be serious problems. On the positive side, fiscal balance had been attained in 1992; inflation was reduced to single digits; and the reforms dismantled layers of protection and regulation. During this period there was a significant

---

[2] On the Mexican reforms up to 1993, see, for example, Loser and Kalter (1992) and Lustig (1992). The book by Pedro Aspe (1993) offers a professional and highly influential insider's assessment of the progress made by Mexico on the reform front.

contrast between Mexico's achievements in terms of reform *policies* and in terms of economic *results*. While the former were massive, and in some areas even spectacular, results in terms of growth and social progress continued to be elusive.[3]

Despite the divergence between policy actions and economic results, the Mexican reforms were consistently praised by the media, financial experts, academics, and the multilaterals—including the World Bank and the IMF—as a major success. It is possible to argue that a Mexican "miracle" was at least partially invented by these institutions. This enthusiastic approach toward Mexico was the result of a number of factors. The most important was perhaps the tremendous faith that many analysts had in the market-oriented reforms themselves; if results were not there, many argued, they were around the corner. This generated a type of self-feeding phenomenon that has historically characterized many "bubbles": optimistic beliefs helped generate an asset price boom, which in turn reassured the believers in the "miracle." Paul Krugman has argued that much of the hoopla on Mexico's prospects represented a "leap of faith, rather than a conclusion based on hard evidence."[4] The U.S. administration's efforts to persuade the public (and Congress) of the benefits of NAFTA also contributed to the popular notion that there was a Mexican "miracle." Moreover, after NAFTA was approved, a large number of observers argued that the free trade pact would accelerate investment and exports in a massive way.[5]

Although the World Bank was clearly an important player in the creation of this great success story, it did this in a rather guarded

---

[3] The selection of Chile and Colombia for comparison is deliberate: Chile is the earliest Latin American reformer, broadly recognized for its achievements; Colombia, on the other hand, has implemented limited reforms, but has maintained a solid economic record throughout the 1980s and early 1990s. A number of things stand out in the comparison: (1) Mexico's GDP growth was significantly lower than that of the two South American countries; (2) in Mexico, total factor productivity growth actually declined between 1978-1982 and 1987-1991, while it grew very quickly in Chile; (3) when compared with the pre-debt crisis period, real wages were significantly higher in the South American nations; (4) Mexico experienced the slowest rate of growth of exports among the three countries; and (5) while in the three countries the extent of poverty declined in the early 1990s relative to the mid- to late 1980s, in Mexico, the number of people in extreme poverty actually increased during this period.

[4] Krugman (1995), p. 33.

[5] Interestingly enough, the Mexican experience was often cited as an example showing that it is possible to undertake *successful* structural reforms within a democratic regime. Mexico, in fact, was often contrasted with the Chilean case, where the bulk of the (truly) successful reforms had been undertaken by an authoritarian military regime. It is possible to speculate, then, that the desire—especially among U.S. officials—to find an example of successful market reforms under a democratic regime contributed to the creation of the notion that Mexico was a super-performer.

way. On this issue as on so many others, the Bank in public, official (or semi-official) documents spoke with two—if not three or four—voices. At times it praised Mexico, and at times it recorded its concerns. For instance, in the abstract of the 1994 *Country Economic Memorandum* (one of the first documents the Bank made available to the public at large through the Internet), it was strongly suggested that Mexico had made great progress, and that after the ratification of NAFTA it was ready for a major take off.[6] Along similar lines, the 1993 *World Bank Annual Report* stated that "almost all countries in the region . . . are implementing adjustment programs. Chile and Mexico, which have established a trend of positive per capita income growth with modest inflation, represent the clearest cases of *success.*"[7] In a document released at the 1993 Annual Meeting, the Bank expressed the view that "in Mexico . . . the reform process is mature and appears consolidated."[8] In other public documents, however, World Bank staff clearly stated that the record had been disappointing, and that many challenges remained. In the 1993 *Trends in Developing Economies*, for example, the staff said: "Growth recovery has, however, been modest . . . [T]he recent slowdown in growth can be traced to a combination of slow productivity growth, a weak US economy, tight fiscal and monetary policies, and *real exchange rate appreciation.*"[9] In the 1993 Annual Meeting document mentioned above, the Bank pointed out that there had been a "*decline* in aggregate total factor productivity growth for Mexico after the reforms" and associated this phenomenon with the fact that the Mexican reforms had been incomplete and had proceeded at an uneven pace as well as with the stiff real appreciation of the peso.[10] An analysis of the causes behind the Mexican crisis by an independent task force sponsored by the Council on Foreign Relations acknowledged that the World Bank had indeed warned of the nonsustainability of the Mexican policies.[11]

The IMF was also quick to praise Mexico's reform policies. For example, a publicly released paper co-authored by the current Director for the Western Hemisphere, Claudio Loser, titled "Mexico: The Strategy to Achieve Sustained Economic Growth," approvingly reviewed the country's policies. According to the authors, "The

---

[6] The World Bank home page address on the World Wide Web is http://www.worldbank.org/.

[7] World Bank (1993a), p. 133. Emphasis added.

[8] World Bank (1993c), p. 9.

[9] World Bank (1993b), pp. 325-30. Emphasis added.

[10] World Bank (1993c), pp. 61-66.

[11] Council on Foreign Relations (1996), p. 26: "In 1994, the World Bank warned that financial flows to Mexico were unsustainable."

success of Mexico's economic strategy since 1989 has led to its gradually regaining access to voluntary international capital market financing after having been virtually excluded for much of the decade. This private sector access to capital, in combination with Mexico's broad economic reform, augurs well for the achievement of sustainable economic growth in the medium term."[12] In October 1994, only a few weeks before the crisis, the IMF's *World Economic Outlook* commented that, although growth had been somewhat sluggish, the economy would recover rapidly. More specifically, it said: "larger output increases are projected for 1995 as aggregate demand—in particular private investment—expands."[13] Along similar lines, the IMF's *International Capital Markets* report issued in September 1994 suggested that the premium paid by Mexican bonds was too high and not fully justified by market fundamentals. And, quite remarkably, in a March 24, 1994, letter to U.S. Secretary of the Treasury Lloyd Bentsen, IMF Managing Director Michel Camdessus said: "Our view is that the Mexican authorities are pursuing fundamentally sound economic policies . . . [T]he economic program for 1994 envisages that inflation will fall further to close to international levels and that there will be a recovery in economic growth. The government is committed to fiscal balance, the maintenance of firm credit policies, and to the consolidation of structural reforms through the granting of autonomy to the Central Bank, the approval of NAFTA, and the adoption of new foreign investment law."[14] Not a word on exchange rate overvaluation. Not one. Interestingly enough, and in contrast with the World Bank, very few warnings— even veiled ones—on the fragility of the Mexican economy were coming out publicly from the IMF.[15]

Despite its public expressions of some of its concerns, the World Bank also endorsed, at least with one of its multiple "voices," the idea that the Mexican reforms were a major success and that the country had a brilliant future.[16] In November of 1994, for example, barely a month before the collapse, the World Bank publicly argued that the election of the Partido Revolucionario Institucional (PRI)

---

[12] Loser and Kalter (1992), p. 12.

[13] International Monetary Fund (1995), p. 24.

[14] Quoted in D'Amato (1995), p. 137.

[15] A report on capital inflows that dealt with six countries, including Mexico, did mention that very large inflows could create some serious economic vulnerabilities. See Schadler, et al. (1993). Also, the Fund's 1994 *Annual Report* mentioned the need for corrective fiscal and monetary policies. Again, however, there was no discussion of the exchange rate policy.

[16] See, for example, the collection of essays by IMF staff on the Mexican reforms, in Loser and Kalter (1992).

presidential candidate would result in a rapid improvement in Mexico's prospects: "Economic growth is expected to surge, reaching the highest level in five years, as a period of post election stability is anticipated."[17] Of course the World Bank and the other multilaterals were not the only, and not even the most vocal, institutions promoting the image of a super-successful Mexican experiment. Investment bankers, mutual fund managers, and financial reporters were even more enthusiastic; some even urged, as late as November 1994, a credit-rating upgrade for Mexico.[18] A forceful example of the private-sector enthusiasm came from Bear Stearns, which argued that Mexico offered a tremendous long-term opportunity. In early November 1994 it stated: "We expect a *strengthening* of the peso in the coming months, creating very high dollar returns on *Cetes*."[19] A few weeks earlier, J.P. Morgan stated: "We view Mexico as investment-grade risk. We do not regard Mexican debt to have predominantly speculative characteristics."[20]

A compilation of major[21] investment banks' views on Mexico during November and December 1994 indicates that the majority continued to be optimistic. Out of twenty written analyses released by major institutions during that period, twelve dismissed the possibility of a devaluation. Of these, two predicted an appreciation of the peso, two urged an upgrade of Mexico's investment rating, and eight argued that, although the current-account deficit was very high, there would be no devaluation.

This enthusiasm for Mexico, and the self-delusion associated with the invention of the "miracle," was captured by Mexico's rapid improvement in country risk tables. For example, in *Euromoney's* country risk ratings—where a lower ranking reflects a lower degree of country risk—Mexico climbed from position 77 in 1985 to 44 in 1994. Astonishingly, Mexico's *Euromoney* country risk ranking improved between March and September 1994! As a result of this perception, and of the sharp decline in interest rates in the United States, Mexico received massive amounts of foreign funds. Between

---

[17] World Bank (1994).

[18] Chemical Bank (November 1994), J.P. Morgan (October 1994), and the Swiss Bank Corporation (December 1994/January 1995) argued that Mexico's rating should be upgraded. See also Fraser (1995), suggestively titled "Who Lost Mexico," for an analysis of Wall Street's views on Mexico in the months preceding the crisis.

[19] Emphasis added. Malpass and Chon (1994). Other private analysts, however, did argue in their newsletters that things were now going quite well south of the border. See the article by Fraser (1995).

[20] J.P. Morgan (1994).

[21] See Fraser (1995).

1990 and 1993 Mexico received more than half of all the monies that moved into Latin America.

Between 1990 and 1993, capital inflows tended to go together with the strengthening of the real value of the currency. Two key and interrelated questions emerge: first, to what extent did this continuous appreciation represent a situation of overvaluation that required corrective policy actions? And, second, was the surge in capital inflows observed after 1989 sustainable? The answers given to these questions are key in interpreting the forces behind the Mexican crisis and in evaluating the appropriateness of Mexican policies after 1990 and, especially, during 1994.

NOMINAL EXCHANGE RATE ANCHORS, INFLATIONARY INERTIA, AND OVERVALUATION

In early 1988, three months into the *Pacto*, the nominal exchange rate was fixed, becoming the fundamental anchor of the anti-inflationary effort.[22] Between 1988 and 1994, Mexico modified its exchange rate system several times, moving first from a completely fixed rate to a system based on a pre-announced rate of devaluation—with the actual devaluation set below the ongoing rate of inflation—and then to an exchange rate band with a sliding ceiling. This policy was justified on two grounds: (1) it was supposed to discourage short-term capital inflows; and (2) it would deal with real exchange rate corrections, in case these were needed.[23] Until October 1993, when the NAFTA controversy heated up in the United States, the actual peso/dollar rate was extremely stable, remaining in the lower half of the band. According to Mexico's former Secretary of Finance Pedro Aspe, once barriers to international trade had been eliminated, it was expected that the exchange rate policy would reduce the degree of "inertial inflation" and would "place an upward boundary on the prices of tradables."[24] At least until 1993, this exchange rate policy was supplemented by prudent fiscal and monetary policies.[25] Throughout 1994, and as a result of political and other developments in Mexico and in the world economy, the

---

[22] During the first months of the *Pacto* nominal wages provided the anchor to the system. According to Vela (1993), the move to an exchange rate anchor in February 1988 was in part the result of pressure from the labor unions.

[23] Bank of Mexico (1993).

[24] Aspe (1993), pp. 23-24.

[25] During the early years of the program, monetary policy was guided by the dual purpose of reducing interest rates while attaining consistency with the predetermined exchange rate (Aspe, 1993).

exchange rate came under considerable pressure, moving toward the top of the band.

Stabilization programs based on an exchange rate anchor have the danger of generating a significant real exchange rate overvaluation, loss of competitiveness, and very large trade deficits. This would be the case if, after the implementation of the stabilization program, inflation continued to exhibit a certain degree of inertia. If this real appreciation trend is not corrected in time, the credibility of the stabilization program will be called into question, inviting speculative attacks on the currency. The Mexican authorities argued that there were three reasons why Mexico would be exempt from this fate: first, the policy started from a situation of undervaluation; second, Mexico had ample international reserves; and, third, a rapid rate of productivity growth was supposed to compensate for the appreciation of the peso.[26]

The Mexican stabilization program succeeded in reducing inertia, but not in eliminating it. As a result, the decline in the rate of inflation was painfully slow. Several authors have estimated econometric models of Mexico's inflationary process during this period and have concluded that, although inertia declined markedly after 1988, it still remained, until 1994, at fairly high levels.[27]

As many had feared, then—and as had been the case a decade earlier in Chile—the process of attempting to reduce inflation while using the exchange rate as nominal anchor was indeed accompanied by a substantial real appreciation. In 1989, a number of observers argued that this trend would become unsustainable, as the country lacked sufficient foreign exchange to finance the rapidly growing trade gap. In early 1990, however, it seemed that the economic situation was about to turn around. The Brady debt reduction agreement was signed, and Mexico began to open its financial sector and to privatize banks. Partially as a result of this and of the perception that an economic "miracle" was taking place, the international capital market rediscovered Mexico. The resulting surge in capital inflows allowed the country to finance very large current-account

---

[26] Later, an additional explanation would be added to this list: NAFTA would furnish enough capital to sustain a more appreciated real exchange rate and would also provide the opportunity to increase exports rapidly (ibid.).

[27] For example, using a dummy variable approach, Edwards, Steiner, and Losada (1996) estimated that the coefficient of lagged inflation—a measure of inflationary inertia or persistence—declined from 0.96 in 1980-88 to 0.40 in 1989-94. Edwards (1996), on the other hand, used a recursive coefficients approach to analyze this issue and found that the coefficient of past inflation in a quarterly inflationary model declined after 1988, but remained at around 0.5.

deficits in 1992-94. The fact that these funds were of a private nature persuaded a number of analysts—and especially senior Mexican officials—that this was a positive development and not a cause for concern. As we will see, however, other observers remained skeptical and pointed out, with increasing alarm, that the accumulated appreciation of the peso was undermining the foundations of the Mexican economy and was bound to generate, sooner rather than later, a major crisis. As was argued in the preceding section, even the World Bank—in one of its multiple voices—pointed out the dangers of overvaluation.

CAPITAL INFLOWS, REAL EXCHANGE RATES, AND THE SUSTAINABLE CURRENT ACCOUNT

For a long time economists have argued about the appropriate sequencing of economic reform. An important component of this debate has referred to the right timing for relaxing capital controls and opening the capital account: Should this policy take place early in the reform process, or should some impediments to capital mobility be retained until the liberalization of trade has been fully consolidated? The central issue is that liberalizing the capital account would, under some conditions, result in large *temporary* capital inflows and in an appreciation of the real exchange rate, sending the "wrong" signal to the real sector, thus frustrating a rapid expansion of exports.[28] The conventional wisdom in this debate—although not accepted by every participant—is that the opening of the capital account should be done gradually, and in a way that avoids "unnecessary" real exchange rate appreciation.

Mexico opted for opening the capital account very early in the reform process, as capital controls were almost completely eliminated in late 1989.[29] The adoption of this sequence of reform—which contradicted the conventional wisdom—responded to a series of factors, including Mexico's long tradition with capital mobility and the country's desire to join the Organisation for Economic Co-operation and Development (OECD). This strategy contrasted with that followed by other Latin American reformers, including Colombia and Chile, which maintained some form of capital impediment in an effort to have some ability to manage the money supply.

In the absence of capital controls, international financial man-

---

[28] See McKinnon (1991, 1982) and Edwards (1984).

[29] Some controls were maintained, however. In particular, it was not possible for nationals to shorten the peso.

agers were free to move very large volumes of funds in and out of Mexico. In 1993 alone, net capital inflows surpassed 8 percent of GDP. Most of the capital flowing into Mexico after 1993 was short term in nature and was invested in the stock market, in private-sector instruments, and in government securities.[30] The composition of these flows added to the vulnerability of the system as a whole. It should be recognized, however, that in the late 1980s, the dangers of a dramatic surge in capital *inflows* were far from the minds of Mexican policy-makers and of independent analysts of the Latin American scene. The concern at the time was in fact the opposite: What could these countries do to stop capital flight, to attract new funds, and to reschedule their foreign debts? Moreover, in early 1990, even after the Brady deal had significantly reduced Mexico's foreign debt, the main concern of the Mexican authorities was to obtain sufficient foreign financing to engineer a reduction of the (very high) real interest rates.[31]

The surge in capital inflows that started in 1990 allowed Mexican nationals to increase their expenditures greatly. Starting in 1990, the country experienced a consumption boom that put additional pressure on an already appreciated real exchange rate and contributed to the creation of a large current-account deficit. A disturbing development after 1989 was the steep decline in private savings.[32] This contrasted sharply with the experience of most East Asian countries during the early 1990s; these countries' capital inflows resulted in significant increases in investment rates without negatively affecting savings. Furthermore, in no other Latin American country did the current-account deficit reflect such an adverse evolution of the savings-investment differential as in Mexico. Moreover, after 1992, the decline in aggregate savings also reflected a reduction in public savings, as fiscal policy was relaxed.[33]

---

[30] See Edwards, Steiner, and Losada (1996).

[31] See the fascinating analysis of the Mexican economic situation by Guillermo Ortiz (1991).

[32] It could be argued that the decline in savings (which is in part the counterpart to the increase in consumption) is quite misleading in situations in which the consumption of durable goods increases significantly. After all, the case can be made that the purchase of certain consumer durables is, to a certain extent, a similar decision to the purchase of, say, a financial asset. In the recent Mexican experience, these classification problems do not seem to have played an important role, as the expenditure on consumer durables as a proportion of GDP *declined* from 7.2 percent in 1987 to 6.3 percent in 1993.

[33] This was so despite the fact that, between 1991 and 1994, there was a slight *increase* in the ratio of taxes (direct and indirect) to GDP. This increase, which *ceteris paribus* implies a decline in private savings, should be reflected in enhanced public savings, unless public expenditure is concomitantly augmented.

Starting in 1992, a debate began on the consequences of the real appreciation that had occurred since 1988. In early 1992, Rudiger Dornbusch claimed that "the current problem of the Mexican economy is the overvalued exchange rate,"[34] and, in November 1992, he argued that the daily rate of devaluation should be *tripled* in 1993 to 120 cents per day.[35] In late 1992, I pointed out that "the rapid real appreciation of the peso in the last few months has contributed to [a] . . . widening trade imbalance, affecting overall credibility."[36] In a public document issued in November 1992, the World Bank noted, with a tragic sense of premonition, that "opening its capital account also exposes Mexico to the volatility of short-term capital movements that can transmit destabilizing external shocks to the economy even if domestic policies are right." The report went on to say that Mexico could "adjust to these risks [of volatile capital movements] through higher interest rates and, possibly, depreciating the peso."[37]

The Mexican authorities responded to these questions by arguing that, since flows were largely private and the fiscal accounts were in surplus, there was nothing to be concerned about. This position was based on a three-part argument: first, it was pointed out that the system had enough built-in flexibility—in the form of flexible interest rates and the exchange rate band—to deal with eventual disequilibria; second, it was argued, a rapid increase in productivity was about to take place, generating a major export expansion that would help close the current-account gap; and, third, it was claimed, the long-term fundamentals remained healthy, especially in light of NAFTA's ratification.[38] As evidence of having matters under control, the authorities argued that non-traditional exports were doing fine, although they were of course lagging considerably with respect to the growth in imports. In 1994, Guillermo Ortiz, the current Secretary of Finance, argued that whether there was a situation of overvaluation "depend[ed] on the equilibrium real exchange rate . . . [T]he appreciation process is a natural, and not necessarily a negative, consequence of the reform process in Mexico."[39] And Miguel Mancera, Governor of the Bank of Mexico, told *The Economist* in January 1994 that the current-account deficit was not a problem—

---

[34] See Dornbusch (1993), p. 369.
[35] See *Excelsior*, November 23, 1992, p. 1.
[36] See Edwards (1994), p. 39.
[37] World Bank (1992), p. 359.
[38] See Bank of Mexico (1993, 1994); and Aspe (1993).
[39] Ortiz (1994), p. 306.

because it was associated with the inflow of foreign funds rather than expansionary fiscal or monetary policy.[40]

The surge in capital inflows led to the idea that Mexico was experiencing an "equilibrium" real exchange rate appreciation. According to this view, the strengthening of the peso was fully justified by fundamentals. Astonishingly, perhaps, even a year after the crisis this continued to be the "official" view from the Bank of Mexico.[41]

The view that an increase in capital flows will lead to an appreciation of the real exchange rate is correct from a simple theoretical perspective. Indeed, in order for the transfer of resources implied by higher capital inflows to become effective, a real appreciation is *required*. A limitation of this interpretation, however, is that it fails to recognize that the rate at which capital was flowing into Mexico in 1991-93—at levels exceeding 7 percent of GDP—was clearly *not sustainable* in the long run. This means that at some point the magnitude of this flow would have to be reduced, requiring a reversal in the real exchange rate movement. Although there are no mechanical rules for determining the volume of capital that can be maintained in the long run, there are some helpful guidelines that analysts can follow in order to detect departures from capital-account sustainability.[42] In general, there will be an "equilibrium" level of a country's liabilities that foreigners will be willing to hold in their portfolios. Naturally, this "equilibrium portfolio share" will not be constant and will depend on, among other variables, interest rate differentials, the perceived degrees of country and exchange risk, and the degree of openness of the economy. Moreover, when countries embark upon (what is perceived to be) a successful reform program, the "equilibrium" level of the country's liabilities that will be willingly held by international investors is likely to increase, as they will be eager to take part in the country's "take-off." In a recent paper, Guillermo Calvo and Enrique Mendoza argued that, in a world with costly information, it is even possible for very large

---

[40] Although Mexico's remarkable fiscal adjustment following the debt crisis cannot be overemphasized, it is important to acknowledge that, upon closer scrutiny, the stance in terms of fiscal policy started to shift as early as 1989. This can only be appreciated when the traditional fiscal accounts are corrected in order to exclude from public expenditure the inflationary component of interest payments. In any event, it is still the case that a significant shift in the fiscal stance took place only beginning in the second semester of 1993. See Leiderman and Thorne (1995).

[41] See its 1995 report and its Governor's remarks at the Inter-American Development Bank conference on "Experiences in Banking Crisis Management," Washington, D.C., October 5-6, 1995.

[42] On the issue of current-account sustainability see, among others, Reisen (1995).

volumes of capital to move across countries on the basis of rumors.[43] They estimate that, in the case of Mexico, belief in a change in domestic returns by one-half could result in capital movements of approximately US$14 billion.

Transitional issues are particularly important when there are large shifts (positive or negative) in the international portfolio demand for a country's liabilities. If, for example, there is a reduction in a country's degree of country risk, foreigners will increase their demand for the country's securities, and in the short run— while the new securities are accumulated—the current-account deficit will overshoot its new long-run equilibrium level. Once portfolio equilibrium is regained, however, the current-account balance will again revert to its long-run equilibrium level. One of the most important dynamic effects of this transition is on the real exchange rate. As capital flows in, there will be an increase in expenditure and an appreciation in the real exchange rate. Once capital stops flowing in, or even when the rate at which it flows in slows down, the real exchange rate will be "overly" appreciated, and a massive adjustment may be required in order to maintain equilibrium. The dynamics of capital inflows and current-account adjustment will require, then, that the equilibrium real exchange rate first appreciate and then depreciate. And while the real exchange rate appreciates without any impediment during the surge in inflows, when the availability of foreign capital declines, nominal wage and price rigidity will make the required real depreciation difficult under a pegged exchange rate.[44] Mexico's clinging to the rigid exchange rate system, the obsession with single-digit inflation, and a succession of negative shocks made the possibility of a smooth landing increasingly unlikely as capital flows declined during 1994.

Naturally, the situation will become even more serious if, as a result of external or internal developments, there is a *decline* in the portfolio demand for a country's securities—as was the case in Mexico after December 20, 1994. In these circumstances, the capital-account balance will suffer a very severe contraction—and the current account may even have to become positive—during the transitional period toward the new equilibrium.

The relevant question regarding events in Mexico was not, as some analysts incorrectly thought during 1994, whether the inflows

---

[43] See Calvo and Mendoza (1996b).

[44] This type of analysis has been made in relationship to the sequencing-of-reform debate. See, for example, Edwards (1984).

observed during 1991-93 were sustainable, but how and when Mexico was going to adjust to a lower availability of foreign resources.[45]

1994: A RECURRENT NIGHTMARE

Although the accumulated disequilibria and the slow growth in productivity had created a vulnerable situation, the market was increasingly enthusiastic about Mexico at the end of 1993. The approval of NAFTA had been key in creating this positive view. The year 1994, however, did not begin well. On January 1, the Zapatista "army" staged an uprising in the southern state of Chiapas, reminding the world that, despite the modernization reforms and the highly acclaimed *Solidaridad* program, Mexico continued to be a country with pressing social problems and tremendous inequalities.[46] Six weeks after the eruption of the Chiapas uprising, the *Financial Times* commented on Mexico's social conditions, pointing out that "low growth has meant that many Mexicans have yet to benefit significantly from economic initiatives that brought inflation down . . . and privatised hundreds of state-owned businesses."[47]

As a result of increased political uncertainty, in late February the exchange rate moved to the upper limit of the band. Surprisingly, perhaps, interest rates on peso-denominated government securities (28-day *cetes*, for example) did not increase substantially, and international reserves did not fall. In fact, from January to mid-February there was a record inflow of foreign direct investment. Moreover, and contrary to what has been intimated by some analysts, neither reserves nor domestic interest rates were affected by the Federal Reserve's decision to tighten U.S. monetary policy in February.[48] By mid-March it seemed that things were at least partially under control. In fact, after the initial scare generated by Chiapas, the financial community was once again betting on Mexico. On January 28, 1994, J.P. Morgan stated in its newsletter that, "while in the

---

[45] In 1993, Oks and van Wijnbergen (1995, p. 174) recognized the temporary nature of the expansion of capital inflows and argued that the key question was "once capital stops flowing, should we expect the current account to improve or is Mexico heading for a major [balance of payments] crisis?" It is worthwhile noting that Oks was at the time the World Bank's country economist for Mexico, and van Wijnbergen had been the Bank's lead economist for Mexico until early 1992.

[46] The *Solidaridad* program was President Salinas's flagship social program aimed at targeting social expenditure to the poorest segment of society in a direct way that eschewed the bureaucracy (see Aspe 1993). This program was strongly endorsed by the multilateral institutions, including the World Bank.

[47] *Financial Times*, February 17, 1994.

[48] In fact, interest rates on *cetes* declined for almost eight weeks following the Federal Reserve's actions of early February.

short term, directional moves in Mexican Bradys . . . will continue to be influenced by exogenous factors such as the rise and fall of global markets, we expect spreads to tighten substantially by year end, as investors begin to price Mexico risk expecting an investment-grade rating."[49]

And then, on March 23, fate struck again. The PRI presidential candidate—Luis Donaldo Colosio—was assassinated while greeting the crowd at a political rally in Lomas Taurinas, Tijuana (Baja California). This time the financial community reacted in panic. Investors, foreign and domestic, reduced their demand for Mexican securities. Under the impression that this was a shock of a temporary nature, the authorities strongly intervened to shore up the peso, spending around US$10 billion. Additionally, there was a rapid increase in peso-denominated interest rates—rates on 28-day *cetes* increased from around 10 percent in February to more than 16 percent in April. With the peso already at the top of the band, further devaluation was not an option within the prevailing exchange rate system. The U.S. authorities reacted to these events with alarm, and, on March 24, Secretary Bentsen and Federal Reserve Board Chairman Alan Greenspan announced that the United States was extending a US$6 billion swap facility to Mexico.

Despite the recurrence of negative shocks, the financial community still appeared to be confident of Mexico's future. This view was neatly reflected in a front-page article in London's *Financial Times* on March 25, 1994: "Even with Mexico's dependence on foreign capital to cover a current account deficit of over Dollars 20bn, a crisis is eminently avoidable." On March 28, a *Financial Times* headline announced: "A Sense of Calm Returns to Mexico."[50] A week after the assassination of Colosio, Ernesto Zedillo was named the PRI's new presidential candidate, and he pledged to continue the Mexican reform path to economic development.

Despite the positive prognosis, Mexico had difficulties rolling over its rapidly maturing peso-denominated debt. The authorities faced a dilemma: Should they allow interest rates to increase further, at the risk of engineering a recession in an election year and weakening an already badly battered banking system, or should they substitute dollar-linked securities that paid a significantly lower rate— *tesobonos*—for the maturing *cetes*? In April, J.P. Morgan commented that "in the near term, the greatest pressure may come from foreign

---

[49] J.P. Morgan (1994).
[50] *Financial Times*, March 25, 1994, p. 1.

investors who decide to sell their investments in domestic securities. If the peso were to come under severe pressure, the final decision by the Mexican government will involve weighting the trade-off between allowing interest rates to rise to whatever level is required, and abandoning a key component of its economic program [the exchange rate system]."[51] In late April, the Mexican authorities decided to (informally) impose a cap on *cetes* peso-denominated interest rates, a policy that came to be known as "drawing the line" ("*tirar la rayita*"), and to issue increasing amounts of dollar-denominated *tesobonos*. Evidently, if market participants had expectations of a devaluation, the risk would now be shouldered by the government, in much the same way that an increase in the interest rate on *cetes* would have increased the cost of servicing domestic debt.

At the same time that the government resisted increasing interest rates on peso-denominated public debt, the central bank sterilized the decline in reserves. The decision to maintain the money-supply target unaltered implied that the decline in reserves had to be compensated with increases in central bank credit. This allowed for important increases in credit by the financial system. Particularly active in lending were the official development banks, whose credit outstanding had increased by 35 percent in the twelve months ending in June. In addition to all these developments, fiscal policy was being (if anything) relaxed in response to a political campaign that turned out to be unexpectedly difficult for the long-governing party.

During the first half of 1994, concerns about the sustainability of Mexico's external situation grew among analysts, including the World Bank staff and U.S. officials. This preoccupation became particularly serious after Colosio's assassination. At the spring meetings of the Brookings Institution Economics Panel, Rudiger Dornbusch and Alejandro Werner argued that the Mexican peso was overvalued by at least 30 percent and that the authorities should rapidly find a way to solve the problem.[52] In their view, whether the realignment should have taken the form of an accelerated rate of crawl or a floating rate depended on the support the government could get from labor unions. At that same meeting, Guillermo Calvo argued that, because of a lack of credibility, any exchange rate adjustment was likely to generate a financial panic and that the solution lay in regaining credibility by obtaining massive support from the U.S.

---

[51] J.P. Morgan (1994).
[52] Dornbusch and Werner (1994).

Treasury—which in his view should have announced that it was ready to buy the outstanding stock of *cetes*.[53] Stanley Fischer, soon to become the IMF's First Deputy Managing Director, also expressed his concerns regarding the external sustainability of the Mexican experiment.[54] Internal U.S. government communications released to the U.S. Senate Banking Committee during 1995 also reflected a mounting concern among some U.S. officials. Several staff members of the Federal Reserve Bank of New York, for example, argued that a devaluation of the peso could not be ruled out. On May 2, 1994, however, Treasury Under Secretary for International Affairs Lawrence Summers stated in a memorandum to Secretary Bentsen that "in our view, Mexico's current exchange rate policy is sustainable."[55] As time passed, the U.S. authorities became increasingly concerned about the evolution of Mexico's international reserves. A May 1994 memo from Treasury Assistant Secretary for International Affairs Jeffrey Shafer points out that the Bank of Mexico had, reportedly, spent US$10 billion since the Colosio assassination to defend the peso.

Between April and October, the *official* stock of international reserves held by the Bank of Mexico—that is, the level of reserves released to the public three times a year—remained stable, and so did interest rates on *cetes*. The exchange rate, on the other hand, rose with the ceiling of the band. After May, interest rates on *cetes* actually declined somewhat, although they never reached the levels observed during the first quarter. The deceiving stability that these developments implied has to be confronted with the fact that, increasingly, the government was replacing peso-denominated debt with *tesobonos*, rapidly changing the currency composition of broad money (M3). This strategy was quite transparent and was even commented on, matter-of-factly, in financial circles. According to J.P. Morgan's *Emerging Markets Outlook*, "half of the 28-day and 91-day *cetes* offered were issued; the central bank would not accept the high yields required by the market to auction the full amount . . . In the *tesobonos* auction, yields . . . trended down modestly."[56] And on July 23, 1994, an article in *The Economist* pointed out that "the central bank has also had to issue plenty of *tesobonos*—dollar-linked bonds that are popular with investors that worried about currency risk."[57]

---

[53] Calvo (1994).
[54] Fischer (1994).
[55] See D'Amato (1995), p. 226.
[56] J.P. Morgan, *Emerging Markets Outlook*, July 22, 1994, p. 22.
[57] "Pounding the peso," *The Economist*, July 23, 1994, p. 76.

As of October, the broadly defined monetary aggregate, M3, was increasing at an annual rate of over 20 percent;[58] its domestic-currency component, however, was increasing at only 6.7 percent. The share of M3 held in dollar-denominated assets, which stood at 9.2 percent at the end of 1993, had reached 21 percent by the end of the third quarter. Moreover, according to Calvo and Mendoza, after March 1994, foreign reserves—even though they had ceased to decline in April—were becoming insufficient backing for the short-term liabilities of the government. By August the amount of *tesobonos* outstanding was roughly equivalent to the stock of international reserves (around $16-17 billion).[59] In what in retrospect proved to be a serious mistake that greatly eroded credibility, the authorities decided to withhold much of the financial information from the public and the multilateral institutions (see the discussion below, however).[60] The *ex post* analysis of indicators of exchange rate and country risk—calculated as the spreads between *tesobonos* and *cetes*, and *tesobonos* and U.S. T-bills, respectively—suggests with some clarity that, after early reactions as a result of the Chiapas uprising and the assassination of Colosio, the market's perception of the Mexican situation remained stable until quite late in the game; risk measures based on interest rate differentials shot up only in the first week of December.[61]

In August, Ernesto Zedillo Ponce de Leon was elected President with one of the smallest margins in Mexico's modern history. In September, the *Pacto* was once again renewed, and, after an active debate within the government, no major policy changes were introduced. In particular, exchange rate, monetary, and fiscal policies were maintained, and the policy of substituting *tesobonos* for maturing *cetes* was continued. These decisions—maintaining the exchange rate system instead of engineering a gradual adjustment under a floating rate regime and continuing the massive issues of *tesobonos*—mystified many analysts, particularly Mexico-watchers in the U.S. government. In fact, the staff of the Federal Reserve Board had

---

[58] M3 = M1 + short term (financial and non-financial sector) liabilities.

[59] Between the end of March and the end of October the amount of *tesobonos* increased by the same amount as the decline in *cetes*, around M$35 billion (or US$10 billion).

[60] After two weeks in the field, the IMF mission returned to Washington in early June without having obtained data from the Bank of Mexico authorities on the recent evolution of international reserves. The World Bank was also kept in the dark on the behavior of some of the variables.

[61] According to Obstfeld and Rogoff (1995), interest rate differentials indicate that, after March 1994, credibility on the sustainability of exchange rate policy was consistently lower than before the events of March.

argued that the renewal of the *Pacto* provided an excellent opportunity for altering the exchange rate regime and gradually eliminating the accumulated overvaluation. In a briefing note to Secretary Bentsen dated October 27, 1994, Treasury staff commented that they were concerned that "exchange rate policy under the new *Pacto* could inhibit attainment of a sustainable external position."[62]

The decision to maintain the policy course unaltered was the result of a combination of factors. It was thought that, with time, investors would understand that the heightened turbulence was temporary and that, consequently, additional funds would once again flow into the country. Second (as pointed out above), there was great reluctance to allow peso interest rates to increase further. At this point, with the presidential election already won by the PRI, the overriding concern was that higher interest rates would adversely affect the banking system. Preoccupation with the financial health of banks had begun in late 1992, when a significant increase in the past-due loans ratio became evident. In 1990, non-performing loans were estimated to be only 2 percent of total loans; but that ratio increased to 4.7 percent in 1992, to 7.3 percent in 1993, and to 8.3 percent at the end of the first quarter of 1994.[63] With the fourth largest bank, Banca Cremi, in serious trouble, the authorities tried to buy additional time as they worked out an emergency plan to strengthen those banks considered to be in a particularly weak position. By the end of the first semester, the State Development Banks had developed a relief program based on some write-offs of commercial banks' past-due interest and on government-issued loan guarantees.

The policy stance remained firm even in late September, when the Secretary General of the PRI, José Francisco Ruíz Massieu, was assassinated. As the number of assassinations and violence and uncertainty grew, investors became even more nervous, and the authorities intensified the substitution of *tesobonos* for *cetes*. On October 21, Governor Miguel Mancera announced that the Bank of Mexico's reserves holdings were US$17.12 billion. Many analysts—including analysts in the U.S. government—believed, however, that the Bank of Mexico had borrowed to bolster the reserves level. In mid-October, the U.S. Treasury debated how the U.S. should react if

---

[62] See D'Amato (1995), pp. 308, 338.

[63] It is important to mention that, in these calculations, past-due loans include only unpaid installments of principal plus interest. Additionally, past-due loans do not include those that have been restructured without having paid interest. These accounting procedures are, to a certain extent, compensated by the fact that installments are considered past due after a relatively short period of time (15 days in general).

the Mexican government requested drawing on the US$6 billion swap. In a note to Secretary Bentsen, Under Secretary Summers said that he "would be very uncomfortable agreeing to a drawing . . . and would like to discourage consideration of any request." And in a memo to Chairman Greenspan dated October 18, 1994, the Federal Reserve staff suggested that he communicate to the Mexicans that "they should not count on financial support via the Federal Reserve and Treasury lines to sustain an inappropriate exchange rate. The swap lines are intended to deal with what are viewed as transitory market disturbances, not to buttress an unsustainable exchange rate regime."[64] In mid-October, major Mexican corporations—including telecommunications giant Teléfonos de México (Telmex)—announced disappointing third-quarter earnings. The stock market tumbled, and the peso weakened further, moving ever closer to the top of the band. Later in the month, and in an effort to attract new foreign capital, Mexico agreed to grant operating licenses to 52 foreign banks and brokerage houses. It was expected that this policy would result, in the short to medium run, in a flow of at least US$5 billion. But this did not happen.

In November, some investors opted to reduce their exposure in Mexico, largely as a result of uncertainties linked to the inauguration of a new administration in December. Ironically, AT&T's announcement that it would enter the Mexican market also contributed to the sell-off of pesos, as a number of Wall Street firms removed Telmex from the recommended list. International reserves declined by around $5 billion, and, as had been the case at the end of the first quarter, the central bank opted to sterilize. Net domestic credit from the central bank, which had been negligible following the events of late March, increased by close to M$20 billion in November alone, its dollar equivalent being roughly equal to the decline in reserves.[65]

By the end of November, reserves stood at $12.5 billion, with short-term public debt in excess of $27 billion—around 70 percent of it in dollar-denominated *tesobonos*. The situation had surpassed the current-account and overvaluation sphere and had all the characteristics of a major financial crisis. Reserves at the central bank had become clearly insufficient backing for short-term domestic public debt. Needless to say, they were much more insufficient when measured against all short-term financial liabilities. According to a

---

[64] See D'Amato (1995), pp. 381, 383-84.

[65] According to the *Wall Street Journal* (July 6, 1995, p. A4), the incoming administration at this point in time favored a devaluation, which the outgoing Finance Minister opposed.

Wall Street Journal story, on the night of November 20, President Salinas met with President-Elect Zedillo and a group of advisors. After a long discussion, the majority of those present concurred that a devaluation was necessary to calm the markets.[66] According to this story, however, Secretary of Finance Pedro Aspe threatened to resign if the parity was abandoned, and the idea of a correction had to be shelved. The new administration took over on December 1, and Pedro Aspe was replaced by Jaime Serra. Although the new team had broad international experience—after all, Serra had successfully negotiated NAFTA—it had not worked closely with the financial community. Moreover, de-classified Treasury documents suggest that, when the decision to devalue was made, the new Mexican authorities had not established an official contact with their U.S. counterparts. In a remarkable memo, presumably dated December 19,[67] to Timothy Geithner, then Deputy Assistant Secretary for International Monetary and Financial Policy, an unidentified staff member in the Office of the Assistant Secretary for International Affairs (OASIA) says: "Sidaoui [then a Deputy Secretary of Finance] is our contact, but contact has not been made." The OASIA staff member then goes on to suggest that it would be advisable for Under Secretary Summers "to establish contact with Sidaoui and at least let the Mexicans know we are concerned."[68]

The decline in reserves that started in November continued into December. In the aftermath of the crisis, Wall Street analysts and operators argued that the lack of current information on Mexico's reserves position played an important role in magnifying the crisis. When Wall Street realized that the country's financial situation was much weaker than it had been led to believe, confidence in the authorities disappeared, and a massive withdrawal of funds took place. The fact that the level of international reserves was disclosed only three times a year by the Bank of Mexico had for some time been particularly disturbing to a number of Wall Street analysts.[69] A postmortem of the crisis sponsored by the Council on Foreign Relations and undertaken by an independent task force chaired by John Whitehead concluded that "full financial information was not forthcoming to all investors."[70] A round table organized by the Group of

---

[66] "Peso Surprise," *Wall Street Journal*, July 6, 1995.

[67] The memo's date has been cut off in the D'Amato papers. Its date can be approximately established by the following statement: "I estimate their reserves were $11.8 at cob Friday, December 16." D'Amato (1995), p. 428.

[68] D'Amato (1995), p. 428.

[69] See, for example, the "'Transition to Transparency," *Institutional Investor*, January 1994, pp. 111-13.

[70] Council on Foreign Relations (1996), p. 27.

Thirty reached a similar conclusion.[71] The Senate Banking Committee documents indicate quite clearly, however, that the U.S. Treasury was well aware of the speed at which reserves were being depleted. On November 18, Assistant Secretary Shafer informed the Secretary of the Treasury that "reserves have now fallen below $14 million," and a December 5 memo to Under Secretary Summers and Shafer said that "reserves are now only slightly above the critical $10 billion threshold. . . . They seem to have used up all the easy ways to boost reserves."[72] The private sector, however, was largely unaware of how fast reserves were falling during November and December.

With reserves reaching dangerously low levels, the authorities on December 20 opted for a change in policy. The exchange rate band was widened to allow for a 15 percent devaluation. Surprisingly, the announcement of the new band was not accompanied by a supporting program, nor did it specify how the authorities planned to handle a possible massive withdrawal of deposits. In disbelief, investors fled, rendering the change in policy ineffective; in one day the Bank of Mexico lost US$4 billion. At that time, the authorities realized that they had no alternative but to float the peso.

CONCLUSIONS

Many analysts were surprised by how rapidly Mexican economic conditions deteriorated after the devaluation. Maturing *tesobonos* and *cetes* were not rolled over, the once-abundant foreign funds disappeared overnight, and what was supposed to be a run-of-the-mill devaluation became a major crisis. Many analysts have asked why Mexico was hit so hard by these developments. After all, a few years earlier, a number of countries—Spain and Canada, to name just two—had experienced major exchange rate adjustments in an orderly way. What made Mexico so special? The answer resides in the almost complete loss of confidence in Mexico, its institutions, and its leaders in the aftermath of the crisis. Financial operators and market observers felt that they had been misled in a grand way and, suddenly, were unsure of how to assess Mexico's true payments capacity and economic potential. This sense of perplexity and massive loss of confidence in turn generated a gigantic decline in the portfolio demand for Mexican securities. As a result, the peso/dollar exchange rate had to be adjusted by an amount that exceeded almost every analyst's expectation. Given Mexico's lack of

---

[71] Group of Thirty (1995).
[72] D'Amato (1995), p. 417.

international reserves, investors were particularly concerned that it would be unable to pay the rapidly maturing *tesobonos*. On December 30, 1994, Salomon Brothers opined that the "possibility of a forced rescheduling of *tesobonos* cannot be ruled out." On February 2, 1995, alone, US$5.2 billion in *tesobonos* was due, and between June and August a further US$8.4 billion was maturing. The rapid reaction by the U.S. government, the International Monetary Fund, and the Bank of International Settlements, which jointly made available close to US$40 billion in credit lines to Mexico, helped prevent a liquidity problem that would have resulted in a systemic global financial debacle.[73] By the third quarter of 1995, the specter of a major default had disappeared, as virtually all *tesobonos* had been paid off.

Only slowly, and through a combination of policies aimed at correcting macroeconomic disequilibria and supporting those affected by the crisis—especially debtors and local banks—has Mexico been able to regain some of its reputation. Overall, 1995 was a terrible year. During 1996, however, there were important improvements. Toward mid-year, there were clear signs of economic recovery, and monthly inflation reached its lowest level since the eruption of the crisis. The year ended with a rate of growth of 4.5 percent, a rate of unemployment of 4.1 percent, and inflation of 28 percent. In early 1997, the international analysts were once again bullish about Mexico, and capital was flowing into the country at increasing rates. Between late October 1994 and mid-January 1997, public-sector debt in the hands of foreigners increased from NP$17 billion to NP$27 billion. Although the figures involved are small relative to the early 1990s, there is no doubt—once again—that this is not a sustainable trend even in the medium run. This abundance of foreign funds has allowed the authorities to maintain a stable peso while relaxing monetary policy and thus reducing domestic interest rates. The key question, then, is whether the recovery of growth and employment will be sustained, or whether it will only be a statistical blip.

For most of 1996-97, the Bank of Mexico followed a nominal exchange rate targeting policy. By manipulating liquidity to the financial sector—and thus targeting domestic interest rates—it tried to maintain the value of the dollar within a very narrowly defined band. This policy has been largely successful, permitting the exchange rate to remain below the threshold of 8 pesos per dollar.

---

[73] For details of the early economic program and of the U.S.–IMF rescue program, see, for example, Burki and Edwards (1996), and Edwards (1995).

This nominal exchange rate targeting policy has had two undesirable side effects. First, throughout most of 1996-97, interest rates were extremely volatile—and relatively high. Second, this policy has resulted in a continuous real appreciation of the peso. Both of these factors, and in particular the appreciating real exchange rate, will slow export growth and may stall the recovery.

Is the real exchange rate overvalued at this time? In light of the rapid inflows of capital into Mexico and of the authorities' policy of targeting the exchange rates, some analysts have begun to argue that the real value of the peso is overvalued, and that we are on the way to _déjà vu_ all over again. Any analysis of the data, however, suggests that at this time these concerns are unfounded. There are a number of reasons to argue that the peso is _not_ overvalued at the time of this writing (November 1997). First, by the end of 1996, the real exchange rate will still be 26 percent more depreciated than it was in December of 1994.[74] Second, there have been some changes in "fundamentals" that justify an equilibrium real exchange rate appreciation. The most important of these fundamental changes are:

- There has been a marked improvement in the terms of trade. This has been largely the result of the increase in the price of oil. Interestingly enough, the CIA oil-market forecast for 1997 suggests that the price of oil will continue to be high throughout the year.

- There have been some important increases in productivity. According to a Ricardo-Balassa principle, countries with rapid productivity growth will experience an equilibrium real exchange rate appreciation. (This has been true in the case of Japan, for example, since the 1950s.)

- Mexico has been more successful than predicted in attracting foreign financing. This has been the case for both the private and public sectors.

- The fiscal adjustment undertaken by the government has been more strict than anticipated.

---

[74] Notice, however, that by December 1996 the real exchange rate was only 7 percent more depreciated than it had been in January 1995!

REFERENCES AND BIBLIOGRAPHY

Aspe, Pedro (1993). *Economic Transformation the Mexican Way*. Cambridge: MIT Press.

Bank of Mexico. *The Mexican Economy*. Mexico City. Several issues.

Buffie, Edward, and Allen Sangines (1988). "Economic Policy and Foreign Debt in Mexico," in Jeffrey Sachs, ed., *Developing Country Debt and Economic Performance vol. 2*. Chicago: University of Chicago Press.

Burki, Shahid Javed, and Sebastian Edwards (1996). *Dismantling the Populist State: Latin America's Unfinished Revolution*. Washington, D.C.: World Bank, Office of the Vice President, Latin America and the Caribbean.

——————— (1995). *Latin America After Mexico: Quickening the Pace*. Washington, D.C.: World Bank, Office of the Vice President, Latin America and the Caribbean.

Calvo, Guillermo (1995). "Varieties of Capital-Markets Crisis." College Park, Md.: University of Maryland. Mimeographed.

——————— (1994). "Comments on Dornbusch and Werner." Brookings Papers on Economic Activity no. 1. Washington, D.C.: Brookings Institution.

Calvo, Guillermo, and Enrique Mendoza (1996a). "Petty Crime and Capital Punishment," *American Economic Review*. May.

——————— (1996b). "Rational Herd Behavior and the Globalization of Security Markets." College Park, Md.: University of Maryland. Mimeographed.

——————— (1995). "Reflections on Mexico's Balance of Payments Crisis: A Chronicle of a Death Foretold." College Park, Md.: University of Maryland. Mimeographed.

Chemical Bank newsletter (1994).

Council on Foreign Relations (1996). *Lessons of the Mexican Peso Crisis: Report of an Independent Task Force*. New York: CFR.

D'Amato, Alfonse (1995). "Report on the Mexican Economic Crisis." Washington, D.C.: United States Senate.

Dornbusch, Rudiger (1993). "Mexico: How to Recover Stability and Growth," in Rudiger Dornbusch, ed., *Stabilization, Debt and Reform*. New Jersey: Prentice Hall.

——————— (1989). "Debt Problems and the World Macro Economy," in Jeffrey Sachs, ed., *Developing Country Debt and The World Macro Economy*. Chicago: University of Chicago Press.

——————— **and Alejandro Werner** (1994). "Mexico: Stabilization, Reform, and No Growth." Brookings Papers on Economic Activity no. 1. Washington, D.C.: Brookings Institution.

Dornbusch, Rudiger, Ilan Goldfajn, and Rodrigo Valdes (1995). "Currency Crises and Collapses." Brookings Papers on Economic Activity no. 2. Washington, D.C.: Brookings Institution.

Edwards, Sebastian (1997). "Latin America's Underperformance," *Foreign Affairs*. March/April.

————— (1996). "Exchange Rate Anchors, Credibility and Inertia: A Tale of Two Crises, Chile and Mexico," *American Economic Review*. May.

————— (1995). *Crisis and Reform in Latin America: From Despair to Hope.* New York: Oxford University Press.

————— (1994). "Trade Liberalization Reforms in Latin America," in Graham Bird and Ann Helwege, eds., *Latin America's Economic Future.* London: Academic Press.

————— (1993). "Exchange Rates as Nominal Anchors," *Welwirtschaftliches Archiv* 129, no 1.

————— (1989). "Structural Adjustment Policies in Highly Indebted Countries," in Jeffrey Sachs, ed., *Developing Country Debt and Economic Performance vol. 2.* Chicago: University of Chicago Press.

————— (1988). *Exchange Rate Misalignment in Developing Countries.* Baltimore: Johns Hopkins University Press.

————— (1984). "The Order of Liberalization of the External Sector in Developing Countries," *Essays in International Finance* 156. New Jersey: Princeton University.

————— and Alejandra Cox-Edwards (1991). *Monetarism and Liberalization: The Chilean Experience.* Chicago: University of Chicago Press.

—————, Roberto Steiner, and Fernando Losada (1996). *Capital Flows, the Real Exchange Rate and the Mexican Crisis.* Washington, D.C.: World Bank, Office of the Chief Economist.

Fischer, Stanley (1994). "Comments on Dornbusch and Werner." Brookings Papers on Economic Activity no. 1. Washington, D.C.: Brookings Institution.

Flood, Robert, and Peter Isard (1988). "Monetary Policy Strategies," *International Monetary Find Staff Papers* 36, no. 3. Washington, D.C.: International Monetary Fund.

Fraser, Kerry (1995). "Who Lost Mexico?" *Emerging Markets Investor*.

Group of Thirty (1995). "Mexico: Why Didn't Wall Street Sound the Alarm?" New York: Group of Thirty.

International Monetary Fund (1995). "Factors Behind the Financial Crisis in Mexico." Annex I in *World Economic Outlook*. Washington, D.C.: IMF, May.

————— (1994). *Annual Report.* Washington, D.C.: IMF.

Ito, Takatoshi (1993). "U.S. Political Pressure and Economic Liberalization in East Asia," in Jeffrey Frankel and Miles Kahler, eds., *Regionalism and*

Rivalry: Japan and the United States in Pacific Asia. Chicago: National Bureau of Economic Research/University of Chicago Press.

J.P. Morgan (1994). *Emerging Markets Outlook*. Several issues.

Krugman, Paul (1995). "Dutch Tulips and Emerging Markets," *Foreign Affairs*. July/August.

Leiderman, Leonardo, and Alfredo Thorne (1995). "Mexico's 1994 Crisis and its Aftermath." Mimeographed.

Loser, Claudio, and Eliot Kalter (1992). "Mexico: The Strategy to Achieve Sustained Economic Growth." Occasional Paper 99. Washington, D.C.: International Monetary Fund.

Lustig, Nora (1992). *Mexico: The Remaking of an Economy*. Washington, D.C.: Brookings Institution.

Malpass, David, and David Chon (1994). "Mexican Pesos and Cetes Are Attractive," Bear Stearns. November 7.

McKinnon, Ronald (1991). *The Order of Economic Liberalization*. Baltimore: Johns Hopkins University Press.

——————— (1982). *The Order of Economic Liberalization: Lessons from Chile and Argentina*. Carnegie-Rochester Conference Series on Public Policy 17. Amsterdam: North Holland.

Naím, Moisés (1995). "Mexico's Larger Story," *Foreign Policy* 99, Summer.

Obstfeld, Maurice, and Ken Rogoff (1995). "The Mirage of Fixed Exchange Rate." National Bureau of Economic Research Working Paper Series no. 5191. Washington, D.C.: NBER.

Oks, Daniel, and Sweder van Wijnbergen (1995). "Mexico After the Debt Crisis: Is Growth Sustainable?" *Journal of Development Economics* 47, no. 1, June.

Ortiz, Guillermo (1994). "Comments on Rudiger Dornbusch: Stabilization and Monetary Reform in Latin America," in J.O. de Beaufort Wijnholds, S.C.W. Eijffinger, and L.H. Hoogduin, eds., *A Framework for Monetary Stability*. Dordrech/Boston: Kluwer Academic Publishers.

——————— (1991). "Mexico Beyond the Debt Crisis: Toward Sustainable Growth With Price Stability," in Michael Bruno, Stanley Fischer, Elhanan Helpman, and Nissan Liviatan, eds., *Lessons of Economic Stabilization and Its Aftermath*. Cambridge: MIT Press.

Reisen, Helmut (1995). "Managing Temporary Capital Inflows: Lessons from Asia and Latin America." Paris: OECD Development Centre. Mimeographed.

Sachs, Jeffrey, Aaron Tornell, and Andres Velasco (1995). "The Collapse of the Mexican Peso: What Have We Learned?" National Bureau for Economic Research Working Paper Series no. 5142. Washington, D.C.: NBER.

Santaella, Julio, and Abraham Vela (1994). "The 1987 Mexican Inflation Stabilization: Matching Stylized Facts and Theory." Washington, D.C.: Research Department, International Monetary Fund. Mimeographed.

Schadler, Susan, Maria Carkovic, Adam Bennett, and Robert Kahn (1993). "Recent Experiences with Surges in Capital Inflows." IMF Occasional Paper no. 108. Washington, D.C.: IMF.

Steiner, Roberto (1995). "The Mexican Crisis: Why Did It Happen and What Can We Learn?" Washington, D.C.: World Bank, Office of the Chief Economist, Latin America and the Caribbean. Mimeographed.

Swiss Bank Corporation newsletter (December 1994/January 1995).

Vela, Abraham (1993). "Three Essays on Inflation and Stabilization: Lessons from the Mexican Solidarity Pact." Unpublished Ph.D. dissertation. Los Angeles: University of California at Los Angeles, Department of Economics.

World Bank (1994). *Global Outlook and the Developing Countries*. Washington, D.C.

————— (1993a). *Annual Report*. Washington, D.C.

————— (1993b). *Trends in Developing Economies*. Washington, D.C.

————— (1993c). *Latin America and the Caribbean a Decade After the Debt Crisis*. Washington, D.C.

————— (1992). *Trends in Developing Economies*. Washington, D.C.

5. THE FOLLY, THE CRASH, AND BEYOND: ECONOMIC POLICIES AND THE CRISIS

RUDI DORNBUSCH

The 1994-95 crash was not the first crisis in Mexico and probably is not the last one either. Mexico has a record of being fundamentally mismanaged—too much borrowing and too little saving, too little competitiveness, too much government, too little transparency, and an unbelievable denial of reality. Of course, it takes two parties to create a crisis: as in every other instance, an overeager capital market supported the unrealistic assumptions of the Mexican strategy. Every crisis, though, has a new angle; the replay is almost the same, but not quite.

The penultimate crisis came as recently as 1982, when Mexico's Secretary of Finance came to New York to reveal that he could not pay the bills, and most of Latin America followed soon. The present crisis has much the same origins as the preceding ones: irresponsible lending by overconfident, overeager creditors and, on the Mexican side, major currency overvaluation. What is new is the exact detail of poor debt management and overlending. Then, it was bank debt; this time around, it was called *tesobonos*, but the principle is the same.

Waves of excitement in supplying developing countries with capital are not unprecedented. It is worth bearing in mind the historical record so as not to lose perspective on the fragility of the financing of large current-account deficits. In 1928, the distinguished Harvard economist Frank Taussig, writing on the eve of widespread debt defaults to comment on the collapse of Latin American credit, described the "unusual" sequence of events:

> The loans from the creditor country begin with a modest amount and proceed crescendo. They are likely to be made in exceptionally large amounts toward the culminating stage of the period of activity and speculative upswing, and during that

stage become larger from month to month so long as the upswing continues. With the advent of crises, they are at once cut down sharply, even cease entirely . . . A sudden reversal takes place in the debtor country's international balance sheet; it feels the consequences abruptly, in an immediate need of increased remittances to the creditor country, in a strain on its banks, high rates of discount, falling prices. And this train of events may ensue not only once."[1]

The overconfident investors who, as in every previous crisis in Latin America, thought there was another El Dorado with extraordinary returns in dollars year after year were disillusioned beyond belief.[2] The very investors who for a year—on far more than one occasion—received personal assurances that this would never, never happen became the most extreme protagonists in selling Mexico out.

At the time of the 1994-95 crisis, it was tempting to argue that ultimately interest in lending to Mexico and the region will return, but only when assets are dirt-cheap. Investors would first lick their wounds and curse their fate. Then they would need to see what Mexico will do to rebuild its image. Just as in real estate, there is always another boom—it just does not come in time to bail out the current holders of the hot potato. In fact, though, the return of capital was surprisingly rapid. Super-high interest rates and the strengthening of the peso (and analogies with Turkey's quick turnaround) brought money back in no time. Far from disillusioning emerging-market investors, the Mexican near-meltdown had little lasting influence; emerging-market finance is here to stay and grow. Of course, a large part of the confident return may be the U.S.–International Monetary Fund (IMF) bailout of Mexico. Much of the background to that operation remains to be disclosed. It may have little to do with protecting Mexico, or with protecting U.S. investors in various emerging-market funds, and much more to do with the huge off–balance sheet positions of some New York institutions.

The crash of the Mexican peso is just one more example of the cycle of exuberant optimism followed by collapse and bottomless skepticism in Latin America finance. As long as the music goes on, more and more ignorant investors are pulled in. And with the prospects so bright, more and more promoters raise capital to take

---

[1] See Taussig (1928), p. 130. See also the wider discussion of international lending following the default of debts in the late 1920s reported in Dornbusch and Cardoso (1989).

[2] More broadly, Kindleberger (1989) reviews the history and atmosphere of financial crises.

investors for a ride on the bubble. The crash of the peso ruined investors' bonuses, and it also dealt a major setback to Mexico's prospects.

PREVIEW

In the end there is always a crash, but it takes much longer than one thinks, and then it happens much faster than one would have thought. A country that only a moment ago was basking in the glory of reform and prosperity falls straight into bankruptcy. Investors feel cheated, economic prospects turn bleak, and the hunt is on for the whodunit—a finance minister who played the wrong music and thus sapped confidence, foreign investors who pulled out and left the country high and dry, or a previous administration that left behind an awesome legacy. A postmortem is instructive. In the case of Mexico, the responsibility lies squarely with former President Carlos Salinas and his obsessive preoccupation with inflation.

Following a borrowing spree in the late 1970s, Mexico last crashed in 1982. Debts to commercial banks around the world went into default; the peso was devalued over and over again in an attempt to gain a trade surplus to meet the demands of creditors. But even as the currency went down, inflation exploded. That vicious cycle of inflation and depreciation came to a peak with inflation well above 200 percent. Under the pressure of events, reform and stabilization became the central objective. Much good was done: privatization; trade liberalization, including NAFTA; deregulation; and budget balancing, including fiscal reform.

Somewhere along the way, external confidence recovered, money started coming, and external deficits ballooned. With easy access to financing and much of the domestic agenda accomplished, reducing inflation to U.S. levels became the central preoccupation. Depreciation of the currency was kept far below the rate of inflation; that helped slow inflation, but it also meant an increasingly uncompetitive trade position. At the outset, that could be rationalized by renewed access to world capital markets and the rewards of a reformed and stabilizing economy.

The trouble is this: Somewhere along the way, a U-turn must come to restore competitiveness—otherwise the currency ultimately goes over the cliff. By 1993, Mexican producer prices had risen *in dollars* by over 45 percent since the late 1980s compared with prices in the United States. An overvaluation of at least 25 percent could be discerned. Growth slowed down (except for election year spending), real interest rates were extremely high when measured by rates on commercial bank loans, and the external balance shifted toward a massive surplus. All the symptoms of a troubled financial situation were in place. Clearly the peso had become overvalued, but Mexican leaders refused to acknowledge the facts, and foreign investors were lulled into holding on to exposed positions. Superior fiscal performance was, of course, a strong point in explaining why Mexico was uniquely attractive. That was not enough.

EXCHANGE RATE–BASED STABILIZATION

In the 1990s, Mexico continued an ambitious reform process that had started during the de la Madrid administration. The key aspects of reform were a settlement of external debt with a Brady Plan, deregulation and trade opening, and privatization. Even though much of reform today has become suspect and is apt to be tainted with corruption, the major accomplishment in economic modernization should not be disregarded. Mexico did take a large and important step toward an open and competitive economy. President Salinas, with his cabinet, deserves lasting credit for the vision and courage.

Accompanying the reform process was a major effort to establish financial stability. The key features of that process were two: balancing the budget and bringing down inflation. At the end of the 1980s, budget deficits of 5-10 percent were by all accounts excessive. In the early 1990s, inflation peaked near 30 percent—a rate far too high for comfort (see Figure 1, p. 130). An all-out effort to secure financial stability was called for.

As Table 1 shows, fiscal consolidation was swift and substantial—as was progress on the inflation front. In looking at the disinflation, it is helpful to assess the inflation rate in terms of past inflation, the acceleration that comes from real depreciation (or the deceleration induced by real appreciation), the acceleration deriving from increasing real public-sector prices, and the impact of the output gap in stimulating higher margins or real wage claims.[3] The problem in disinflation is that there is no volunteer to start the process. Wages tend to be indexed, explicitly or implicitly. Public-sector prices follow the rate of inflation, or else there is a risk of widening deficits. The exchange rate must offset the prevailing rate

---

[3] This can be expressed as $\pi = \pi_{-1} + \alpha (e-\pi_{-1}) + \beta(p-\pi_{-1}) + \phi y; \alpha+\beta =1$, where π is the rate of inflation; e, the current rate of depreciation; p, the current rate of increase in public-sector prices; and y, the output gap.

Table 1. Macro Indicators

	1990	1991	1992	1993	1994	1995
	(percentage change)					
Growth	4.5	3.6	2.8	0.6	3.5	-6.9
Inflation	29.9	18.8	11.9	8.0	7.1	52.0
Depreciation	14.4	7.3	2.7	0.6	8.3	90.2
	(as percentage of GDP)					
Budget	2.8	0.5	-1.6	-0.7	0.1	-0.1
Current Account	-3.0	-5.1	-7.4	-6.5	-7.9	-0.3

Source: Bank of Mexico.

of inflation, or else there is a loss of competitiveness. Finally, a recessionary squeeze of real wages or margins is unpopular. Thus, inflation yesterday becomes inflation today.

Incomes policy is one way to cut through the inflation cycle. If wages, prices, and the exchange rate at some all point started to decelerate together, then inflation would be down without cuts in real wages, real appreciation of the exchange rate, or declining real prices in the public sector. Mexico did well with that strategy in the mid-1980s, but increasingly the *Pacto* strategy became strained—there was too much wage inflation and too little currency depreciation. Figure 1 shows the result: Inflation did come down steadily—by 1993-94 it had fallen below 10 percent. But at the same time the real exchange rate appreciated steadily, reaching an all-time high in late 1994. The real exchange rate is shown in Figure 2 here by Mexican wholesale prices in dollars relative to the U.S. wholesale price level.[4] As always, there is a question as to an appropriate base period. Surely the peak level of competitiveness in 1987 is not suitable. But by the same token, an all-time-high real appreciation must

---

[4] There is a further discussion of the particular measure of competitiveness below. Suffice it to say here that we avoid using consumer prices in the calculation to avoid the influence of the various subsidy removals for consumer goods associated with the budget correction.

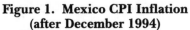

**Figure 1. Mexico CPI Inflation
(after December 1994)**

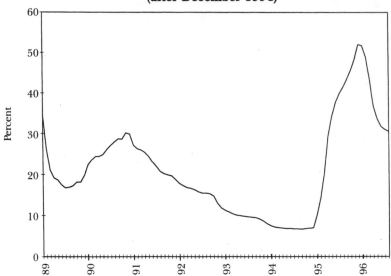

**Figure 2. Mexico–U.S. Relative Price Level
(WPI, 1980: 1=100)**

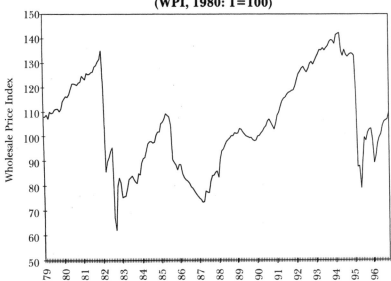

be explained. The contention here is that the reform measures called for real depreciation, not real appreciation. If that is correct, the issue of base period or measure of real appreciation misses the basic point.

Exchange rate–based stabilization goes through three phases: The first one is very useful and perhaps even indispensable. In this short phase, exchange rate pegging helps bring under way a stabilization. It achieves some concrete stabilization objectives and creates results—and hence confidence. Moreover, the first phase often benefits from an initial undervaluation that creates a cushion for real appreciation. Even so, phase one cannot last very long, because much of what is done here is in fact borrowed: It is to be validated by policy improvements down the road. The more is borrowed, the worse the prospects that it can be repaid—i.e., that the stabilization will last. In the second phase, increasing real appreciation becomes apparent, it is increasingly recognized, but it is inconvenient to do something. The reluctance to act in part involves the very realistic issue of what exactly to do. Not doing anything is easy; doing something is much harder. Not surprisingly, this phase lasts quite a while, and it feels good, since an overabundance of capital inflows suggests that something is being done right. Finally, in the third phase, it is too late to do something. Real appreciation has come to a point where a major devaluation is necessary. But the politics will not allow that. Some more time is spent in denial, and then—sometime— enough bad news piles up to cause the crash.

Mexico's exchange rate story of 1991-94 follows very much that pattern. In 1992-93, the question of excessive real appreciation and overvaluation was increasingly discussed. But with no concrete ideas about another strategy, with no wish to give up on disinflation, nothing was done. And then the election year of 1994 came in sight. Last opportunities to do something in 1993 just went unused—and then 1994 was there, and doing anything was completely out.

In 1993, a devaluation was still a possibility; certainly President Salinas considered it an option in the spring of that year—or at least he privately said so. But soon the government had political priorities that conflicted with reality and perhaps even fooled itself that the problems would go away or the financing would become easier. The rest is history: Reserves were run down to unmanageably low levels, debts were dollarized, maturities were shortened—just keep the music going so nobody finds out that the emperor has no clothes. Of course, these very steps to try and squeeze an extra year of life out of a moribund strategy help explain the extreme severity of the following crisis.

Mexico's policy-makers rationalized that real appreciation was unproblematic: NAFTA would bring direct investment and trade opportunities. Deficits were large now, but would be small in the future—and, in any event, money was no object, since investors had fallen in love with Mexican stocks and T-bills. Overvaluation turned problematic when the upcoming 1994 election brought with it the possibility of changes in economic strategy or a show of weakness by the official party.

Indeed, politics turned nasty (Chiapas, the assassination of the candidate, and more), and that caused some eyebrows to be raised. But no day passed without fresh assurances to the investors that all was well: the peso would never be allowed to fall. The foreign loans kept coming but at higher interest rates. High interest rates and lack of competitiveness increasingly strangled growth. No growth and a gigantic external deficit—almost 8 percent of GDP—made for a classical prediction: the peso would yield, sooner or later. But continuity and credibility babble can hold off problems only so long.

Yet President Salinas held on to the strategy of no waves—politics first, reality later. The myth of a super-performing Mexico was kept alive; criticism was not allowed, certainly not from cabinet members who hoped to get the magic nomination to be the next holder of absolute power. Chilean dictator Augusto Pinochet had put himself in the same position in the late 1970s. Just as Pinochet and his cabinet were impervious to common sense in currency matters, Salinas thought that with enough manipulation and censorship he could keep the peso afloat. Ultimately, both turned out to be very wrong and in a strikingly similar manner.

Without Chiapas, the crisis might not have happened. But that is unlikely; there is always *some* extraneous event that makes the glass run over, and if the currency is badly out of line, it does not take much. But why the seemingly bottomless drop of the peso? The analogy here is a bank run. Mexico dissipated its reserves in an attempt to sustain various levels of the peso. Nobody wants to be caught as the last one out or the first one in; investors left *en masse*.

Mexico's per capita income today is still 5 percent less than it was in 1982, at the time of the last crisis. The easy money is gone, and real income will be falling further. Salinas's brilliant reforms were about to put Mexico on the path to prosperity; instead, his utterly misguided currency experiments plunged the country into economic and possibly political turmoil.

Massive selling, fund redemptions, and forced liquidation with price collapses chasing yet further redemptions marked the period immediately preceding the collapse. Markets simply vanished. The financial chaos, the sheer lack of a market, and the inability in early 1995 to raise even a few hundred million dollars in new credits all conjure up the image of a gigantic fraud—Mexico had never reformed, there was no substance, and the other shoe (whichever that might be) was about to drop.

Of course, that is an extreme and totally unwarranted assessment of where Mexico has come. A better analogy is a company where the engineers have developed great technology, the workers have done a special job in raising productivity, and the sales people have excelled in developing markets. Yet, in this rendition, while nobody was watching, the CEO and the CFO were playing the markets, speculating in currency, and rigging up a gigantic loss that overshadowed all the gains made in the years of reform. Mexico had sort of an "Orange County problem"—to draw an analogy from recent financial scandals in the United States. Moreover, whoever is in charge of financial supervision in the international system closed an eye to what was going on.

REFORM WITHOUT GROWTH

The interesting question in analyzing the latest Mexican collapse is just how it was possible that the government persuaded itself that there was no problem. The thrust may well be that the cabinet was fully aware of the problem but simply insisted on getting through the election and into a new government—and dealing with issues later. But it is also possible that, in the isolated atmosphere of Mexican government, denial of reality was dominant.

The most striking fact of Mexican performance that should have aroused attention was surely the lack of growth. In the period 1985-94 Mexican output grew at an average rate of 2 percent. Labor-force growth over that period was at least 3 percent per year. Accordingly, productivity fell on average over the whole decade. In the more recent period, 1990-94, growth averaged 2.6 percent per year—still below the growth of the labor force. By 1993, growth had basically vanished. The election year brought back growth, driven by a significant and targeted fiscal expansion. But clearly the government could not have taken that to be anything other than election pump-priming.

The basic contention is that the lack of growth—not the current account or the real exchange rate taken in isolation—is the evidence

133

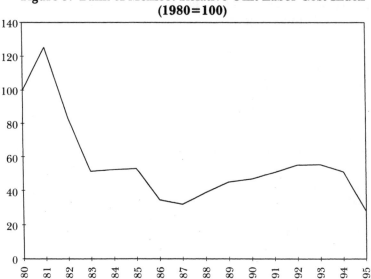

Figure 3. Bank of Mexico: Relative Unit Labor Cost Index
(1980=100)

of an overvaluation problem. Even though the lack of growth ought to have caused alarm, the government was confirmed in its prejudices by two important propositions: first, that Mexico was experiencing high productivity growth and hence surely had no competitiveness problem; and, second, that modernization and reform ought to imply an increased valuation in the stock market and in the real exchange rate—not an overvaluation.

THE PRODUCTIVITY ISSUE

The Organisation for Economic Co-operation and Development (OECD), of which Mexico is a member, does not report productivity data for the Mexican economy. The reason is the absence of reliable employment data. But the Mexican government does report productivity in manufacturing, and the central bank makes much of the major gain in competitiveness implied by the data. Specifically, a Bank of Mexico series based on relative unit labor costs shows a competitiveness loss of only 7 percent between 1990 and 1994-95.[5] This contrasts sharply with the data reported in Figure 3.

---

[5] Bank of Mexico (1996), p. 282.

The reason is an average growth rate of productivity reported as 5.7 percent per year.[6] This rate exceeds the rate Japan experienced in its best years, 1960-73.[7] There are a number of reasons to be suspicious. First, employment is poorly recorded, at least in the judgment of the OECD. Second, it is not obvious that the distinction between gross output and value added is consistently applied. At a time of significant growth in outsourcing, this difference is critical.

But even if the numbers were accurate, there are two further caveats. First, many firms can learn to live with virtually *any* exchange rate. They just become more capital-intensive. Of course, it is not the case that the economy, as opposed to firms, can do this. The labor redundancy that emerges needs an answer. In Mexico, output has barely grown at the rate of labor-force growth; thus, if productivity growth was significant, labor market conditions must have deteriorated year after year for many years. The point then is that competitiveness has to do not only with firms but also with an economy's ability to have full employment. In Mexico that was patently not the case.

TRADE LIBERALIZATION AND THE REAL EXCHANGE RATE

Another critical issue in the overvaluation discussion is trade liberalization and deregulation. The argument is often made that reforms warrant real appreciation. But this is an inappropriate identification. Reforms have two features: On one side, they lead to a more efficient use of resources; on the other side, they free resources. The former justifies higher stock-market valuation (or higher real wages); the latter begs the question of where resources will move. If wages and prices were *fully* flexible, liberalization would be accompanied by a fall in wages and prices in dollars.[8] The resulting gain in competitiveness would create demand and hence employment. In the absence of wage-price flexibility, a real depreciation is required via devaluation. It is instructive to look at Argentina's experience in the 1990s. Massive unemployment is the counterpart of dramatic restructuring, including in the public sector, and of trade liberalization. Wage-price flexibility is not working fast enough—there is only ever so slight deflation. Since the exchange rate cannot be used, an extended period of muddling on seems to be the likely course. In Mexico, by contrast, the exchange

---

[6] Average real wage growth over the period is reported as only 1.8 percent. See ibid., p. 290.

[7] See Maddison (1991), p. 275.

[8] See Dornbusch (1974).

rate could have been used as a counterpart to reform and as a way to translate it into a high-growth experience. Of course, real depreciation would not only solve the employment issue—it would also help on the external side in containing the trade deficit induced by trade liberalization.

ALTERNATIVE HYPOTHESES

This paper has argued that overvaluation is the reason for the Mexican crisis of 1994-95. Alternative hypotheses have been advanced and are at least plausible.[9] One highly visible contention has to do with Mexican credit expansion in the election year. In the face of reserve losses, Mexico's central bank fully sterilized these outflows, while development banks kept up a significant credit expansion. Too much money, motivated by the election year, is in this view the central contention. There is no question that central bank policy helped promote and presumably aggravate the crisis. It is right to believe that high interest rates could have avoided the crisis then and there. But it is also likely to be true that an extended period of high interest rates would ultimately have raised credibility questions: growth was becoming insignificant except for credit creation and election-year spending, and non-performing loans were rising steadily. High interest rates could have affected the timing; they could not have undone the overvaluation. Of course, in expanding demand and widening the external deficit, the credit policy of the central bank and the development banks contributed to the extent of the crisis. The same is true of the debt management strategy in the form of dollarization and shortening of maturities. These were part of a desperate game to get beyond the election, and they suggest just how aware the administration was of the underlying unsustainability of its policies.

In summary, Mexico's reforms should have set the country off on a path to high growth. The failure is not, of course, due to the reforms. Overvaluation was the key mistake. Bad credit policies and mismanagement of debt were important aggravating factors. Thus the lesson is this: Don't overvalue. Just as in Argentina since 1994, sound credit policy is not enough when there is a substantial overvaluation.

---

[9] Note in particular Bank of Mexico (1996, 1995); Blejer and del Castillo (1996); Calvo (1996a, 1996b); Calvo and Mendoza (1996); Cole and Kehoe (1996); Gil-Díaz and Carstens (1996); IMF (1995b); J.P. Morgan (1996a, 1996b); Lustig (1995); Mancera (1995); Masson and Agenor (1996); Roberts (1996); Sachs, Tornell, and Velasco (1996); Santella and Vela (1996); and U.S. GAO (1996).

POSTSCRIPT: CRAWL NOW OR CRASH LATER

One would have thought that the severity of the recent experience might have taught Mexican policy-makers a lesson—stay far, far away from an exchange rate–based stabilization. Yet precisely that same strategy is being pursued once again. By late 1996, much less than half of the huge real depreciation of 1995 was left. Even in the face of more than 20 percent inflation, monetary policy kept the peso flat for an entire year rather than depreciating at the pace of inflation. The peso is said to be a "flexible" rate, but in between interest rate and aggregate policy it manages to keep the peso flat, keep the capital coming, and risk preparing yet another instance of overvaluation. It is early to express that concern, but it is the appropriate time, since correction of the course remains easy. It is difficult to expect that inflation can fall sufficiently rapidly below world trends to bring a remedy. The experience with real appreciation reported by Goldfajn and Valdes[10] shows clearly that large overvaluations have little chance of a mild end.

Countries with 15-20 percent inflation per *year* should not belittle inflation; they must see it as one of a number of priorities, and they should view getting it under control as a process of five or even ten years. Accepting the right perspective on moderate inflation is important, because otherwise severe recession, super-high real interest rates with resulting banking problems, and currency overvaluation—with the risk of a collapse—might be the result rather than the dramatic success hoped for on the inflation front.

Chile offers an excellent example of good policy. Over the past decade, the country has had an average inflation rate of 17 percent. At the outset, it was 30 percent; in the early 1990s, it was still double-digit; and today it is down to 7 percent. The average growth for the ten-year period was 7 percent. Chile's approach has been exemplary, particularly in the past few years, when the central bank has refused to overreach and squeeze inflation down to the fashionable 2 percent of the industrialized countries. Chile's policy-makers recognize that strong growth, modernization, and integration in the world economy are not held back by 6, 10, or even 15 percent inflation, but could be seriously hampered if overambitious disinflation created a macroeconomic problem.

The central lesson in stabilizing inflation is that it is very perilous indeed to use the exchange rate for anything but a very transitory, initial consolidation effort. The exchange rate cannot carry

---

[10] See Goldfajn and Valdes (1996).

most or even much of the burden of stabilization. Nor can monetary policy do the job all by itself. Fiscal policy and competition must do a very substantial portion of the work.

The concern for inflation is altogether appropriate, but single-mindedness is not. In the face of moderate inflation, growth must also be part of the discussion. It is not correct to argue that there can be no growth in the presence of inflation; nor is it right to state that even moderate inflation is a detriment to growth.

It might be argued, of course, that the only stable inflation is zero inflation. But that would be a dogmatic posture without any empirical foundation. For the past decade or more, countries have been at work reducing inflation—or at least containing it. Countries with moderate inflation rates, such as Chile, have managed perfectly well to achieve *gradual* reductions without either compromising the credibility of that strategy or sacrificing growth. The fact that inflation was falling steadily over twelve years while growth was strong throughout actually made the program a textbook case of successful inflation-fighting. Mexico's case, by contrast, is a series of failures and blunders as a result of half-baked ideas about credibility, inflation kills, and the like. Chile today is a low-inflation country. Mexico is once again back to intolerably high inflation. The right message is that inflation must come down and that there is never room for complacency; that is not the same as inflation reduction first, growth later. Comparing Mexico's and Chile's per capita GDP over the fifteen years leaves no question. Mexico's currency experiments have been expensive—and if there is one more building up, who needs it?

REFERENCES AND BIBLIOGRAPHY

Andrews, David, and Shogo Ishii (1995). "The Mexican Financial Crisis: A Test of the Resilience of the Markets for Developing Country Securities." International Monetary Fund Working Paper. Washington, D.C.: IMF. December.

Bank of Mexico (1996). *The Mexican Economy*. Mexico City: Bank of Mexico.

——— (1995). *The Mexican Economy*. Mexico City: Bank of Mexico.

Blejer, Mario I., and Graciana del Castillo (1996). "*Déjà Vu* All Over Again? The Mexican Crisis and the Stabilization of Uruguay in the 1970s." International Monetary Fund Working Paper. Washington, D.C.: IMF. July.

Bosworth, Barry (1996). "The Decline in Mexican Saving: A Cost Reform?" Paper prepared by the LAC-Country Department II of the World Bank. Washington, D.C.: World Bank. May 10.

Calvo, Guillermo A. (1996a). "Capital Flows and Macroeconomic Management: Tequila Lessons." Unpublished paper. College Park, Md.: University of Maryland.

————— (1996b). "Why is 'The Market' So Unforgiving?" Unpublished paper. College Park, Md.: University of Maryland.

————— and Enrique G. Mendoza (1996). "Mexico's Balance-of-Payments Crisis: A Chronicle of a Death Foretold." Working papers in International Economics no. 20. College Park, Md.: Center for International Economics, Department of Economics, University of Maryland. March.

Cole, Harold L., and Timothy J. Kehoe (1996). "A Self-Fulfilling Model of Mexico's 1994-95 Debt Crises." Minneapolis, Minn.: Staff Report 210, Research Department, Federal Reserve Bank. April.

Dornbusch, Rudiger (1996). "Exchange Rates and Disinflation." Unpublished manuscript. Cambridge, Mass.: Massachusetts Institute of Technology.

————— (1974). "Tariffs and Nontraded Goods," *Journal of International Economics* 4. May.

————— and Alejandro Werner (1994). "Mexico: Reform Without Growth." Brookings Papers no. 1. Washington, D.C.: Brookings Institution.

————— and Eliana Cardoso (1989). "Foreign Private Capital Flows," in Hollis Chenery and T.N. Srinivasan, eds., *Handbook of Development Economics*. Amsterdam: North-Holland.

Gil-Díaz, Francisco, and Agustín Carstens (1996). "Some Hypotheses Related to the Mexican 1994-95 Crisis." Serie Documentos De Investigacion. Mexico City: Banco de Mexico, Direccion General De Investigacion Economica.

Goldfajn, I., and R.Valdes (1996). "The Aftermath of Appreciations." Working Paper no. 5650. Washington, D.C.: National Bureau of Economic Research.

Gonzalez-Hermosillo, Brenda (1996). "Banking Sector Fragility and Systemic Sources of Fragility." International Monetary Fund Working Paper. Washington, D.C.: IMF.

Hanke, Steve H. (1996). "Currency Board for Mexico," *Central Banking* 4, no. 4. Spring.

International Monetary Fund (1995a). *International Capital Markets*. Washington, D.C.: IMF.

————— (1995b). *World Economic Outlook*. Washington, D.C.: IMF.

J.P. Morgan (1996a). "Mexico's 1994 Crisis and its Aftermath." *Economic Research Note*. Mexico City: Banco J.P. Morgan, S.A. April 5.

————— (1996b). "The Banking Problems in Mexico's Recovery." *Economic Research Note*. Mexico City: Banco J.P. Morgan, S.A. March 1.

Kindleberger, Charles P. (1989). *Financial Panics and Mania*. New York, N.Y.: Basic Books.

Krugman, Paul (1996). "Are Currency Crises Self-Fulfilling?" in O. Blanchard, ed., *Macroeconomics Annual*. Washington, D.C.: National Bureau of Economic Research.

Lustig, Nora (1995). "The Mexican Peso Crisis: The Foreseeable and the Surprise." Brookings Discussion Papers in International Economics. Washington, D.C.: Brookings Institution. June.

Maddison, Angus (1991). *Dynamic Forces in Capitalist Development: A Long-Run Comparative View*. Oxford: Oxford University Press.

Mancera, Miguel (1995). "Don't Blame Monetary Policy," *Wall Street Journal*. January 31.

Masson, Paul R., and Pierre-Richard Agenor (1996). "The Mexican Peso Crisis: Overview and Analysis of Credibility Factors." International Monetary Fund Working Paper. Washington, D.C.: IMF. January.

Roberts, Craig (1996). "Mexico: Don't Blame Salinas for Zedillo's Mistakes," *Business Week Economic Viewpoint*. March 4.

Sachs, Jeffrey, Aaron Tornell, and Andres Velasco (1996). "Financial Crises in Emerging Markets: The Lessons From 1995." Brookings Papers on Economic Activity no. 1. Washington, D.C.: Brookings Institution.

Santella, Julio A., and Abraham E. Vela (1996). "The 1987 Mexican Disinflation Program: An Exchange Rate-Based Stabilization?" International Monetary Fund Working Paper. Washington, D.C.: IMF. March.

Taussig, Frank (1928). *International Trade*. New York: Macmillan.

Tornell, Aaron, and Gerardo Esquivel (1990). "The Political Economy of Mexico's Entry to NAFTA." Working Paper no. 5322. Washington, D.C.: National Bureau of Economic Research. October.

U.S. General Accounting Office (1996). *Mexico's Financial Crises: Origins, Awareness, Assistance, and Initial Efforts to Recover*. Report to the Chairman, Committee on Banking and Financial Services. Washington, D.C.: House of Representatives. February.

Uribe, Martin (1996). "The Tequila Effect: Theory and Evidence from Argentina." Unpublished paper. Division of International Finance, Board of Governors of the Federal Reserve System. April.

Williamson, John (1996). *The Crawling Bank as an Exchange Rate Regime*. Washington, D.C.: Institute for International Economics.

Zedillo, Ernesto (1996). *Second State of the Nation Report*. Message to the Honorable Congress of the Union from the President of Mexico Ernesto Zedillo Ponce de Leon, at the presentation of his Second State of the Nation Report. Mexico City, Mexico. January.

6. THE PESO FOLKLÓRICO: DANCING AWAY FROM MONETARY STABILITY

ROBERT L. BARTLEY

MEXICO'S CYCLE OF DEVALUATION

To most observers, including those in the financial markets, the Mexican economic crisis of 1994 was a bolt from the blue. It erupted at the end of an apparently triumphant Mexican administration and on the heels of the supposedly historic North American Free Trade Agreement—just as Mexico seemed to be leaving the ranks of "developing nations" to join the Asian tigers as "newly industrialized." Yet to anyone who had paid special attention to Mexico over the last decade or two, the crisis evoked less surprise than *déjà vu*.

This was, after all, the fourth Mexican economic crisis in fewer than twenty years. The Echeverría devaluation in 1976 broke the 12.5 peso/dollar exchange rate that had prevailed since 1954. The López Portillo devaluation of 1982 punctured a heady boom built on oil exports. The succeeding bust, deepened by such end-of-term lunacy as bank nationalization, left President Miguel de la Madrid to pick up the pieces in the excruciating debt negotiations of 1985 and 1986, with further declines in the peso and a crisis devaluation to open the election year 1988. With this as a record, what could be less surprising than another devaluation at the transition from the Salinas administration to the Zedillo administration?

The *de facto* exchange rate policy of one devaluation per president had indeed become a highly choreographed *folklórico*. An administration would run a boom into a bust and devalue. The incoming administration would announce a drive against the corruption of the old—jailing, say, the former head of Pemex or the Pemex union. By the end of the *sexenio*, it would be time for another devaluation and another cycle. Much of the anger in Mexico directed at Carlos Salinas indeed derives from a feeling that he did not dance to script. He should have taken responsibility for

141

his devaluation, the feeling runs, rather than leave it to his unhappy successor to pull the trigger.

The real promise of the Salinas administration—at least to this friend and admirer of the former president—was a break with the cycle of devaluation. The final year of his presidency was plagued with not only atrocious luck but also policy blunders. In particular, when the Federal Reserve tightened in 1994, Mexico failed to protect the peso by following suit. But every earlier act under President Salinas and Secretary of Finance Pedro Aspe—and for that matter the final refusal to devalue—reflected a thrust toward price and exchange-rate stability. The Salinas administration revalued the currency to one new peso to 1,000 old pesos, put heavy emphasis on curbing inflation, and kept the exchange rate within a narrow and highly predictable band. In the event, as well, the final decision to devalue was taken by the incoming administration—in my view, even at this late date the last in a string of mistakes.

Successive devaluations, after all, are not the only policy option open to developing nations. Mexico itself, after three postwar devaluations, maintained its 12.5 rate for more than two decades. As one authority describes the mood of the times, "Devaluations had become the scourge of the political system, both within the private sector and among the increasingly important independent consultants, lawyers, economists, and the like. These professionals criticized the government for constantly mismanaging the economy and bringing about continual devaluations."[1]

With two decades of fixed rates followed by two decades of devaluation, Mexico can indeed be seen as something of a case study. In early 1996, the peso stood at about 7.5 to the dollar, or 7,500 on an old peso basis, compared with 12.5 in 1979. This record of massive depreciation corresponded with a growth rate of 2.7 percent between 1975 and 1995 (see Table 1). This is paltry by any standard, let alone for a developing country with rapid population growth and large oil reserves. In dollar terms, perhaps a more relevant deflator, the record is somewhat more respectable, with a rate of 5.8 percent.

These growth rates, though, are less than half those of the earlier period of exchange rate stability—healthy annual rates of 6.7 percent in constant internal prices and 13.5 percent in dollar terms. Comparing the two twenty-year periods, the verdict has to be that a simple and straightforward policy of exchange rate stability outperforms clever experiments with exchange rate manipulation. (It would

---

[1] Roberto and Luiz (1984), p.103.

Table 1. Mexico: Exchange Rates and Growth

	Nominal GDP (bn Npeso)	Real GDP (1990 prices)	Average Growth (20 years)	peso/$ (1000/1-1993)	US $ GDP (bn)	Average Growth (20 years)
1955	0.088	115.0		12.5	7.1	
1975	1.100	424.6	6.7%	12.5	88.9	13.5%
1995	1,785.700	728.0	2.7%	6,413	274.7	5.8%

Source: Bear Stearns & Co.

of course be possible to make too much of this comparison. I certainly would not recommend returning to the autarkic development policies of the earlier period, which in any event probably would be impossible in today's increasingly fluid world economy.)

In terms of an economic-political dynamic, the policy of "stabilizing development" brought about its own downfall. The economic development was not accompanied by political opening—a dilemma that came to a head in 1968, when troops massacred student protesters in Tlatelolco—the same site where the Aztecs made their final stand against Cortés in 1521. Directly in the line of command as Interior Minister at the time of the slaughter, President Echeverría lurched to the left upon inauguration, setting off an inflationary spiral that destroyed the 12.5 rate and started the devaluationist spiral.

In any event, growth rates all around the world fell by about half after 1973.[2] So perhaps Mexico's experience was typical, rather than a result of its exchange rate policy. Of course, Mexico was an oil exporter, and should have been expected to gain from high prices after the 1973 "oil shocks" (often blamed for the growth slowdown among importers). Then too, the collapse in world growth may have been largely or partly the result of the breakdown of the Bretton Woods monetary system and the advent of generalized floating exchange rates.[3] Even the oil shocks were presaged by an official

---

[2] See Maddison (1995; 1989).

[3] For a discussion of the reasons for the post-1973 world slowdown, including the collapse of the Bretton Woods monetary arrangements, see Maddison (1989), pp. 85-90, and Maddison (1995), pp. 82-86. On Latin America, see Maddison (1995), p. 52: "Although most of Latin America became politically independent in the 1820s, and like North America has very large natural resources, it is very different in its institutional background. In the Western Offshoots [U.S., Canada, Australia, and New Zealand] the indigenous populations were marginalized; in Latin America they were

OPEC declaration after the closing of the Bretton Woods gold window.[4]

Despite the caveats, the raw fact remains that growth was much higher with exchange rate stability than with periodic devaluation—and without the turmoil that Mexico has had to endure four times in the last twenty years. Certainly it would be silly to argue that more devaluation would have helped—that Mexico would have had better growth had it taken its 12.5 rate not merely to 7,500 but to 15,000 or 150,000.

EXCHANGE RATES IN AN INTEGRATED WORLD

I subscribe to a view that sees the world economy as not merely "interdependent" but organically integrated. That is, the world does not consist of various national economies connected by pipes and valves called the trade account, the investment account, and so on. Rather, it is an organic whole; in Robert Mundell's aphorism, "the only closed economy is the world economy."

In a perfectly integrated world, hypothetically with instant equilibrium, exchange rates would have no impact on the real economy. In a two-nation world, the relative values of currency A and

---

assimilated, but became an underclass. Peonage and slavery led to very wide disparities in income, wealth, education and economic opportunity. . . . There has been continuing neglect of population education, heavy-handed regulatory tendencies in government, a long history of debt default and fiscal irresponsibility. These characteristics were important in keeping Latin American growth and levels of income well below those in North America."

[4] Organisation of Petroleum Exporting Countries, (1971):

The Conference,

Having considered the report of the Secretary General concerning the recent international monetary developments and their adverse effects on the purchasing power of the oil revenues of Member countries; *noting* that these developments have resulted in a de facto devaluation of the United States dollar, the currency in which posted prices are established, vis-a-vis the currencies of the major industrialized countries; *recalling* Resolution XXI.122 which calls, inter alia, for adjustment in posted or tax-reference prices so as to offset any adverse effect resulting from de facto or de jure changes in the parity of monies of major industrialized countries:

Resolves:

1. that Member Countries shall take necessary action and/or shall establish negotiations, individually or in groups, with the oil companies with a view to adopting ways and means top offset any adverse effects on the per barrel real income of Member Countries resulting from the international monetary developments as of 15th August 1971.
2. that the results of negotiations shall be submitted to the next Conference. In case such negotiations fail to achieve their purpose, the Conference shall determine such action as necessary for the implementation of this Resolution.

currency B would simply be a manifestation of money creation by central bank A and central bank B. If one central bank doubled its money supply, its currency would fall by half—or conversely, if it wanted to devalue by 50 percent, it would double some relevant monetary aggregate. In the real sector, meanwhile, nothing would change. If one country exported bread and the other wine, the same number of loaves would be worth the same number of bottles. So a devaluation could not possibly change the balance of trade between a wine exporter and a bread exporter; the devaluation could only affect domestic prices. The devaluing country would simply have double the inflation rate of its partner, that's all. In this hypothetical world, you cannot change the terms of trade by playing with the unit of account.

In this frictionless world, devaluation would obviously be pointless, except perhaps as an expression of preferences about internal rates of inflation. The two nations might as well effect a monetary union with one currency and one monetary policy. After all, the division of labor, comparative advantage, and all the good things Adam Smith wrote about depend on the price mechanism, and it would transmit its signals most simply and efficiently in a single currency.[5] Of course, if national pride dictated currencies with different names, a single currency could be simulated by a fixed exchange rate. Each currency could be converted at par value into gold, say, or moon rocks, or another scarce commodity. Or all the nations of the world could fix their currency to nation n, leaving the nth nation free to set world monetary policy, as in the heyday of Bretton Woods.

"External accounts" become a mere curiosity in this frictionless world. No one bothers to calculate the exports and imports of, say, Manhattan Island—which would show a horrifying trade deficit if any place ever did. Even between nations, the international accounts are of course accounting identities that must by definition balance. A trade deficit *must* be offset by an investment surplus, and vice versa. In this great circle of transactions, what logic is there to drawing

---

[5] Paul Volcker, for example, said in a 1995 lecture at the University of London: "The system of floating exchange rates simply isn't working well. During the past 20 years, currency prices have been prone to abrupt and erratic fluctuations. . . . [S]wings, up and down, as large as 30% or 40% over the course of a year or two, have not been uncommon. Quite obviously, international trade and investment have grown even in the face of that volatility. But surely the persistence of such fluctuations, with the consequence of enormous uncertainty in relative price levels among countries, is inconsistent with the kind of cool appraisals of relative cost and comparative advantage implied by the theoretical underpinning for open markets."

arbitrary toll gates called "balance of payments," or "merchandise trade," or "current account"?[6]

Under such circumstances, what conceivably could be the meaning of the phrase "external equilibrium"? The usual notion seems to be that it is a bad thing to have too much trade offset by too much investment, or, as is more likely the case, too much investment offset by too much trade. If one watches how "external equilibrium" is used in practice, one often finds a tacit assumption that the ideal trade deficit is zero. This of course also means zero investment, and since no one will explicitly defend any such conclusion, the zero-trade deficit assumption remains tacit. In a frictionless world, trade and investment flows depend on relative rates of economic growth; rapidly developing countries will attract more than their share of the world's investment and use more than their share of the world's goods. That is, a big trade deficit is a healthy sign.

To descend from hyperbole, even today's consummately integrated world of course does not have instant equilibrium. Different prices adjust to devaluation at different rates. Traded goods adjust first (unless you count sensitive commodities such as gold, which probably will start to adjust before the devaluation). Untraded goods adjust later, and domestic wages probably last of all. Differences in economic scale also matter; a big economy with a big internal market behaves in one way; a small economy dependent on trade, in quite another. Furthermore, monies are not perfectly substitutable. The demand for as well as the supply of a currency can change, which is why devaluations nearly always overshoot the intended parity.

For the academic researcher, of course, an eventual equilibrium may be less intriguing than the frictions and lags along the way. Conceivably, though barely so, that may also be true of the policy-maker operating on the margin. If the underlying equilibrium model is correct, the policy-maker is *only* dealing with frictions and lags, and identifying them takes more information and insight than policy-makers typically display. Especially so since one of the big frictions in the real world is called politics—the uneasy art of mobilizing support for a policy among the public and relevant elites. The disciplines

---

[6] In 1976, the Treasury received a report from a special Advisory Committee on the Presentation of Balance of Payments Statistics, comprising nine prominent international economists. The report recommended that "the words 'surplus' and 'deficit' be avoided insofar as possible," and noted that "these words are frequently taken to mean that the developments are 'good' or 'bad' respectively. Since that interpretation is often incorrect, the terms may be widely misunderstood and used in lieu of analysis." See Special Advisory Committee on the Presentation of Balance of Payment Statistics (1976), pp. 18-27.

of a fixed exchange rate are hard for political elites to accept, whether in a developing nation such as Mexico, or a reserve-currency nation such as Germany (with the European Currency Union), or the United States (with Bretton Woods).

For the economic analyst, the ultimate issue is how closely the real world approximates the frictionless ideal. If one believes in national economies connected by pipes and valves, one is likely to believe that governments can manipulate exchange rates for one advantage or another, perhaps to achieve external equilibrium, or perhaps to invoke "money illusion" during an election campaign. If one believes the world economy is consummately integrated, one is likely to believe that devaluations are folly—indeed, that, precisely because different prices adjust at different rates, devaluations are themselves shocks likely to disrupt real growth.

ANATOMY OF A CRISIS

Maintaining a fixed exchange rate parity of course means devoting monetary policy to that purpose—above all, for a small economy linked to a giant neighbor. To link the peso to the dollar, Mexico has to accept the monetary policy set by the U.S. Federal Reserve. If the Federal Reserve slows the creation of dollars, the Bank of Mexico has to slow the creation of pesos or face an unsustainable inconsistency. It seems clear enough that this was the essence of the 1994 crisis. The principal dispute is at what point it became too late to turn back. When, that is, did the costs of tightening monetary policy to defend the peso exceed the costs of devaluing?

At the onset of 1994, or even well into it, Mexico did not look like a devaluing nation. The classic symptom of devaluation is soaring inflation, fed by large fiscal deficits and burgeoning official debt. Yet by the end of 1993, the yearly rate of peso inflation had been reduced to about 8 percent—down from more than 150 percent in 1987. Outstanding debt had been cut by half and by some measures was less than the average for the member countries of the Organisation for Economic Co-operation and Development (OECD). The official government accounts were essentially in balance, with a deficit of merely 0.3 percent of GDP. And Mexico started the year with $25 billion in foreign exchange reserves. This scarcely made Mexico a classic devaluation candidate.

True, those who fret about external balance cite the current-account deficit, which ended the year at $28.8 billion, or 7.7 percent of GDP. But Mexico had sustained current-account deficits of $23.4 billion (6.4 percent of GDP) in 1993 and $24.4 billion (7.4 percent) in 1992—accumulating foreign exchange reserves the whole while. The usual conception is that this large trade deficit had to be financed by foreign borrowing. It is equally plausible to argue that foreign investors, attracted by the promise of NAFTA, were showering Mexico with investment, and that because the numbers are an accounting identity, this *had* to result in a large current-account deficit.

The current-account deficits are also the basis for the assertion that the peso was "overvalued"—a term more often used than defined. Most of the time, it is merely a market prediction, subject to the usual caveat that anyone who can outguess markets will be rich. It might have some more rigorous meaning as a deviation from purchasing power parity, but this is seldom what anyone means. To the extent that "overvalued" has a meaning, it is based on the selection of some hypothetical year of "external balance" when the current-account deficit was lower if not zero. If in subsequent years Mexico has more inflation than the United States, its currency is deemed "overvalued," but it all depends on what one considers the original definition of balance. An overvalued currency is supposed to stimulate imports and starve exports; in 1994, Mexico's exports grew by 24 percent.

As 1994 progressed, it became clear that the picture was not as rosy as it initially seemed. While the federal budget was in balance, there is some statistical confusion about spending by industrial development banks and state governments. Some calculations of the 1994 fiscal deficit put it as high as 4.7 percent of GDP.[7] This was an election year, and as is by now well known, political events were disruptive: a curious peasant uprising in the remote state of Chiapas in January, and the assassinations of PRI presidential candidate Luís Donaldo Colosio in March and PRI General Secretary José Francisco Ruíz Massieu in September. And just before President Ernesto Zedillo took office on December 1, Deputy Attorney General Mario Ruíz Massieu charged that PRI officials had obstructed his probe of his brother's murder.

During all this, monetary policy was especially problematic. In the wake of the crisis, Bank of Mexico Governor Miguel Mancera published his analysis, "Don't Blame Monetary Policy," in the *Wall Street Journal*.[8] He cited a series of "unfortunate political or criminal events." He blamed the Colosio assassination for the initial loss of

---

[7] See Council on Foreign Relations (1996), p. 8.
[8] Mancera (1995).

reserves, and the accusations by Mario Ruíz Massieu for starting the final run on the peso, concluding that "Mexican monetary policy should not be blamed for not having contemplated a series of political shocks that were entirely unexpected, and indeed, that had been unknown in Mexico for several decades."

Clearly political events were crucial, and indeed continue to roil the Mexican economy, but Governor Mancera's article persuaded many serious observers that monetary policy *was* to blame. In particular, he explained that, "as is the case with most central banks, Mexico's central bank followed a classic sterilization strategy." That is, it offset foreign currency transactions with domestic ones, leaving the supply of pesos unaffected. When pesos were redeemed for dollars, the Bank of Mexico merely created some new pesos to replace them. If it had done otherwise, "interest rates would have soared to levels that would have caused severe economic disruptions." The redemptions, though, were a sure sign that the supply of pesos exceeded the demand. Redeeming them automatically reduced the outstanding peso supply, but this effect was "sterilized" by issuing new pesos to replace them. As is typically the case in any devaluation, the heart of the crisis was sterilization to offset the natural effects of the market.

This was taking place at a time when the Federal Reserve was steadily tightening money. It started to increase its federal funds rate in February with a 25 basis point increase from the 3.0 percent low. This was followed by two more 25 point increases, then 50 basis point increases in May and August. On November 15, the day after Mario Ruíz Massieu aired his accusations on Mexican television, the Federal Reserve boosted its target rate by 75 basis points. It did not top out until the following spring, after another 50 point increase to 6.0 percent.

All this while, the Bank of Mexico was trying to maintain the peso parity by spending its reserves. Its end-of-month reserve position peaked at $29.2 billion in February.[9] By April, after the Colosio assassination, it had declined to $17.3 billion. After fluctuating as low as $16.1 billion, it was $17.2 billion at the end of October. These figures were released after the crisis. Previously reserves were formally reported only three times a year, though President Salinas made a personal announcement of the October figure.

The day after the Colosio assassination, a new foreign exchange swap position was announced with the United States. In April,

---

[9] See U.S. General Accounting Office (1996), p. 50.

Mexican authorities started a big expansion of dollar-linked *tesobonos*. Reserves fell to $13 billion by November 18,[10] in the wake of the Ruíz Massieu accusations and the Federal Reserve's aggressive interest-rate boost. On December 21, the day after a 15 percent devaluation was announced, the bank lost another $5 billion in foreign exchange reserves, in addition to issuing $8 billion in new *tesobonos*. With the peso left to float, the bank reported $6.2 billion in reserves as the year ended.

Obviously something went terribly wrong. Mexican officials have a point in noting that the whole reason reserves were accumulated was for use in offsetting market shocks. There is no compelling reason why Mexico needs $30 billion in foreign exchange reserves. Even at the $16-17 billion level as late as October, the bank's dollar holdings exceeded Mexico's monetary base—meaning that every peso bill in circulation could have been replaced with dollars. The reserves buy time, giving policy-makers room to make choices about accepting devaluation or tightening money to avert it. The interesting issue is when the crucial mistakes occurred. The prime candidates might be the Colosio shock, the $16 billion plateau between shocks, the Ruíz Massieu shock, the inauguration, or the devaluation shock of December 20.

With the Colosio shock, interestingly, Mexican officials did three different things. They did spend reserves, buying pesos for dollars to protect the exchange rate. But, sterilization policy or no, they also allowed short-term interest rates to rise; the yield on *cetes*, domestic short-term Treasury debt, finished March at just over 10 percent, and went to more than 17 percent at the end of April. Finally, they devalued, taking the peso to 3.4 per dollar from 3.1, or from the top of the preannounced band to the bottom. This was a 15 percent devaluation, but the authorities then in charge were careful to observe their previously announced policy, preserving the confidence of investors that they would not devalue in attempts to manipulate trade flows or other variables.

There followed a plateau of several months, with reserves at $16-$17 billion, and *cetes* yields settling to 14 percent. A great deal of *cetes* borrowing was displaced by *tesobonos*, however, which swelled from $3.1 billion at the end of March to $29.2 billion before the December devaluation.[11] Some argue that the December devaluation would have been less painful if it had been done earlier, and this would have been the most plausible period—when signs of trouble

---

[10] Ibid., p. 70.
[11] Ibid., p. 11.

were clear but, the argument goes, reserves were still plentiful enough to scare speculators into protecting a lower parity. But if a 15 percent devaluation did not cure "overvaluation," how much was needed? And of course, the larger the devaluation, the higher the eventual bill to redeem *tesobonos*—that is, the higher the implicit future increase in the peso money supply. On December 21, counting the direct loss and the new *tesobonos*, Mexico spent $13 billion in one day, even at a lower parity. With this kind of loss of confidence, how much longer would $17 billion have lasted?

Also, with reserves exceeding the money supply, Mexico at this point had the opposite option: establishing a currency board like the one associated with Finance Minister Domingo Cavallo in Argentina to guarantee that there would be no sterilization and that any peso redemptions would automatically reduce the money supply in defense of the exchange rate. The plateau surely provided options, of which devaluation was only one, but they were complicated by the necessities of the election and presidential succession.

The Ruíz Massieu shock was certainly spectacular, in both political and economic terms. After the former Deputy Attorney General fled Mexico and was arrested in the United States, American judges refused to extradite him. He was found to have $9 million in unexplained bank deposits in the United States; unexplained wealth is a crime under Mexican law but not U.S. law. In Mexico, meanwhile, rumors associated President Salinas with the assassinations of the PRI's presidential candidate and its Secretary General, though he had appointed both to their positions. And Ruíz Massieu's cover-up charges implicated the former President's brother Raúl, who himself was attached to some $200 million in unexplained funds in Switzerland. These baroque events hint not only at official corruption, but at a deliberate conspiracy to destabilize Mexico, as drug gangs earlier destabilized Colombia. They also greatly complicate not only economic analysis but U.S.–Mexican relations.

The Ruíz Massieu shock came at a time when crisp decisions were practically impossible. President Salinas had two weeks left in office, and President Ernesto Zedillo was forming his cabinet in preparation for inauguration. On November 20, President-elect Zedillo met with outgoing officials and agreed to reaffirm the existing exchange rate; this served to stabilize reserves at around $12 billion through the first two weeks of December.[12] Investor confidence was weakened with the announcement of the Zedillo cabinet and

---

[12] Ibid., p. 71.

budget; investors worried over the absence of the Cavallo-like Pedro Aspe.

With reserves dropping to $10.5 billion, the Bank of Mexico proposed a float, and government officials convened their fateful December 19 meeting. When business leaders opposed a float, the 15 percent devaluation was a compromise, proving disastrous to reserves and delaying the float by one day.

The point of this narrative is to frame the issue of when Mexican officials no longer had the choice of tightening money but could only devalue. Or, to put it another way, were they *forced* to devalue, or did they *choose* to devalue? And if it was the latter, was it the best of the available poor choices or, given the subsequent state of the Mexican economy, a mistake? And if a mistake, what kinds of political calculations and economic advice contributed?

Clearly, there is plenty of blame to go around. The Salinas administration handled the Colosio shock deftly enough, but its issuance of *tesobonos* turned out to be a disastrous mistake. They would have been as easy to redeem as *cetes*, and at a smaller interest cost, if the peso had held the parity at which they were issued. But the peso's fall from 3.4 to 6.8 doubled the peso cost of redeeming the dollar-linked instruments, further swelling the peso money supply and increasing pressure on the exchange rate.

More generally, the Salinas administration was clearly too expansive during 1994. Since reserves were not unlimited, a policy of sterilization could not persist indefinitely. At some point, election or no, money had to be tightened if the peso was to be defended.

Further, continuing with the Salinas administration balance sheet: What was it doing with $29 billion of reserves in the first place? This accumulation only served to obscure and delay the needed monetary adjustment. To put the question even more pointedly, why was economic growth so disappointing in 1993? No doubt the main blame lies with structural problems in the Mexican economy, in particular difficulties in developing small and mid-sized businesses—a point frequently made by President Zedillo before he was swept up in devaluation difficulties. But with real growth low, and the peso at the top of its band, Mexico was accumulating foreign exchange reserves. This suggests that while monetary policy was too easy in 1994, it was too tight in 1993.

At the political level, the Salinas officials may have wanted a kind of monetary nest egg to draw upon in an election year. But at the intellectual level, they thought in terms not merely of maintaining a predictable parity with the dollar, but of bringing statistical inflation rates down to U.S. levels. While this seems entirely ortho-dox, I have come to doubt that it is an appropriate goal for a devel-oping nation. In technical terms, just as you cannot change the terms of trade by manipulating the unit of account, an exogenous change in the terms of trade will not affect the exchange rate.

To take a real-world example, Hong Kong has for many years experienced high rates of increase in measured inflation even while its dollar was fixed to the U.S. currency. The reason seems to be that its wage rates are being arbitraged to world levels, which naturally raises price indexes. To put it another way, since the price mecha-nism is supposed to show where resources are needed, rapidly devel-oping regions will have unusually sharp increases in prices. If that is how the system works, exchange rate parity is ambitious enough as a goal.

Finally, the Salinas administration clearly felt strongly about the stability of the peso and the need to preserve confidence, but not strongly enough to fully institutionalize it. In the Argentine case, the currency board arrangement came as a last resort, after the financial system went through a hyperinflation not experienced by Mexico even at the worst of its crisis. But Salinas and Aspe, who knew the financial history of their country, probably could have constructed such arrangements. In their last year in office, after all, they passed legislation for an independent central bank.

Ultimately, of course, the choice of devaluation was made by the Zedillo administration. Obviously there was a debate about exchange rate policy during the transition; that is why Pedro Aspe was not in the new cabinet. The new president could have organized his cabinet and his budget around his November 20 pledge to main-tain the rate, which did perceptibly stiffen investor confidence.

Even as late as December 19, I would stoutly argue, there was the choice of tightening money instead of toying with devaluation. If the central bank had tightened to defend the exchange rate at this point, when the currency still had a semblance of confidence, how high would interest rates have gone? In the last *cetes* auction before the event, December 14, the rate was 13.75 percent; if tightening had doubled rates, they would have soared to 27.5 percent. With the devaluation, they went to 39 percent. They peaked at 92.5 percent in March 1995, and still stood at 43 percent in the spring of 1996. Heavy foreign borrowings, at expensive interest rates, succeeded in stabilizing the peso at around 7.5 in early 1996, but with Mexico in the throes of a deep recession. The case against a monetary tighten-ing to preserve the 3.4 rate was that interest rates would go too high, foreign exchange reserves would be lost, and a recession would ensue. How much worse could the opposite choice have been?

President Zedillo, it should be stressed, was dealt an exceedingly bad hand. With everyone thinking the Mexican economy was a success story, his priorities lay elsewhere, with political and judicial reform, both clearly essential to his country's long-term success. The political accidents were catastrophic, if indeed they were accidents, and we now see that the Salinas economic success was far from institutionalized. It would have taken a superman to see the depth and speed of the coming economic crisis and to organize a new economic team to confront it.

The new president was handicapped, too, by the tenor of economic thinking he could scarcely help but imbue. Nearly everywhere he could turn, to his academic training in the Yale economics department, to what he heard from the United States, to the standard recipe books of the international financial institutions, he would be told that devaluation is a useful policy tool—that indeed at some point it was essential, or at least inevitable, to expand exports and cure external imbalance. In Mexico, the intellectual advocates of devaluation got their way but are not exactly volunteering to accept the responsibility for the result.

THE ARGENTINE ALTERNATIVE

The prevailing wisdom suffers even more if one compares Mexico with Argentina, which chose the opposite course when hit by the fallout from the Mexican crisis. When Mexico devalued, investors naturally took another look at developing nations everywhere, and started to withdraw funds. Indeed, currency speculators shifted their focus from Mexico to Argentina, next on their list of "overvalued" currencies. But instead of sterilizing these outflows, Argentina took the opposite course, directly allowing the redemption of Argentine pesos to reduce the money supply.

Indeed, the Argentine episode was important as a test of the theory of currency boards, a proposal increasingly debated in the wake of the latest Latin debt crisis.[13] The principle is that the local currency should be backed 100 percent by holdings of a reserve currency, and should be convertible into the reserve currency at a fixed exchange rate. This rule gives the local monetary authority no discretion; if market participants redeem the local currency, these

---

[13] See Hanke and Walters (1994), p. 161; Williamson (1995); Hanke and Schuler (1994); Hanke (1996); Barro (1995).

redemptions automatically produce a monetary contraction, just as gold outflows did under the classic gold standard.

Argentina instituted a currency board with the Convertibility Law of April 1991, under President Carlos Menem, who was elected in the midst of hyperinflation in 1989, and Finance Minister Domingo Cavallo. They announced that the nation's foreign exchange holdings belonged to the citizens and would be used to redeem any outstanding peso at one per dollar. The result was a sudden end to inflation and an economic boom. From 1992 through 1994, economic growth averaged 7 percent a year, whether measured in pesos or U.S. dollars.

The currency board, however, had never been tested by adversity. When Mexico devalued, worried investors fled other emerging markets. Currency speculators started to short the Argentine peso, betting that the Menem regime would not have enough determination to stick with the policy. It was easy enough to predict that the monetary contraction would boost interest rates, and that this would cause a recession; and national elections were scheduled for May 1995. So speculators calculated that, faced with a monetary shock and recession, President Menem would of course choose devaluation now and risk more inflation later.

The shorts were burned when the President made the other choice. President Menem and Finance Minister Cavallo continued to redeem every peso presented for dollars—indeed, they removed a previous bid-asked spread to make the rate absolutely fixed. Then they proceeded with a series of measures to deal with the ensuing damage: accelerating privatizations, reducing government spending, cutting the wages of senior government officials, and increasing certain taxes—in particular, temporarily increasing the value-added tax from 18 percent to 21 percent.

Predictably, the pressure focused on the banking system. Any modern banking system is susceptible to runs, and a currency board cannot act as lender of last resort. Foreign exchange holdings may cover outstanding currency, but they cannot conceivably be large enough to cover all the loans of the banking system. And banking systems in countries such as Argentina and Mexico are not likely to be the soundest around. The shock was magnified in February 1995, when international banks cut off credit lines to their Argentine branches, forcing them onto local markets.

So the Argentine efforts focused on preventing a banking collapse. They consolidated banks, including setting up a fund to privatize the particularly suspect banks owned by provincial governments. They jiggered with reserve requirements to ease the liquidity crisis. They established a limited lender-of-last-resort function with 2 percent of existing reserves. And they sought loans from international lenders, which finally resulted in a package including $4.7 billion in loans from the IMF, the World Bank, and the Inter-American Development Bank. In effect, instead of lending money to the Argentine central bank to support the peso, the International Monetary Fund and the rest became lenders of last resort to the Argentine banking system.

The short-term economic results were impressive (see Table 2). Argentina did suffer a recession, with a 4.6 percent contraction in its economy during 1995. But in U.S. dollar terms, the measure of worldwide purchasing power of Argentine citizens, the fall was less than 1 percent, compared with the 32 percent shock experienced by devaluing Mexico. The inflation rate actually fell in 1995, and the spike in interest rates quickly subsided; by early 1996, 30-day deposits were actually below their pre-crisis levels.

In retrospect, support of the Argentine program was an excellent example of the utility of support organized by the international financial institutions and the U.S. Treasury. With $5 billion in timely credit, the IMF, the World Bank, and the Inter-American Development Bank played an important part in averting the collapse of the Argentine banking system and lancing the financial boil. This is certainly an example of how these institutions can ease the costs of adjustment to external shocks. The key is simplicity itself: The international institutions should support policies that work.

Politically, the Argentine results were even more impressive. The May 1995 elections were held during recession, but President Carlos Menem won over 50 percent of the vote in the first round of the May election, averting the need for a run-off. Notably, his two leading opponents also supported the Convertibility Law. What burned speculators missed was that Argentine society in the 1990s, like Mexican society back in the 1950s, had forged a consensus against devaluation. Indeed, the crisis turned the corner less with the IMF agreement than with the "Patriotic Loan," a US$1 billion domestic bond issue; Argentine citizens expressed their support of the Convertibility Law by oversubscribing. The Argentine business community was solidly behind the Menem program.[14] This consensus was forged in the hyperinflationary crisis and the economic boom that followed the convertibility law.

---

[14] See Moffett and Friedland (1995).

Table 2. Comparison: Mexico and Argentina

	Mexico	Argentina
Exchange Rate		
Dec-94	3.4[a]	1
Dec-95	7.68	1
Dec-96	7.88	1
Dec-97	8.16	1
Short-Term Interest Rates[b]	*(percentages)*	
Dec-94	14	9.8
peak	93	28.0
Mar-96	43	7.6
Dec-97	19	7.0
CPI Increase (Dec./Dec.)	*(percentages)*	
1994	7.1	3.9
1995	52.0	1.6
1996	27.7	0.1
1997	15.0	1.4
GDP Growth **(adjusted for internal prices)**	*(percentages)*	
1994	4.5	8.5
1995	-6.2	-4.6
1996	5.1	4.3
1997	7.0	7.5
GDP	*(US$ billions)*	
1994	421	282
1995	287	280
1996	335	297
1997	404	322
GDP (in US$ billions, change from 1994)	*(percentages)*	
1994	----	----
1995	-31.8	-0.7
1996	20.4	+ 5.3
1997	-4.0	+14.2

a Prior to devaluation
b Mexico, 28-day *cetes*; Argentina, 30-day deposits
Note: 1997 figures are year-end estimates.
Source: Bear, Stearns & Co.

In the 1997 elections, the campaign was dominated by the issue of corruption. Finance Minister Cavallo persisted in raising this issue and was forced from government in 1996; in 1997 he won a parliamentary seat with his own minor political party. With larger opposition parties also raising the issue, President Menem's party lost its majority. The 1991 convertibility law was not an issue, being again accepted across the political spectrum. I once had the opportunity to ask President Menem if he felt less sovereign because the peso was fixed to the dollar. He said that before, he had had only dollars, but now he had both dollars and pesos, so he felt more sovereign.

The initial economic success holds promise of lasting, since the three-year results are even more impressive than those of the first year. In the three years ending in 1997, Argentina managed to grow its dollar-measured GDP by 14 percent.

MEXICO SINCE THE CRISIS

By 1997, Mexico's GDP in dollars was still below its 1994 level, but the Mexican program is widely hailed as a success. Clearly the Mexican economy had emerged from the crisis, as it had three times before in the last two decades. In internal prices, its real growth reached 7 percent in 1997, with declining inflation and interest rates.

The peso held at around 7.5 to the dollar from January 1996 to October 1996, and at around 7.8 until October of 1997, when the Asian currency crisis started to spread. The peso weathered that crisis reasonably, falling to around 8.3 and then recovering to nearly 8.0.

In January 1996, the Bank of Mexico announced new procedures that adjusted the supply of pesos to demand—in effect withdrawing liquidity when the exchange rate showed signs of falling. In 1996 and 1997, it accumulated dollar reserves. By September 1997, it said it would increase liquidity under certain circumstances, including an exchange rate appreciating at an unsustainable rate. That is to say, the central bank announced it was prepared to stop sterilizing capital flows; it would withdraw pesos when the exchange rate fell and supply them when it rose. This is the essential mechanism of a currency board, though Mexico was not prepared to take the full measure of making it automatic.

As capital inflows resumed and the current-account deficit inevitably rose, indeed, some sectors of Mexican opinion began worrying that the peso would again become "overvalued," as measured by the "real" exchange rate. The fear, that is to say, is that the hoped-for

export advantages of devaluation will be wiped out by internal inflation. Indeed. The peso was at 3.4 in 1994, and held at 7.8 through
most of 1997—a drop from 29.4 cents to 12.8 cents, or a devaluation
of 56 percent. However, between December 1994 and November
1997, Mexico's price index rose from 103 to 229, or 125 percent. The
peso fell by half, neatly offset by a doubling of internal prices.
Exporters won three years of advantage, at the expense of Mexican living standards, and may want to do it again in the new *sexenio.*

Not surprisingly, the internal political scene remained roiled.
No progress was evident in investigations of the assassinations, the
case of Raúl Salinas dragged on, and the principal investigator of
these events, Pablo Chapa Bezanilla, has himself been arrested. In
the 1997 elections, the PRI lost the lower house of the legislature
and the mayoralty of Mexico City. Within the dominant party, voices have been raised, notably at its September 1996 Congress, against
economic liberalization and against President Zedillo. Crime, most
spectacularly kidnapping, became widely perceived as a crisis, especially in Mexico City. In some perverse sense, this may be a symptom
of reform; President Zedillo has taken important initiatives to clean
up the judicial system and police. In terms of economic policy, no
societal consensus seemed to be emerging.

Mexico's recovery was christened a success, at least in many
eyes, when it was able to repay its loans from the United States in
1996. After the Congress balked at a $40 billion loan program, the
Clinton administration arranged a multilateral stand-by package of
$48.8 billion, with $20 billion coming from the U.S. Exchange Stabilization Fund and Federal Reserve swaps. The United States ultimately advanced $12.5 billion; by July 1996, Mexico had repaid the
principal to $10.5 billion and had arranged to repay an additional
$7 billion—in, as one news report put it, "a gesture of good faith
during the U.S. election year."[15] The money was refinanced in the
private sector, with J.P. Morgan & Co. and Swiss Bank Corp. acting
as lead managers. This willingness to buy Mexican debt can be seen
as a sign of strength for the Mexican economy, or, alternatively, as a
calculation that even the high-flying *tesobonos* proved ultimately to be
backed by the full faith and credit of the U.S. Treasury.

The alternative to the Mexican package would have been to
"let the market solve Mexico's woes," as urged by L. William Seidman, a prominent former U.S. financial official.[16] This view gained

---

[15] See U.S. GAO (1996), p. 16.
[16] Seidman (1995). Seidman also presented similar testimony to congressional
committees.

currency in the U.S. Congress. Three senators from the Joint Economic and Banking committees—Connie Mack, Alfonse D'Amato, and Jim Saxton—wrote the central bank governors and finance ministers of G-7 countries to say, "Countries following unsound economic policies and speculators who invest in those countries should not be protected from the consequences of their actions."[17]

U.S. Treasury Secretary Robert Rubin expressed some of the same reservations. "A by-product—not a purpose—of these kind of support programs is that investors are being paid off," he mused to reporters after a speech in September 1997. "What we don't want to have is a situation where people can do unwise things and not pay a price for it."

Yet when financial crisis struck in Asia, the Mexican model was the refuge of first resort for the U.S. Treasury and the international financial institutions. Large loan packages were assembled for Thailand, Malaysia, Indonesia, the Philippines, and Korea after the devaluation of their currencies. Doubts about whether Hong Kong's currency board could maintain its "peg" echoed similar doubts about Argentina in 1994 and 1995. Though the U.S. Treasury Exchange Stabilization Fund was again tapped, the loan packages implied a large increase in the resources of the IMF, and at this writing the U.S. Congress has yet to be heard from. Almost certainly there will be a large debate about the Mexican experience; its 1994-97 recovery bids to be a model not only for its own future development, but for emerging economies everywhere.

A VISION OF MONETARY UNION

Yet both Mexican economic history and the recent experiences of Mexico and Argentina argue that the correct advice is not more and quicker devaluation but exchange rate stability. One can argue over whether the whole world is organically integrated as in the theoretical discussion above, but Mexico shares a 2,000-mile border with the world's biggest and most advanced economy. Pigs and cows regularly ford the Rio Grande; further West, the border is sometimes three strands of barbed wire through the *mesquite*. El Paso is the upscale suburb of Ciudad Juarez; Laredo, the entry port of the industrial power of Monterrey. All of this is now joined in a free-trade zone.

The Mexican policy elite attends school at Harvard and Yale and Stanford. The Mexican financial elite, sprinkled with billionaires,

---

[17] D'Amato (1995), Appendix C.

is anything but unsophisticated—of course the first money to flee the prospect of devaluation was Mexican. In the face of this organic integration, it is simply preposterous to believe that the Bank of Mexico can sow anything but mischief in trying to follow a different monetary policy from that of the Federal Reserve. Like it or not, the Mexican monetary authorities have to face reality: so far from God, so close to the United States.

Given this kind of integration, indeed, the question is whether the polite fiction of a currency board would suffice. It was from a Mexican, businessman and author Gabriel Zaid, that I first heard the suggestion that the United States create Mexican and Canadian seats on the Federal Reserve Board and let everyone use dollars. Francisco Gil-Díaz, then Vice Governor of the Bank of Mexico, was quoted in the Mexican press as saying: *"La 'unión monetaria' con los socios del TLC, en el mejor de los mundos sería el arreglo ideal"* [Monetary union with the NAFTA partners, in the best possible world, would be an ideal arrangement].[18]

Gabriel Zaid's proposal would require a vision and a generosity that U.S. authorities only very occasionally display. But given increasing suspicion within the U.S. Congress, a duplicate of the 1995 Mexican package seems unlikely, and perhaps it is not too soon to float this alternative. Monetary union would also require that Mexican authorities adopt Carlos Menem's attitude toward monetary sovereignty—which is not asking little, given the history of Mexico's relations with the northern colossus. Still, it might be easier if Mexican leaders recognized what the policy of one devaluation per *sexenio* is doing to their people.

The devaluation cut Mexican wages in half. One of the sharpest expressions of annoyance I encountered in the wake of the Mexican devaluation came from Senator Bob Bennett. During Banking Committee Hearings on NAFTA, he had accepted a $10,000 wager with free-trade opponent Ross Perot that, over ten years, Mexican and American wages would converge. A successful entrepreneur himself, Senator Bennett could afford the money but was galled by the prospect of paying it to Perot, thanks to the peso devaluation.

Yet for Mexico or any other developing country, isn't wage convergence the ultimate test of a successful policy? Or would Mexican leaders prefer to keep domestic wages depressed for the passing benefit of exporters—multinational corporations and domestic billionaires? As important, the most serious structural problems of the

---

[18] Estévez (1996).

Mexican economy revolve around the difficulty of nurturing small and mid-size businesses dependent on the accumulation of capital by those with access to pesos rather than dollars. The choice of devaluation destroys this capital overnight. Similarly, it cuts off the development of a broad middle class—the bank clerk who took out a modern floating-rate home mortgage and found it unserviceable as devaluation and inflation boosted rates. Since the end of its incredible civil war in the 1920s, Mexico has been a profoundly conservative society. The Indian rebellion in Chiapas is dramatic, but middle-class populism, the *El Barzón* debt protest, and ire at rising crime may be more important.

From these perspectives, devaluing is not a bloodless exercise in "adjusting" currency bands. The Mexicans of the 1950s and the Argentines of the 1990s had it right: Toying with a little devaluation sooner or later leads to a lot—and is a scourge to be avoided. In the end, any other choice will be less painful.

REFERENCES AND BIBLIOGRAPHY

Barro, Robert J. (1995). "Latin Lessons in Monetary Policy," *Wall Street Journal*. May 1.

Council on Foreign Relations (1996). *Lessons of the Mexican Peso Crisis: Report of an Independent Task Force*. New York: CFR.

D'Amato, Alfonse (1995). *Report on the Mexican Economic Crisis*. Washington, D.C.: United States Senate.

Estévez, Dolia (1996). "Hacienda y BdeM pelean sobre el futuiro de las política combiaria," *El Financiero*. February 22.

Hanke, Steve H. (1996). "Reflections on Exchange Rate Regimes: A Tale of Two Pesos." Unpublished paper prepared for the Mont Pelerin Society regional meeting. Cancun. January.

———— and Alan Walters (1994). "The Wobbly Peso," *Forbes*. July 4.

———— and Kurt Schuler (1994). *Currency Boards for Developing Countries: A Handbook*. San Francisco: ICS Press.

Maddison, Angus (1995). *Monitoring the World Economy, 1820-1992*. Paris: Organisation for Economic Co-operation and Development.

———— (1989). *The World Economy in the 20th Century*. Paris: Organisation for Economic Co-operation and Development.

Mancera, Miguel (1995). "Don't Blame Monetary Policy," *Wall Street Journal*. January 31.

Moffett, Matt, and Jonathan Friedland (1995). "The Big Gamble: Taking a Huge Risk, Argentina Intentionally Deflates its Economy," *Wall Street Journal*. March 21.

Organisation of Petroleum Exporting Countries (1971). Conference Resolution XXV.140. Beirut, Lebanon. September 21.

Roberto, Newell G., and Rubio F. Luiz (1984). *Mexico's Dilemma: The Political Origins of Economic Crisis*. Boulder, Co.: Westview Press.

Seidman, L. William (1995). "Block the Bailout: Let Market Solve Mexico's Woes," *Wall Street Journal*. January 23.

Special Advisory Committee on the Presentation of Balance of Payments Statistics (1976). "Report of the Advisory Committee on the Presentation of Balance of Payment Statistics," *Survey of Current Business* 56, no. 6. June.

United States General Accounting Office (1996). *Mexico's Financial Crisis*. Washington, D.C.: GAO. February.

Williamson, John (1995). *What Role for Currency Boards?* Washington, D.C.: Institute for International Economics.

7. PRIDE AND PREJUDICE: THE ECONOMICS PROFESSION AND MEXICO'S FINANCIAL CRISIS*

FRANCISCO GIL-DÍAZ AND AGUSTÍN CARSTENS

INTRODUCTION

An explosion of scholarly papers, seminars, and news articles has sprouted around the 1994-95 Mexican economic crisis. This is partly because the crisis was quite unexpected and contrary to the forecasts and expectations of the great majority of professional economists[1] and market participants. In this chapter, after briefly outlining Mexico's economic performance and policies from 1987 to 1994, we review critically the different hypotheses that have been proffered to explain Mexico's crisis. We then offer our own views, enriched by the analysis and insights presented in the literature.

Mexico's economy changed radically in the past ten years. The debt crisis of 1982 had been followed by five years of stagflation, culminating in an abrupt devaluation in November 1987. At that point an integral set of reforms was introduced that included the acceleration of trade liberalization and the creation of a formal Pact between the government and labor and rural and private-sector representatives on the contents of an economic program. Key elements of the Pact were the adoption of the exchange rate as a nominal anchor and a fiscal adjustment made necessary by the ongoing decline in Mexico's terms of trade.

The Pact was successfully renewed twelve times between December 1987 and November 1994. During this period, the

---

* The contents of this paper are the sole responsibility of its authors and should not be attributed to the Bank of Mexico, of which the authors were at the time of writing, respectively, Vice-Governor and General Director of Economic Research. A summary of this paper was published in the Papers and Proceedings, June 1996, of the *American Economic Review*. A fuller version was presented at the 1996 Annual Meeting of the American Economic Association.

[1] The only exception of which we are aware is Calvo (1994).

exchange rate regime evolved from a brief fixed rate in 1988, to a modestly rising crawling peg, and, eventually (from January 1991 to December 1994), to the adoption of a band that was widened gradually until it reached almost 15 percent. Exchange rate fluctuations within the band would not trigger pressures for increased wages or prices, as agreed within the Pact. This "bellows" absorbed strong upward and downward pressures from the foreign exchange market (though it was to collapse under the speculative attack unchained by the political events of 1994).

The above macroeconomic program was complemented with a far-reaching microeconomic reform that included:

- Deregulation of areas including foreign investment, transportation, and the financial sector;
- Privatization of around 1,000 corporations, generating $25 billion in revenues that were used to reduce government debt;
- Reform of the rural land tenure system;
- Private-sector investment in many infrastructure sectors;
- Unilateral adoption of free-trade policies, starting in 1985 and leading to NAFTA and other trade agreements;
- Tax reform through reduced rates, fewer taxes, and increased compliance; and
- An incipient pension and housing fund reform.

Under the influence of the reforms, the government's share of the economy, measured by its overall spending with respect to GDP, was reduced from 44 percent in 1987 to 24.6 percent in 1994—a substantially lower share than in most other OECD member countries. Economic growth resumed at positive per capita rates[2] and, from 1988, average labor productivity in the manufacturing sector increased at an annual rate of 5.6 percent (in 1994 it reached an even more impressive 8.0 percent). These improvements were reflected in average annual wage-earnings growth in the sector of 5.9 percent over the 1988-94 period.

The proceeds of privatization were used to permanently improve public finances through debt reductions. The average net debt of the public sector[3] as a proportion of GDP fell from 74 percent in 1987 to 21 percent in 1994. A fourth of the 1994 total was

---

[2] This statement is true even for 1993, when growth was reduced to 2 percent as the result of the uncertainty associated with the passage of NAFTA, which postponed private investment. Population growth for that year is estimated at 1.9 percent.

[3] Consolidated with the Bank of Mexico.

domestic debt. Simultaneously, the development of a wider private credit market allowed the gradual conversion of non-marketable public debt, derived mostly from a transfer of central bank credits to the government, into marketable securities placed among investors.[4] The share of total financial resources used to finance the public sector fell from 65 percent in 1987 to just 8 percent by the end of 1994. As inflation receded, the process of "financial deepening" (defined as the ratio of M4 to GDP) took off, increasing from 28.2 percent in 1977 to 34.2 percent in 1988, and it grew by more than 60 percent in the following six years, reaching 55 percent in 1994. Meanwhile, the share of private foreign debt in the country's total indebtedness more than quadrupled, from 8.5 percent in 1988 to 35.4 percent in 1994.

Mexico seemed to be another example of how market-oriented reforms can be the passport out of economic backwardness. At the end of 1993, all the pieces of the economic jigsaw puzzle were falling into their proper places, including the recent approval of NAFTA by the U.S. Congress. Higher private investment and large and growing deficits in the current account were the opposite sides of the same mirror showing that Mexico was perceived as an attractive investment destination for the international financial community, complementing the country's domestic savings.

Then everything collapsed. The rundown of international reserves brought about by political unease forced a devaluation in December 1994 that triggered the suspension of external financial flows. Under these circumstances, a current-account deficit was impossible to finance. A collapse in production and spending was unavoidable, and internal adjustment measures ensued. Output fell by 6.2 percent in 1995, and inflation reached 52 percent. Unemployment, business failures, serious bank portfolio problems, and political unrest followed as natural short-run outcomes of the crisis.

A LOOK AT HYPOTHESES
ABOUT THE CAUSES OF THE CRISIS

What went wrong? What role did the reforms play, and how could the situation have turned out so disastrously? In the search for answers, the 1994 political nightmare is sometimes mentioned as an afterthought, or merely as the trigger of a foretold conclusion. The different—not necessarily competing—eco-

---

[4] The share of marketable to total debt went from 48.5 percent in 1985 to 100 percent in 1991.

nomic hypotheses put forward to explain the crisis fall into the following broad categories:

- An overvalued currency
- Central bank credit expansion
- Excessive growth of the money supply
- Opaque, incomplete, or asymmetric information
- Excessive stimulus to aggregate demand
- Insufficient savings

Each of these hypotheses is examined below.

WAS THE REAL EXCHANGE RATE OVERVALUED?

The crisis of the Mexican economy has been ascribed by numerous economists, journalists, and others to trends in the real exchange rate. It is somewhat perplexing that these commentators devote so much attention to the public policies supposedly required to maintain the right or at least competitive real exchange rate (RER)—a real variable that, together with other real aggregate economic variables such as the real interest rate and the real wage rate, is market-determined (endogenous) and cannot be set by monetary, budget, or nominal exchange rate manipulations. Movements in the RER have been enthroned as the explanatory concept for all kinds of economic events: balance-of-payments crises, weak economic growth, the behavior of the current account in the balance of payments, etc. While there may be cause for concern about an overvalued real exchange rate measured through labor unit costs, the attention given to this subject has been excessive and misleading.

Measurements of the Real Exchange Rate. There is no way to pinpoint a critical benchmark equilibrium RER. If such a concept exists, it is very likely to be a moving target.

In the literature and in this paper, several different practical measures of the RER are employed:

- *A bilateral RER* (e_1). It is calculated by comparing movements in the consumer price index (CPI) in Mexico and in the United States, respectively.
- *A multilateral RER* (e_2). In this case, not only the United States, but a number of trading partners are incorporated in the calculation, suitably weighted.
- *A multilateral (or bilateral, but not shown here) labor unit costs RER* (e_3). In this calculation, we use indices of labor costs rather than consumer prices.

Figure 1. Alternative Measures of Real Exchange Rates

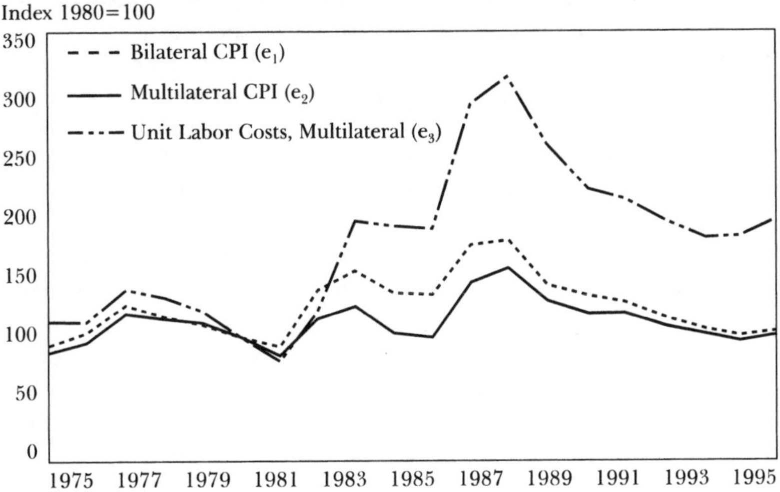

Index 1980=100

Source: Bank of Mexico.

As illustrated in Figure 1, e_1 rose in December 1987 as a result of the November 1987 devaluation. After that, it fell almost continuously until December 1993 but depreciated gradually in 1994 as the nominal exchange rate moved to within its predetermined bands. The amount of appreciation over the period considered, December 1987 to November 1994, was 39 percent (105.8 vs. 172.87). Meanwhile, e_2 went from 157.7 in December 1987 to 104.3 in November 1994, which implies an appreciation of 33.9 percent.

It is interesting to compare these numbers with those produced by several of the most vocal critics of Mexico's former exchange rate policy: "From the 1987 level, the real appreciation measures as much as 76 percent."[5] In another paper, it is argued that "the overvaluation hypothesis starts by noting that in the past few years Mexico has built up a huge real appreciation."[6] Huge compared with what? Mexico's own history? Such a statement ignores the effect of Mexico's vast economic reforms on its competitiveness. An appreciation of 33.9 percent, or even of 40.3 percent in such a timeframe, given the size of the initial nominal devaluation, is not something "unnatural" or excessive.

To see this, it is useful to look into the effect of a nominal devaluation on the domestic price level. If we assume initially that

---

[5] IMF (1995a).
[6] See Dornbusch and Werner (1994), p. 11.

169

$e_1 = 100$, the day after a 100 percent devaluation, e_1 will rise to 200, and it will fall to 100 when internal prices have fully adjusted to the devaluation. When comparing 100 with 200, there will have been a 50 percent appreciation in real terms. With these magnitudes present, one can interpret the 33.9 percent appreciation experienced by the peso as measured by e_2, or 38.8 percent as measured by e_1, over the December 1987–November 1994 period. It does not seem "huge"—nor does it seem rapid, taking into account the seven-year time lapse. In the longer version of this paper, the authors show in greater detail how a simulation model incorporating parity changes and plausible adjustment lags can track Mexico's actual experience of inflation over the period in question.

One remaining definition, e_3, deserves some serious consideration, as it is related to the competitiveness of the economy and is the only one left out of most (perhaps all) recent discussions of the viability of Mexico's exchange rate policy up to 1994.

In an open economy, the one factor of production whose cost may become misaligned with the rest of the world is labor. Credit may be costlier in a developing country, but its higher cost cannot be compensated by moving the RER. Technology can be readily assimilated, as can entrepreneurial and organizational talent. But the domestic cost of labor can get out of line. It can do so because of any of an array of possibilities: increased unionization; increased union aggressiveness; false business-labor-wage contracting, which anticipates higher than realized inflation; or backward wage-price indexation, among others.

To measure competitiveness, in turn, it makes little sense to compare indices of consumer prices (unless this is the only indicator available). Firms do not pay tuition or household rents, or buy hamburgers in order to compete. They pay for labor and other inputs. This makes e_3 the most relevant of our three measures.

Figure 1 therefore also shows the trend of e_3, the multilateral labor unit cost comparison. The index depreciated from 112 in 1975-76 to 139 in 1977—following the devaluation of almost 100 percent in September 1976, after which it appreciated steadily until it reached 80 in 1981. The 1982 devaluations brought it up to 120, and then to 195 in 1983. Given the levels attained by the series, we do not believe anyone could interpret an index of 195 in 1983 as anything but an extremely competitive number. As the series shows, the number for 1992 was 182—only 6 percent below the 1983 number, where it remained in 1993. It then depreciated even more, to 202 in the third quarter of 1994—again, a very competitive historical level. This is far removed from an appreciating trend or an uncompetitive level.

It is baffling that the writers who have analyzed the Mexican crisis fail to even mention, much less to analyze, this RER index. Is this a case of conventional ignorance dominating *a priori* conclusion?

Before ending this section, it is interesting to observe the Mexican private sector's opinion regarding its competitive position compared with the rest of the world at that time. They were evidently unaware of any lack of international competitiveness. In 1994, the Center for Economic Studies of the Private Sector (CEESP) published the results of a questionnaire that asked firms to rank the main export limitations they faced. Of seven factors, the exchange rate ranked in sixth place in the first semester, and last in the second semester, and it was mentioned by only 10 percent of the firms. More revealing than the percentages of the survey were the opinions regarding exchange rate policy. The CEESP document states,

> Another interesting aspect [of the responses to the survey] was the perception of exchange rate policy this past November. For four fifths (80 percent) of the firms this policy should either stay the same, or the slippage of the peso should be reduced or the nominal exchange rate fixed. Only 20 percent suggested that the exchange rate slippage should be increased (not a single firm mentioned a devaluation as warranted).[7]

The Real Exchange Rate and Growth. Some analysts have cited the alleged lackluster growth performance of the Mexican economy in the 1988-94 period as further evidence for the supposed overvaluation of the real exchange rate.[8] It may be noted that neither theory nor comparative international experience supports the notion that a real appreciation will *per se* have a negative impact on GDP growth (unless, of course, internal costs have gotten out of line). However, the more immediate problem with the above argument is that Mexico's allegedly slow growth is, in part, a result of flawed statistics.

Mexican GDP weights, dating from 1980, gave a disproportionate importance to sectors that stagnated or had output declines; at the same time they underweighted sectors that turned out to be star performers. One must keep in mind that the structural reform that began in 1983 and has continued had a strong impact on the

---

[7] Center for Economic Studies of the Private Sector (1994).

[8] See, for example, Dornbusch and Werner (1994), p. 11; Dornbusch, Goldfajn, and Valdes (1995), p. 3; Krugman (1995), p. 40.

Table 1. Growth of Gross Domestic Product

Annual Rates of Growth							Average Annual Rate of Growth
1988	1989	1990	1991	1992	1993	1994	1988-1994
(1993 Weights)							
1.3	4.2	5.1	4.2	3.6	2.0	4.5	3.86
(1980 Weights)							
1.3	3.3	4.5	3.6	2.8	0.7	3.5	3.02

Source: National Accounts System, INEGI, and Banco de México Economic Research Department.

relative growth of economic sectors. In a previous paper, we published our own estimates of what GDP figures would look like if we used 1993 weights to recalculate annual growth rates.[9] These estimates were unofficial and were modified, *upward*, by Mexico's Statistical Institute (INEGI). The revised growth figures represent a far better performance of the Mexican economy (Table 1).

In the 1989-94 period, growth in output was higher than Mexico's population growth—even in 1993, when a 2 percent rise in GDP occurred as population rose 1.9 percent. The cumulative growth of the revised GDP series over the 1988-94 period is 26 percent, compared with 21.4 percent with the original 1980 weights. The implied annual rate is 4 percent. Furthermore, the year-to-year performance gives credence to our private investment behavior hypothesis and none to the "reform-and-no-growth" of Dornbusch and Werner, Krugman, and others.[10]

Another piece of evidence is a study by Pérez-López (1995) based on co-integration analysis, in which the RER is the single most important factor explaining GDP fluctuations in Mexico. Its sign confirms an appreciation-growth relationship for the Mexican economy. Moreover, Kamin and Rogers (1997) found evidence that real devaluation has led to high inflation and economic contraction in Mexico.

There is at least one hypothesis worth exploring to see why some growth-inducing behavior, namely private investment, was

---

[9] See Gil-Díaz and Carstens (1996a).
[10] Dornbusch and Werner (1994) and Krugman (1995).

Figure 2. Fixed Gross Real Private Investment*

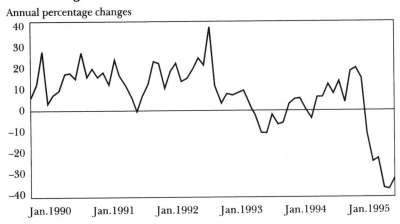

Annual percentage changes

* The series portrayed here excludes private investment, the amount and timing of which were decided by the government (such as toll speed highways, prisons, water treatment plants, thermal electric generating plants, and some water projects). However, the unadjusted private investment series does not differ markedly from this one.
Source: Bank of Mexico.

partially postponed. When NAFTA negotiations were concluded on August 12, 1992, the perception among investors was that its formalization was going to be a speedy process. But the expected date of completion kept being pushed back, as unforeseen technical and political difficulties were encountered. As time passed, fears of a possible failure to gain ratification began to grow, especially as vocal opponents appeared to be gaining support. The significance of the slower process for Mexican economic performance is that private investment, which had a clear upward trend until the third quarter of 1992, fell abruptly in the last quarter and even had negative growth rates in 1993. It resumed an upward trend only after NAFTA's approval (Figure 2).

Slow Export Growth. Presumably claims about slow export growth are related to the overvaluation hypothesis.[11] As in the arguments referred to previously, the numbers in this case also speak for themselves. Mexico's exports reached $60.9 billion in 1994, continuing a growth trend without parallel even among the legendary Asian tigers (Figure 3). Total export growth that year was 17.3 percent, while

[11] See Krugman (1995).

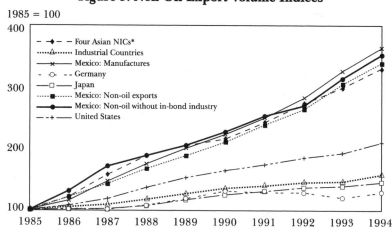

Figure 3. Non-Oil Export Volume Indices

* Newly Industrialized Countries (NICs): Hong Kong, Korea, Singapore, and Taiwan.
Source: Bank of Mexico and I.M.F. *World Economic Outlook.*

non-oil exports grew 20.2 percent. Manufacturing non-*maquiladora* exports grew 21.7 percent. These rates are not the statistical result of being based on a tiny export foundation, since a fairly high export platform already had been achieved. Non-oil exports, for example, multiplied by a factor of 32 times in the period 1983-94.

Other indicators of a possible overvaluation are sometimes looked for in the behavior of incoming and outgoing foreign tourism. In 1994 the outlays of Mexican tourists abroad decreased 4 percent, and the income from foreign tourists increased 3.2 percent (despite some J curve effects from that year's devaluation of the peso, prior to its December collapse).

DID CENTRAL BANK CREDIT EXPAND AND SET THE STAGE FOR DEVALUATION?

One of the first reactions of institutional investors and other observers to the crisis was to blame it on an allegedly excessive expansion of the domestic credit of the central bank. Later, economists wrote articles presenting the same arguments more formally. Some, like Robert Barro, or Andrew Atkenson and José-Victor Ríos-Rull, correctly interpreted the facts as a post-crisis increase in internal central bank credit caused by the fall in international reserves[12]

---

[12] Barro (1996), p. 49; and Atkenson and Ríos-Rull (1995).

Figure 4. Exchange Rate and International Reserves (1994)

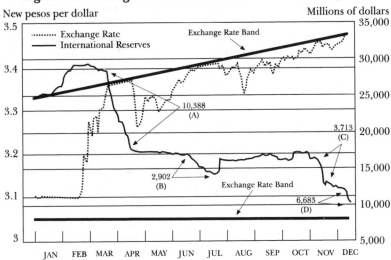

(A) Murder of the PRI's candidate for President.
(B) Resignation of the Secretary of the Interior.
(C) Deputy Attorney General's claims.
(D) Intensified hostility of the EZLN.
Source: Bank of Mexico.

(although Barro, incredibly, states that after November a central bank credit contraction could have averted the devaluation). Others, like Jeffrey Sachs, simply ignored the sequence of events and therefore argued the opposite.[13] In a revised interpretation, Sachs, Aaron Tornell, and Andres Velasco repeated some of the factual mistakes common in the literature.[14] By contrast, Rudiger Dornbusch, et al. question how effective a different monetary policy could have been over anything more than the short term.[15]

Everything worth stating on the subject of the allegedly excessive central bank credit expansion is contained in Miguel Mancera's 1995 *Wall Street Journal* article and in the Bank of Mexico's 1994 *Annual Report* (Figure 4).[16] Three tenets are essential on this score:

1. All the foreign exchange losses that occurred in 1994 coincide with a distinctly identifiable negative political shock and not with an *ex ante* expansion of the central bank's credit and/or the money supply.

---

[13] Sachs (1995).
[14] Sachs, Tornell, and Velasco (1995).
[15] Dornbusch, Goldfajn, and Valdes (1995).
[16] Mancera (1995) and Bank of Mexico (1994).

2. A massive speculative attack on a currency whose authorities are committed to maintaining a band cannot be resisted—certainly not in the present environment where the speed and amount of resources that move every day in world financial markets quite simply overwhelm them (intervention in the 1994 Mexican case involved $25 billion in reserves plus $30 billion in *tesobonos*).

3. The foreign exchange market was in equilibrium, i.e., the current-account deficit was being financed by a surplus in the capital account, and the exchange rate remained below the top of the band through November 1994, except for the brief interludes when speculative attacks were taking place.

Others discover monetary laxity in the behavior of interest rates: Leonardo Leiderman and Alfredo Thorne wrote that "while short term interest rates were raised after the Colosio assassination in March, and the interest rate differential vis-à-vis the U.S. reached 12 percentage points in April . . . this differential showed a declining trend, which reflected mainly rises in U.S. interest rates. Thus, despite a marked fall in foreign exchange reserves, and despite the substantial exchange rate pressure, monetary aggregates were growing quite rapidly in 1994, and there was no active reliance on interest rate hikes to defend international reserves and the exchange rate band."[17] In contrast, Steven Kamin and John Rogers found econometric evidence that Mexican monetary authorities merely accommodated shifts in the demand for money during 1994.[18]

If monetary policy, measured through the evolution of interest rates in 1994, is to be judged, one has to choose the appropriate indicator. Figure 5 compares the LIBOR rate with the Mexican interbank borrowing rate. This is a better indicator than the segmented *cetes* market, because the *cetes'* privileged status as bank collateral resulted in their carrying an artificially high price (note also that *cetes* were fast disappearing as *tesobonos* took their place). It is true that after rising almost 20 percentage points—not 12—above LIBOR, the differential fell somewhat after the Colosio assassination. Still, the excess of Mexican over LIBOR rates remained at 10 percentage points or higher throughout a period when the exchange rate fluctuated *within* the confines of its predetermined band and not at its top. This performance cannot be characterized as monetary looseness.

---

[17] Leiderman and Thorne (1995).
[18] Kamin and Rogers (1995).

**Figure 5. Interbank Average Interest Rate (TIIP)–Libor
(Weekly Observations)**

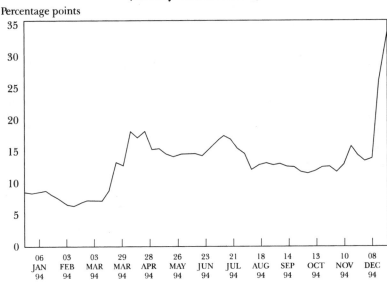

Percentage points

Source: Bank of Mexico.

The conclusions above hold independently of arguments related to the arrangement of monetary institutions. This said, many writers fail to point out that Mexico's monetary institutions were not designed to fight off a speculative attack through sudden quantitative adjustments in credit—nor could they have been adapted overnight. Therefore, beyond allowing interest rates to rise, the country was not prepared to conduct even a modest mop-up of liquidity, much less to perform a currency board type of non-sterilization.

A currency-board mechanism, contrary to central bank sterilization, will allow a fall in the money supply that matches the fall in international reserves. However, this requires: a) large amounts of commercial bank (foreign currency) reserves to draw upon at the central bank; b) a history of non-sterilization practices by the central bank—otherwise commercial banks will not know how to react, especially to wide and abrupt foreign exchange movements; and c) if not ample reserves at the central bank, then at least large foreign credit lines to the commercial banks. Either a and b, or b and c, is necessary to allow commercial banks to cushion the day-to-day currency movements and other fluctuations in the payments mechanism. None of the three conditions listed above was present when the speculative attacks took place in 1994. Mexico had a payments mechanism that left it no alternative but to sterilize movements in its foreign exchange reserves and raise interest rates. Thus, there was nothing for the central bank to do but to allow substantial rises in interest rates, which it did.

WAS THERE EXCESSIVE EXPANSION OF THE MONEY SUPPLY?

A related interpretation of excessive monetary expansion deals instead with the growth of the money supply. According to some observers, like Meltzer, "the central bank pumped in money to hold down the rise in interest rates on the government's debt" and "the principal net buyer of government securities was the Bank of Mexico. In the same two months (February to April), the bank almost tripled its holdings, purchasing more than 80 billion pesos ($24 billion) of government securities from Mexicans, foreigners, and new issues from the Mexican government." Also, "the bank financed its purchases of bonds and part of the government budget by starting another round of inflationary policy."[19]

The figures certainly do not confirm such assertions. The Treasury's account at the Bank of Mexico did not exhibit the loan of a single peso throughout 1994. The central bank bought Treasury bonds from the market, not from the government. The explanation for the increased holdings of government securities by the Bank of Mexico from February to April 1994 is the Bank's collateralized credits to Mexican financial intermediaries issued to sterilize the losses of international reserves. There is no other source for such an increase. Credits were granted in the form of repurchase agreements (REPOs). Mexican financial intermediaries issued liabilities to the Bank of Mexico, collateralized with part of their holdings of government securities. According to accounting procedures, the securities received in a REPO are included as part of the Bank of Mexico's position.

This could be the data Meltzer refers to when he arrives at the mistaken conclusion that the central bank financed government expenditures. In the two-month period referred to, the central bank purchased 27.3 billion pesos, or $8.3 billion. With a balanced federal budget, the Treasury was obviously not issuing net debt to finance deficit spending. Central bank accounts show that it purchased securities or extended loans to the banking sector only to partially compensate for the monetary impact of its losses of international

---

[19] Meltzer (1996b) and (1996a), respectively.

reserves, which for the period considered were $11.8 billion. The Bank of Mexico bought smaller amounts of government securities than it lost in reserves—the opposite of Meltzer's assertion.

There is no way the holdings of government securities above can be accounted for as a net increase in aggregate demand or as a source of finance for additional government expenditures. Beyond the peso credits that mirror the fall in international reserves, the bank only extended credit to provide for the growth in the demand for base money.

Meltzer also claims that: "The money directly controlled by the bank, known as the monetary base—bank reserves and currency— accelerated from a lower than 4 percent annual rate in the spring of 1993 to a rate higher than 10 percent in January and February 1994. In March, the annual growth rate was 26 percent. Growth of the base declined from this peak but remained high and was 19 percent or more annually in each month from July through December. This policy was highly inflationary." When discussing the summer-fall period of 1994, Meltzer states: "Although the exchange rate was gen- erally close to the upper intervention point, the Bank of Mexico did not lose reserves or raise interest rates."[20]

The monetary base does not include "bank reserves," as Meltzer states, since there are none in Mexico; the country's mone- tary base contains only currency. Beyond this factual error, if mone- tary policy was highly inflationary, is it not puzzling that the exchange rate remained below the top of the band, that no addi- tional reserves were lost, and that inflation continued coming down? To state that the growth in currency was excessive, some model of currency demand must be formulated—something that Meltzer fails to do. A model developed at the central bank (a highly stable one despite the turbulent periods included in its estimation) shows that the expansion of the monetary base during 1994 was in conformity with demand estimates. Two other econometric estimates produce similar results, and we know of none that contradicts them.[21]

Moreover, beyond econometrics, Meltzer should know that the demand for currency usually perks up when there is an increase in uncertainty—in this case as the result of political disturbances. If one compares the ratio of currency to M1 for 1976, 1982, and 1988—all difficult political years in which presidential terms ended—with the preceding years' ratios, it will be seen that the ratio increased signif-

[20] Meltzer (1996a).
[21] See Kamin and Rogers (1995) and Atkenson and Ríos-Rull (1995).

icantly. As is well known, the public determines the ratio as well as the demand for real currency. The latter *fell* in real terms by 3.07 percent in December. Even though M1 has been very unstable because of the shifts between checks and other liabilities, if one wishes to follow M1, it can be seen that its December increase was only 3.8 percent compared with that of currency, which was 20 percent.

But month-to-month numbers do not adequately reflect monetary behavior, especially during 1994, when monthly increases showed some variability. The average increase in M1 for the year was 12 percent, an amount consistent with the increase in nominal output for that year, since the growth of GDP was 4.5 percent and average consumer price index inflation was 6.95 percent in the same period.

Finally, international empirical evidence shows that the variation in the rate of inflation represents the most important reason for fluctuations in the real demand for financial assets. Mexico was no exception. From 1989 to 1992 an important re-monetization was registered as the annual inflation rate fell from 160 percent to less that 12 percent.

WHAT ABOUT THE OPAQUE DATA ISSUE?

Timeliness and Completeness of Data. The quotes here are also numerous. Take a typical damning sentence: "Mexico's foreign reserves fell with each new shock. At the start of the year they stood at $25 billion, by the end they had dwindled to 6 billion; worse, deliberately slow publication of the figures hid the extent of the problem until it was too late."[22] That is what the *Economist* and many others claimed. Let us inspect the facts:

Ever since the 1940s and up to 1994, the amount of the central bank's international reserves was released on only three occasions within any given year: the *Annual Report* of the Bank of Mexico in the spring; the Address of the Central Bank Governor at the Mexican Bankers' Convention, usually in the summer; and the President's Report to the Congress in the autumn.

One might surmise that this policy, unaltered for more than fifty years, was well known within and outside of Mexico. Nobody can

---

[22] "Mexico Survey," the *Economist*, October 28, 1995. Here the *Economist* contradicts itself. In the same article, it had already stated: "the ministers and their friends in the supposedly independent Bank of Mexico were more inclined to ease fiscal and monetary policies than to tighten them." Did reserves fall because of shocks or because of expansionary policies?

claim to have been cheated or lied to. In 1994, and according to schedule, the central bank's reserves were announced through the Bank of Mexico's *Annual Report,* delivered to the Congress in March; in Governor Mancera's speech at the Bankers' Convention in October; and again by President Salinas in his annual address to the Congress on November 1. By November, the trajectory of reserves could have been easily followed, including their considerable fall, with ample time before the devaluation almost two months later.

Other relevant information, such as the monthly balance-of-trade figures, was released earlier than is customary in most developed countries. The quarterly balance of payments, which contains changes in international reserves, was published with its customary seven-week lag.

As a matter of fact, "central bank watchers" emerged early in the 1990s at domestic and foreign banks. They were able to figure out with amazing precision the amount of international reserves on a daily basis by analyzing the central bank's day-to-day open market operations and its sterilization policies, with the help of the seasonal behavior of currency demand. The Bank of Mexico provided all the elements needed for this exercise, so that even the Bank's critics could surmise accurately what transpired within the Mexican economy.

All this information, plus data known and analyzed by the markets, contributed to a clear and continuous picture throughout the year of the level and trend of Mexico's international reserves, as well as other relevant data. The Appendix to this chapter (see p. 197) contains extensive references from the press and experts in various sources concerning the level of or movements in international reserves.

The Claim that Information Favored Nationals. An argument contained in an IMF publication[23] had a great echo in the world press: implying that Mexican nationals—not foreigners—attacked the Mexican currency in the critical first three weeks of December 1994. The IMF of course was not interested in the issue of who was to blame but in what it considered asymmetric information opportunities

---

[23] "In the run-up to the devaluation, that is, from November 30 to December 19, foreign investors had net sales of about $326 million in Mexican government debt securities, and there were net purchases of equity, while reserves fell by $2.8 billion. For the entire month of December 1994, foreign investors were net sellers of about $370 million of debt and equity, while Mexican foreign exchange reserves fell by $6.7 billion, only $1.7 billion of which was accounted for by the trade deficit. Indeed, foreign investors did not start to sell their Mexican equity holdings in any sizable quantity until February 1995." IMF (1995c), pp. 7-8.

regarding local emerging-market investors versus foreign investors, with the locals supposedly having better first-hand knowledge.

Whatever value this argument may have for other so-called emerging markets, it certainly does not fit the following facts about Mexico:

- To an extent comparable to developed economies, Mexico does not restrict capital flows. Market makers, arbitrageurs, investment fund managers, bank treasurers, etc., from all over the world continuously exchange information on Mexican market events. It is difficult to imagine how a nation could attract such an important share of total net capital flows to developing countries from 1989 to 1994 if such investors—most of them with substantial experience in international markets—did not consider the information they had available to be reliable and sufficient.

- The IMF report cited above also describes the large purchases of *tesobonos* that took place, most of them by foreigners. Evidently, besides the already large drops in international reserves that took place from March to November—a large amount also purchased by foreigners—the latter had already hedged their peso exposure precisely because of their large increases in *tesobono* holdings and their also large purchases of *coberturas* ("forwards") at Mexican banks. Therefore, the December currency purchases, even if they had been made mostly by Mexican residents, would have represented a late response and not opportunistic purchases resulting from privileged information.

- Some of the peso sales in the days of the devaluation were conducted by Mexican banks as a consequence of their hedging of short positions in dollars that they had contracted to offer foreign residents a hedge against a peso devaluation.

- Finally, the IMF conjectures on the residency of investors are based on the nationality of the custodian institutions of an incomplete sample of financial instruments. It seems questionable, to say no more, to identify the nationality of the custodians with the residency of the investors.

EXCESSIVE STIMULUS TO AGGREGATE DEMAND?

The relevant quotes on this subject are also rich and varied. They go from Dornbusch, Goldfajn, and Valdes's: "For the election year fiscal spending was turned up, concentrated on the third quarter. But other than for the fiscal stimulus, growth clearly was low"; to Krugman's: "The approach of the presidential election seems to have led

Table 2. Contribution of Aggregate Demand to Growth of GDP

Year		Contribution to Growth of:			Sum=Growth of GDP
		Public Expenditures	Private Expenditures	Net Exports	
1992	**I**	0.26	6.51	-2.85	3.93
	II	-0.51	5.09	-3.27	1.31
	III	-0.83	7.89	-3.16	3.90
	IV	1.09	3.15	-2.14	2.10
1993	**I**	-0.17	3.87	-1.33	2.40
	II	0.43	-1.20	1.01	0.24
	III	0.33	-2.66	1.48	-0.85
	IV	-0.36	-1.01	2.34	0.97
1994	**I**	0.87	0.11	-0.30	0.68
	II	1.00	4.80	-0.99	4.81
	III	1.22	4.10	-0.79	4.54
	IV	-0.47	5.86	-1.39	4.01
1995	**I**	-0.99	-9.34	9.54	-0.79
	II	-1.84	-19.54	10.87	-10.51

Source: Bank of Mexico, from the National Accounts.

the Mexicans neither to devalue nor to accept slow growth, but rather to reflate the economy by loosening up government spending."[24] Dornbusch's quote, in particular, raises the question of whether he really believes that a GDP expansion is brought about by fiscal spending in the same quarter.

Table 2 shows a rather large contribution to final demand from the private sector in 1994 and a very small one from public expenditures—certainly not the stuff that would lead one to associate 1994 with a pump-priming year. Moreover, the balance of the public sector presented in the Public Accounts showed a deficit of 0.09 percent of GDP for that year—not exactly what one would characterize as irresponsible spending for electoral purposes.[25] The issue of expansion of credit from development banks during 1994 has also been raised; this is a topic we return to later in the paper.

---

[24] Dornbusch, Goldfajn, and Valdes (1995); the *Economist,* October 28, 1995; and Krugman (1995).

[25] Cuenta Pública (1995).

INSUFFICIENT SAVINGS?

The information on savings referred to by analysts and quoted in the press refers to a concept defined as gross domestic savings (GDS), calculated by INEGI, with the exception of a recent calculation by J.P. Morgan that delves into the numerical subtleties surrounding the estimates of savings in Mexico and utilizes national account figures.[26] From the GDS series, people have inferred that there was a substantial fall in the country's savings during President Salinas's administration. It is also asserted that the savings ratio became abnormally low: "Mexican domestic savings are currently at very low levels, reaching only 13.7 percent of GDP in 1994, having fallen from above 20 percent of GDP in 1987."[27] Another illustrative quote is: "Private saving, on the other hand, dropped from a peak in 1988 of 19 percent to a low of 9 percent of GDP in 1994."[28]

Such low numbers and wide swings in a short period should have motivated analysts to dig deeper into the concept's definition and into their sources, since such low numbers do not appear published anywhere. However, they were taken at face value and led some analysts to conclude that some government policy was at fault and that private consumption had somehow been artificially stimulated and had, therefore, contributed to the import boom. The most casual inspection of import figures will reveal, however, that this was not the case, and it became obvious that the definition of savings merited careful scrutiny—such as J.P. Morgan's, for instance.

At a macroeconomic level, the problem with GDS is that it does not measure the full thrift effort, since it estimates savings after net payments to factors abroad are deducted from it. Another measure widely quoted in the literature, for instance in Velasco, is gross national savings (GNS), equal to GDS plus net payments to factors abroad.[29] Measured in this way (Table 3), savings fell 4.13 percentage points of GDP from 1989 to 1994. This reduction in savings is a fraction of the number most frequently used and results in a figure for 1994 far greater than the ridiculously low one suggested by some authors. A drop in the savings ratio of the order of magnitude rendered with this revised method can hardly be considered the cause of a balance-of-payments crisis. J.P. Morgan's adjustments, on the other hand, led them to conclude that private savings *increased* from 1989 to 1994, although they also claim that the level was still low.[30]

---

[26] J.P. Morgan (1996).
[27] See Fraser (1995).
[28] See Atkenson and Ríos-Rull (1995).
[29] Velasco (1991).
[30] J.P. Morgan (1996).

Table 3. Domestic Savings as a Percentage of GDP

	1983	1989	1994
Gross National Savings (GNS)	30.33	21.24	17.11
Gross Domestic Savings (GDS)	24.69	19.37	15.58
Private (GDS)	21.77	16.49	11.93

Source: Bank of Mexico.

Table 4. Gross National Savings

	1983	1989	1994
Gross National Savings (Public Sector)	3.49	1.74	3.73
Gross National Savings (Private Sector)	26.85	19.50	13.38

Source: National Income Accounts, INEGI.

Nevertheless, they estimate private savings to be 18 percent of GDP. What follows is an exercise similar to J.P. Morgan's, although it does not take into account, as they do, revisions based on changes in the terms of trade or on the government's revenue from the inflation tax.

The breakdown of GNS into public and private can be appreciated in Table 4. Public savings are obtained directly and merit a brief definition; they result from taking the operational financial balance of the public sector and adding to it public investment from the national accounts.[31] For completeness, real interest expenses from the off-budget amounts were subtracted. There are two distinct periods involved in these series. From 1983 to 1989, a sharp fall in savings correlated, as would be expected, with the collapse in Mexico's terms of trade. Before the oil boom, in the 1950s and 1960s, GNS averaged 16.1 percent and 19.8 percent of GDP, respectively. As oil revenues mounted during the 1970s, savings increased to 22.3

---

[31] Therefore Public Sector Savings (Sp) would be equal to $Sp = OFB + Ip$, where OFB, the Operational Financial Balance of the Public Sector, is defined as the fiscal surplus/deficit of the consolidated public sector minus the sum of the inflationary amortization of the public debt and Ip = Public Sector Investment. The latter is added because the objective is to obtain a savings concept equal to current income minus current expenditure, but the Sp number is defined as income minus total expenditures.

Figure 6. Gross Domestic Savings and Gross National Savings*

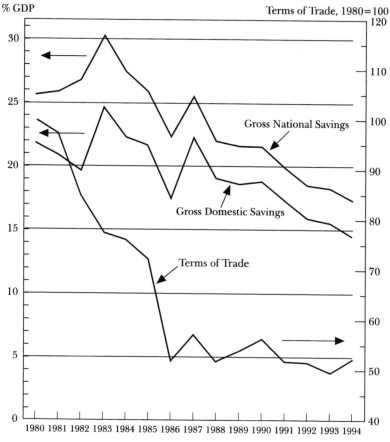

*Gross Domestic Savings = Gross National Savings – Net Payments to Factors
Abroad (interest, profits, royalties, etc.) + Transfers (mostly workers' remittances).
Source: Bank of Mexico.

percent of GDP. Figure 6 depicts the strong fall in the savings ratio
as the terms of trade collapsed in 1983. To interpret the figure, it
must be remembered that just as the adjustment year 1995 shows an
atypical, sharp increase in domestic savings, so did the adjustment
year 1983.

Besides the gradual increase in public savings from 1989 to
1994, one should underscore the substantial public-debt reductions

Table 5. Shares of Private Consumption to GDP

	1990	1991	1992	1993
Share of Private Consumption/GDP (%)	70.8	71.8	72.2	71.5
Share of Private Consumption/ Disposable Income (%)	79.7	80.6	81.4	81.2

Source: National Income Accounts, INEGI.

that took place during this period, which generated an improvement in the government's financial position as the average net consolidated public debt diminished from 74 percent of GDP in 1987 to 21.3 percent of GDP in 1994.

Even though private savings fell during 1989-94, the non-residual figures in the national accounts shown in Table 5 are relatively stable. The broad picture seems to be that the lower aggregate savings ratio by 1989 is a reflection of the drastic fall in Mexico's terms of trade—not of a profligate government or population—and that its more recent levels reflect the pre–oil boom observations.

Had government savings not increased gradually from the 1.7 percent of GDP they represented in 1989, the current-account deficit might have been higher. One cannot be certain as to whether more savings would have avoided the crisis, but the magnitudes handled do not suggest a dramatically different outcome.

There is considerable discussion in the economic literature on whether savings can be influenced through public policy. A Barro-Ricardian economist would argue that individual behavior will offset government saving increases. A growth theorist might question the ethics of forcing lower consumption today in order to increase the consumption of future generations. But, aside from positions that imply a wise-benevolent but manipulating government that knows best, the one unmistakable lesson that can be derived from theory is that savings and their allocation are negatively influenced by interest rate controls and economic instability. The first did not happen, and the latter was in the process of being successfully brought under control.

187

FLAWED EXPLANATIONS: A RECAPITULATION

Summing up our discussion so far, the evidence does not support most of the hypotheses that have been offered concerning the crisis. The list of themes examined covers:

1. An overvalued exchange rate that supposedly led to punishingly high interest rates that in turn suffocated growth. The known facts attest, instead, to a highly competitive economy. Moreover, not only was economic growth not compromised, but instead the economy managed to come out from a six-year doldrums caused by depressed terms of trade, the foreign debt overhang (1983-88), and twelve previous years of economic mismanagement (1971-82).

Our interpretation of movements in the exchange rate suggests that a proper analysis of the chain of causality of price movements is the following: Exchange rate movement led to a change in the general price level through the prices of tradables, which led to changes in the contracts related to such non-tradables as rents, tuitions, and wages. This in turn led to changes in the nominal demand for money due to increased prices, resulting in changes in the money supply due to the need to accommodate shifts in the demand for money.

Inflation is a monetary phenomenon, but the relevant monetary variable under the circumstances described above is the exchange rate. Central banks, like virtually every monopoly, are humble institutions that can only influence the quantity demanded of their product or its price.

When there is inflation, price movements unchained in the manner described adjust in a fashion that some economists have called "inertia." But inertia has an economic cause: In most cases it is the natural, if protracted, adjustment to a higher nominal exchange rate. Thus movements in the real exchange rate measured through relative general price indices are meaningless. Comparative labor unit costs are the pertinent variables to observe in order to reach relevant conclusions about competitiveness.[32]

2. Central bank credit expansion did not cause but was the result of the huge, instantaneous drain on international reserves in 1994. Mexico was in no position to reduce the amount of currency (its monetary base) in circulation several times over. There was no excessive lending to the government. After several politically trig-

---

[32] Krugman's 1994 comparison of wage and productivity growth in the United States with respect to the rest of the world is an excellent example of this approach (pp. 274-80).

gered speculative attacks that managed to drain international reserves, Mexico's currency collapse was no more avoidable than those experienced by several European countries in 1992.

3. Information from Mexico was neither hidden nor released differently from the manner to which market participants were accustomed. On many key statistics, Mexico was already providing more timely and thorough information than many industrialized countries.

4. Demand in 1994 was driven by exports and by private investment and consumption. Not only did the government avoid pump-priming in an election year, but, according to the national accounts, its contribution to expenditure grew below the overall growth in aggregate demand.

5. Private savings gauged as a residual did not show the drastic falls attributed to them by some authors. Measured by the national accounts, they remained constant. A revision of the data by J.P. Morgan, with these apparent contradictions in mind, even reaches the conclusion that private savings *rose* as a proportion of GDP during 1989-94.[33] At any rate, savings behavior cannot be pinpointed as the cause of the growing imbalance in the current account.

A DIFFERENT VIEW

We find clear evidence that Mexico experienced a politically triggered speculative attack, not a crisis based on the misalignment of real phenomena. However, some internal developments did create a favorable environment for a speculative attack. Prior to the 1994-95 economic collapse, the private sector's financial situation evolved from an unprecedented net-asset position to considerable debt. A coincidence of converging events and policy measures combined to produce the substantial and quick indebtedness of the private sector:

- The financial sector was liberalized, lending and borrowing rates were freed, and directed credit was abolished.
- Bank reserve requirements were eliminated.
- To calculate non-performing loans, banks applied "due payments" criteria: misleadingly, the amount of payments due after 90 days was recorded as delinquent loans instead of the value of the loans themselves.
- Banks were hastily privatized—in many instances with no due

[33] J.P. Morgan (1996).

189

respect to "fit and proper" criteria in the selection of new shareholders or their top officers.

- Several banks were purchased without their new owners proceeding to their proper capitalization, since shareholders often leveraged their stock acquisitions, sometimes with loans provided by the very banks that had been bought out.

- Taxes on inter-country capital flows (dividends, interest, etc.) were drastically reduced or eliminated.

- Foreigners were allowed to hold short-term "domestic" government debt.

- Short-term, dollar-indexed, peso-denominated Mexican government securities, *tesobonos*, were issued at the end of 1991.

- Unprecedented and huge amounts of foreign capital (much of it securitized) became available worldwide and particularly to Mexico.

- Commercial banks had lost a substantial amount of human capital at the higher echelons while under public management. With these officials, institutional memory migrated as well.

- The problem of "moral hazard" (or perverse incentives) was enhanced by the full government backing of bank deposits. This backing did not distinguish between inter-bank borrowings, borrowings from abroad, or deposits by large treasuries. In addition, homogeneous premiums were applied to all banks, regardless of their creditworthiness.

- There were no capitalization rules based on portfolio market risk. This encouraged asset-liability mismatches that in turn led to a highly liquid liability structure—more than two-thirds overnight for the banks—with the potential to create huge strains on the lender-of-last-resort capabilities of the central bank.

- Banking supervision capacity was weak to begin with, and it became overwhelmed by the great increase in the portfolio of banks.

- Some commercial banks were able to have access in disproportionate amounts to money market funds because of their confidence that, on any particular day, they could rely on an unlimited supply of daylight overdraft facilities.

- Mexico did not have efficient credit bureaus.

- There was a phenomenal expansion of credit from the development banks.

This combination of factors constitutes an almost unique experience[34] of how, despite important economic achievements, financial liberalization[35] can go astray in an environment that has no adequate safeguards against the predatory practices banks can be induced to undertake by full deposit protection. Fast credit growth and its aftermath is not, however, an exclusive feature of Chile and Mexico: Graciela Kaminsky and Carmen Reinhart reviewed the experiences of 20 countries that experienced banking and balance-of-payments crises and found that, in about half of these countries, the banking crisis preceded the balance-of-payments crisis.[36]

The numbers related to the expansion of credit during the Salinas administration are impressive. From December 1988 to November 1994, the amount of credit outstanding from local commercial banks to the private sector rose in real terms from 90.3 billion pesos to 340 billion pesos (an increase over the six-year period of 277 percent, or 25 percent per year).[37] Over the same period (also in real terms) credit card liabilities rose at 31 percent per year, direct credit for consumer durables rose at a yearly 67 percent, and mortgage loans at an annual 39 percent.

In dollars, external credit flows to the private sector went from a negative $193 million in 1988 to $23,198 million in 1993. The flow fell to $8,864 million in 1994, but this decrease was more than compensated by the fall in the international reserves of the Bank of Mexico that year, which went down by $18,884 million. Therefore, the total use of external resources was $27,748 million in 1994.

But the story is not yet complete. The government broke with a long and healthy practice of including in the definition of its consolidated deficit the amounts channeled through government development banks—a concept known as the deficit or surplus, as the case might be, due to "financial intermediation." The deficit due to financial intermediation went from 1.07 percent of GDP in 1990, to 2.8, 2.66, 3.33, and 3.68 percent of GDP in the succeeding years. Such a volume contributed to careless lending: "During the past government, *Nacional Financiera* extended 470,000 credits, of which half were not viable," and "they were not viable even before the cri-

---

34 Chile's 1982-83 crisis has many parallels with Mexico's. See Gil-Díaz (1995).

35 Mancera (1997) discusses the causes of the increase in private debt and provides a full presentation of the diverse financial salvage operations required in the aftermath of the crisis.

36 Kaminsky and Reinhart (1996).

37 All the figures quoted in this section were provided directly by the Economic Research Department of the Bank of Mexico.

sis."[38] The size of financial intermediation to GDP was not negligible to explain the size of current-account deficits, which were 3.0 percent, 5.1 percent, 7.4 percent, 6.5 percent, and 7.9 percent each year between 1990 and 1994.

The unseemly attraction of foreign resources and the liquidation of large amounts of government debt, which helped fuel a boom in bank lending—combined with the moral hazard cocktail concocted by the various measures already enumerated—led to a rapidly increasing current-account deficit financed by a large proportion of short-term capital. This deficit was combined with the commitment (consecrated in the Pacts) to contain the exchange rate within a widening but relatively tight band. We believe that the economic literature does not sufficiently emphasize the vulnerability of fixed exchange rates under fast-moving and potentially huge transfers of short-run capital. The implicit or explicit policy recommendations of many authors would have mitigated the depth and violence of the 1994-95 Mexican economic crisis, but none would have avoided it.

David Hale's chapter in this volume points to the huge increase in securitized lending over recent years. This development represented a truly fundamental difference for two reasons: when banks are the foreign creditor, there is an interlocutor when the crisis arrives, and banks have capital to absorb losses, which allows them to engage in calm negotiations. These two facts may account for the nervous behavior of investors before and after the crisis erupted. A quote from Hale is relevant: "The magnitude of the recent Mexican crisis suggests that developing countries will have to re-examine their assumptions about monetary policy . . . Some countries will be able to establish investor confidence simply by establishing independent central banks, while others should consider converting their central banks into currency boards similar to those which now exist in Hong Kong or Argentina."[39]

Given the proven fragility of fixed exchange rates, there is a need to choose the appropriate monetary institutions. Hale and others favor a currency board because it presents several advantages: The money supply is demand-determined; foreign reserves are hostage to money-demand movements, which reassures investors; and the public sector is ultimately constrained to budgetary equilibrium. One of the outcomes of this arrangement is that interest rates and inflation mirror those prevailing in the country chosen for the

---

[38] Gilberto Borja, CEO of Nacional Financiera, quoted in *El Economista* (Mexico D.F.) September 9, 1996, p. 20.
[39] Hale (1995), p. 5.

currency peg, thus achieving a lower cost of capital and greater price stability. Speculative activities are reduced to their bare essentials; economic growth is higher; and a longer-term horizon allows exporters to plan for permanent investments. But a lender of last resort is needed and requires ample availability of foreign reserves or lines of credit. An independent central bank, on the other hand, is an improvement over a dependent one, because it focuses the public's attention on central bank actions and improves accountability.

REFERENCES AND BIBLIOGRAPHY

Atkenson, Andrew, and Jose-Victor Ríos-Rull (1995). "How Mexico Lost Its Foreign Exchange Reserves." Preliminary manuscript. Philadelphia and Minneapolis: University of Pennsylvania and Federal Reserve Bank of Minneapolis. September.

Bank of Mexico (1994). *Annual Report*. Mexico City: Bank of Mexico.

Bank of Mexico (various years). *The Mexican Economy*. Mexico City: Bank of Mexico.

Barro, Robert J. (1996). *Getting It Right: Markets and Choices in a Free Society*. Cambridge: MIT Press.

Buira, Ariel (1995). "The Mexican Crisis of 1994: An Assessment." Paper presented at the Conference on Private Capital Flows to Emerging Markets after the Mexican Crisis. Institute for International Economics, Washington, D.C., and the Austrian National Bank, Vienna. September.

Calvo, Guillermo (1994). *Comments on Dornbusch and Werner*. Brookings Papers on Economic Activity no. 1. Washington, D.C.: Brookings Institution.

———— and Enrique G. Mendoza (1995). "Reflections on Mexico's Balance-of-Payments Crisis: A Chronicle of a Death Foretold." Preliminary manuscript. College Park and Washington, D.C.: University of Maryland and Federal Reserve. October.

Center for Economic Studies of the Private Sector (1995). *Actividad Economica* 187. Mexico City: CEESP.

———— (1994). *Actividad Economica* 183. Mexico City: CEESP.

Cole, Harold L., and Timothy J. Kehoe (1995). "Self-fulfilling Debt Crisis." Preliminary manuscript. Minneapolis: Federal Reserve Bank and the University of Minnesota. November.

Cuenta Pública (Public Accounts) (1995). México, D.F., Secretaría de Hacienda y Crédito Publico.

Dornbusch, Rudiger, Ilan Goldfajn, and Rodrigo Valdes (1995). *Currency Crises and Collapses*. Cambridge: MIT.

Dornbusch, Rudiger, and Alejandro Werner (1994). "Mexico: Stabilization, Reform, and No Growth." Preliminary manuscript. Cambridge: MIT. April.

Fraser, Damian (1995). *How Can Mexico Save More?* London: Barings Securities International Ltd. September.

Gil-Díaz, Francisco (1995). "A Comparison of Economic Crisis: Chile in 1982, Mexico in 1995." Paper presented at "Forum 95: The Forum for Managed Futures and Derivatives." Chicago: Managed Futures Association. July.

Gil-Díaz, Francisco, and Agustín Carstens (1996a). "Some Hypotheses Related to the Mexican 1994-95 Crisis." Bank of Mexico Research Paper 9601. Mexico City: Bank of Mexico. January.

———— (1996b). "One Year of Solitude: Some Pilgrim Tales About the Mexican 1994-95 Crisis," *American Economic Review*. June.

Gil-Díaz, Francisco, and Raul Ramos-Tercero (1988). "Lessons from Mexico," in Michael Bruno, Guido di Tella, Rudiger Dornbusch, and Stanley Fischer, eds., *Inflation Stabilization: The Experience of Israel, Argentina, Brazil, Bolivia and Mexico*. Boston: MIT Press.

Hale, David (1995). "Lessons from the Mexican Peso Crisis of 1995 for International Economic Policy." Preliminary manuscript. Oesterreichische Nationalbank, Vienna. September.

International Monetary Fund (1995a). *World Economic Outlook*. Washington, D.C.: IMF. March.

———— (1995b). *International Capital Markets: Developments, Prospects, and Key Policy Issues*. Washington, D.C.: IMF. May.

———— (1995c). *Developments in 1994. Annex I: Factors Behind the Financial Crisis in Mexico*. Washington, D.C.: IMF. June.

J.P. Morgan (1996). "How low is Mexico's private saving?" *Emerging Markets Data Watch*. September 6.

Kamin, Steven B., and John H. Rogers (1997). *Output and the Real Exchange Rate in Developing Countries: An Application to Mexico*. International Finance Discussion Papers, No. 580. Washington, D.C.: Board of Governors of the Federal Reserve System. May.

———— (1995). *Monetary Policy in the End-Game to Exchange-Rate Based Stabilizations: The Case of Mexico*. Washington, D.C.: Board of Governors of the Federal Reserve System. September.

Kaminsky, Graciela L., and Carmen M. Reinhart (1996). *The Twin Crises: The Causes of Banking and Balance-of-Payments Problems*. International Finance Discussion Papers, No. 544. Washington, D.C.: Board of Governors of the Federal Reserve System.

Kiel Institute of World Economics (1995). "The Mexican Reform Process: Improving Long-Run Perspectives. Mastering Short-Run Turbulences."

194

Study commissioned by the Mexican-German Chamber of Commerce and Industry. Kiel, Germany: Kiel Institute of World Economics. June.

Krugman, Paul (1995). "Emerging Market Blues," *Foreign Affairs*. July/August.

——— (1994). *Peddling Prosperity*. New York: W.W. Norton.

Leiderman, Leonardo, and Alfredo Thorne (1995). "Mexico's 1994 Crisis and its Aftermath: Is the Worst Over?" Unpublished manuscript. Tel Aviv: University of Tel Aviv. August.

Mancera, Miguel (1997). "Problems of Bank Soundness: Mexico's Recent Experience." Paper presented at "Seminar on Banking Soundness and Monetary Policy in a World of Global Capital Markets." Washington, D.C.: International Monetary Fund. January 28.

——— (1995). "Don't Blame Monetary Policy," *Wall Street Journal*. January 31.

McKinnon, Ronald I., and Huw Pill (1995). "Credible Liberalizations & International Capital Flows: The Overborrowing Syndrome." Unpublished manuscript. Palo Alto: Stanford University. June.

Melick, William R. (1996). *Estimation of Speculative Attack Models: Mexico Yet Again*. Basel, Switzerland: Bank for International Settlements. August.

Meltzer, Alan H. (1996a). *A Mexican Tragedy*. Washington, D.C.: American Enterprise Institute. January.

——— (1996b). "Clinton Bailout Was No Favor to Mexicans," *Wall Street Journal*. February 2.

Naím, Moisés (1995). "Sobering Growth Realities," *Foreign Affairs*. July/August.

Organisation for Economic Co-Operation and Development (1995). *1994-95 Annual Review: Mexico*. Paris: OECD. July.

Pérez-López, Alejandro (1995). "Un Modelo de Cointegracion para Pronosticar el PIB de Mexico." Bank of Mexico Research Paper 9504. Mexico City: Bank of Mexico. July.

Rebelo, Sergio, and Carlos Vegh (1996). "Real Effects of Exchange-Rate-Based Stabilization: An Analysis of Competing Theories," in NBER's *Macroeconomic Annual 1995*. Cambridge: MIT Press.

Sachs, Jeffrey (1995). "The Mexican Peso Crisis: Sudden Death or Death Foretold?" Unpublished manuscript. Cambridge and New York: Harvard University and New York University. November.

Sachs, Jeffrey, Aaron Tornell, and Andres Velasco (1995). "Lessons from Mexico." Unpublished manuscript. Cambridge and New York: Harvard University and New York University. March.

Shelton, Judy (1994). *Money Meltdown: Restoring Order to the Global Currency System*. New York: The Free Press.

Velasco, Andres (1991). "Liberalization, Crisis, and Intervention: The Chilean Financial System, 1975-85," in V. Sundararajan and T. Baliño, eds., *Banking Crises: Cases and Issues*. Washington, D.C.: International Monetary Fund.

APPENDIX

Dates of Public Awareness of Bank of Mexico's Foreign Reserves

1	2	3
Opinions Recorded in the Mexican Press (US dollars)	Net International Reserves Actual Figures (US dollars)	Differences between 1 and 2 (%)
Afin Brokerage House (Jan. 25, 1994): "International reserves decreased from 23,017 mn in October, 1993 to 18,554 mn in December of 1993. By the end of 1994 they will reach 23 bn"	Oct. 93 = 23,017.4 mn Dec. 93 = 24,951.7 mn Dec. 94 = 6,148.2 mn	-0.0017 -25.6 274.1
Inverméxico Brokerage House (Jan. 26, 1994): "International reserves fell from 23 bn in October of 1993 to 19.4 bn in November of 1993"	Oct. 93 = 23,017.4 mn Nov. 93 = 18,689.9 mn	-0.076 3.8
Vector Brokerage House (June 14, 1994): "There will be a loss of reserves of 5 bn throughout 1994"	Loss of reserves between Dec. 93 and Dec. 94 = 18,803.5 mn	-73.4
Mexico City Chamber of Commerce, Canaco (July, 1994): "Foreign reserves have increased throughout (President Salinas's) six year term from 6,859 mn in 1989 to 26,135 mn in March of 1994"	March 94 = 24,425.3 mn	7.0
'Financial analysts' (July 25, 1994): "Foreign reserves currently are 18 bn"	22 July 94 = 14,168.3 mn	27.0
Banorte (July 25, 1994): "(International) reserves are above 20 bn"	22 July 94 = 14,168.3 mn	41.2
El Financiero (July 26, 1994): "According to Banco de México, international reserves were 17,064.3 mn at the end of April"	April 94 = 17,296.8 mn	-1.3
Vector Brokerage House (July 26, 1994): "Foreign reserves, 17,959 mn in April"	April 94 = 17,296.8 mn	3.8
Foreign Trade National Council, Conacex (July 27, 1994): "Reserves are 21 bn"	26 July 94 = 14,381.5 mn	46
La Jornada (Aug. 29, 1994): "[Reserves] were 18,175 mn at the end of May, compared to 29,585.8 mn in February"	Feb. 94 = 29,155.4 mn May 94 = 17,142.3 mn	1.5 6
Vector Brokerage House (Sept. 1994): "Reserves are 19 bn"	21 Sept. 94 = 16,891.9 mn	12.5

Dates of Public Awareness of Bank of Mexico's Foreign Reserves

1	2	3
Opinions Recorded in the Mexican Press (US dollars)	Net International Reserves Actual Figures (US dollars)	Differences between 1 and 2 (%)
Enrique Quintana, financial analyst (Sept. 28, 1994): "reserves were 15,900 mn at the end of June"	June 94 = 15,997.7 mn	-0.61
Banorte Financial Group (Oct. 9, 1994): ". . . are 15,884 mn in June"	June 94 = 15,997.7 mn	-0.71
Senator Carlos Sales, Chairman of the Foreign Trade Commission (Oct. 1994): ". . . [reserves were] 15 bn in June"	June 94 = 15,997.7 mn	-6.2
'Specialists' of the private sector (Oct. 11, 1994): ". . . 16 bn until September"	Sept. 94 = 16,139.7 mn	-0.86
José Madariaga, President of the Mexican Bankers Association (October 12, 1994): "International reserves fluctuate between 17 bn and 20 bn"	11 Oct. 94 = 16,166.4 mn	between 5.2 and 23.7
Vector Brokerage House (Oct. 12, 1994): "International reserves oscillate between 18 bn and 19 bn"	11 Oct. 94 = 16,166.4 mn	between 11.3 and 17.5
Arturo Damm, financial analyst (Nov. 4, 1994): ". . . 17 bn"	3 Nov. 94 = 16,320.6 mn	4.2
El Financiero (Nov. 18, 1994): "International reserves fell by more than 11 bn between February and October. In February they were 28.7 bn"	Feb. 94 = 29,155 mn Oct. 94 = 17,242.2 mn Difference = -11,913.2 mn	-1.6 2.7 -7.6
El Economista (Nov. 18, 1994): "International reserves fell by 8 bn so far this year"	Jan. 94 = 26,274.5 mn 18 Nov. 94 = 12,790.7 mn Diff. = 13,483.8 mn	- 40.7
Macroasesoría, Economics think-tank (Nov. 30, 1994): "International reserves will be 16 bn by the end of 1994"	Dec. 94 = 6,148.2 mn	160.2

Dates of Public Awareness of Bank of Mexico's Foreign Reserves

1 Opinions Recorded in the Mexican Press (US dollars)	2 Net International Reserves Actual Figures (US dollars)	3 Differences between 1 and 2 (%)
El Economista (Dec. 1, 1994): "In March [reserves] were 24 bn. By the time of the [6th. State of the Union Address of President Salinas] they were 17.2 bn"	March 94 = 24,425 mn 31 Oct. 94 = 17,242.2 mn	-1.7 - 0.24
Economic Research Institute, National University of Mexico (Dec. 5, 1994): "In December, 1993 [reserves] were 24,537.1 mn. At the end of 1994 they will be 16,850 mn"	Dec. 93 = 24,951.7 mn Dec. 94 = 6,148.2 mn	-1.6 174
'Financial analysts and experts' (Dec. 5, 1994): "At the beginning of November, 1994, international reserves equaled 17.2 bn plus credit lines for another 17 bn to face speculative attacks"	31 Oct. 94 = 17,242.2 mn	98.4
'Various analysts' (Dec. 5, 1994): "In the previous week to the ratification of the Pact [between businessmen, workers and the government] reserves fell around 2 bn"	19 Sep. 94 = 16,821 mn 23 Sep. 94 = 16,645 mn Difference = 176 mn	10,363
Probursa Financial Group (Dec. 5, 1994): "There are 30 bn between international reserves and credit lines"	31 Oct. 94 = 17,242.2 mn	74
Bear Stearns (Dec. 5, 1994): "In February of 1994, R = 29,329 mn and in September, R = 17,220. Variation = 12,120 mn.	Feb. 94 = 29,155.4 mn Sep. 94 = 16,139.7 mn Difference = 13,015.7 mn	0.56 6.7 - 6.9
'Currency traders' (Dec. 5, 1994). ". . . estimated that capital flight was 2.4 bn between November 14 and 18"	14 Nov. 94 = 15,941.5 mn 18 Nov. 94 = 12,790.7 mn Diff. = 3,150.8 mn	-23.8
'High ranking financial executives' (Dec. 21, 1994): "[International] reserves are between 10 bn and 15 bn"	20 Dec. 94 = 10,359 mn 21 Dec. 94 = 5,853.5 mn	between -3.5 and 44.8 between 70.8 and 156

APPENDIX (continued)

Dates of Public Awareness of Bank of Mexico's Foreign Reserves

1	2	3
Opinions Recorded in the Mexican Press (US dollars)	Net International Reserves Actual Figures (US dollars)	Differences between 1 and 2 (%)
El Universal (Dec. 21, 1994): ". . . [foreign] reserves of approximately 17 bn"	20 Dec. 94 = 10,359 mn 21 Dec. 94 = 5,853.5 mn	64.1 190.4
Reforma (Dec. 21, 1994): ". . . probably they [reserves] were yesterday around 11 bn or 12 bn"	20 Dec. 94 = 10,359 mn	6.2 or 15.8
Excelsior (Dec. 21, 1994): "Quoting the Fed and the State Department, [Mexico's] reserves fell in the year from 24.1 bn to 17.2 bn"	Dec. 93 = 24,951.7 mn 20 Dec. 94 = 10,359 mn Difference 14,592.7 mn	- 3.4 66.2 - 52.7

8. THE MARKETS AND MEXICO: THE SUPPLY-SIDE STORY

DAVID D. HALE

INTRODUCTION

The Mexican economic crisis of 1995 was the fifth great Latin American financial crisis since the continent received independence from Spain, and the first major crisis of the post–Cold War boomlet in securitized capital flows to what the World Bank calls developing countries and Wall Street refers to as emerging markets.

As Mexico was one of the countries that played a pioneering role in promoting market-oriented economic reform in Latin America after the debt crisis of the early 1980s, the magnitude of the peso's devaluation and the Mexican economy's contraction after 1994 came as a shock to practically everyone. In 1994, there had been numerous 50th anniversary celebrations of the Bretton Woods conference, featuring scholarly papers suggesting that developing countries would now be able to finance economic development through private capital flows and that organizations such as the World Bank or the IMF should focus primarily on assisting very poor countries in Africa or South Asia. In the summer of 1994, it was widely believed that the end of the Cold War had set the stage for a new global economic order analogous to the world before 1914, when there were large flows of private portfolio capital between rich and poor countries. But as the world's economic policy-makers were celebrating the founding of the Bretton Woods institutions, Mexico's foreign exchange reserves were eroding because of investor concern about two political assassinations, a guerrilla insurgency in Chiapas, and uncertainty over how the new Mexican president would resolve the policy trade-offs between promoting economic growth and restraining the country's large current-account deficit. In the closing weeks of 1994, a run on Mexico's foreign exchange reserves forced the government to abandon its long-standing commitment to a stable peso. The resulting loss of investor confidence was so great that the U.S. Treasury and the IMF had to offer Mexico emergency loans of over $40 billion in order to prevent a default on the dollar-linked securities that the government had issued to sustain capital inflows after the assassination of the PRI presidential candidate. There was widespread criticism of the aid package in both the U.S. Congress and many European finance ministries, but the Clinton administration persevered because of concerns about the political stability of Mexico, the secondary effects of the crisis on other developing countries with large current-account deficits, and the feedback effects on the U.S. economy.

The rescue package for Mexico was the largest international aid program since the Marshall Plan and represented a clear commitment by both the IMF and the U.S. Treasury to protect the market-oriented economic reforms that had begun under President Carlos Salinas and were being increasingly embraced by other developing countries. Despite the rescue program, however, capital flows to all developing-country equity markets slumped to about $27 billion during 1995 from a level of over $62 billion during 1993. The sudden suspension of capital flows to the emerging stock markets forced several countries to hike interest rates in order to protect their currencies; Argentina was also forced to borrow from the IMF.

Although the rescue package allowed Mexico to avoid default on its existing securities, the sudden suspension of private capital flows forced interest rates to rise sharply and drove the economy into such a severe downturn that the consumption share of GDP fell by nearly 10 percent during the first half of 1995. But while the rescue package could not prevent the most severe economic downturn in Mexico since the 1930s, it nevertheless can be regarded as a success for three reasons:

1. The rescue package permitted Mexico to resume borrowing in the international capital markets only six months after the peso devaluation—whereas after its 1980s default, Mexico had lost access for seven years.

2. The impact of the Mexican crisis on other developing countries faded after only a few months. According to data from the Institute of International Finance, total capital flows to developing countries were remarkably resilient during 1995, despite the Mexican crisis. Private capital flows held at $205 billion during 1995 compared with $163 billion in 1994. Private flows were sustained by a sharp rise in the level of bank lending to developing countries as well as steady expansion of foreign direct investment. Bank lending rose to $86 billion in 1995 from $33 billion in 1994. Direct equity investment was at $76 billion, compared with $64 billion in 1994. Total capital flows to developing countries rose to $246 billion in 1995 from $187 billion in 1994— because of a sharp rise in official transfers to $41.2 billion (from $23.9

billion in 1994 and $22.3 billion in 1993). The rise in official transfers resulted from the IMF and U.S. Treasury loan to Mexico.

3. No developing country abandoned market-oriented economic reform as a result of the Mexican crisis. Politicians in India and Korea often cited the Mexican crisis as a reason to slow financial liberalization, but there has been no major reversal of the movement toward reducing trade and capital controls in developing countries. Meanwhile, the ability of Argentina to withstand the strains on its banking system despite the sudden suspension of private capital flows has given a significant boost to investor confidence in the long-term viability of its currency board monetary regime. Argentina's approach has been to bolster its trade account not through a devaluation but through more aggressive microeconomic reform of its labor market, enterprises owned by the provincial governments, and other government polices that have inhibited productivity in the past.

It is not difficult to construct scenarios in which, in the absence of the Mexican aid package, the impact of the Mexican crisis could have been much worse. Without assistance from the IMF and U.S. Treasury, Mexico would have defaulted on its *tesobono* securities and thus probably lost access to the international capital markets again for several quarters, if not years. The shock of a Mexican default would have encouraged even more aggressive selling of the Argentine peso and the currencies of other developing countries with large current-account deficits. While Argentina would have permitted interest rates to rise very sharply, it is questionable whether the banking system and currency board could have survived a prolonged period of high-cost money. Other developing countries would also have permitted their interest rates to rise in defense of their currencies, but, with the exception of Hong Kong, it is doubtful that they would have resisted devaluation as dogmatically as Argentina. If Mexico had defaulted, it also is doubtful that commercial banks would have been as willing to expand their lending to developing countries on the scale that occurred during 1995 and 1996.

While the Mexican economic slump of 1995 was the first great crisis of securitized capital flows in the post–Cold War era, it was not dissimilar to the crises that often gripped capital-importing nations during the late nineteenth century. In that period, the United States suffered many comparable crises because of its dependence upon the London capital markets for the money needed to finance its Western railways and other infrastructure projects. As a result of the strong financial link between New York and London, all major crises in the U.S. financial markets during the late nineteenth century stemmed either from rising interest rates in London or some political event in the United States that called into question the dollar's exchange-rate link to the pound sterling through the gold standard.

The greatest crisis occurred in 1893, when the advent of a new Democratic administration under Grover Cleveland triggered a run on the U.S. gold reserve. Interest rates rose sharply, and Cleveland had to obtain emergency loans from J.P. Morgan and the Rothschilds in order to retain the dollar's link to gold. The loan helped to stabilize the dollar, but it did not prevent the U.S. economy from experiencing a severe recession and continuing agitation for a devaluation of the dollar against gold. In 1896, populist opponents of the gold standard captured control of the Democratic Party and nominated William Jennings Bryan for the presidency. In the weeks after his nomination, some investors sold dollar bonds for fear of a devaluation, and New York brokerage houses kept their trading rooms open throughout election night so that their clients could trade U.S. securities listed in London as polling results came in from the Western states. The defeat of Bryan produced an immediate rally in U.S. bonds, but there was a subsequent recovery in commodity prices without a devaluation of the dollar because of large South African gold discoveries that boosted the world money supply.

Mexico's problem at the end of 1994 was its greater vulnerability to an investor crisis of confidence—compared with that of the 19th century United States—because of both the scope of its need for foreign capital and its brief history as a capital importer through security markets. In the late nineteenth century, the United States had typically imported capital on a scale of 1-2 percent of GDP annually. During the period 1990-94, Mexico's capital imports had averaged 6 percent of GDP annually. The United States was a former British colony that had been importing capital from London since the first days of settlement. Mexico has experienced major fluctuations in its sentiment toward foreign investment since it became independent during the early nineteenth century. Like the United States, it welcomed foreign investment and even had a few companies listed on European stock exchanges during the late nineteenth century. But after the Revolution of 1910, Mexico embraced a policy of economic nationalism and restricted most forms of foreign trade and investment. It shifted to a policy of economic liberalization only after the debt crisis of 1982 and then accelerated the process of "market opening" when the collapse of communism made it clear that there was no alternative to a market-based economic system. As a result of these contrasting historical circumstances, Mexico has always been more vulnerable to fluctuations of investor sentiment.

Economic analysts will be debating the causes and consequences of the Mexican economic crisis for many years, but there is a broad consensus among observers about four major themes:

1. Developing countries should bolster their domestic savings rates and not run current-account deficits as large as 7-8 percent of GDP (Mexico's level in 1994) when their investment rates have increased by much less.

2. Developing countries should attempt to finance their current-account deficits through expanded foreign direct investment, not just sales of stocks and bonds to foreign investors. In the period 1990-94, Mexico financed about three-quarters of its external deficit through securitized capital flows, whereas most other developing countries financed only about one-quarter of their deficits through such portfolio capital inflows.

3. Developing countries emerging from periods of high inflation should be cautious about using their exchange rates as targets for monetary policy. While stabilization of the exchange rate can help to accelerate the transition to lower inflation, there is also a risk that it will produce a tendency toward overvaluation that undermines commercial competitiveness.

4. Finally, developing countries should improve the supervision of their commercial banking systems in order to enhance the ability of their central banks to conduct credible monetary policies. Mexico privatized its commercial banks in 1991, primarily by selling them to highly leveraged stock brokers. They in turn attempted to finance the takeovers by aggressively expanding both consumer and corporate lending. As there was a huge demand for credit in Mexico after a long period of high inflation and state control of the banks, lending expanded so rapidly that many institutions did not maintain adequate credit quality standards, and the stock of non-performing loans was approaching 8 percent even before the onset of the 1995 slump. The central bank was aware of these credit quality problems and therefore was reluctant to raise interest rates sharply in defense of the peso during 1994. If there had been more effective bank supervision, it would have been easier for the Mexican central bank to defend the peso through monetary tightening when foreign exchange reserves declined.

All of these conclusions about the Mexican crisis are understandable in view of the economy's performance during the period before the devaluation. Mexico was running a current-account deficit equal to 7-8 percent of GDP despite the fact that its economy was expanding at an annual rate of only about 3 percent. The private domestic savings rate had fallen by several percentage points since 1990, while the investment share of GDP had increased only modestly. The country had a large stock of short-term dollar liabilities and had funded itself heavily through the sale of dollar-linked *tesobono* securities after the Colosio assassination in March 1994. There was sufficient investor concern about the condition of Mexico's banks that their share price had slumped through most of 1994, and attempts to resolve balance-sheet problems through mergers had collapsed. All of the tensions in Mexico's policy mix also had been magnified during 1994 by a large rise in the level of U.S. short-term interest rates—after four years in which U.S. interest rates had either fallen sharply or been stable. Yet the magnitude of the crisis that resulted from Mexico's devaluation was nevertheless extraordinary in view of the enthusiasm with which foreign investors had deployed capital there during the early 1990s.

WALL STREET VIEWS BEFORE THE DEVALUATION

In the period before the peso was devalued, many Wall Street brokerage houses had produced reports discussing Mexico's economic risks, but none had predicted a crisis of the severity that subsequently ensued.

At **Bankers Trust**, the November 7 report on emerging markets reviewed the bond market problems that had resulted from Federal Reserve tightening but ended on an optimistic note about Mexico:

> Latin American economies clearly look stronger than they were a year ago. As this year can attest, though, economic growth alone does not necessarily translate into strong equity markets. Valuations and expectations for corporate earnings are high for some markets, notably Brazil. By contrast, parts of the Mexican and Argentine markets are cheap, especially construction and banks in the case of Mexico, and services, commodities and utilities in the case of Argentina, and both corporate and economic performances could easily exceed expectations. There are also likely to be more turnaround stories as corporate restructuring has begun to bear fruit in raising productivity and profitability.[1]

---

[1] See Gay (1994), p. 4.

At **Bear Stearns**, the research department also took a sanguine view of Mexico's prospects, linking its optimism to President Ernesto Zedillo's pursuit of a variety of tax and microeconomic reforms in 1995:

> Mexico's economic policy needs a substantial amount of Zedillo's attention early in his administration to convert it from moderate growth (3%-4% average) to faster growth (6% average). A 6% growth rate for Mexico is possible later in the decade given its commercial relations with the U.S. . . .
>
> We expect a technocratic economic policy, with numerous improvements in regulatory policy, continuing efforts toward deregulation and banking competition, and private sector expansion at the margins of the oil monopoly.
>
> We expect the peso to strengthen somewhat as short-term capital flows back in. It is highly unlikely that the peso band will be breached, given the government's very sound financial position, tight monetary policy, constitutional mandate to maintain purchasing power, and *Pacto* commitments.
>
> However, peso lending rates are likely to remain dauntingly high. The government seems insistent on building uncertainty (and therefore high costs) into its future exchange rate through the ever-widening exchange rate and band and the preference for a discretionary monetary policy. Its goal seems to be a floating exchange rate system patterned on Canada's—not a good choice for an emerging market.
>
> We expect Mexico's stock market to outperform most other world equity markets as investors recognize the stability of the economic program and the significance of Mexico's commercial relationship with the U.S. However, we expect the market to be correlated with the U.S. market and to have some upside limit (well above current levels) unless Zedillo turns out to be as strong in his first year as Salinas was.[2]

Other firms were more cautious about the risks facing the peso exchange rate. In a strategy review of Latin America published shortly after the Mexican presidential election, **Baring Securities** warned investors about the policy trade-offs between exchange-rate stabilization and protection of the banking system:

---

[2] See Malpass (1994), p. 5.

Looking ahead, there are as yet no signs of a change in exchange rate policy. The peso briefly traded up just before and after the election, but this may well have formed part of the government's strategy of ensuring that confidence was maintained through a potentially troublesome period. Since then the peso has traded at around NP3.40/US dollar, implying a weaker exchange rate than was earlier forecast by most observers. Banco de Mexico's quick decision to narrow the intervention band was reportedly taken to reduce potential volatility, but clearly also reflects the authorities' realization that the excessively strong peso would be unhealthy for the economy. Although exports are growing rapidly and growth has picked up, eliminating two potential justifications for adjusting the peso parity, pressure in that direction may now come from the problems faced by the financial sector. Excessive credit growth in recent years combined with the slowdown of the economy in 1993 and early 1994 has led to a deterioration of asset quality. Without a more significant reduction in interest rates, companies and individuals will continue to find it difficult to service their obligations. By allowing the peso to weaken, the government could reduce the need for foreign financing, thus permitting a more rapid reduction of interest rates. An adjustment of the parity is still a possibility, albeit remote, leaving an increase in the daily slippage of the upper limit of Banco de Mexico's intervention band as the more likely option.[3]

The **Morgan Bank** also recognized that policy-makers faced some difficult choices in reconciling their desire for a stable currency with a stronger economy, but it did go so far as to predict a devaluation. The Morgan report noted:

Despite a sharp decline in international reserves, Mexico's current account balance has deteriorated sharply in 1994. In effect, looser fiscal policy and a more accommodating monetary policy have prevented the Mexican economy in general, and the trade balance in particular, from adjusting to reduced net capital inflow. Unless there is a substantial rise in capital flow to Mexico in 1995, fiscal and monetary policy will need to tighten if Mexico is to achieve its exchange rate objectives.

---

[3] See Schonander (1994), p. 13.

Policymakers, therefore, may face a very real trade-off between higher economic growth in 1995 and maintenance of the exchange rate policy.

The greatest weakness of Mexico's economic "model" over the past few years has been the reliance on short-term capital inflows to finance an extremely large current account deficit. In 1994, this model has been maintained at the cost of a sharp drop in international reserves. Since the stock of international reserves is finite, the sustainability of current policies in 1995 will depend critically on the evolution of capital flows.

No one can predict capital flows with any reliability. Nonetheless, there are reasons for believing that the external environment facing Mexico may be as unfavorable in 1995 as it was in 1994. First, despite the recent rise in U.S. interest rates, J.P. Morgan forecasts another 200 basis-point rise in short-term U.S. interest rates during 1995. Second, the relative attractiveness of other Latin American markets, such as Brazil, appears to have increased. Both these developments may negatively affect the flow of funds to Mexico. If so the government will need to tighten macroeconomic policy in 1995 in order to meet its exchange rate objective. Tighter macroeconomic policy, however, may render the government's 4% economic growth target for 1995 overly ambitious.[4]

The above commentaries indicate that Wall Street analysts were aware of the contradiction in Mexico's economic program and large current-account deficit but, after five years of steady growth in capital inflows, could not imagine as abrupt a change in the direction of investor sentiment as subsequently did occur. The problem that confronted analysts and fund managers in allocating capital to Mexico during late 1994 was that the country had an expensive equity market compared with the risks posed by the country's political problems and large current-account deficit. In September 1994, the Mexican equity market had a price to earnings (P/E) multiple of 19.34 and a price to book value ratio of 2.34, compared with low single-digit P/E multiples and a discount to book value during much of the late 1980s (Table 1). The New York market's P/E multiple during September 1994 was 18, and its ratio of price to book value was 2.4. The Mexican market's value was not extravagant compared with other Latin American markets during late 1994. The Brazilian market had

---

[4] See Skiles (1994), p. 1-2.

Table 1. Valuation of Selected Stock Markets							
		United States		Mexico		Brazil	
		P/E	P/BV	P/E	P/BV	P/E	P/BV
1989	January	12.10	1.94	3.47	.58	4.57	.46
	March	11.70	1.87	3.74	.60	5.46	.64
	June	12.30	1.96	4.82	.75	4.75	.52
	September	13.40	2.14	6.24	.89	5.07	.63
	December	14.10	2.16	8.40	.90	5.87	.72
1990	January	13.80	2.01	8.81	.92	6.53	.80
	March	14.10	2.03	7.39	.73	3.64	.27
	June	15.50	2.08	8.82	.94	6.24	.41
	September	13.70	1.77	8.83	.87	7.07	.36
	December	14.10	1.92	10.33	.99	4.69	.33
1991	January	14.60	2.00	10.03	.92	5.34	.45
	March	16.80	2.14	12.09	1.12	6.30	.39
	June	17.50	2.07	13.05	1.49	7.35	.60
	September	18.80	2.15	12.85	1.66	7.48	.57
	December	21.70	2.32	14.40	1.84	15.47	.76
1992	January	23.20	2.27	15.93	2.07	20.82	1.07
	March	24.30	2.23	15.52	2.30	738.96	.64
	June	23.60	2.22	12.10	1.87	-98.06	.38
	September	23.00	2.26	9.44	1.54	-296.68	.43
	December	22.70	2.36	12.28	1.99	-24.43	.37
1993	January	22.90	2.37	11.93	1.92	-23.18	.32
	March	23.80	2.45	12.54	1.99	16.11	.36
	June	22.50	2.56	12.40	1.70	16.73	.48
	September	21.70	2.60	14.11	1.79	14.08	.55
	December	22.10	2.64	19.45	2.59	12.59	.55
1994	January	23.00	2.72	19.81	2.59	18.56	.72
	March	19.70	2.53	16.36	2.47	19.54	.75
	June	18.80	2.50	16.58	2.21	14.37	.57
	September	18.80	2.63	19.34	2.63	20.17	.79
	December	16.90	2.61	17.07	2.16	13.09	.63
1995	January	16.50	2.67	15.02	1.89	12.37	.57
	March	16.40	2.77	57.90	1.52	9.25	.44
	June	16.90	2.91	-115.93	1.58	9.35	.49
	September	17.00	3.08	27.66	1.60	12.27	.51
	December	17.20	3.21	—	—	—	—

Source: Baring Securities.

Table 1, continued							
Argentina		**Chile**		**Singapore**		**Hong Kong**	
P/E	**P/BV**	**P/E**	**P/BV**	**P/E**	**P/BV**	**P/E**	**P/BV**
.55	.08	4.10	.78	23.60	1.96	13.30	1.87
13.2	.25	4.25	.84	22.00	2.04	11.80	1.82
462.57	7.92	4.10	.80	21.30	2.17	8.50	1.10
80.3	3.51	3.90	.71	20.60	2.21	9.90	1.30
9.15	1.13	5.61	.89	20.70	2.35	10.00	1.20
5.73	.69	5.97	.91	48.80	2.39	9.70	1.16
-35.01	1.76	6.31	.96	20.40	2.37	9.80	1.29
-4.93	.61	6.00	.88	20.30	2.29	10.80	1.22
-6.41	.42	5.96	.79	14.00	1.52	8.90	1.00
-3.07	.26	7.87	1.04	15.70	1.64	9.60	1.07
-15.26	.50	7.89	1.20	16.50	1.70	10.30	1.13
-10.74	.86	10.69	1.42	18.80	1.99	12.40	1.31
-11.45	.58	14.45	1.59	19.50	1.90	12.00	1.31
-28.87	1.25	17.89	2.03	17.60	1.63	11.80	1.39
-405.97	1.68	15.87	1.73	19.10	1.74	12.30	1.43
-46.73	1.67	16.76	1.63	19.50	1.78	13.30	1.56
-75.71	1.93	16.59	2.00	18.00	1.66	12.80	1.67
-205.04	1.73	14.97	1.98	17.90	1.63	15.70	1.92
55.28	1.18	13.39	1.72	16.90	1.57	14.10	1.69
37.99	1.20	12.99	1.71	18.80	1.70	13.60	1.59
31.97	1.19	14.50	1.95	18.90	1.69	14.60	2.03
36.84	1.23	13.11	1.62	18.60	1.69	14.60	2.21
32.63	1.23	15.83	1.64	18.10	1.56	15.60	2.16
39.27	1.53	16.89	1.72	19.70	1.75	15.40	2.31
41.90	1.94	20.04	2.11	25.80	2.21	22.60	3.32
42.09	2.09	24.35	2.63	24.90	2.12	21.70	3.19
31.62	1.80	20.71	2.07	19.20	1.88	16.00	2.39
26.59	1.66	20.46	2.22	19.90	1.82	15.20	1.97
27.01	1.92	23.80	2.62	20.70	1.98	15.80	2.08
17.71	1.42	21.38	2.51	19.50	1.92	13.30	1.64
16.16	1.35	20.82	2.47	17.90	1.76	11.70	1.44
14.83	1.21	19.89	2.34	17.60	1.82	13.50	1.66
12.28	1.22	20.12	2.37	17.70	1.68	14.30	1.67
12.33	1.18	17.59	2.10	16.60	1.57	14.10	1.74
—	—	—	—	17.80	1.69	14.30	1.77

a P/E of 20.2 and sold at a 20 percent discount to book value. The Argentine market sold at a P/E multiple of 27 and at 1.92 times book value. The Chilean market sold at a P/E multiple of 23.8 and at 2.62 times book value. But investors were able to rationalize these superior valuations because other Latin countries had much smaller current-account deficits than Mexico's and thus appeared to be poised for higher rates of economic growth.

In 1994, Brazil also had a presidential election and a currency reform program that greatly enhanced investor optimism about the country's economic growth prospects. As a result, many investment funds significantly increased their asset allocations in Brazil at the expense of Mexico. Ironically, if the Marxist candidate had won the Brazilian election, international investors would have shunned Brazil and kept much higher asset allocation weightings for Mexico.

The high valuation of Mexico's stock market did not discourage foreign demand for Mexican securities during the early months of 1994. There was considerable optimism at the start of the year because of the enactment of NAFTA by the U.S. Congress in November 1993. But there was a sharp decline in foreign demand for Mexican equities and peso-denominated government securities after the Colosio assassination. As a result, Mexico had to defend the peso by running down its foreign exchange reserves from $29 billion to $16 billion and by increasing the role of the dollar-linked *tesobono* security in its external financing. The peso value of *tesobonos* owned by foreign investors grew from only 4.5 billion in January 1994 to 23.9 billion in April, 53.5 billion in August, and 54.9 billion in November. The stock of foreign-owned *cetes*, by contrast, fell from 70.3 billion pesos in January to 24.4 billion pesos in the month before the peso devaluation. The sharp rise in *tesobono* financing indicated that there was a major disequilibrium in Mexico's balance-of-payments position.

Foreign demand for Mexican equities and peso-denominated debt fell sharply because of investor apprehension about political risk and the slow growth of the economy, forcing the Mexican government to assume the currency risk in its external financing. In the absence of the *tesobono* financing, Mexico probably would have been forced to raise interest rates sharply and to permit its stock market to fall in order to make peso-denominated assets more attractive for foreign investors. Mexico did raise interest rates from less than 10 percent in mid-March 1994 to over 20 percent in April, but interest rates then declined and fluctuated in a range of 10-15 percent during the final months of the year. This level of interest rates was not sufficiently high to prevent a rundown of foreign ownership of *cetes*, while the demand for Mexican equities continued to be inhibited by uncertainty about the economic outlook as well as rising U.S. interest rates. After tightening at a gradual pace through most of 1994, the Federal Reserve surprised the market with a 75 basis-point rate hike in November, and most Wall Street analysts expected further tightening in the new year. The incoming Zedillo administration would probably have had to announce a radical new agenda for privatization or growth-enhancing economic reforms in order to achieve its initial goal of financing a $32 billion current-account deficit policy through private capital inflows during 1995.

Professor Alan Meltzer of Carnegie Mellon University has argued that monetary tightening alone would have stabilized the peso in late 1994. In a paper for the American Enterprise Institute, he stated:[5]

> The distinctive facts about 1994 are not the low saving rate or the prevalence of short-term debt. The critical change was in the policies of the Mexican central bank and government during an election year. To make the economy appear strong on election day, the Mexican government increased spending and lending, much of it off-budget. A 22 percent increase in credit to the public sector from the state development banks was planned for 1994, compared with a 7 percent increase in 1993. And the central bank pumped in money to hold down the rise in interest rates on the government's debt.
>
> The bank financed its purchases of bonds and part of the government budget by starting another round of inflationary policy. The money directly controlled by the bank, known as the monetary base—bank reserves and currency—accelerated from a lower than 4 percent annual rate in the spring of 1993 to a rate higher than 10 percent in January and February 1994. In March, the annual growth rate was 26 percent. Growth of the base declined from this peak but remained high and was 19 percent or more annually in each month from July through December. This policy was highly inflationary.
>
> The main disturbing influence is the government's fiscal policy. The election was not followed by a reduction in monetary growth or in government budget and off-budget spending and lending. The retiring government sat on its hands or, perhaps, rested on its earlier accomplishments.

---

[5] Meltzer (1996).

From August to November of 1994, the Bank of Mexico continued to pump money into the economy. The monetary base rose at annual rates between 20 percent and 25 percent. On the basis of their experience in past elections, the public may not have been surprised by the election-year policy. But the policy did not end with the election, and neither the incoming nor the outgoing government gave a sign that inflationary policy would be checked. The 1995 budget plan showed no reduction in spending and no plan to tighten fiscal policy.

There is no doubt that some monetary and fiscal tightening after the presidential election would have enhanced the prospects of holding the peso's exchange rate in its target band. But as the European devaluations of 1992 illustrated, there are limits to how far interest rates can be raised without undermining the credibility of monetary policy itself. As a result of the rising debt delinquency ratios at Mexico's banks, investors might well have regarded a large interest-rate hike as a sign that the country's current-account deficit had become unsustainable and that there was no alternative to devaluation. In fact, foreign investors had purchased Mexican equities during the early 1990s in order to profit from a potentially superior rate of economic growth. In 1994, the government had been able to plug the financing gap resulting from reduced equity capital inflows with sales of *tesobonos*. But it could not expect to persist with such a financing mix indefinitely. A central bank move to jack up interest rates might have boosted foreign demand for *cetes* temporarily, but, as such a rate hike would have depressed economic growth expectations, it might also have encouraged a further withdrawal of foreign capital from the equity market.

THE REACTION OF INVESTORS TO THE DEVALUATION

In many countries, a currency devaluation is often perceived as a "buy" signal for the equity market because it signals a move toward an economic adjustment program designed to squeeze consumption and boost the profit share of GDP. The Mexican devaluation, by contrast, had a very negative impact on investor confidence and set the stage for a complete collapse in portfolio capital flows to the country. The devaluation failed to bolster investor confidence for several reasons:

1. The devaluation took most foreign investors by surprise. They had believed the promises of Secretary of Finance Pedro Aspe that the Mexican government would not resort to the election-year tradition of devaluing the currency at the end of the president's term. As Mexico had devalued in 1976, 1982, and 1988, sophisticated foreign investors had long been concerned about the risk of an exchange-rate adjustment during the period after the August 1994 election. But when the Salinas government let the post-election window pass without any change in policy, foreign investors assumed that the Zedillo government would also maintain the peso's exchange rate indefinitely. When Secretary of Finance Aspe stepped down at the start of December, investors had no reason to expect his replacement to change policy—but they did not know him as well as they knew Aspe; consequently he did not have an existing stock of personal credibility with foreign investors to use in defending the peso when Mexico's foreign exchange reserves began to plummet because of local selling.

2. The decision by the U.S. Treasury to provide emergency loans in order to support the peso at the time of the Colosio assassination produced excessive complacency on the part of many foreign investors about exchange rate risks. After the enactment of NAFTA, many investors believed that the U.S. government would encourage a strong peso to promote American exports to Mexico as well as to prevent an upsurge of imports from Mexico that might further inflame protectionist sentiment. When the United States provided Mexico with a large swap line during the spring of 1994, it appeared to validate those perceptions and helped to lessen investors' concerns about peso overvaluation. As we know from the D'Amato Report on U.S. Treasury policy toward Mexico, many Treasury officials had long been concerned about Mexico's large current-account deficit forcing a devaluation, but they could not express such sentiments in public. The problem for the U.S. Treasury was defining the circumstances under which it should intervene on behalf of the peso. The shock of the Colosio assassination was so great that it was easy to justify intervention. But the assassination of PRI Secretary General José Francisco Ruíz Massieu and the renewed insurgency in Chiapas during the autumn of 1994 were not so conspicuously destabilizing as to justify further U.S. Treasury assistance. Yet the Ruiz murder had a very negative impact on investor sentiment in Mexico, while the television and newspaper photos of the Chiapas insurgents caused foreign investors to remain apprehensive during the critical weeks after the inauguration of President Zedillo.

3. A third reason why the devaluation had such a negative impact on investor sentiment was the composition of the Mexican equity market itself in late 1994. Investors could not reallocate funds within the equity market to benefit from the devaluation because the market capitalization of companies in export-sensitive industries was very small compared with the market capitalization of companies focused on domestic consumption sectors, such as telecommunications, cement, retailing, and beverages. Among the large capitalization companies, only Alfa, GI Minerva, Panoles, Cydsa, and Empressa Moderna were potential beneficiaries of the devaluation. Their combined capitalization was equal to less than 12 percent of Mexico's potential market capitalization. Telmex, CIFRA, and Cemex, by contrast, accounted for almost 23 percent of Mexico's total market capitalization. In fact, Telmex had the largest capitalization of all the companies listed on Latin America's stock markets. In Europe and Asia, by contrast, the export sector accounted for a much larger share of stock market capitalization, helping to provide investors with alternative investment opportunities if the exchange rate depreciated. The sectoral imbalance in Mexico's equity market reflected the country's long history of protectionism and the fact that a large share of the country's tradable goods are produced by multinational firms without local equity market listings.

The changing composition of Mexico's capital inflows during 1994 provided useful leading indicators of the country's increasing devaluation risk. According to a report by the Bank of Mexico published in June 1995 (see Table 2), the total stock of foreign portfolio investment in the Mexican equity market in January 1994 was about $61 billion (compared with only $4.5 billion at the end of 1990). About $38 billion of this investment was held in the form of American Depositary Receipts listed on U.S. equity markets and about $14 billion was held in the form of ordinary equity. The value of foreign investment in Mexican equities peaked in January 1994 and declined erratically during the next twelve months as a result of the weakness of equity prices and some selling, but it was still $50.4 billion before the peso devaluation. The value of foreign investment in Mexican government securities, by contrast, did not peak until late 1994. Before the peso devaluation, it was about 80 billion pesos—compared with 68 billion pesos at the end of 1993 and 9.9 billion pesos at the end of 1990. But there was a major change in the composition of foreign-owned Mexican government debt during 1994 (Table 3). At the end of 1993, the distribution of foreign investment in Mexican government securities was about 70 percent *cetes*, 3.9 percent *bondes*, 20.1 percent *ajustabonos*, and only 5.9 percent dollar-linked *tesobonos*. One month before the peso devaluation of December 1994, by contrast, the distribution of holdings was 24 percent *cetes*, 4 percent *ajustabonos*, and 55 percent *tesobonos*. During 1994, foreign investors had effectively reduced their vulnerability to

216

Table 2. Foreign Investment in Mexican Stock Market
Amount Outstanding at Market Value
(billions of dollars)

Month	ADRs[a]		FREE SUBSCRIPTION		NEUTRAL FUND		MEXICO FUND		TOTAL[b]	
	Amount	%	Amount	%	Amount	%	Amount	%	Amount	%
1989										
December	0.4	49.8	0.1	13.2	*	4.3	0.3	32.7	0.8	100.0
1990										
December	2.1	47.0	1.4	31.0	0.7	15.1	0.3	6.8	4.5	100.0
1991										
December	13.7	73.9	3.0	16.2	1.3	7.2	0.5	2.6	18.6	100.0
1992										
December	21.2	73.8	5.1	17.8	1.8	6.2	0.6	2.2	28.7	100.0
1993										
December	34.0	62.2	12.9	23.6	6.4	11.7	1.4	2.5	54.6	100.0
1994										
December	21.2	61.5	8.1	23.5	4.3	12.6	0.8	2.2	34.4	100.0
1994										
January	38.1	62.6	14.1	23.1	7.2	11.8	1.5	2.4	60.9	100.0
February	34.9	62.1	13.2	23.5	6.8	12.1	1.3	2.4	56.2	100.0
March	31.1	61.8	11.7	23.3	6.3	12.5	1.2	2.4	50.3	100.0
April	30.0	62.0	11.1	23.0	6.1	12.5	1.2	2.4	48.3	100.0
May	31.9	61.6	12.0	23.2	6.6	12.8	1.2	2.4	51.8	100.0
June	28.6	61.6	10.7	23.0	6.0	13.0	1.1	2.4	46.4	100.0
July	31.7	62.1	11.8	23.2	6.3	12.4	1.2	2.3	51.1	100.0
August	33.4	60.2	13.5	24.4	7.2	13.0	1.3	2.4	55.4	100.0
September	33.4	59.7	13.8	24.7	7.4	13.2	1.3	2.4	55.9	100.0
October	29.9	58.5	12.9	25.2	7.0	13.8	1.2	2.4	51.0	100.0
November	29.1	57.7	13.0	25.7	7.1	14.1	1.3	2.5	50.4	100.0
December	21.2	61.5	8.1	23.5	4.3	12.6	0.8	2.2	34.4	100.0

(percentage changes)					
Dec. 90/Dec. 89	429.1	1,212.1	1,857.1	16.7	459.9
Dec. 91/Dec. 90	546.1	115.1	96.2	58.8	311.0
Dec. 92/Dec. 91	53.9	69.1	33.2	26.6	54.2
Dec. 93/Dec. 92	60.6	152.7	256.5	120.4	90.6
Dec. 94/Dec. 93	-37.7	-37.2	-31.9	-43.8	-37.0

[a]Includes global depositary receipts.
[b]Total for 1993 and 1994 includes warrants and investments in the intermediate market.
*Figures less than 50 million dollars.
Source: Bolsa Mexicana de Valores.

Table 3. Foreign Investment in Mexican Government Securities
Amount Outstanding at Face Value at End of Period

	CETES		BONDES		TESOBONOS		AJUSTABONOS		TOTAL	
	(New peso billions)	*(%)*	*(New peso billions)*	*(%)*	*(New peso billions)*	*(%)*	*(New peso billions)*	*(%)*	*(New peso billions)*	*(%)*
1991										
January	4.1	41.1	4.6	47.0	0.1	0.5	0.9	8.7	9.9[a]	100.0
December	9.1	54.0	2.2	13.3	0.8	4.7	4.6	27.6	16.8[b]	100.0
1992										
December	28.5	64.3	3.9	8.7	0.6	1.4	11.4	25.6	44.4	100.0
1993										
December	47.7	70.2	2.6	3.9	4.0	5.9	13.7	20.1	68.0	100.0
1994										
December	13.5	12.9	0.2	0.1	87.8	84.2	2.8	2.7	104.2	100.0
1994										
January	49.1	70.3	3.0	4.3	4.5	6.4	13.3	19.0	69.8	100.0
February	53.4	71.0	2.3	3.0	5.7	7.5	13.9	18.5	75.3	100.0
March	50.8	65.1	2.5	3.2	10.3	13.2	14.4	18.5	78.1	100.0
April	35.9	49.5	0.8	1.1	23.9	33.0	11.9	16.4	72.6	100.0
May	32.9	43.1	0.9	1.1	30.9	40.5	11.7	15.3	76.3	100.0
June	30.8	39.4	1.9	2.5	35.5	45.4	9.9	12.7	78.2	100.0
July	26.8	32.5	1.7	2.1	45.5	55.2	8.4	10.2	82.4	100.0
August	25.1	29.6	0.6	0.7	53.5	63.1	5.6	6.6	84.8	100.0
September	24.1	28.9	0.5	0.6	52.6	63.0	6.3	7.5	83.5	100.0
October	24.7	29.9	0.6	0.7	51.6	62.4	5.7	6.9	82.7	100.0
November	19.0	24.4	0.2	0.3	54.9	70.2	4.0	5.1	78.1	100.0
December	13.5	12.9	0.2	0.1	87.8	84.2	2.8	2.7	104.2	100.0
	(percentage changes)									
Dec. 91/Jan. 91	123.7		-51.9		1,379.6		438.3		70.3	
Dec. 92/Dec. 91	214.5		72.9		-22.1		144.7		164.1	
Dec. 93/Dec. 92	67.1		-32.0		547.7		20.3		53.2	
Dec. 94/Dec. 93	-71.7		-94.2		2,102.4		-79.5		53.4	

[a]Includes 262.1 millions of new pesos (2.7 percent) corresponding to PAGAFES.
[b]Includes 64.8 millions of new pesos (0.4 percent) corresponding to PAGAFES.
Source: Bank of Mexico.

exchange-rate risk by converting their holdings of peso-denominated *cetes* into dollar-linked *tesobono* securities. But while owners of the *tesobonos* reduced their nominal currency risk, they continued to face a credit risk that Mexico would lack the foreign exchange required to repay the securities in dollars. The *tesobonos* had a short maturity and a nominal dollar value in excess of $30 billion; yet Mexico entered 1995 with only $5-$6 billion of foreign-exchange reserves. There was concern among investors about the ability of Mexico to redeem the *tesobonos* as scheduled. The potential threat that the *tesobonos* posed to Mexico's dwindling foreign-exchange reserves also called into question the ability of Mexican private companies, especially the banks, to service their dollar-denominated liabilities. The sharp deterioration in market perceptions of all forms of Mexican credit risk after December 1994 further undermined the country's ability to import portfolio capital.

THE INVESTMENT INSTITUTIONS
AND INVESTORS INVOLVED

The nature of the investment institutions that had helped to finance the Mexican current-account deficit during the early 1990s also contributed to the abruptness and severity of the interruption in capital flows after 1994. At the start of the 1990s, Mexico attracted capital primarily from specialist investment institutions with a high appetite for risk. These institutions included hedge funds, international mutual funds, and a newly evolving group of funds focused on developing countries or emerging markets. As U.S. interest rates fell and more investment institutions became familiar with Mexico, both the dollar volume of flows and the variety of fund managers with Mexican exposure expanded. In 1993, officially recorded equity capital flows to Mexico from the United States rose to $5.1 billion (compared with $2.8 billion in 1992, $2.1 billion in 1991, and $918 million in 1990). Many Mexican companies also encouraged this investment by seeking ADR listings on the New York Stock Exchange. In the fixed-income markets, U.S. investors purchased a large volume of Mexican securities immediately after the debt restructuring negotiations with the commercial banks were completed and again during the period of low interest rates after 1992. U.S. investors purchased $6.8 billion of Mexican fixed-income instruments in 1990, $6.4 billion in 1993, and $10.6 billion in 1994. The debt share of Mexican capital inflows rose sharply during 1994 because of the introduction of the *tesobono* security and the reduced investor demand for equities resulting from uncertainties about the economy and rising U.S. interest rates.

219

The U.S. mutual fund industry played a major role in promoting demand for Mexican equity and debt securities during the early 1990s. As a result of the low level of U.S. short-term interest rates, the American household sector vastly expanded its holdings of mutual funds. The size of the equity fund industry grew from $117 billion in 1985 to $245 billion in 1990, $749 billion in 1993, and $1.3 trillion in 1995. Bond funds expanded from $135 billion in 1985 to $323 billion in 1990 and $761 billion in 1993. In 1993 and early 1994, international funds attracted almost 40 percent of total mutual fund purchases by retail investors because of the low yields on U.S. money market assets. There were three major markets for Mexican securities in the mutual fund industry: equity funds focused on emerging markets in general or Latin America in particular, fixed-income funds concentrating on high-yield securities, and generalist global equity and bond funds giving a modest weighting to Mexican financial assets. According to a survey of 64 emerging-market mutual funds by Emerging Markets Funds Research, the exposure of these closed-end and open-end funds to Mexico in mid-1994 was about $4.1 billion. In 1994, there also were about 15 closed-end and open-end mutual funds with $1.7 billion of assets focused exclusively on Mexican securities. The specialist funds focusing on emerging markets and Latin America appear to have accounted for about 7-8 percent of the $75 billion of foreign investment in Mexican securities in mid-1994. The managers of such funds did not like Mexico's devaluation, but as their mandate was to focus on Latin America and other developing countries, it did not cause them to abandon the market totally.

Mutual fund industry data indicates that specialized Latin American fixed-income funds suffered redemptions of about $550 million during the fourth quarter of 1994 and the first quarter of 1995 compared with net money inflows of just over $400 million during the first half of 1994. These redemptions reinforced the weakness of the market for Mexican securities, but they did not play a dominant role in reducing the country's foreign exchange reserves. Fixed-income funds focusing on emerging markets had positive money flows all through 1994 and the first quarter of 1995. Their net sales actually expanded during early 1995 because of investor bargain-hunting for value after the Mexican crisis.

The investors who suspended capital flows to Mexico after December 1994 were the generalist global bond and equity funds that had many alternative outlets for their money. As the crisis intensified, foreign commercial banks exacerbated it by suspending credit lines to Mexican companies. The U.S. high-yield fixed-income mutual funds were most reluctant to recommit capital to Mexico because they had either lost heavily on their *cetes* as a result of the devaluation or faced a surprise upsurge of credit risk on their *tesobonos* as a result of the country's dwindling foreign exchange reserves. Despite the fact that they did not experience large redemptions, several of the generalist bond managers sold Mexican securities heavily during the first quarter and in some cases took Mexico off their approved list. If there was a weak link in Mexico's capacity to import capital, it was comprised of the large money flows that had come from generalist fixed-income and equity mutual funds after 1992. Taking one example of a generalist fund management firm withdrawing its capital from Mexico, according to brokers, Fidelity reduced its stock of capital in developing-country fixed-income securities from $7 billion in early 1994 to barely $1 billion by mid-1995. The managers of such funds had believed the Mexican government's promises that there would not be a devaluation. Some even assigned their domestic equity analysts to follow Mexican companies as if they were part of a new North American economic zone without any exchange rate risk. As a result, they were totally unprepared for the political shocks of 1994 and experienced both anger and humiliation when the peso collapsed. Many also felt a personal sense of betrayal because of the numerous meetings they had had with senior Mexican officials promising to defend the exchange rate.

According to U.S. government data, American investors did not play a dominant role in causing the Mexican devaluation; nor did they engage in wholesale liquidation of securities after it happened. The government's capital flow data indicate that U.S. investors sold $378 million of Mexican equities during the fourth quarter of 1994 and purchased $199 million during the first quarter of 1995. In the fixed-income market, they purchased $671 million of securities during the fourth quarter and added another $276 million during the first quarter of 1995. In the second quarter, they sold only $24 million of equities and $38 million of fixed-income assets. Much of this selling probably occurred after the Mexican market rallied. The U.S. Treasury data is surprising because some large American mutual funds sold Mexican fixed-income securities heavily during early 1995. If there was net buying by U.S. investors, it must have resulted from dealers and hedge funds purchasing Mexican securities after their prices had fallen sharply. But since the Mexican government was projecting a current-account deficit of over $32 billion in 1995 and had to roll over $55 billion of maturing liabilities, the simple absence of net selling by foreign investors would not have been enough to ensure economic stability.

Mexico entered the final month of 1995 with only about $12 billion of foreign exchange reserves—compared with $29 billion one year before—and a projected current-account deficit in excess of $32 billion. When the reserves were severely depleted by a rush for dollars from Mexican investors, a crisis was unavoidable. Foreign investors may not have caused the peso to collapse, but a simple absence of buying by them turned the devaluation into a financial crisis because of the sheer scope of Mexico's need for external savings.

HOW MEXICO ATTRACTED SO MUCH CAPITAL

The Wall Street enthusiasm for Mexico during the early 1990s followed the pattern of many traditional investment manias. What began as a modest flow of money into a good opportunity attracted so much capital that it produced a self-reinforcing market boomlet that caused prices to rise sharply and thus made it difficult for investors to cope with bad news. Several factors encouraged American investors to flock to Mexico during the early 1990s—and then to experience profound disappointment when the peso was devalued at the end of 1994:

1. Many American investors were very excited about the revolution in economic policy that occurred under President Salinas, especially his support for the North American Free Trade Agreement (NAFTA). It was widely felt that Mexico had the opportunity to become a new Asian-style growth "tiger" driven by robust exports and much higher levels of foreign direct investment. Mexico's actual growth rate during the early 1990s remained quite modest (it averaged only 2.8 percent) compared with East Asia, but it was expected that growth would accelerate after NAFTA took effect. At the start of the 1990s, Mexican equities were also quite cheap compared with equities in other developing countries. In early 1990, the Mexican stock market sold at a price to earnings (P/E) multiple of 8.8 and a price to book value ratio of 0.92, whereas many East Asian markets had P/E multiples in the 20-30 range (the U.S. market has traditionally sold at a P/E multiple of 14-18). Many Mexican dollar bonds also offered interest rate premiums 300-400 basis points above U.S. securities.

2. The surge of foreign capital to Mexico's financial markets was reinforced by the general investor enthusiasm for the concept of "emerging markets." The end of the Cold War and the spread of liberal economic ideas to hitherto mercantilist developing countries persuaded investors that Latin America, Eastern Europe, and South Asia would be able to follow the example of the export-led economic takeoff established by East Asia during the 1970s and 1980s. Before 1989, only about one-fourth of the world's population had been living in market economies truly open to foreign trade and investment. After 1989, practically all countries had some form of market-based economic system and were receptive to foreign investment.

In 1988, there were 91 equity funds focusing on emerging markets with $6.1 billion of assets. Seventy-two of the funds, with $4.5 billion of assets, were focused on Asia, while four funds, with $520 million of assets, were focused on Latin America. The number of emerging-market funds mushroomed to 465 with $29 billion of assets in 1992, and to 820 funds with $123 billion of assets by 1994. Meanwhile, the number of Latin American funds expanded to 55 with $4.9 billion of assets in 1992 and to 105 with $14.7 billion of assets in 1994 (Table 4).

Total equity capital flows to emerging markets rose to a peak of $62.3 billion in 1993—compared to $21.2 billion in 1992, $15.9 billion in 1991, and $13.2 billion in 1990. The Institute of International Finance estimates that portfolio capital to developing-country emerging markets declined to $27.2 billion during 1995 and then rebounded to $48.2 billion in 1996. In the case of Latin America, equity capital flows rose from $9.9 billion in 1990 to a peak of $20 billion in 1993 and then slumped to only $4.0 billion during 1995.

3. A sharp decline in the level of U.S. interest rates during the early 1990s had increased the risk tolerance of U.S. investors. As a result of the real-estate lending crisis in the American banking system, the Federal Reserve had reduced money market yields from levels as high as 9-10 percent in 1989 to 3 percent by the end of 1992. With yields on U.S. assets so low, American investors were anxious to diversify their portfolios into higher-yield assets, and the fixed-income securities of developing countries became one of the favorite alternatives. Such a development was not unprecedented. After the Federal Reserve easing of the early 1980s, there had been a strong upsurge of demand for high-yield, low-grade U.S. corporate bonds (junk bonds). Under the leadership of Drexel Burnham, this market grew rapidly until the credit squeeze and recession of the early 1990s produced a sharp rise in the default rate. After 1992, there was a healthy rebound in the level of investor demand for high-yield corporate bonds as well as for the debt securities of developing countries.

What was unique about the early 1990s was the magnitude of the demand for Latin American paper. American retail and institutional investors had not purchased Latin American securities on

Table 4. Growth in Emerging-Market Mutual Funds

	1988		1989	
	Net Assets (U.S. $ millions)	Number of Funds	Net Assets (U.S. $ millions)	Number of Funds
EQUITIES	**5,857**	**91**	**9,975**	**142**
Global	900	15	1,350	18
Asia	4,437	72	7,435	112
Regional	1,750	35	3,100	50
China	47	2	50	2
Hong Kong	...	...	...	...
India	270	3	300	4
Indonesia	35	1	260	7
Korea	990	10	1,215	13
Malaysia and Singapore	75	3	240	7
Pakistan	—	—	—	—
Philippines	45	3	280	7
Sri Lanka	—	—	—	—
Taiwan	80	4	600	4
Thailand	845	11	1,390	18
Vietnam	—	—	—	—
Latin America	520	4	985	9
Regional	—	—	175	2
Argentina	—	—	—	—
Brazil	220	3	320	3
Chile	—	—	160	2
Colombia	—	—	—	—
Mexico	**300**	**1**	**330**	**2**
Peru	—	—	—	—
Europe	—	—	205	3
Regional	—	—	90	2
Turkey	—	—	115	1
Africa	—	—	—	—
BONDS	**275**	...	**500**	...
TOTAL FUNDS	**6,132**	...	**10,475**	...

Sources: Emerging Market Funds Research, Inc.; and Lipper Analytical Services, Inc.

Table 4, continued

1990		1991		1992		1993	
Net Assets (U.S. $ millions)	Number of Funds	Net Assets (U.S. $ millions)	Number of Funds	Net Assets (U.S. $ millions)	Number of Funds	Net Assets (U.S. $ millions)	Number of Funds
13,320	**225**	**19,180**	**290**	**29,535**	**465**	**73,043**	**573**
2,300	29	3,750	39	7,750	78	24,750	108
9,240	174	11,575	211	16,823	312	38,465	372
4,000	75	5,350	92	8,000	115	21,500	130
60	3	110	4	1,300	34	3,220	48
...	...	...	...	348	19	591	20
830	6	970	6	1,090	7	2,055	13
525	18	400	18	440	21	860	22
1,205	17	1,310	24	1,710	38	3,420	56
505	17	600	17	645	23	1,039	21
—	—	65	2	65	3	310	6
240	8	290	8	350	9	670	10
—	—	—	—	—	—	30	1
475	5	890	13	925	15	1,860	16
1,400	25	1,580	26	1,920	26	2,860	26
—	—	10	1	30	2	50	3
1,455	16	3,525	33	4,517	64	9,068	78
380	5	1,510	18	2,000	40	5,200	53
—	—	115	2	105	2	170	3
165	3	380	4	485	8	625	8
380	4	740	4	850	4	1,115	4
—	—	—	—	17	1	63	1
530	**4**	**780**	**5**	**1,040**	**8**	**1,865**	**8**
—	—	—	—	20	1	30	1
325	6	330	7	430	10	715	13
210	4	240	5	350	8	570	11
115	2	90	2	80	2	145	2
—	—	—	—	15	1	45	2
900	...	1,700	...	3,750	...	8,500	...
14,220	...	**20,880**	...	**33,285**	...	**81,543**	...

such a large scale for over half a century. (In the 1920s, U.S. retail investors had purchased a large volume of Latin American bonds because of the low yields on domestic securities and a policy of government support for capital outflows in order to promote exports. In that period, American commercial banks had also enjoyed stock brokering powers, and some took advantage of them by securitizing bad Latin American loans into bonds and selling them to naive retail investors. This was one of the factors that led to the enactment of the Glass Steagall law in 1933.) While the Mexican debacle of 1995 has led cynics to say that history repeated itself, the upsurge in U.S. demand for Latin American securities after 1990 was far more soundly based than the investment boomlet of the inter-war years. The 1990s upsurge in U.S. buying came after a period of debt restructuring and improvement in Latin American credit quality. It was also accompanied by a movement to the most far-reaching implementation of market-oriented policies in the region since the Great Depression, or, in the case of Mexico, since the Revolution of 1910. Finally, it is doubtful that the world economy will experience a slump on a scale comparable with the 1930s in the foreseeable future. It was that era's commodity price deflation that caused Latin America's default rate to rise so sharply.

4. The tremendous expansion that occurred in the size of the U.S. mutual fund industry and its share of total household savings also encouraged a strong upsurge of U.S. demand for Mexican and other Latin American securities during the early 1990s. As interest rates fell from 10 percent to 3 percent, American households shifted billions of dollars out of bank deposits and money market funds into equity and bond mutual funds. The assets of equity and bond mutual funds mushroomed from $550 billion in 1990 to over $2 trillion by the end of 1995. The securitization of retail savings in stock and bond funds vastly expanded the potential supply of capital available for investment in foreign security markets. The assets of mutual funds focused solely on foreign markets grew from a few billion dollars in the late 1980s to $116 billion in 1995, while global bond and equity funds had another $105 billion in assets. The rapid growth of defined-contribution pension-fund plans in the United States will continue to encourage further expansion of the mutual fund industry, including funds focused on foreign securities.

American pension funds also became active players in many developing-country security markets during the early 1990s. The U.S. pension fund sector began to diversify on a global basis during the mid-1980s, and the process accelerated during the 1990s as a result of academic research showing that such diversification would enhance return while reducing risk. According to Intersec Research, U.S. pension funds had $366 billion of foreign assets in late 1995 compared with $151 billion at the end of 1992. About $291 billion was invested in equities, while $62 billion was invested in fixed-income securities and $13 billion in balanced funds and derivatives. Net flows of pension fund money to global funds also has been more steady than the mutual fund flows to global managers. Between 1993 and 1995, the share of mutual fund cash flow going to international assets fell from 40 percent to 7 percent, while pension fund contributions to international funds have been holding in a range of $30-$40 billion per year. American pension funds now have about 7-8 percent of their total assets in foreign securities and typically allocate about 15 percent of those international assets to emerging markets. As the capitalization of the so-called emerging market countries is expanding far more rapidly than the capitalization of other countries, these weightings will probably increase further in the future.

As a result of the Mexican crisis, many commentators have suggested that securitized capital flows from mutual funds and pension funds are far more volatile and unpredictable than other forms of financial intermediation. While portfolio capital flows certainly have the potential to be volatile, there is no automatic reason why they have to behave more erratically than other forms of investment. On the contrary, the pool of capital held by institutions investing primarily in stocks and bonds, such as pension funds or mutual funds, is now expanding far more rapidly than any other form of savings. In the G-7 industrialized countries, pension fund assets exceed $12 trillion and are likely to expand significantly in the future. In the United States, Britain, and Switzerland, pension fund assets are now 50-70 percent of GDP, but in Japan, Germany, France, and other European countries, they are a much smaller share of GDP despite the fact that the population of those countries is aging rapidly (see Table 5). Successful developing countries are also boosting their savings rates by promoting the development of pension funds, but their populations are typically much younger than those of the old industrial countries. As the world financial system becomes more integrated, it would be natural for countries with older populations to lend some of their surplus savings to countries with younger populations, because the younger populations typically have greater investment needs. In fact, the primary role of the financial system in the old industrial countries is to recycle to young borrowers the savings of older people preparing for retirement. In the United States, for example, the Federal Reserve estimates that about 80 percent of all financial savings belongs to people over the age of 55, whereas most of the mortgage and installment debt belongs to younger people establishing families.

Table 5. Private Pension Fund Assets

Country	Assets (percent of GDP)
Switzerland	70
United Kingdom	60
United States	51
Netherlands	46
Sweden	33
Canada	32
Denmark	16
Japan	5
Germany	3

Source: Pension Funds, E.P. Davis.

The tremendous expansion of household wealth in the form of tax-deferred retirement savings also stands in sharp contrast with the poverty of the public sector in the old industrial countries. As a result of the growth in government-funded entitlement programs for retirement and health care, many industrial countries now have ratios of public debt to GDP as well as unfunded future entitlement claims two or three times as large as their current national income. The relative poverty of the public sector in the old industrial countries will thus further magnify the importance of private capital flows from pension funds and mutual funds in the post–Cold War global economy. At the end of World War II, by contrast, the ratio of government debt to GDP was 125 percent in the United States and 200 percent in the United Kingdom. The high levels of public-sector debt and unfunded entitlement programs in the old industrial countries today suggest that transfers of government assistance to finance economic development are going to remain at very modest levels compared with the official aid transfers that occurred during the first two decades after World War II. In 1994, the countries of the Organisation for Economic Co-operation and Development (OECD) spent about 0.3 percent of GDP on official aid transfers compared with numbers in the 0.5-0.6 percent range during the 1960s. In the

United States, aid spending has fallen from 0.55 percent of GDP to 0.15 percent, while Japan has increased its outlays from 0.22 percent of GDP to 0.29 percent. Some European countries still devote over 0.5 percent of GDP to official aid, but as these countries face major fiscal crises, it is unclear for how much longer spending can remain at such a high level. The relative poverty of the public sector in the old industrial countries will thus further magnify the importance of private capital flows from pension funds and mutual funds in the post–Cold War global economy compared with the period after World War II.

5. Another factor that helped to set the stage for the recent Mexican crisis was the inevitable tendency of Wall Street firms to create such large marketing and trading infrastructures for their new emerging-market products that some felt compelled to oversell the concept. Before 1991, there was practically no coverage of Latin American stock markets by Wall Street research departments, while a significant portion of the research on Asia came from British firms with long-standing links to Hong Kong and Singapore. As investor interest in emerging markets developed, Wall Street created new groups of traders, analysts, and investment bankers to accommodate it. Although the establishment of research departments should have encouraged more sophisticated decision-making, it also produced the "moral hazard" problems of high overhead costs encouraging excessive competition for transaction fees. In 1994, Wall Street had to generate the trading revenue and transactions fees from its new emerging-market departments to maintain profitability in the face of a severe global bear market in bonds and a slump in its other traditional business lines. As doubts about Mexico's economy began to mount during 1994, investment bankers sometimes lobbied analysts and strategists to remain optimistic in order to protect their firms' deal flow. In 1994, Bear Stearns even took public on the New York Stock Exchange a Mexican bank, Banpais, with such a poor reputation that it would have been difficult to obtain new equity capital for the institution in Mexico itself. (Banpais was seized by the government in March 1995 because of concerns about accounting irregularities and management integrity.)

Wall Street perceptions of how to define appropriate financial risk for retail and institutional investors are never static. After long periods of low interest rates and buoyant equity markets, the appetite for risk increases. After prolonged bear markets, investors are usually very cautious. The volatility of U.S. interest rates in the 1980s and early 1990s produced major fluctuations in the appetite of American investors for risk. In the mid-1980s, the sudden collapse of short-term interest rates left the American investing public very dissatisfied with the low returns available on the money market funds that had mushroomed in size during the Volcker monetary squeeze of the early 1980s. Hence they diverted large sums of money into the high-yield, low-grade domestic bond funds promoted by Drexel Burnham and other Wall Street firms.

The search for higher yields also produced a brief flurry of demand for Australian bonds because they, too, offered yields several hundred basis points above the yields available on U.S. bonds, and most American investors perceived Australia to be a stable Anglo-Saxon country with good economic prospects. In 1986, Prudential Bache Securities launched a new Australian bond fund in order to capitalize on this search for higher yields and hoped to raise a few hundred million dollars. Instead it stunned both Wall Street and Australia by attracting nearly $1 billion of retail savings, setting a record for fund-raising by a new investment trust. But, sadly for the buyers, the fund launch coincided with a sharp decline in commodity prices and Australia's terms of trade, which caused the country's current-account deficit to rise sharply. When Finance Minister Paul Keating compared Australia's deteriorating balance-of-payments position with that of a banana republic, the Australian dollar plunged from 0.73 at the time of the fund launch to 0.59 a few months later. There were lawsuits from a few shareholders to protest the price decline, but such complaints faded when commodity prices and the Australian dollar rallied in the late 1980s.

As Australia is classified as an OECD member country, its experience with volatile securitized capital inflows was largely forgotten by 1990, but there are a number of striking analogies between the recent Mexican crisis and the volatility of Australia's capital account during the late 1980s. In 1983, the new Hawke government launched an economic reform program that included floating the Australian dollar, abolition of most capital controls, and deregulation of the financial system. Despite a declining budget deficit in the late 1980s, there was a large current-account deficit because of an upsurge in private investment encouraged partly by the aggressive lending policies of the sixteen foreign banks that had entered the domestic marketplace after the country liberalized the financial system. As commodity prices were depressed until the late 1980s, much of this bank lending financed an upsurge of corporate takeover activity, not an expansion of the country's traditional export-generating industries. The central bank raised interest rates in order to restrain inflation, but financial deregulation encouraged such intense competition to make loans that the credit boom continued until there were highly publicized corporate bankruptcies. As a result of the high natural resource content of its exports, Australia has long experienced cyclical volatility in its economy, and commodity-driven changes in its terms of trade. But what was instructive about the Australian experience of the 1980s was the capacity of the private banking sector to engage in such high-risk lending policies that it produced a large current-account deficit in the face of cautious fiscal policies. The resulting capital inflows also produced a period of exchange-rate overvaluation that boosted consumption at the expense of exports and profits in the country's tradable goods industries.

Like Australia, Mexico did not have a large government deficit during the early 1990s, but its newly privatized financial institutions did expand credit very aggressively and worked closely with Wall Street securities firms to import large amounts of capital for use by Mexico's corporate and household sectors. The private bank credit share of GDP rose from 10 percent to 40 percent in five years. The lesson from both countries is that governments cannot always assume that the private sector will make sensible decisions about resource allocation when the financial system is suddenly liberalized after a long period of controls. In such circumstances, there will often be pent-up credit demand (which Mexico clearly had), or bankers may feel compelled to fight for market share by lowering credit quality standards (as happened in Australia). The tragedy of Mexico is that its policy-makers learned little from the great banking crises that had engulfed the United States, Australia, Sweden, and other countries as it began the privatization of its banking system during 1991.

6. A sixth factor encouraging the large flows of private capital to Mexico during the early 1990s was the excellent salesmanship of senior Mexican economic officials—especially President Salinas and Secretary of Finance Pedro Aspe, a polished and articulate spokesman for the country's reform program. Like Australia's Paul Keating in the mid-1980s, Aspe was named Finance Minister of the Year by *Euromoney* and was a highly acclaimed speaker at many international investment conferences. With the expansion of capital flows to Mexico, he increasingly came to resemble a corporate chief financial officer taking direct responsibility for investor relations during periods of uncertainty by holding conference calls with large investment institutions. When fund managers had doubts about Mexico's policy contradictions, they found solace chatting with him. His trips to New York were often followed by peso rallies. When investors were unwilling to purchase peso-denominated securities at moderate interest rates after the assassination of presidential candidate Colosio, he collaborated with Wall Street to create the new dollar-linked *tesobono* instrument, which became very popular in the months before the devaluation. His departure in December 1994 created a great vacuum because the new Secretary of Finance, Jaime Serra, did not have Aspe's personal experience managing investor confidence.

There is no way of telling whether the retention of Pedro Aspe as Secretary of Finance during the early months of the Zedillo administration would have altered the timing of Mexico's devaluation and its subsequent negative impact on investor confidence. Aspe undoubtedly would have been more sensitive to their perceptions of what was happening in Mexico during late 1994 than officials arriving for the first time. But his retention would not have eliminated the economic imbalances that threatened investor confidence in the peso, especially the low level of foreign exchange reserves compared with the country's projected current-account deficit and short-term dollar liabilities. Instead, Aspe probably would have pursued a strategy of using his personal capital with investors to play for time. As reserves dwindled, he most likely would have sought U.S. Treasury assistance to defend the peso's existing target band while developing a new economic package for enhancing the investment appeal of Mexico as the central bank moved toward a wider target band for the peso or simply floated the currency. Aspe would not have prevented a devaluation, but in trying to guide the adjustment process through well-timed announcements of new economic initiatives focused on foreign investor confidence, he probably could have prevented Mexican interest-rate risk premiums from rising to levels that forced the economy into a far more severe recession than was justified on the basis of the country's economic potential after the enactment of NAFTA.

EMERGING MARKETS AFTER THE MEXICAN CRISIS

After Mexico defaulted on its dollar obligations in 1982, it did not regain access to the international financial markets for seven years. In early 1995, Mexico came close to defaulting on its *tesobono* securities, but an emergency loan from the U.S. Treasury and the IMF replenished its foreign exchange reserves in time to prevent such an outcome. The total aid package was the largest international financial assistance program since the Marshall Plan. As a result of the support showed by the IMF and the U.S. Treasury, Mexico was able to resume borrowing from the international markets only six months after the peso devaluation.

DEBATE ON THE AID PACKAGE

There has been great controversy about whether the Mexican default risk in early 1995 constituted a systemic threat to the international financial markets that justified official intervention by a lender of last resort such as the IMF. Some argue that the bailout created new moral hazard problems by rescuing investors who had purchased *tesobono* securities with a high yield because they contained some element of default risk. Others contend that Mexico should simply have defaulted on its dollar-linked debt and regressed to a more mercantilist economic policy with capital controls in order to escape from the severe recession that engulfed the economy despite the IMF–U.S. Treasury loan.

There were several good arguments for the U.S. Treasury and the IMF to help Mexico avoid the problems of investor perception that would have resulted from a formal default:

1. Because Mexico was one of the pioneers of market-oriented economic reform in the Third World during the late 1980s, a default would have had a much greater psychological impact on the economic reform process in other developing countries than a default by a smaller country or one pursuing irresponsible economic policies, such as Venezuela. In the weeks after the crisis, officials in countries as diverse as Korea and India cited the Mexican crisis as a reason to slow their own economic liberalization programs. While no country has reversed its economic reforms because of the Mexican crisis, the opponents of liberalization might have been more successful if Mexico had actually gone into default and lost access to the international capital markets again for a prolonged period.

2. If Mexico had defaulted, the so-called "tequila effect" of investors liquidating securities in other emerging-market countries might have gone further, producing even larger interest-rate hikes than actually occurred in Argentina, Brazil, the Philippines, and other developing countries with large current-account deficits. There was no logical reason for investors to sell the securities of the Philippines or Poland because of a crisis in Mexico—but it is certain that the trading losses on the bonds of a country as important as Mexico had major negative effects on the liquidity of the whole market for developing-country debt. It should also be noted that most emerging-market trading departments in early 1995 were less than four years old and were often staffed by people who had only experienced rising asset prices. A Mexican default would have curtailed the upsurge of bank lending to developing countries that occurred in 1995.

3. The factors that led to the Mexican crisis had such a large political content that one can argue they justified a political response from the United States and the IMF. In contrast with the early 1980s, Mexico was not running large fiscal deficits or practicing inflationary monetary policies. It is true that the government boosted spending and development lending during the run-up to the election, and that the central bank offset the loss of foreign exchange reserves with faster growth of the domestic monetary base, but the budget deficit remained modest, and interest rates increased by several hundred basis points after the Colosio assassination. It is doubtful that concerns about monetary and fiscal policy alone would have provoked a suspension of capital flows or encouraged large capital outflows by Mexicans without the shock of political assassinations and the Chiapas insurgency. Mexico had not experienced such political shocks since the 1920s, so they had an unnerving impact on domestic investor confidence, not just foreign investor attitudes. This investor apprehension also was magnified by the fact that such events coincided with the inauguration of a new president who had not even been on the original short list of contenders for the presidency before the selection of Colosio in November 1993.

Investor interest in developing-country debt and equity markets would have recovered at some point even if Mexico had defaulted during early 1995. The economic attractions of the developing countries for growth-oriented equity investors and yield-oriented, fixed-income investors are so compelling that they would have overcome the shock of a Mexican default. At present, developing-country equity markets account for only about 15 percent of world stock market capitalization, whereas the same countries account for over 40 percent of world output, 70 percent of the world's land area, and 85 percent of the world's population. The gap between the developing countries' market capitalization and their factor endowments should shrink dramatically in the future as the economies develop further. In fact, several East Asian countries already have ratios of stock market capitalization to GDP well in excess of 100 percent. But there can be no doubt that a Mexican default in early 1995 would have generated major shock effects in other countries and probably slowed the integration of developing-country financial markets into the world financial system by at least two or three years.

LESSONS FOR INVESTORS

Since the Mexican rescue package was announced, there has been extensive discussion about establishing a new framework for restructuring securitized sovereign debt during periods of

Table 6. Emerging-Market "Meltdowns" (Stock Indices)

Country	Peak	Trough	Decline	Recovered to Prior Peaks	Jan. 95 Level
Argentina	939 (2/80)	40 (5/85)	-96	6 yrs., 3 mos. (8/91)	1582
	682 (6/89)	239 (7/89)	-65	2 yrs., 1 mo. (8/91)	1582
	2256 (5/92)	1040 (11/92)	-54	2 yrs., 2 mos. (1/94)	1582
Brazil	314 (4/86)	54 (12/87)	-83	5 yrs., 11 mos. (11/93)	497
	78 (5/82)	38 (5/83)	-51	1 yr., 6 mos. (11/84)	497
Hong Kong	1297 (3/73)	125 (11/74)	-90	13 yrs., 11 mos. (2/87)	4076
	1198 (11/80)	334 (9/83)	-72	6 yrs., 1 mo. (12/86)	4076
Indonesia	150 (3/90)	51 (10/91)	-66	not yet	93.3
Mexico	**377 (4/79)**	**54 (3/83)**	**-86**	**4 yrs. (3/87)**	**1583**
	998 (9/87)	**222 (12/87)**	**-76**	**2 yrs., 4 mos. (4/90)**	**1583**
	4208 (1/94)	**1583 (1/95)**	**-62**	**not yet**	**1583**
Taiwan	1829 (1/90)	418 (9/90)	-77	not yet	1028
Turkey	1678 (7/90)	225 (11/92)	-87	not yet	409
	759 (12/93)	237 (4/94)	-69	not yet	409
Venezuela	984 (2/92)	390 (3/93)	-60	not yet	341
	201 (2/88)	82 (1/90)	-59	6 mos. (7/90)	341
	146 (11/85)	63 (2/86)	-57	1 yr. (2/87)	341

Source: Morgan Stanley Research, IFC, and MSCI (Hong Kong).

economic crisis—much as U.S. corporations restructure under the bankruptcy law. It is more difficult to restructure bonds than commercial bank loans because of the large number of potential players involved, but in view of the dramatic growth now occurring in securitized forms of lending and investment in developing countries, the odds are high that during the next global economic slump there will be financial accidents requiring both governments and companies to restructure some of their debt.

As even a simple discussion of restructuring alternatives would make it difficult for some highly indebted countries to import capital, it is doubtful that there will be a consensus about the optimal formula for resolving future liquidity or solvency problems with securitized lenders until the next global economic slump forces action. During the interim, private investors themselves will attempt to avoid a repetition of the Mexican experience by focusing more carefully on the vulnerabilities in the post–Cold War global financial system that the Mexican crisis has illustrated.

1. Investors will now pay far more attention to *the structure of a country's capital account and the quality of the capital flows financing its external deficit.* What are the levels of foreign direct investment, commercial bank lending, and securitized forms of capital inflow compared with the current-account deficit? What is the distribution of the securitized capital flows between equity, short-term debt, and long-term bonds? How stable are the funding sources of the institutions that are purchasing the securitized debt of the developing countries? Are they long-term investors with stable cash flows, such as pension funds, or are they mutual funds, which could suffer redemptions if there were a sudden deterioration in their investment performance?

In retrospect, Mexico was highly vulnerable to a funding crisis because it financed over 70 percent of its external deficit through the sales of bonds and equities to foreign investors. A large share of the capital also came from mutual funds, which were vulnerable to redemptions if their performance suffered as a result of some financial shock. It also could be argued that the heavy reliance on U.S. mutual funds created an extra element of jeopardy, since the United States itself does not have any surplus savings. Like all countries in the Western Hemisphere, the United States is an external debtor and capital importer. American investment firms were able to purchase Mexican securities because the United States was able to sell a large volume of securities to foreign investors or to borrow heavily from the Bank of Japan during the early and mid-1990s.

The recent financial crisis in East Asia resulted from a different form of financial intermediation than Mexico's. During the past decade, the countries of East Asia have relied far more heavily on bank lending and direct investment to finance their external deficits. Portfolio capital flows accounted for only about 20-30 percent of their external fund raising. As a result of the exchange rate peg that many Asian countries had with the U.S. dollar, their local corporations borrowed heavily in dollars in order to reduce their cost of capital. Such borrowing was attractive when exchange rates were stable, but after the devaluation of the Thai baht in July 1997, it helped to set in motion a financial crisis that quickly got out of control. Once Asian companies realized their exchange rates were vulnerable, they rushed to hedge their dollar exposure and generated a cascading wave of selling pressure that caused Asian currencies to overshoot massively on the downside. The Malaysian ringitt fell from 2.6 to almost 5.0 to the dollar. The Indonesian rupiah plunged from 2,300 to over 15,000 to the dollar. The Korean won fell from 800 to 2,000 to the dollar. The Thai baht slumped from 26 to 55. As the Asian countries had had moderate ratios of external debt to GDP, few investors had perceived them to be as vulnerable as Mexico in 1994. But the large volume of short-maturity dollar debt that Asian firms had accumulated produced a liquidity crisis that quickly evolved into a solvency crisis.

2. Another issue that investors will study more carefully because of the Mexican and the East Asian crises is *the quality of a country's bank supervision.* Does the country have a long tradition of strong commercial banks, or were the banks privatized very recently? Is the banking marketplace open to foreign competition, or is it a local cartel? If the market is being opened to foreign competition, will the local banks be able to maintain profitability without undermining their credit quality? If the banking sector was state-owned, did the government ration credit through interest rates or through lending controls that have created a large, pent-up demand for credit? The lesson from the United States, Australia, and Mexico during the past decade is that bank deregulation and privatization require enhanced financial supervision to deal with the risk that excessive lending competition will depress credit quality standards and create significant resource misallocation in favor of domestic consumption sectors such as property development.

3. A third issue that investors will scrutinize more carefully is *the nature of the country's monetary regime.* Does the central bank have true autonomy, or is it easily manipulated by politicians? Does the central bank have a coherent framework for achieving economic growth with low inflation compared with the government's fiscal policy and other economic objectives? If the central bank is pursuing an exchange rate target, how much support does it enjoy from the business community and other groups sensitive to the level of the exchange rate? If the country is pursuing its exchange rate target through a currency board, does the banking system have sufficient strength to survive the interest-rate shocks that might periodically occur as the system is tested by volatility in capital flows? What is the quality and transparency of the data flow from the country's monetary institutions?

There is no consensus among economists about the optimal monetary regime for developing countries, because the feasibility of each model depends so heavily upon historical circumstances. Argentina has been able to retain its currency board in the face of severe austerity, because its history of hyperinflation had a profound impact on public attitudes toward the policy trade-offs between growth and inflation. Mexico suffered from severe inflation crises three times in the modern era, but most analysts believe that it should still attempt to operate an independent central bank focused on domestic economic indicators, such as inflation, and not switch to an Argentina-style currency board. Yet the success of the Argentine system in the face of the 1995 shocks will probably invite investors to become more supportive of the currency board concept for Mexico and other developing countries. Mexico is becoming so heavily integrated with the U.S. economy that there are more compelling arguments for Mexico to link its exchange rate to the dollar through a currency board than there are for Argentina to do so. It also should be noted that during the last great era of securitized capital flows between rich and poor countries, most nations had a fixed exchange rate link to the gold standard.

The revival of securitized capital flows via debt and equity markets will inevitably force developing countries to view their exchange-rate policy from the perspective of financial competitiveness and not just commercial competitiveness. Most economists continue to regard exchange-rate policy as a sub-component of trade policy, but the tremendous growth now occurring in securitized capital flows suggest that promoting investor confidence will become a more important factor for exchange-rate policy than it has been at any time since the breakdown of the Bretton Woods system or the pre-1914 gold standard.

4. A fourth factor that investors will attempt to monitor more carefully as a result of the Mexican crisis is *the behavior of a country's local investors.* In recent months, both the IMF and private analysts have suggested that the Mexican crisis resulted from capital flight by local investors—not from selling by foreign mutual funds. It is difficult to quantify capital flight, but the Bank Credit Analyst (BCA) of Montreal has attempted to measure it by examining the Bank of International Settlements (BIS) data on bank deposit holdings by countries as well as changes in official measures of capital flows, service trade, and foreign exchange reserves (see Table 10). The BCA found that the return of flight capital to Latin America played a major role in driving equity prices higher during the early 1990s while a resumption of capital flight contributed to the exhaustion of Mexico's foreign exchange reserves during late 1994. As a result, the BCA warned that it would be difficult for the Latin American equity markets to enjoy a sustained recovery unless local investor confidence also recovered.

238

In the case of the great Asian financial crisis of 1997, local borrowers also played the decisive role in generating massive selling pressure on local currencies. When exchange rate expectations suddenly changed, local corporations felt compelled to cover their dollar liabilities and set in motion a wave of selling that was too powerful to be contained by speculative buying from other investors.

5. A final factor that investors will focus upon more carefully as a result of the Mexican crisis is *a country's potential access to a lender of last resort in the event that it experiences a funding crisis*. The United States offered swap lines to Mexico during 1994 and then lobbied for a large IMF loan package during early 1995 because of the close relationship that it has developed with Mexico as a result of NAFTA and a 2,000-mile land frontier. Some European countries resented the special treatment for Mexico (its loan was three times larger than any previous IMF credit), but the United States had sufficient power to impose its will on the IMF board.

ASIAN POSTSCRIPT

One of the factors that caused the Asian crisis to get out of control during 1997 was the failure of the United States to play a decisive role at an early stage of the crisis. As a result of the congressional hostility to the Mexican loan in 1995, the U.S. Treasury was unable to use the Exchange Stabilization Fund to contribute to the Thai rescue package. Japan contributed $4 billion to the Thai loan, but since Japan has such large direct investment and banking exposure to Thailand, many investors had expected it to play a larger role. The United States did offer a modest contribution to the Indonesia loan program because of the expiration of the congressional restrictions on the Exchange Stabilization Fund, but the United States was not viewed as a major player. When Korea began to experience a bank run and turned to the IMF for help, the United States also stressed that it would play only a secondary role in the support operation. It was not until Korea's foreign exchange reserves were nearly exhausted that the United States acted decisively to provide support and use moral suasion over its commercial banks in order to prevent a formal default. The U.S. government was able to rationalize its intervention in Korea partly on national security grounds—because it has nearly 40,000 troops there. Investors will conclude from the U.S. approach to the crisis that American lending will always have a political as well as an economic agenda attached to it.

The great surprise of the Asian crisis in 1997 was the unwillingness of Japan to play a more decisive role. During 1995 and 1996, Japanese officials had often stressed the need for more regional monetary cooperation. They also supported a protocol among several Asian central banks pledging to recycle liquidity during periods of crisis. But as the Thai crisis evolved, Japan was prepared to offer only moderate bilateral assistance within the framework of a traditional IMF program. Japan later proposed the establishment of a regional monetary fund to help troubled countries but withdrew the proposal when the U.S. government stressed the need for collaboration through the IMF.

What now remains to be seen is whether the IMF will be able to obtain additional funding to support its new role as lender of last resort to developing countries. In early 1997, the industrial countries planned to expand the IMF's capital through a New Agreement to Borrow, but the U.S. Congress has refused to enact the legislation. As a result, the IMF now has a high level of resource utilization and would not be able to duplicate its recent upsurge of emergency lending to East Asia. The scope of the East Asian crisis demonstrates even more clearly than the Latin American crisis of 1995 that the developing countries need a lender of last resort. But since there are still great philosophical disagreements about the role of the IMF and the moral hazard risks that it creates for lenders, it is far from clear that it will obtain the funding needed to play an effective role in the future.

CONCLUSION

The economic slump that engulfed Mexico after the late 1994 peso devaluation was the first major test of the international economic order created by the end of the Cold War and the spread of liberal economic ideas to developing countries. The U.S. Treasury and the IMF intervened to prevent Mexico's liquidity crisis from forcing a default on its dollar-linked government securities, but they could not prevent the country from experiencing one of the most severe economic slumps to occur in Latin America during the modern era. The magnitude of the Mexican recession shocked everyone because of the international acclaim that the country enjoyed only two years earlier, but it is precisely because everyone underestimated Mexico's potential vulnerability to a liquidity crisis that the downturn was so severe.

Mexico financed a large current-account deficit for nearly five years through the sale of corporate equities and government bonds to foreign investors. No developing country had depended so heavily upon securitized capital flows to finance a large external deficit since the last great age of global capitalism before 1914. It was never inevitable that Mexico would experience a liquidity crisis; one occurred because of the interaction of several factors converging at the same time, including a tumultuous presidential election year, the assassination of two reform-minded politicians, a sharp rise in the level of U.S. interest rates, steady deterioration in the quality of Mexican bank loan portfolios, and the retirement of the Finance Minister who had played a major role in persuading global fund mangers to purchase over $75 billion in Mexican securities. Mexico was also importing most of its capital from a country that was itself savings deficient and thus had to recycle the surplus savings of East Asia and Europe. In fact, every country in the Western Hemisphere is a net external debtor.

Policy-makers are still debating the implications of the Mexican crisis for the role of the IMF and other potential lenders of last resort. In 1995, the IMF expanded its lending to $51 billion, or the highest level since 1985. The Fund's new disbursements during 1995 were the largest ever; in contrast with previous years, however, they were heavily concentrated in only three countries: Mexico, Argentina, and Russia. These countries absorbed over 90 percent of new loans during 1995 compared with a previous peak for loan concentration of 37 percent in 1983, when the largest recipients were Argentina, Brazil, and India. IMF Managing Director Michel Camdessus has been lobbying for expanded IMF capital since early 1994, and the Mexican crisis has increased the credibility of his arguments, but it will be difficult to obtain any additional IMF funding from the current U.S. Congress.

As a result of the constraints on expanding the IMF's role, the major impact of the Mexican crisis will be on how private investors adjust their behavior to the perceived lessons from Mexico's recent experience. In the future, they will be far more sensitive to the composition of a country's capital inflows, the quality of its banking regulation, and the level of its foreign-exchange reserves compared to both the size of the current-account deficit and the magnitude of foreign currency debt maturing within one year. They will also focus more attention on the country's potential access to a lender of last resort in the event of a liquidity crisis.

The level of private capital flows to emerging markets plunged to only $27.2 billion during 1995 from over $62 billion two years earlier as a result of the Mexican crisis, but with the Latin American economies stabilizing and the G-7 countries easing monetary policy again, there should be a rebound in private capital flows to emerging market countries during 1996. The developing countries still account for only about 15 percent of world stock market capitalization, despite the fact that they represent 40 percent of world output, 70 percent of the world's land area, and 85 percent of its population. They should be able to offer very attractive investment returns as their level of stock market capitalization catches up with their economic potential. Mexico has also boosted its non-oil export share of GDP to 30 percent from 5 percent in the 1980s, and the total current-account deficit of Latin America will be 2 percent of GDP in 1996 compared with 3.5 percent two years earlier.

While the Mexican crisis has demonstrated the potential vulnerabilities of financing a large current-account deficit primarily through the sale of securities, it is difficult to imagine the importance of securitized capital flows in the world financial system diminishing. The value of assets in the pension funds of the old industrial countries now exceeds $12 trillion and is growing steadily. The U.S. household sector now has more assets in equity and bond mutual funds than bank deposits, and the role of the mutual fund sector is likely to expand further because of the increasing importance of defined-contribution retirement programs. The developing countries are themselves also trying to bolster their savings rates by creating new retirement saving programs. This trend will increase the importance of securities markets for domestic savers, not just for foreign investors.

The challenge now facing developing countries is not merely to attract a respectable share of the world's expanding stock of securitized foreign investment. It is also to develop effective monetary policies for coping with potential volatility resulting from exogenous shocks beyond their control, such as rising U.S. interest rates, or political assassinations. Chile has distinguished itself from other developing countries by maintaining official controls on the magnitude of portfolio capital inflows. Countries that want to pursue more liberal financial policies may have to expand their stock of foreign exchange reserves if they have a capital account dominated by portfolio capital flows rather than foreign direct investment.

During the last great age of securitized capital flows, there was far more commonality of economic institutions between capital-exporting and capital-importing nations than existed subsequently between 1914 and 1989. Much of Africa and Asia were under European colonial rule. In the Western Hemisphere, Japan, and the self-governing dominions of the British Empire, there was a general acceptance of market-oriented economic systems, private property, and the gold standard as a guardian of monetary stability. Despite this commonality of institutions, though, there were periodic interruptions in the flow of capital resulting from political and economic shocks, such as the impact of the Franco-Prussian War on European interest rates, opposition to the gold standard in countries with large agricultural populations suffering from depressed commodity prices, and revolutions in Latin America that led to defaults on securities widely owned by foreign investors. The level of world commodity prices fell by 40 percent in the late nineteenth century and created a far less benign economic environment than exists today for countries with large agricultural and mineral producing sectors. But despite such shocks, the flow of capital between rich and poor nations never ceased for a prolonged period. In the years before the outbreak of World War I, Britain was exporting capital on a scale approaching 9 percent of GDP, while France and Germany were becoming increasingly more important foreign investors. British foreign investment was equal to about 140 percent of that country's national income, while French foreign investment was close to 100 percent of GDP. What shattered the last great age of global financial integration was not economic failure but a European civil war that began in 1914 and persisted in various forms until the collapse of Nazi Germany in 1945.

As a result of the political shocks resulting from the two World Wars and the Great Depression in the period between them, the process of global economic integration broke down. Communist revolutionaries took over Russia in 1917 and China in 1949. After the dismantling of the European colonial empires, nearly two-thirds of humankind lived under economic systems characterized by state domination, including severe restrictions on foreign trade and investment. Although Latin America emerged from World War II with large foreign exchange reserves and eight of the world's nine convertible currencies, its political elites also joined the trend toward an expanded government role in the economy and trade policies focused on import substitution.

But since the collapse of communism and the acceptance of liberal economic ideas by developing countries six years ago, the private sector in both the industrial and the developing countries has been rapidly re-creating the global marketplace for goods and capital that existed before 1914. Mexico's near default in early 1995 threatened to slow this process by undermining one of the star role models of economic liberalization. So far, however, both Mexico and most other Latin American countries have responded to the crisis by reaffirming their commitment to market-oriented economic reform. The debate of the more recent past in Mexico has not been about whether President Salinas was right to pursue NAFTA and dismantle Mexico's traditional barriers to foreign trade and investment. It

Table 7. The Role of Foreign Direct Investment
in World Economic Activity, Selected Years

	1913	1960	1975	1980	1985	1991
World FDI Stock as a Share of World Output	9.0[a]	4.4	4.5	4.8	6.4	8.5
World FDI Inflows as a Share of World Output	—	0.3	0.3	0.5	0.5	0.7
World FDI Inflows as a Share of World Gross Fixed Capital Formation	—	1.1	1.4	2.0	1.8	3.5
World Sales of Foreign Affiliates as a Share of World Exports	—	84[b]	97[c]	99[d]	99[d]	122

[a] Estimate.
[b] 1967 based on United States figures.
[c] Based on United States and Japanese figures.
[d] 1982 based on German, Japanese, and United States data.

Source: Deutsche Morgan Grenfell, based on United Nations Conference on Trade & Development Division on Transnational Corporations and Investment, *World Investment Report 1994.*

has instead focused on the policy lessons that the crisis has to offer about how to manage the exchange rate, promote effective supervision of the banking system, diversify capital inflows, and enhance the credibility of monetary policy. If any analysts could have predicted the severity of Mexico's recession five years ago, they would almost certainly have expected Mexico to renounce NAFTA and return to a mercantilist economic policy. As a result, the historians of the early twenty-first century will probably look upon the Mexican crisis of 1994-95 as not only the first great financial shock of the post–Cold War international economic order but also as the crisis that confirmed the enduring nature of the liberal revolution in economic ideology that swept through the Third World at the end of the 1980s. It was easy for Mexico's politicians to defend market-oriented economic ideas when their economy was booming. It is the resilience of those ideas in the face of 10 percent GDP contraction that demonstrates the magnitude of the intellectual transformation that has occurred in Mexico and other Latin American nations since the end of the Cold War.

REFERENCES AND BIBLIOGRAPHY

Gay, Robert S. (1994). "Looking Beyond the Haze into 1995." *Perspectives on Emerging Markets*. Bankers Trust Research. November 7.

Malpass, David (1994). *Latin America Outlook 1995*. Bear Stearns Global Development. November 16.

Schonander, Lars (1994). *Latin America Economic Overview*. Baring Securities. September.

Skiles, Marilyn E. (1994). "Financing Mexico's Current Account." *Economic Research Note*. J.P. Morgan. November 18.

Meltzer, Alan (1996). *A Mexican Tragedy*. Washington, D.C.: American Enterprise Institute. January.

9. A FATE FORETOLD: THE WORLD BANK AND THE MEXICAN CRISIS*

SHAHID JAVED BURKI

INTRODUCTION

For the World Bank as for the many other institutions represented in this volume, the Mexico crisis was a pivotal event. The Bank was, rightly, seen as intimately involved in the Mexican reform effort, and therefore as implicated when the financial crisis struck. As other contributors have extensively analyzed the economic and political sources of the crisis, I will focus particularly on the economic dialogue between the Bank and Mexico in the period leading up to and including the crisis. My purpose in doing so is to illustrate the difficulties and dilemmas that necessarily arise in handling sensitive relationships with governments on the one hand, and with the public and financial markets on the other. I hope that this narrative will also shed light on the range of instruments and resources that the World Bank uses in its intellectual interaction with countries—a process that is not always well understood.

To summarize the conclusions of the paper, I believe that the Bank's analysts clearly identified the medium-term financial risks facing Mexico and successfully mobilized the institution to communicate their concerns to the Mexicans. But the Bank was not able to persuade the authorities to change course, nor were we willing to risk destabilizing financial markets through a forthright public critique of Mexican policy. The Bank's guarded public attempts to point out the vulnerability in the Mexican situation were largely ignored by both the markets and the Mexicans.

---

* This paper draws on an unpublished review undertaken by Sebastian Edwards while he was Chief Economist for the Latin America and the Caribbean (LAC) Regional Office of the World Bank. All interpretations are, however, entirely mine, and should not be attributed in any manner to the World Bank or its affiliated organizations, or to members of its Board of Executive Directors or the countries they represent.

247

The above comments are not intended to imply that the Bank's analyses were perfect. Like many others, we missed the full implications of some developments in 1994: the increasing use of *tesobonos* (treasury debt indexed to the U.S. dollar), the expansion of credit, and the sharp loss of reserves at the end of the year.

I have come to call the Bank's behavior during the pre-crisis period "speaking with two voices." With its first voice, the Bank was strong and clear in communicating its concerns to the Mexican authorities; of this I have no doubt. With its more muted second voice, the Bank aimed to reassure financial markets by stressing Mexico's very real accomplishments in an attempt to buy time for Mexico to complete the process of adjustment on which it had embarked. Even with the benefit of hindsight, it is difficult to see how these two voices could have become more unified, desirable though this might have been.

THE REFORM EFFORT

The World Bank was involved with the Mexican reform effort essentially from the beginning. From the mid-1980s on, Bank staff maintained a fruitful and frank dialogue with the Mexican authorities and assisted them in a number of programs, including the trade reform process. By assigning some of its strongest professionals to work on Mexico, the Bank signaled its degree of commitment to the reform program. This was clearly appreciated by the authorities during the de la Madrid administration and, after 1988, by the Salinas government.

Despite a vigorous reform effort, and the benefits of debt reduction under the Brady Plan, the actual performance of the Mexican economy was rather modest. Real growth between 1988 and 1994 averaged 2.8 percent—significantly lower than that of Chile (7.1 percent) or Colombia (4.1 percent), for example. Productivity growth was almost flat until 1993; export expansion was not overly impressive; real wages, while increasing, barely regained their 1980 level; the real exchange rate appreciated significantly; private savings experienced a major decline; and poverty and income distribution continued to be serious problems. On the positive side, fiscal balance was attained in 1992; inflation was reduced to single digits; and the reforms dismantled successive layers of protection and regulation.

Despite this divergence between Mexico's achievements in terms of reform *policies* and economic *results*, Mexico was consistently praised by the media, financial experts, academics, and the multilateral institutions as a major success. It is sometimes suggested that a Mexican "miracle" was, at least in part, invented by these institutions. This enthusiasm was the consequence of a number of factors. The most important, perhaps, was the tremendous faith that many analysts had in market-oriented reforms; if results were not visible, many argued, they were around the corner. Paul Krugman has commented that much of the hoopla on Mexico's prospects represented a "leap of faith, rather than a conclusion based on hard evidence."[1] The U.S. administration's efforts to persuade the public and Congress of the benefits of the North American Free Trade Agreement (NAFTA) also contributed to the popular notion that there was a Mexican "miracle."[2]

THE BUILD-UP TO THE CRISIS: 1990-93

In analyzing the crisis, it is useful to distinguish between two periods: 1990 to 1993, when the economy became increasingly vulnerable; and 1994, when external and domestic political shocks precipitated the collapse of the peso. Mexico was in fact seen to be growing vulnerable to unfavorable external developments as far back as the early 1990s. Among factors at play, the most important were the real appreciation of the peso, the very large current-account deficit financed by massive portfolio capital inflows, the slow growth of productivity, and the decline in private savings. Starting in 1992, a debate began to take place both outside and inside the World Bank regarding the possible consequences of the real appreciation that had occurred since 1988. Partly at the request of the Mexicans, the Bank's macroeconomic work from 1992 to 1994 focused on the exchange rate regime and associated issues of monetary and financial management, using a combination of Bank staff and expert external consultants.

In mid-1992, the Bank sent a team—led by a senior World Bank economist and including a respected international consultant—to review the macroeconomic situation and to analyze the sustainability of the exchange rate system and the widening current-account imbalance. A confidential report was prepared and passed on to the Mexican authorities in early October of that year. It suggested that the time had come for Mexico to introduce a more flex-

---

[1] Krugman (1995), p. 33.
[2] The Mexican experience was often cited as an example that it is possible to undertake successful structural reforms within a democratic regime. Mexico was in fact often contrasted with Chile, where the most radical reforms had been undertaken by an authoritarian regime.

ible exchange rate regime. This report recognized the existence of potential trade-offs between a more flexible exchange rate regime and other objectives of the program, notably reduction of the rate of inflation. The report argued, however, on the basis of the experiences of Chile and Israel, that as long as fiscal and monetary policies were prudent, there was no reason to expect greater nominal exchange rate flexibility to generate an acceleration in inflation. A more flexible exchange rate regime would probably slow the speed at which inflation was being reduced. This potential shortcoming had to be weighed against the increased degrees of freedom that a more flexible system provided and the potentially positive effect on economic activity and growth. Although the specifics of this suggestion were not followed by the authorities, the rate of daily devaluation was increased from 20 to 40 (old) pesos in mid-October 1992.

This measure proved to be insufficient. During the rest of 1992, the real appreciation of the peso deepened while the current-account deficit remained remarkably large. The Bank's staff continued to be concerned. A Private Sector Assessment mission that visited Mexico in January 1993 was clear as to the risks being run. It noted that the economy was dependent on high levels of foreign capital inflows, which were subject to rapid shifts in expectations. If flows were to fall, this would provoke a sharp rise in interest rates.

The mission drew attention to the vulnerability of the banking sector due to the high real interest rates needed to attract foreign capital and to the high failure rates among firms rendered uncompetitive by the mix of an appreciated real exchange rate and high real interest rates. It also highlighted another channel of vulnerability: High domestic interest rates resulting from this macro policy stance were leading many of the larger firms to shift their borrowing abroad, exposing even these firms to significant cross-currency risk. If a crash landing was to be avoided, it was important for Mexico to start moving toward greater exchange rate flexibility and toward a reduction in the current-account deficit from the existing levels of 6.5-7.0 percent of GDP to a level of about half that amount.

While the Mexican authorities appreciated the Bank's concerns and technical analysis, they argued that the widening of the exchange rate band had already provided enough flexibility, that the private character of capital inflows evidenced confidence in Mexican policies, and that any further changes in exchange rate policy would be reviewed by them later in the light of experience. The authorities also pointed out that the impending approval of NAFTA would result in a major change in Mexico's external conditions, allowing it to continue to attract large volumes of foreign funds.

250

DEVELOPMENTS IN 1994

The Bank's analytic and policy work on monetary management, exchange rate policy, and the banking system (as well as on a range of other policy issues, including poverty, infrastructure, and the environment) continued in 1993 and 1994—through the approval of NAFTA in the fall of 1993 to the inauguration of the Zedillo government in the fall of 1994. An active dialogue with the Mexican authorities was maintained on all these issues. In 1994, after the Mexican Parliament enacted legislation giving the central bank full legal independence, the Mexicans requested that the World Bank assist the central bank in developing a policy framework to guide its macroeconomic management. As before, the method of work was for World Bank staff to identify issues and maintain a dialogue with the Mexicans while mobilizing international experts (often at the specific request of the Mexicans) to provide additional depth and credibility. There was consensus between these outside experts and the Bank's staff that the exchange rate anchor had fulfilled its purpose of reducing inflation. However, having brought about a substantial real appreciation, and a concurrent trade deficit that required increasing amounts of uncertain and volatile foreign capital, it was time to introduce additional exchange rate flexibility. The World Bank's repeated counsel accordingly was that the central bank anchor its monetary policy to an inflation rate target rather than an exchange rate target, leaving the nominal exchange rate available as an instrument to absorb external shocks. Bank staff were also successful in drawing the government's attention to the mounting risks in the banking system resulting from inadequate supervision and heightened currency risk. At the government's request, the Bank prepared an action plan for the consolidated supervision of financial groups (later supported by World Bank lending), and the Bank's analyses also were probably influential in measures taken by the authorities to limit the open foreign-exchange position of banks.

These concerns regarding macroeconomic policy were communicated to the Bank's Executive Board in May 1994, in the context of an overall review of the Bank's strategy toward Mexico. The Board was advised of the risks posed by shifts in the supply of capital, and also that the authorities were aware of the risks.

In 1994, an active and continuous dialogue on macroeconomic and exchange rate policy was maintained between the World Bank and the Mexican authorities at every level. In early 1994, on my first visit to Mexico as the incoming Regional Vice President, my predecessor and I met with members of the cabinet and with President

Carlos Salinas de Gortari. We raised our concerns with regard to the vulnerability of the external sector to the overvaluation of the exchange rate. I again raised the issue when I met with Secretary of Finance Pedro Aspe in April 1994, on the occasion of the Inter-American Development Bank (IDB) annual meeting in Guadalajara, Mexico.

The Mexican response was polite but firm: they appreciated the Bank's concerns, but did not agree with our conclusions and recommendations. They advanced three arguments. First, the system had enough built-in flexibility, in the form of flexible interest rates and the exchange rate band, to deal with disequilibria. Second, in their view, a rapid increase in productivity was about to take place, generating a major export expansion that would help close the current-account gap. Third, they argued, the long-term fundamentals remained healthy, especially in light of NAFTA's ratification. As evidence that the economy was under control, the authorities maintained that non-traditional exports were doing fine, although lagging considerably behind the growth in imports. A senior Mexican official argued that the question of the peso's overvaluation "depend[ed] on the equilibrium real exchange rate . . . The appreciation process is a natural, and not necessarily a negative, consequence of the reform process in Mexico."[3] The Governor of the Bank of Mexico told the *Economist* in January 1994 that the current-account deficit was not a problem because it was associated with the inflow of foreign funds rather than with expansionary fiscal or monetary policy.[4]

In 1994, with the elections a few months away, and at the request of the government, the Bank prepared a set of 18 papers on basic policy issues—including education, labor, environment, exchange rate, fiscal, and macroeconomic policies—that the new administration would need to face. The overview on macroeconomics stated that the fight to maintain the current exchange rate regime had contributed to sluggish economic growth, surging imports and sustained large current-account deficits, financial distress and bankruptcy in many otherwise-healthy companies, and the banks' grow-

---

[3] Ortiz (1994).

[4] Although Mexico's remarkable fiscal adjustment following the debt crisis is impressive, it is also important to note that the stance in terms of fiscal policy started to shift as early as 1989. This can only be appreciated when the traditional fiscal accounts are corrected in order to exclude from public expenditure the inflationary component of interest payments. In any event, it is still the case that a significant shift in the fiscal stance took place only beginning in the second semester of 1993. See Leiderman and Thorne (1995).

ing portfolio of non-performing loans. It went on to suggest that *moderate* economic growth (of 3-4 percent) could only be attained in the context of a positive macroeconomic environment, comprising a lower real interest rate, a more depreciated exchange rate, tight fiscal policy, and sustained recovery of the international economy.

The Bank's advice on exchange rate policy was not acted upon, after some internal debate among high-level Mexican officials, and the *Pacto* renewal basically maintained the exchange rate regime and overall macroeconomic policy. At the same time, Bank staff as well as the financial community were not aware of the day-to-day behavior of international reserves. In October, the issue of exchange rate policy and current-account sustainability was again brought up with the Mexicans at the highest level, at the World Bank Group's Annual Meetings in Madrid. The reply was, once again, along prior lines: The country had been subjected to a series of political shocks, but productivity was increasing; exchange rate flexibility was available; and the existence of a US$6 billion currency stabilization fund set by NAFTA in early 1994 was additional insurance.

As the final months of 1994 unfolded, the Bank's concerns did not dissipate. In early December, the staff suggested that a very high-level meeting on macroeconomics and exchange rate policy be held between the incoming economic authorities and senior officials of the World Bank and the International Monetary Fund (IMF), including the Bank's Chief Economist and the IMF's First Deputy Managing Director. The Mexican authorities agreed with the suggestion and proposed that the meeting be held the week between Christmas and the New Year. In mid-December, however, they requested a postponement of the meeting until February.

During most of 1994, the Bank's macroeconomic advice to Mexico was strategic in nature; it dealt mostly with exchange rate issues and with the need to introduce greater flexibility. Little was said, however, on the dangers associated with the rapid substitution of *tesobonos* for *cetes*. This reflected two factors: First, staff quite simply missed the significance of the rapid accumulation of dollar-linked debt. Second, in the absence of timely data on international reserves, it was thought that a currency collapse—although a clear risk at some point if policies were not changed—was not imminent.

Several contacts were made during December with Mexican senior authorities—mostly from the Bank of Mexico—regarding the strength of Mexico's external position. Despite the long tradition of frank dialogue and World Bank support for the program, staff had no access to precise information on reserves—although government officials did indicate privately that reserves had been falling rapidly since mid-November—nor was World Bank staff informed in advance of the decision announced on December 20 to widen the band.

THE BANK'S "SECOND VOICE": THE EXTERNAL ARENA

While these discussions were taking place internally, some outside commentators, though still a minority, were also raising alarms on the increasing external vulnerability of the Mexican economy. As early as November 1992, Rudiger Dornbusch argued in a newspaper article that the daily rate of devaluation should be tripled in 1993 to 120 cents per day, and Sebastian Edwards subsequently pointed out that "the rapid real appreciation of the peso in the last few months has contributed to [a] . . . widening trade imbalance, affecting overall credibility."[5] In a cautious fashion, the Bank began to share its internal misgivings with a broader audience. In a public document issued in November 1992, the Bank noted: "Opening its capital account also exposes Mexico to the volatility of short-term capital movements that can transmit destabilizing external shocks to the economy even if domestic policies are right."[6] That report went on to say that Mexico could "adjust to these risks [of volatile capital movements] through higher interest rates and, possibly, depreciating the peso."[7] In the World Bank's *Trends in Developing Economies 1993*, Bank staff expressed apprehension in more vivid terms, stating that: "In 1992 about two-thirds of the widening of the current account deficit can be ascribed to lower private savings . . . If this trend continues, it could renew fears about Mexico's inability to generate enough foreign exchange to service debt or remit dividends."[8]

After 1993, as fiscal policy was relaxed and public savings also experienced a decline, the drop in savings became more serious. Yet as of the end of 1993, and despite this vulnerability, international capital markets had high expectations for Mexico. The Mexican authorities, for their part, believed that the decline in savings was a temporary phenomenon, not dissimilar to the impact on savings in other situations of rapid adjustment. The authorities were also convinced that the current-account deficit would be solved through pro-

---

[5] Dornbusch in *Excelsior*, November 23, 1992, p. 1, and Edwards (1994), p. 39, respectively.
[6] World Bank (1992), p. 359.
[7] Ibid., p. 359.
[8] World Bank (1993), p. 330.

ductivity increases and that, because of access to NAFTA markets, capital would continue to flow in at the rate of 1992-93, providing time to adjust the external accounts. The increase in capital inflows exacerbated the real exchange rate appreciation generated by the rigid exchange rate regime. For the transfer of resources implied by the higher capital inflows to become effective, a real appreciation was *required*. This was indeed the position taken by the Mexican authorities. However, the rate at which capital was flowing in clearly was *not* sustainable for the long run.[9] At those rates, the volume of Mexican securities held by foreigners as a proportion of the country's GDP grew continuously and with no limits. This clearly was a short-term phenomenon that would have to be partially reversed.[10]

THE BANK'S ROLE—IN RETROSPECT

In providing an overall assessment of the Bank's role as an advisor to the Mexican government, it is useful to address the following three questions: Was the message the correct one? Was the message backed by technically sound analysis? And were the messengers the appropriate ones?

Was the message the correct one? There is no doubt that, very early on, the Bank's staff was aware of the increasing vulnerability of the Mexican economy and of the need to regain competitiveness by abandoning the exchange rate as the nominal anchor. The staff was aware of the implicit trade-offs involved in allowing the exchange rate to depreciate. As was documented above, on the fundamental topics of exchange rate overvaluation and unsustainable current-account deficits, the Bank issued several warning signals as early as the end of 1992.

However, as events in 1994 unfolded, Mexico's already weak external position became even more so. Increased use of *tesobonos* and a rapid decline in reserves made Mexico even more vulnerable to changed perceptions in the markets about the country's creditworthiness. The Mexican authorities did not provide information on

---

[9] Given the rate of growth of the economy during this period, sustainable inflows were closer to the 2-4 percent of GDP range than to the 7 percent level observed during 1992-93.

[10] In 1993, Oks and van Wijnbergen recognized the temporary nature of the expansion of capital inflows and argued that the key question was: "once capital stops flowing, should we expect the current account to improve, or is Mexico heading for a major [balance of payments] crisis?" (1995, p. 174). It should be noted that Oks was at the time the World Bank's country economist for Mexico, and that van Wijnbergen had been the Bank's Lead Economist for Mexico until early 1992.

reserves; nor did the Bank fully track changes in short-term obligations. The lack of full information throughout most of 1994 greatly affected the nature of the Bank's message during that year. In fact, crucial policy decisions—the relaxation of fiscal policy in late 1993, the sterilization of the reserves decline in late March 1994, and the switch to short-term, dollar-indexed domestic debt—were not identified as matters of extreme concern by the Bank.

Was the message based on sound technical analysis? This is a difficult question. What is "sound analysis" for some may be "weak analysis" for others. Yet the World Bank clearly made a significant effort to engage some of its most experienced analysts in studying the Mexican economy. Moreover, the Bank consistently used consultants held in high esteem internationally as well as by the Mexican authorities—as evidenced by the decision of the Mexicans to retain some of the same consultants for an independent view of their macro policies.

Was the message conveyed by the appropriate "messenger" to the appropriate interlocutor? The World Bank's position was transmitted to the Mexican authorities at different levels. The economists in charge of Mexico repeatedly had the opportunity to express their opinion to the technical staff on the Mexican economic team. The World Bank Department Director responsible for Mexico and the Vice President for Latin America and the Caribbean conveyed the staff's misgivings at the sub-cabinet and cabinet levels. On more than one occasion, the Bank's President discussed the need for greater exchange rate flexibility and pointed out to top-level Mexican authorities the dangers of very large current-account deficits. For the most part, the World Bank's message was appreciated but did not bring about changes in the government's policies. It is fair to say, then, that the message was transmitted by the right messengers; in fact, the Bank used its complete battery of interlocutors to relate its views to the Mexican authorities at every level.

If the message was largely correct, the analysis sound, and the right intermediaries were used, why wasn't the World Bank's advice accepted? The answer to this lies in genuine differences of opinion. While the Bank staff believed that the Mexican external sector was increasingly vulnerable and that adjustment had to be undertaken as early as late 1992, the Mexican authorities were convinced that the situation was under control and that NAFTA provided them with significant time to engineer an eventual correction in the external accounts. Until the first quarter of 1994, the financial markets seemed to back up the Mexican perspective, making the Bank position appear unduly pessimistic. As the 1994 events unfolded, the

Mexican authorities reacted time and time again as if these were temporary shocks, not realizing that they were rapidly running out of time to correct the real exchange-rate overvaluation and to reduce their dependence on capital inflows. In a paper presented at the Brookings Panel on Economic Activity, Rudiger Dornbusch and collaborators argue that differences of opinion between different actors—including the Mexican authorities, financial analysts, academics, and the multilateral institutions—lie at the heart of any explanation of why Mexico's crisis took the course it did.[11] In the absence of a Bank-financed adjustment program, such differences of opinion between the Bank's staff and the Mexican authorities persisted, with no immediate consequences for the country's economic policy.

In retrospect, were there ways for the World Bank to be more effective in influencing Mexican decision-making? Some have argued that if the Bank had gone public with its concerns early on, the Mexican authorities would have been forced to react in a timely fashion. Although this may appear superficially to be an attractive option, it would have been a highly risky course to follow. There is little doubt that, if the World Bank were to make public its assessment that a country's balance of payments is unsustainable, this in itself would help precipitate a crisis. In most cases, the Bank cannot persuade by withholding disbursements, as such an action only makes matters worse. The test on providing good—and especially useful—advice is not always whether the country follows it. What really matters is whether the message is clear, sound, and appropriately delivered. In some cases the Bank's advice will be accepted; in others, genuine differences of opinion will prevent its being adopted.

One final point should be made: the Bank came to be closely identified with the Mexican reforms from 1987 to 1991 through the series of large policy-based adjustment operations, culminating in the financial support provided to the Brady Plan commercial bank debt agreement. As part of this support, the Bank very publicly provided high praise for the Mexican reforms, and it was in part on the basis of these statements of support that the commercial banks accepted the debt-reduction agreement. The Mexican authorities welcomed these expressions of public endorsement and were very keen to maintain a highly positive public image with the Bank's support. The image did remain positive, and led to capital inflows at a rate of almost $30 billion per year. But with the Bank in this role, it was then often difficult for staff at the working level, who saw direct-

---

[11] Dornbusch et al. (1995).

ly the problems that still existed in Mexico, to make themselves heard. The results were clearly unfortunate. A primary lesson for the Bank is that while there is no problem with public expressions of our assessment of the situation in a country (and Mexico *did* do much that was positive in 1987-1991—taking major steps forward, even if it was not everything that was needed), we need to ensure that such statements are accurate and complete, and that they do not hinder the expression of concerns that develop later.

REFERENCES

Dornbusch, Rudiger, Ilan Goldfajn, and Rodrigo Valdes (1995). "Currency Crises and Collapses." Brookings Papers on Economic Activity no. 2. Washington, D.C.: Brookings Institution.

Edwards, Sebastian (1994). "Trade Liberalization Reforms in Latin America," in Graham Bird and Ann Helwege, eds., *Latin America's Economic Future*. London: Academic Press.

Krugman, Paul (1995). "Dutch Tulips and Emerging Markets," *Foreign Affairs*. July/August.

Leiderman, Leonardo, and Alfredo Thorne (1995). "Mexico's 1994 Crisis and Its Aftermath." Mimeographed.

Oks, Daniel, and Sweder van Wijnbergen (1995). "Mexico After the Debt Crisis: Is Growth Sustainable?" *Journal of Development Economics* 47, no. 1. June.

Ortiz, Guillermo (1994). "Comment on Rudiger Dornbusch: Stabilization and Monetary Reform in Latin America," in O. de Beaufort Wijnholds, S.C. de Eijffinger, and L.H. Hoogduin, eds., *A Framework for Monetary Stability: Papers and Proceedings of an International Conference Organized by De Nederlandsche Bank & the Center for Economic Research at Amsterdam, The Netherlands, October 1993*. Amsterdam: Kluwer Academic Publishers.

World Bank (1992). *Trends in Developing Economies*. Washington, D.C.: World Bank.

World Bank (1993). *Trends in Developing Economies*. Washington, D.C.: World Bank.

10. THE MEXICAN CRISIS AND ITS AFTERMATH: AN IMF PERSPECTIVE*

CLAUDIO M. LOSER AND EWART S. WILLIAMS

Economic developments in Mexico have been the subject of considerable scrutiny over the past two and a half years. There has been much discussion of the causes that led to the balance-of-payments crisis of late December 1994 and had contagious effects on other emerging markets. The significant policy efforts of the Mexican authorities to reestablish financial stability and market confidence after the crisis and the role that the International Monetary Fund (IMF), among other international organizations, played in this process have received relatively less attention. This paper focuses on these latter two issues and discusses new initiatives taken by the Fund since then to reduce the risk and the impact of similar crises in the future.

MEXICO'S STRUCTURAL TRANSFORMATION

DEVELOPMENTS DURING 1988-93

From 1988 to 1993, Mexico followed a strategy of economic adjustment and reform that strengthened the process of macroeconomic stabilization and structural transformation that was initiated after the onset of the 1982 debt crisis.[1] The strategy aimed at laying the foundations for private sector–led growth by reducing macroeconomic imbalances and the role of the public sector in the economy.

* This paper was originally prepared for publication in the last quarter of 1995, when Mexico was in the early stages of emerging from the peso crisis of late 1994 and early 1995. It has been updated to take into account the latest economic developments in Mexico and the evolution of Fund policies in the areas of Fund surveillance and resource availability. The views expressed are those of the authors, and do not necessarily reflect the official position of the management or the Board of Directors of the International Monetary Fund.

[1] Economic developments and policies in the period are discussed in Loser and Kalter (1992), Aspe (1993), and Lustig (1992).

The key elements of the strategy were a managed exchange rate regime, the maintenance of restrained financial policies, a comprehensive program of structural reforms, and a path-breaking external debt restructuring agreement. An important aspect of the strategy was an explicit agreement on policies between labor, business, and the government in the context of a series of wage-price pacts that enhanced the credibility of the program, reduced inflation expectations, and helped to reestablish the confidence of foreign investors in Mexico's transformation efforts.

In the 1988-93 period, fiscal policy aimed at consolidating the considerable gains achieved from around 1982. A major tax reform undertaken in 1987 broadened the tax base, reduced marginal tax rates, and improved tax administration; public-sector prices were kept at competitive levels; the privatization of several large public enterprises was completed; and strict control was exercised over non-interest expenditures. A crucial element in the process of fiscal consolidation was the reduction in interest payments—a result of lower real domestic interest rates, the rescheduling of official external debt, and the completion of an innovative debt-reduction agreement with foreign commercial banks in 1989-90. The agreement with the banks was the first implemented under the Brady initiative and was financed in part with resources from the IMF, the World Bank, and Japan. Mainly reflecting the reduction in interest payments, the overall balance of the non-financial public sector shifted from a deficit of 15 percent of GDP in 1986-87 to a surplus of around 1 percent of GDP in 1992-93.

Beginning in the late 1980s, monetary policy focused on the partial sterilization of capital inflows to keep the increase in the monetary base broadly in line with targeted nominal GDP growth. This strategy contributed to the reduction in inflation from around 160 percent at the end of 1987 to under 10 percent in 1993 and was complemented by a program of financial liberalization that included the freeing of interest rates, the elimination of credit controls, and the abolition of reserve requirements and compulsory liquidity ratios. Between mid-1990 and mid-1992, Mexico's 18 commercial banks (which had been expropriated in 1982) were privatized, and in 1993 a constitutional amendment was approved granting autonomy to the Bank of Mexico.

The structural reform agenda in this period comprised the privatization of several large public enterprises (including two airlines, the banks, the copper mining company, and the telecommunications company); an ambitious trade reform involving further cuts in import tariffs; and the negotiation of free trade agreements with several Western Hemisphere countries, including the North American Free Trade Agreement (NAFTA) with the United States and Canada. Restrictions on foreign investment and ownership were eased, and a number of key sectors—including agriculture, mining, telecommunications, and transportation—were deregulated. Overall, these reforms signaled a strong commitment of the authorities to deepen Mexico's transformation into a market-based economy.

The macroeconomic adjustment and reform program, together with the comprehensive external debt restructuring, paved the way for a resumption of Mexico's access to international financial markets. Private capital inflows surged to an average of over 6 percent of GDP in the period 1990-93; about one-fifth of these inflows was in the form of foreign direct investment, while the rest consisted of portfolio investment, borrowing by private-sector firms and financial entities, and the repatriation of flight capital. The inflows resulted in a marked strengthening of Mexico's gross international reserves, which rose from US$6.6 billion at the end of 1988 to US$25.5 billion at the end of 1993.

The transformation strategy, however, had its adverse consequences. In particular, the use of the exchange rate as a nominal anchor[2] led to a real effective appreciation of the peso of over 80 percent from end-1987 to end-1993. This appreciation, in the context of the major financial and trade liberalization, contributed to a rapid rise in private consumption. As private investment was also buoyant, imports (in U.S. dollar terms) grew at an average annual rate of 24 percent during 1989-92, while export growth averaged just 9 percent a year. In these circumstances, the external current-account deficit increased from around 2 percent of GDP in 1988-89 to close to 7 percent in 1992.

Real GDP growth increased from an annual average of half of 1 percent a year over the period 1985-88 to an average of 4 percent a year in the period 1989-92 before declining to 2 percent in 1993. The relatively modest growth performance since 1989 (compared with that of a number of other countries that have undertaken market-based reforms) has been explained in terms of the real appreciation of the currency and the initial impact of trade liberalization, which promoted a substitution of imports for domestic production; the transition costs of the restructuring process; and insufficient

---

[2] The peso was fixed to the U.S. dollar from March to December 1988 and was allowed to depreciate for the following three years at a preannounced rate. In November 1991, the authorities created a publicly announced intervention band, the floor of which was kept constant while the ceiling depreciated at a predetermined rate.

reform in some key areas, notably agriculture and the non-tradable goods sectors.

DEVELOPMENTS IN 1994

At the beginning of 1994, economic prospects were considered to be very favorable—following the entry into force of NAFTA and an expected surge in foreign direct investment. After two months of record capital inflows, which helped raise gross reserves to US$29.7 billion at end-February, Mexico began to experience financial turbulence in March 1994, reflecting a series of adverse external and domestic shocks. On the external front, strong output growth in the United States and the general pickup in activity in industrial economies placed upward pressures on interest rates in these countries, which prompted investors to reassess the share of their portfolios invested in emerging markets, including Mexico. On the domestic front, political disturbances, in particular the assassination of presidential candidate Luis Donaldo Colosio on March 23, greatly heightened investor concern.

Capital flight out of Mexico reached alarming proportions in late March and April (gross international reserves dropped US$8.2 billion in April). To stem the outflows, the authorities allowed the peso to depreciate to the top (the most depreciated level) of the exchange rate band, doubled short-term interest rates to 18 percent, and obtained commitments of financial support through a stand-by line of credit from the United States and Canada (in the context of the North American Financial Agreement) and from central banks under the aegis of the Bank of International Settlements (BIS). In addition, they sought to address investor fears about a possible major depreciation of the peso by replacing peso-denominated government debt with short-term instruments indexed to the U.S. dollar (*tesobonos*). In the period March-August 1994, the stock of *tesobonos* increased by around US$22 billion. While this move may have helped stabilize financial markets temporarily, it increased the vulnerability of the economy.

The results of the presidential election in August, together with the renewal of the wage-price pact in September, helped ease turbulence in financial markets. However, in late October, just before the incoming administration was about to take office, a new burst of political instability sparked by the assassination of the PRI Secretary General—and coupled with spreading rumors about possible changes in exchange rate policy—led to renewed pressures on the Mexican peso. In contrast with the response of the authorities to the market instability in March-April, monetary and credit policy was on this occasion more accommodating. In these circumstances, from end-October to December 19, gross international reserves declined by about US$7 billion—to around US$11 billion.

On December 20, the exchange rate band was widened by raising the ceiling by 15 percent. This did not stem the loss in reserves, and two days later, with gross international reserves at around US$6 billion, the peso was allowed to float. The need to abandon the managed exchange-rate regime, following repeated pronouncements to the contrary, had strongly adverse effects on financial markets. This change in market sentiment, together with questions about Mexico's ability to service its short-term external debt, in large measure explains the upheaval and sharp peso depreciation of early 1995.

THE RESPONSE TO THE CRISIS

Massive capital outflows and the high level of short-term external nal indebtedness relative to international reserves presented the authorities with the choice of adopting capital controls or some form of involuntary rescheduling. In fact, at the time several analysts advocated the unilateral suspension of debt payments pending the reestablishment of market access—ignoring the effect that this could have on the financial markets in Mexico and more broadly. Much to their credit, the Mexican authorities rejected this view and adopted a tough market-based economic stabilization program, designed in close consultation with the Fund and supported by a large-scale international financial rescue package in which the Fund also played a major role.

THE ECONOMIC PROGRAM

The initial economic program, launched in early January 1995, was formulated in the context of an agreement between the government and representatives of various private-sector interests (the Agreement of Unity to Overcome the Economic Emergency) and was based on rather optimistic assumptions, including real GDP growth of 1.5 percent and an average exchange rate of MexN$4.5 per U.S. dollar, representing a nominal depreciation of 14 percent from the level of the peso as of December 20. The program had an inflation target of 19 percent in 1995 (on an end-of-year basis) and, with the aid of restrained financial and incomes policies, aimed at reducing the external current-account deficit by about one-half, to 4 percent of GDP in 1995. The authorities thought, at that time, that an external current-account deficit of this size might be financeable, largely with official financing. They recognized, however, that in the absence of adequate official assistance, a further substantive adjustment in demand management policies would be necessary.

The immediate stabilization of Mexican financial markets did not materialize as hoped, and the period from end-December 1994 to early March 1995 witnessed a sharp depreciation of the peso and a steady fall in the demand for peso-denominated financial assets. The factors behind the continued market instability appeared to include doubts about the strength of the program, rumors that capital controls were to be reintroduced, concern about the availability of foreign assistance to finance the maturing short-term foreign exchange liabilities of the government, and fears about the collapse of the banking system. In January and February, other equity and currency markets—most noticeably in Latin America, but also in a number of more distant emerging market economies—also came under pressure.

Against this background, the authorities in early March announced a substantial tightening of policies. The revised program was predicated on a real GDP decline of 2 percent for 1995 and envisaged a sharper depreciation of the peso: Thus, the inflation target was revised upward to 42 percent. Fiscal policy was tightened through an increase in the value-added tax rate from 10 percent to 15 percent, a further adjustment in energy prices, and additional cuts in government expenditure, in real terms. The monetary and credit targets of the program were left broadly unchanged in nominal terms, implying a substantial tightening in real terms. All in all, the new program was expected to slash the external current-account deficit to the equivalent of around 1 percent of GDP in 1995 (compared with 4 percent in the original program)—more in keeping with expected net capital inflows.

The authorities recognized that the recession and the sharp increase in interest rates expected under the program would aggravate the already serious problems faced by the banking system. Accordingly, an array of special programs was introduced to help ease the liquidity shortages of the banks, to strengthen banks' capital and reserves, and to give breathing space to hard-pressed debtors. The World Bank and the Inter-American Development Bank (IDB) collaborated in the design of these measures and also provided support to the banking system through a financial-sector loan.

The reinforced program included several measures designed to ease the hardships that the crisis was likely to inflict on the poor. Expenditure on priority health and education programs was to be maintained in real terms; workers earning less than four times the minimum salary were granted nominal wage increases of 10 percent, compared with 7 percent for other workers; health insurance benefits under the social security system were extended from two months to six months for recently unemployed workers; a road construction program employing the rural poor was initiated; and a subsidy on electricity consumption by households was introduced.

Finally, the structural component of the program was strengthened with the decision to broaden the privatization and deregulation strategy to include sectors and activities previously reserved for the public sector, including rail transportation, telecommunications, electricity generation, and certain petrochemical operations. Implementation of the strategy required some amendments to the Constitution, which had classified some of these sectors as strategic, and an extensive revision of the legal and regulatory framework.

PROGRAM FINANCING

In the Fund's view, the strength of Mexico's economic program and the country's track record of macroeconomic and structural adjustment in themselves justified exceptional financial assistance. In addition, early-1995 developments in world markets underscored the systemic risk posed by the Mexican situation.[3] These immediate spill-over effects indicated that Mexico's crisis could raise doubts, unwarranted by fundamentals, about the viability of many other emerging economies, precipitating a major interruption in the flow of capital—one of the driving forces of global growth in recent years—to these countries. In these circumstances, the Fund saw the need to make a significant contribution to what was truly an unprecedented international rescue package.

In early January 1995, at the start of the Mexican crisis, the Mexican authorities set out to arrange a financing package in the amount of US$18 billion.[4] These plans evolved over the following weeks as the crisis deepened and as a better idea of Mexico's potential financing needs was gained. As part of the international effort to support Mexico, the United States proposed increasing its financing from US$9 billion to US$40 billion.

---

[3] The systemic risk posed by the Mexican crisis and the need for exceptional financing is discussed in Bergsten (1995) and Bergsten and Cline (1995).

[4] Comprising support from the United States (US$9 billion), Canada (around US$1 billion), the BIS (US$5 billion), and the international private banking community (US$3 billion).

Following discussions between the IMF staff and the Mexican authorities in early January 1995, consideration was given to allowing Mexico exceptional Fund access of 300 percent of quota (equivalent to US$7.6 billion). By end-January 1995, however, it became clear that the envisaged US$40 billion in U.S. loan guarantees would not receive congressional approval, and the U.S. administration announced alternative plans for short- and medium-term loans that could be effected without congressional approval. The Exchange Stabilization Fund (ESF), which included a small contribution from Canada, amounted to US$20 billion. In order to counter the possible danger that this could leave Mexico's adjustment efforts underfinanced, steps were taken to broaden the international financing package. As part of this effort, the BIS doubled its planned contribution to US$10 billion, and the Fund increased its potential commitment. Specifically, on February 1, 1995, the Fund's Executive Board approved an 18-month stand-by arrangement with Mexico for Special Drawing Rights (SDR) of 12.1 billion (US$17.8 billion).[5] However, the Fund undertook, at the time, to seek US$10 billion from non-G10 central banks, with funds under this initiative intended to reduce, *pari passu*, its commitment under the arrangement. Fund resources were to be re-phased, with 300 percent of quota (US$7.8 billion) to be made available on approval of the program and the remaining amount to be determined at the time of the June program review, once the results of the efforts to raise funds from non-G10 central banks had been determined. Following the decision later in the year to discontinue efforts to seek non-G10 financing, the augmentation of the stand-by arrangement to SDR 12.1 billion was formalized.

At the time, the Fund arrangement with Mexico was the largest ever approved for a member country both in absolute amount and in relation to the country's quota in the Fund. The first purchase also represented a level of front-loading that was unprecedented in Fund arrangements. The exceptional level of Fund support is consistent with the Fund's mandate, which, as described in Article I of the Articles of Agreement, is "to give confidence to members by making the general resources of the Fund temporarily available to them under adequate safeguards, thus providing them with the opportunity to correct maladjustments in their balance of payments without resorting to measures destructive of national or international prosperity." The Mexican financial crisis had presented such a challenge: Large-scale financial assistance needed to be put in place quickly to

---

[5] On August 2,1996, the stand-by arrangement was extended for six months, through February15, 1997.

complement resources that were being made available by the United States, and the IMF was the only institution in a position to make the resources available in the required timeframe. In the absence of adequate financing, Mexico may well have had no option but to resort to "measures destructive of national or international prosperity," such as a moratorium on foreign debt payments or a reimposition of trade and exchange restrictions, with a risk that such measures could have spread to a number of other countries.

DEVELOPMENTS UNDER THE PROGRAM

Mexico has made remarkable progress in coming out of the economic crisis. Existing external imbalances have been eliminated, inflation has been lowered significantly, and economic growth has resumed—after a sharp recession in 1995. Mexico has also regained access to international capital markets, following a short hiatus in 1995. Some of the major performance highlights are:

- *The external current-account deficit* has narrowed from 7 percent of GDP in 1994 to about 0.5 percent of GDP in 1995-96, as national savings have risen by close to 6 percentage points of GDP. *Private capital inflows* have resumed after a sharp decline in 1995, and there has been a decided shift in favor of direct investment and longer-term flows.

- *Net international reserves*, which fell to around negative US$4 billion in March 1995, increased to about US$9 billion as of mid-February 1997.

- After declining by 6 percent in 1995, *real GDP growth* rebounded by 5 percent in 1996, led by strong growth in exports and in private investment.

- Reflecting the sharp depreciation of the peso and corrective price adjustments, the 12-month *inflation rate* accelerated to 52 percent by end-1995, but was almost halved to 28 percent by end-1996.

- While safeguarding government expenditures on social programs, the *primary fiscal surplus* was increased from 2.2 percent of GDP in 1994 to an average of 3.8 percent of GDP in 1995-96.

- As a result of the various support programs and the sharp reduction in interest rates, the feared collapse of *the banking system* was avoided, and a comprehensive restructuring process is under way. Foreign investment in the banking sector is increasing, banks' capitalization levels have risen, and major progress has been made in strengthening prudential and accounting regulations and in tightening bank supervision.

- Strict implementation of the economic program and the positive results have led to a rapid improvement in *Mexico's access to international capital markets*. Accordingly, Mexico purchased only SDR 8.8 billion (close to three-quarters) of the resources available under the stand-by arrangement and utilized US$12.5 billion (roughly 63 percent) of the Exchange Stabilization Fund (ESF) financing package.[6] In 1996-97, Mexico prepaid the loans from the ESF and made sizable advance repurchases to the Fund. Mexico's ability to borrow longer maturities at declining interest rates has also facilitated a smoothing out of the public debt service profile.

POLICY LESSONS FROM THE CRISIS

Of the many policy lessons that have been cited from the Mexican experience, the following appear to be of particular importance:[7]

First, it is no paradox that one of Mexico's major successes—its openness and integration into international financial markets—made it more vulnerable to a reversal in market sentiment. The lesson here, which is relevant to all emerging-market economies, is that openness imposes a strict obligation of economic policy discipline. Mexico's crisis demonstrated clearly the costs that can arise when a country lowers (or is perceived to lower) its guard and allows markets to exercise their discipline instead. The rapid improvement in market sentiment following the government's reinforcement of its program also underscores the fact that policies matter.

Second, large external current-account deficits, regardless of the factors underlying them, are likely to be unsustainable. As U.S. Deputy Secretary of the Treasury Lawrence Summers cautioned at the 1995 IDB Annual Meeting in Jerusalem, "current account deficits cannot be assumed to be benign because the private sector generated them." His suggestion that policy-makers should assume that capital inflows are temporary and outflows permanent, rather than the other way around, also should be seen as sound advice.

---

[6] No drawings were made under the BIS package, which was heavily collateralized.

[7] Lessons from the crisis for economic policy and for the role of the IMF are discussed in Cline (1995), Bergsten and Cline (1995), in a series of speeches and press briefings by the IMF Managing Director (see, for example, Camdessus 1995), and in a series of articles in the *IMF Survey* (for example, the issues of May 8, May 22, and August 14, 1995).

Third, the Mexican crisis illustrated the importance of regular and timely publication of economic data. The crisis was aggravated because the markets were surprised by the magnitude of the imbalances—as reflected in the drop in international reserves and the build-up in short-term dollar-indexed debt—that had developed in the course of 1994. More timely information might have improved the chances of a smoother adjustment. Following the crisis, the Mexican authorities took major steps to expand the coverage and improve the timeliness of published economic data.

LESSONS FOR THE IMF

SURVEILLANCE

Developments in Mexico in late December 1994 gave added impetus to initiatives to strengthen Fund surveillance and to have in place an early warning system to help reduce the risk and severity of balance-of-payments crises. Prior to the crisis, the IMF had been taking action to make surveillance more continuous and effective, but the Mexican experience showed that further adaptations were needed in the following areas:

1. *More continuous policy dialogue between the IMF and member countries, particularly in the intervals between regular annual policy consultations.*

2. *The establishment of stricter requirements concerning the regular and timely submission of key economic and financial data to the Fund* and of standards for the publication of the kinds of economic data needed to enable markets to work more efficiently.

3. *More focused surveillance.* More scrutiny than was previously given to the capital account of the balance of payments and to the sustainability of capital flows, and more attention to developments in the financial sector and to external debt management.

4. *More pointed and candid surveillance.* The Mexican crisis showed the need for the Fund to be more pointed and more critical in its policy dialogue with member countries while respecting the confidentiality in Fund relations with its members.

FINANCING

The crisis also made it clear that the Fund needed to have the capacity to respond rapidly and with sufficient resources to address and manage shocks effectively. It brought to the fore the urgent need for an increase in members' quotas, which had not been keeping pace with the growth of world trade or with the increased scale of international financial flows. As a quota increase could take considerable time, the Fund began to explore ways to increase resources through borrowing from member countries—including through an enlargement of the General Agreement to Borrow (GAB). A third option for increasing resources was through the issue of Special Drawing Rights (SDRs). Prompted by the Mexican crisis, the Fund began to consider the possible scope for a temporary and conditional issue of SDRs to countries facing financial market crises, or for part of an issue of SDRs to be on-lent by the Fund to support adjustment by such members.

POSTSCRIPT

Since the initial preparation of this paper, the turnaround of the Mexican economy has continued to strengthen, and there have been important developments in the area of Fund policies on surveillance and on the enlargement of Fund resources to assist countries in crisis. Some of these developments are listed below.

Based on data for the first three quarters of the year, real GDP growth in 1997 would be around 7.3 percent, reinforcing the economic recovery initiated in 1996. The stock market has recovered to close to its pre-crisis level in U.S. dollar terms; inflation is now projected at around 15-16 percent in 1997; and Mexico's net international reserves have risen significantly.

In mid-1997, Mexico unveiled a medium-term economic program covering the period 1997-2000 and designed to consolidate the stabilization gains made since 1995 and to set the stage for faster and more sustainable growth over the medium term. The program provides a broad, clear, and consistent policy framework for the next few years and has served to reassure markets of the government's intention to continue with its adjustment and reform efforts.

As regards the *evolution of Fund policies*, the Fund has moved to further increase the effectiveness of its *surveillance operations* in the areas of bank soundness, transparency, and good governance. In light of the rapid growth and closer integration of capital markets, the Fund has increased its focus on the capital account of the balance of payments, and progress is being made in amending the Articles of Agreement to make the promotion of capital-account liberalization a specific purpose of the IMF and to give the IMF the appropriate jurisdiction over capital movements.

On the *data front*, the Fund in April 1996 established the Special Data Dissemination Standard (SDDS) for the voluntary dissemination of economic and financial data by member countries that have or seek access to international financial markets. In September 1996, the Dissemination Standards Bulletin Board (DSBB) was introduced, and in April 1997 a hyperlink facility that enables users to move directly from the DSBB to actual country economic and financial data on the Internet was established. As of July 31, 1997, forty-two countries subscribed to the SDDS, and hyperlinks for eight countries had been established. Mexico participates in SDDS and DSBB and also subscribes to the hyperlink. The Fund is currently developing a General Data Dissemination System (GDDS), the primary focus of which is to encourage all members to improve the production and dissemination of core economic data.

The Fund's Executive Board has continued to work on the *Eleventh Review of Quotas* and reached agreement on a 45 percent increase in total Fund quotas, with 75 percent of the overall increase to be distributed in proportion to present quotas and the remaining 25 percent to be distributed selectively so as to better reflect the relative economic positions of member countries. To become effective, this agreement must be approved by the Fund's Board of Governors, hopefully by March 31, 1998.

Meanwhile, the Executive Board took steps to strengthen the Fund's ability to borrow by approving *new arrangements to borrow* (NAB) in January 1997. Under the NAB, twenty-five participating countries would stand ready to lend the Fund up to SDR 34 billion (about US$47 billion) to supplement its regular quota resources, under exceptional circumstances.[8]

The Executive Board and Board of Governors have agreed on an amendment of the Articles to provide all members with an equitable share in the *cumulative allocation of SDRs*. If this amendment is accepted by the membership, there will be a one-time allocation of SDRs to all members that will raise the net cumulative allocations of all members to a common benchmark ratio of their quotas and will double the amount currently in existence.

Finally, it should be pointed out that the experience gained from the Mexican crisis was successfully put to use in dealing with the recent problems in Thailand, Indonesia, and South Korea. Specifically, in a matter of days, the Fund was able to put together urgently needed programs and to catalyze massive international support. The

---

[8] The NAB will enter into force when the decision has been adhered to by potential participants with credit arrangements amounting to no less than SDR 28.9 billion (85 percent of the total).

Fund also activated the new emergency financial mechanisms, which were put in place in 1995, and had recourse to the accelerated procedures for approval of these programs by the Executive Board.

The new surveillance procedures, the ability to count on enlarged resources, and the flexibility to move quickly and effectively when needed may not preclude the emergence of another Mexican-type crisis in this globalized world, as has become evident in recent months. However, these improvements certainly have enhanced the Fund's capacity to deal with and limit the adverse effects of such crises whenever they occur.

REFERENCES AND BIBLIOGRAPHY

Aspe, P. (1993). *Economic transformation the Mexican way.* Cambridge, Mass.: The Press.

Bergsten, C.F. (1995). "Lessons of the Peso Crisis." Statement before the Committee on Banking and Financial Services. Washington, D.C.: U.S. House of Representatives. February 10.

Bergsten, C.F., and W.R. Cline (1995). "The Peso Crisis and Financial Support for Mexico." Statement before the Committee on International Relations. Washington, D.C.: U.S. House of Representatives. February 1.

Camdessus, M. (1995). "Drawing Lessons from the Mexican Crisis: Preventing and Resolving Financial Crises—the Role of the IMF." Address to the 25th Washington Conference of the Council of the Americas. Washington, D.C. May 22.

Cline, W.R. (1995). "Capital Markets After the Peso Crisis." Paper presented to the Annual World Bank Conference on Development in Latin America and the Caribbean. Rio de Janeiro, Brazil. June 12-13.

Dornbusch, R., and A. Werner (1994). "Mexico: Stabilization, Reform and No Growth." Brookings Papers on Economic Activity no. 1. Washington, D.C.: Brookings Institution.

Frankel, J. (1995). "The 'Obvious Peso Blunder' at Treasury." Statement before the Committee on Banking, Housing, and Urban Affairs. Washington, D.C.: U.S. Senate. March 9.

IMF Survey, May 8, May 22, and August 14, 1995.

Loser, C., and E. Kalter, eds. (1992). "Mexico: The Strategy to Achieve Sustained Economic Growth." International Monetary Fund Occasional Paper no. 99. Washington, D.C.: IMF.

Lustig, N. (1995). "The Mexican Peso Crisis: The Foreseeable and the Surprise." Brookings Discussion Papers in International Economics. Washington, D.C.: Brookings Institution. June.

———————— (1992). *Mexico: The Remaking of an Economy.* Washington, D.C.: Brookings Institution.

Savastano, M.A., J. Roldós, and J. Santaella (1995). "Factors Behind the Financial Crisis in Mexico." *World Economic Outlook.* Washington, D.C.: Brookings Institution. May.

11. GETTING THE LESSONS RIGHT: A VIEW FROM THE INTER-AMERICAN DEVELOPMENT BANK*

NANCY BIRDSALL, MICHAEL GAVIN, AND RICARDO HAUSMANN

The 1997 financial crisis in Asia started with the unraveling of a credit boom in Thailand. It was as apparently unexpected as its emerging market precursor in Mexico less than three years earlier. What lessons had the international community learned from Mexico—or failed to learn? In this essay, we discuss plausible but fundamentally misconceived diagnoses of the Mexican crisis that, by focusing on symptoms, had little to say about underlying causes. These diagnoses explained the crisis as the outcome of policy mistakes which were pretty well understood while the Mexicans were making them; against which the Mexicans are supposed to have been warned before it was too late; and from which, therefore, little that was new could be learned—for Mexico or for other emerging markets.

As we discuss in more detail below, we do not believe that the fundamental causes of the Mexican crisis can be found in what became the conventional wisdom of what went wrong: a misguided exchange rate policy, low domestic savings, large current-account deficits, or the infamous *tesobonos*. Instead, we suggest that the crisis resulted from economic and financial vulnerabilities that were generated during the 1989-94 period of recovery and adjustment to Mexico's economic stabilization and "Washington consensus" reforms—vulnerabilities that have also emerged in other reforming countries of the region, and that were not well understood while Mexico and other countries in the region were implementing their economic stabilization and reform programs. These are vulnerabilities to which post-stabilization Latin America is particularly

---

* This chapter reflects the views of the authors and does not necessarily reflect the official position of the management or Board of Directors of the Inter-American Development Bank.

exposed—but which are likely to emerge in any economy where an economic boom is combined with a weak financial sector.

Moreover, we think that the crisis was a true surprise, one that contains important new lessons for the management of macroeconomic policy. Thus, the errors that generated the Mexican crisis were in most cases *not* avoidable by faithfully implementing the policy wisdom of the time, which was in crucial areas either silent or even counterproductive in reinforcing economic and financial fragilities (and which, in a different form, failed for too long to warn of problems in Asia). There is much in the Mexican experience to support the benefits of "Washington consensus" reforms, but there is also much to support the need for key modifications in their implementation.

In this chapter, we present our ideas as follows. In section 1, we discuss salient aspects of the Mexican reforms and the country's 1989-94 recovery, making no attempt to be comprehensive, but instead focusing on developments of direct relevance to our argument. In section 2, we discuss three important features of the period of crisis and renewed recovery. With this background, we turn in section 3 to an evaluation of what seems to us to be the conventional wisdom about the Mexican crisis and explain why we consider it to be incomplete and in important ways misleading. Section 4 then proposes three alternative lessons of the Mexican crisis, and section 5 presents our concluding remarks.

1. THE MEXICAN REFORMS AND RECOVERY, 1989-94

Mexico's economic policies in the period leading up to the crisis, outlined in Mexico's *Plan de Desarrollo Nacional 1989-1994*, were a fairly faithful reflection of the "Washington consensus." They included market deregulation and trade liberalization, reduced state participation in productive processes, renewed fiscal discipline, and intensified efforts to improve living standards for the population at large.[1] The massive and in many respects very courageous reform program was supported on a very large scale by the International Monetary Fund (IMF), the World Bank, and the Inter-American Development Bank (IDB), and by commercial debt relief under the Brady initiative.

---

[1] Aspe (1993) describes the Mexican reforms in some detail. Inter-American Development Bank (1996) provides a progress report on economic reforms in the entire region; among other things, this report indicates that the Mexican reform program was in its essential respects typical of the reform programs followed by other countries.

These structural reforms had important effects on the efficiency, competitiveness, and openness of the Mexican economy, and, while the jury is still out, there remains good reason to believe that they have thereby improved long-run prospects for economic and social development. Moreover, as we shall argue below, the reforms played an important role in facilitating rapid recovery from the 1995 crisis.

THE MEXICAN RECOVERY, 1989-94

The reforms also had very important short-term macroeconomic consequences, most of them quite welcome. The first and arguably most dramatic event was the successful disinflation. Inflation was brought down sharply, from a rate of 160 percent in 1987 to 20 percent in 1989. The renewed confidence in financial stability that was created by this disinflation, and by the impressive fiscal consolidation that underlay it, generated an increase in domestic money demand. This provided the newly privatized domestic financial system with ample financial resources to lend. At the same time, the government was using privatization revenue to retire its domestic debt to the banks, so that the capacity of banks to lend to the private sector was expanded even further. And lend they did: Bank credit to the private sector rose from less than 10 percent of GDP in 1989 to about 40 percent in 1994.

This lending boom helped to support a boom in private consumption and investment spending. The private spending boom generated large current-account deficits, which were financed with even larger capital inflows. It also improved the fiscal accounts—albeit temporarily—because of Mexico's substantial reliance upon expenditure taxes, which were boosted by the (necessarily transitory) bulge in private spending.

THE STABILIZATION AND REFORM CYCLE IN LATIN AMERICA

In these short-term macroeconomic dynamics, the Mexican economy followed a pattern that has also been observed in many other reforming countries of Latin America, though the Mexican experience was somewhat exaggerated in some key respects. In the IDB's 1996 *Report on Economic and Social Progress in Latin America*, we investigated the macroeconomic response to the stabilization and reform programs undertaken by most countries of the region. We identified a typical pattern that comprises fairly well-defined stages and that applies in general outline to almost 20 episodes of stabilization and reform in the late 1980s and early 1990s.[2] The process, which is not

---

[2] The main exception is Chile, where the reforms began in the mid-1970s.

deterministic but varies according to local conditions and policy responses, begins[3] with a period of recovery or boom after the reforms are implemented that typically generates economic and financial vulnerabilities. These vulnerabilities often lead to a period of stress, which may be followed by a period of correction or crisis. We devote a few paragraphs to these findings because they suggest that, while the Mexican case is extreme, it is not unique, and to emphasize that the Mexican case holds lessons for other reforming economies.

In Latin America, the period of *recovery* that typically follows a major stabilization and reform program is characterized by output growth roughly 4 percentage points higher than during a typical year.[4] The boom in spending, especially investment spending, is even more pronounced: consumption growth is typically more than 4 percentage points higher, and investment nearly 12 percentage points higher, than in normal years. The period of recovery has also involved important changes in the demand for financial assets. As confidence in domestic financial stability increases, the demand for domestic financial assets rises, leading to higher money demand and capital inflows. The capital inflows and the increase in demand for money and other domestic financial assets that accompanies the return of financial stability provide the domestic financial system with resources to lend to domestic individuals and firms. Thus, during periods of recovery in Latin America, real domestic credit to the private sector has grown by about 9 percent a year more than during a normal year. Thus the private spending boom is often accompanied—and amplified—by a boom in bank lending, which may also be promoted both by the reduced public-sector use of bank credit that results from fiscal consolidation and by the financial liberalization that is often a part of the reform package.

The Mexican recovery follows this pattern in many respects (see Table 1). Real consumption grew roughly 3.8 percent per year, while real GDP grew about 2.9 percent. There was a lag between the 1988 stabilization and the onset of recovery in 1990, but once the recovery began in 1990, real physical investment grew at an annualized

---

[3] In many cases, there is a substantial delay between the initiation of stabilization and reform and the recovery. In some countries, such as Argentina, recovery began almost immediately. Recovery tended to be faster when the reforms involved an exchange rate–based stabilization and may also have been hastened during the 1990s by the abundance of international capital ready to flow to reforming economies.

[4] For details, see Inter-American Development Bank (1996). While there is substantial variation in the experience of different countries, the patterns that emerge from the data are generally statistically significant at conventional confidence levels.

**Table 1. Characteristics of the Mexican Adjustment
to Stabilization and Reform**

	"Boom" or "Recovery" 1990-93	"Stress" 1994	"Crisis" 1995	"Renewed Recovery" 1996
Annualized growth rate of:				
Real GDP	2.9	4.5	-6.2	3.7
Real Consumption	3.8	4.4	-6.9	1.4
Real Investment	7.4	9.9	-42.7	11.8
Percent of GDP:				
Net Capital Inflows	8.0	3.4	4.1	1.9
Current Account Balance	-6.3	-9.6	-0.2	-0.9

Source: IDB Economic and Social Database. Net capital flows include errors and omissions.

rate of 7.4 percent—less rapidly than is typical for the "boom" phase, but substantially more rapidly than either output or production. Capital inflows averaged 8 percent of GDP during the boom phase, and the current account averaged nearly 6.5 percent of GDP.

As the boom phase of adjustment to stabilization and reform proceeds, it often leaves the economy in an increasingly vulnerable position. A "vulnerable" economy is one in which even small disturbances can trigger highly disruptive reactions. This vulnerability emerges during the boom phase for three main reasons:

1. Domestic financial systems often become vulnerable because an extended period of very rapid bank lending leaves banks holding a large stock of loans to increasingly leveraged individuals and firms that may have difficulty servicing the loans if economic growth slows or if interest rates rise.[5] The difficulty will be compounded if a drop in domestic money demand forces banks unexpectedly and sharply to curtail their lending, creating unexpected demands for borrowers to repay their loans more rapidly than they are able. The link between lending booms and fragile bank balance sheets arises in part because, during such booms, banks expand their lending to

---

[5] Gavin and Hausmann (1996a) document the close link between financial crises and lending booms such as the one Mexico experienced in both the industrial economies and in Latin America. The paper also provides some theoretical arguments as to why lending booms might worsen information problems that are inherent in financial markets, thus contributing to financial fragility.

new customers, about whom they have little information. It is, moreover, difficult to learn about the creditworthiness of borrowers because, during the macroeconomic boom that typically accompanies a credit boom, most borrowers are at least temporarily profitable and liquid, independent of their fundamental creditworthiness: in this sense, "good times are bad times for learning."

2. Vulnerability often results because the spending boom leads to a transitory increase in government revenue, since most Latin American governments depend on taxes based on private spending. This fiscal revenue boom can mask underlying fiscal disequilibria that may be politically difficult to correct, promptly and efficiently, when the spending boom subsides.

3. As the period of boom subsides, it becomes increasingly clear that the economy has developed imbalances that will eventually require a correction; current-account deficits are typically larger than could be financed indefinitely; credit growth must slow from the rapid rates observed during recovery; and the required adjustment in private spending may lead to fiscal imbalances that require correction. International investors may begin to contemplate the need for a major adjustment and, knowing that such an adjustment may impose costs on owners of the country's debt, begin to demand short-term debt. If this demand is accommodated by policy-makers, it can create a dangerous debt structure that exposes the economy to the danger of a self-fulfilling panic by international investors.

There often follows a period when the economy comes under stress. One source of stress is a natural reduction in the growth of domestic spending and production as the stock adjustments described above come to an end, and as the economy's reservoir of underutilized capacity is exhausted. During periods in which Latin American countries have been in the "stress" phase, the rate of economic growth has fallen by about 2 percentage points below that recorded during the boom, while consumption growth and investment growth have declined much more dramatically. In this respect, Mexico was somewhat atypical, for during the period of stress the country's production and spending actually accelerated somewhat. Real GDP is estimated to have grown about 4.5 percent during 1994; consumption growth roughly matched this; and real physical investment grew by nearly 10 percent.

Similarly, when money demand stabilizes at its new higher level, growth in bank lending slows to more sustainable rates. As economies have moved from the "recovery" to the "stress" phase of the adjustment process, the growth rate of real credit to the private sector has declined by more than 5 percentage points per year. This lower rate of credit growth contributes to higher real interest rates. During the "stress" phase of the process, interest rates rise sharply, to about 9 percentage points above the levels that typified the pre-reform period. Here Mexico was typical, though not extreme. Partly because of the decelerating money growth and partly because problems of credit quality were surfacing in some banks by the end of 1993, credit growth slowed during the stress phase, and there seemed to be some evidence of a "credit crunch."

Higher interest rates, slower growth in output and domestic demand, and less rapid growth in bank lending put pressure on borrowers, bringing to the surface problems of credit quality that had been hidden during the boom and rendering the banking system increasingly fragile. In a similar way, higher interest rates and slower growth may bring to the surface underlying fiscal disequilibria that had been masked by the fiscal revenue boom experienced in the recovery phase. As the fiscal situation deteriorates, investors may lose confidence in the ability of the political system to generate the fiscal adjustment required to maintain public solvency, putting additional pressure on interest rates. Finally, market participants' gradually increasing awareness that a correction of spending imbalances will sooner or later be required may generate concerns that a sharp devaluation will be part of the correction, leading to reserve losses, a weaker currency, and higher interest rates.

If dealt with promptly and effectively, the fiscal and financial vulnerabilities that result from the boom and become apparent during the period of "stress" may not generate a crisis. However, these vulnerabilities make the economy highly sensitive to external or domestic shocks and leave little room for policy maneuver. Foreign investors, already nervously contemplating the need for an eventual correction, are being asked to finance large external deficits; governments must rely on markets to finance deficits while they attempt to make a potentially large fiscal adjustment in an orderly fashion; and the banking system must overcome the excesses generated during the boom in an environment of slower growth and higher interest rates. In such an environment, even a small shock can be severely disruptive if it leads to a self-fulfilling panic by international investors or pushes the domestic banking system into crisis. As is well known, Mexico did not get lucky, receiving major political shocks in early 1994 that complicated economic management.

In Latin America, the "correction" phase has in fact tended to be traumatic; output growth falls nearly 5 percentage points below the rate typically recorded during periods of "stress," consumption growth drops by nearly 7 percentage points, and investment growth declines by more than 16 percent. The recent experiences of Argentina and Mexico are of course even more extreme than this; in Mexico, real GDP declined by 6 percent, consumption by 7 percent, and real investment by a massive 43 percent.

MACROECONOMIC AND FINANCIAL VULNERABILITY IN MEXICO

To recapitulate, although there are some differences, in the most important respects Mexico was no exception to the Latin American pattern of adjustment to economic stabilization and reform; indeed, in many respects the country followed that pattern in exaggerated form. Throughout its recovery, the economic and financial vulnerabilities described above were being accumulated. The enormous boom in lending to the private sector was followed by clear signs that the financial position of domestic banks had deteriorated. While the actual fiscal position appeared sound, the observed fiscal balance was attributable in part to a fiscal revenue boom that was associated with the (necessarily transitory) boom in private spending. This revenue boom masked underlying fiscal disequilibria that became visible only when private spending declined. The authorities permitted a large stock of very short-term debt to accumulate and thus exposed themselves to the danger of a self-fulfilling panic by domestic and international investors. We argue that these vulnerabilities—and ultimately the management of financial and fiscal policies that worsened the vulnerabilities—were what lay behind the 1995 crisis.

2. CRISIS AND RENEWED RECOVERY

The financial crisis that enveloped Mexico after its December 1994 devaluation has been discussed at length elsewhere, so here we simply highlight three points about the crisis that are relevant to our argument.

RECOVERY WAS RAPID

The first of these is the rapidity of the recovery—particularly in the financial dimension, but also in broader macroeconomic terms. By 1997, after just two years of recovery from the crisis, the economy was operating at near normal capacity, and a rapid recovery had brought real investment well above its pre-crisis level. It is true that unemployment, though declining, remained relatively high and that recovery has only begun to ease the costs for the poor, who were almost certainly most gravely affected by the crisis. But with all these important caveats made, the fact remains that the crisis was surmounted, and a solid investment- and export-led recovery had taken hold much more rapidly than after the 1982 crisis, and substantially more rapidly than most observers predicted in 1995.

The country's recovery in financial markets has been even more impressive. In March 1995, anyone hazarding a guess that Mexico would within a year be issuing thirty-year government paper would probably have been laughed out of the international financial and policy-making community. Yet in 1996, there was Mexico—having made a highly successful return to international financial markets, having repaid a large part of the official support provided during 1995, and having begun what appears to be a solid economic recovery from the deep recession of 1995.

The rapidity of this economic and financial recovery contrasts sharply with the experience of the 1980s. Recovery this time was clearly facilitated by relatively favorable international conditions, including the plentiful supply of international capital flows to emerging market economies in 1996, and by a hardheaded and courageous policy response to the crisis in Mexico, which succeeded in rapidly reestablishing the country's fiscal and financial stability. But recovery was also facilitated in important ways by the structural reforms that preceded the crisis. The extensive liberalization of domestic markets and the opening to world trade created a substantially more competitive Mexican economy, able to redirect its production to external markets when domestic demand collapsed, while NAFTA provided ready access to U.S. and Canadian markets. Together, these structural reforms contributed to the rapid growth of exports—more than 30 percent in 1995 and another 17 percent in 1996—that was crucial in containing the crisis. Also important was the tax reform, which provided Mexico with a relatively efficient value-added tax (VAT) that could be, and was, raised to contain the potential fiscal imbalances created by the crisis. This increase in fiscal revenue was instrumental in counteracting inflationary pressures unleashed by the crisis and, more importantly, in reestablishing confidence in the country's medium-term fiscal viability.

THE DOMESTIC FINANCIAL SYSTEM WAS PIVOTAL

The other two points pertain to the evolution of the crisis and the required policy response. It is now commonplace but nevertheless crucial to observe that the Mexican banking crisis was very closely associated with the macroeconomic crisis. And the former was not the mere consequence of the latter. Mexican banks were weak, and understood to be so, by the end of 1993—well before the political turbulence and capital outflows of 1994. This financial vulnerability contributed to the macroeconomic crisis in two ways. First, the fragile banks were an important constraint on monetary policy in 1994. With the benefit of hindsight, at least, it now appears obvious that the capital outflows of that year should have triggered a more determined tightening of monetary policy. But the resulting higher interest rates and tighter credit would have seriously undermined an already debilitated financial system, risking the creation of a financial crisis via the banks, rather than the capital flight that actually occurred. In short, given the weakened state of the financial system, it is not completely clear that any monetary policy response to the capital outflows of 1994 could have prevented a financial crisis.

The financial fragility was in all likelihood caused, in part, by the fact that the privatization and liberalization of the financial system got ahead of the regulatory and supervisory framework. The Mexican experience thus reinforces the importance—already made obvious by the Chilean and Uruguayan financial crises of the early 1980s—of combining financial liberalization with improvements in the regulatory and supervisory structure. But having noted that, it is far from clear that any plausible supervisory structure could have prevented the development of the financial vulnerabilities that materialized in Mexico during the financial boom of 1990-94. Even in the best-regulated financial systems, bank lending booms are almost invariably associated with financial crisis,[6] and a substantial responsibility for the financial fragilities must rest with the macroeconomic policies that made the lending boom possible. We will expand upon this point below.

FISCAL POLICY WAS CONTRACTIONARY

A third observation is that resolution of the crisis required an enormous fiscal contraction, one that can only have aggravated the collapse in domestic demand and production that was experienced during 1995. In other words, fiscal policy was highly pro-cyclical, at least during the crisis, and was forced to be so because financial market participants were fleeing and would only return once confidence in Mexico's fiscal viability was restored.[7] The fact that such a fiscal

---

[6] Lending booms are also associated with financial crisis in industrial economies, where the financial regulatory structures, while far from perfect, are as good as one can reasonably expect Latin American supervision to be over the policy-relevant time horizon.

[7] This destabilizing fiscal policy is all too typical of the region. Gavin, Hausmann, Perotti, and Talvi (1996) document that fiscal policy is typically pro-cyclical in Latin America, particularly during recessions, when a more stabilizing response would be most valuable and when, in the industrial countries, fiscal policy is in fact highly counter-cyclical.

adjustment was needed suggests that, before the crisis, public spending in Mexico was based on current revenues, not on a realistic estimate of what could be financed when the temporarily favorable budgetary circumstances changed for the worse.

This suggests a natural benchmark against which to measure Mexican fiscal policy during the pre-crisis period. While most discussions of pre-crisis fiscal policy in Mexico ask whether it was sustainable according to some medium- or long-run solvency criteria, we would pose the question differently: Was fiscal management conservative enough to permit a stabilizing response to a bad macroeconomic outcome? The answer is obviously "no," which suggests that, whether or not fiscal policy was a fundamental cause of the crisis, its management left something important to be desired, because it left the authorities in a position from which a counter-cyclical response to the crisis was impossible and an undesirable fiscal contraction was necessary. Again, we shall have more to say on this below.

3. FOUR MISLEADING DIAGNOSES

With this background established, we now discuss four lessons that seem to make up an emerging conventional wisdom about the causes of the Mexican crisis. These place responsibility for the crisis on a faulty exchange rate policy; low domestic saving; large current-account deficits; and the issuance, mainly during 1994, of the *tesobonos*—short-term, dollar-indexed government debt.

"EXCHANGE RATE POLICY WAS THE CULPRIT"

Part of the conventional wisdom is that a key cause of the Mexican crisis was an overvalued peso. This overvaluation is commonly attributed to the Mexican authorities' nominal exchange rate policies, and specifically their use of a crawling exchange rate band to provide an "anchor" for inflationary expectations. The conclusion is then drawn that a more flexible exchange rate policy could have reduced the magnitude of the overvaluation and perhaps prevented the crisis.

This argument makes some logical sense, but it misses the factual mark. Until around February 1994, the exchange rate had been driven by large capital inflows to the floor of the band, and if the band had been widened it is therefore likely that the exchange rate would have become even more overvalued, not less. Thus Mexican exchange rate policy was not promoting exchange rate overvaluation but acting as a check on it. In February this situation changed, and the exchange rate band probably kept the peso stronger than it otherwise would have been. But, for reasons that we have discussed above, the damage to the Mexican economy was by then largely done.

Put somewhat differently, explanations for the financial crisis that attempt to give a causal role to exchange rate policy need to be more explicit about the source of the exchange rate misalignment. The fact that the authorities struggled to keep the exchange rate above the floor (most appreciated portion) of the band for most of the relevant time period, when the problem was excessive capital inflows and undesired reserve accumulation, undercuts explanations based upon management of the nominal exchange rate. To us it is more plausible that the spending boom generated the real exchange rate appreciation, which means that the exchange rate misalignment was more symptom than fundamental cause. In this sense, exchange rate policy was to a large extent a sideshow to the crisis.

"LOW DOMESTIC SAVINGS WAS THE CULPRIT"

It is commonly felt that an important contributor to financial instability in Mexico, and other countries in Latin America, is the unwillingness of domestic residents to save enough and to direct their savings toward domestic financial systems, where they can promote domestic investment. In the absence of such savings, countries are forced to choose between low rates of investment and growth, and an excessive reliance upon volatile foreign capital.

Here there are differing views. Some analysts argue that high domestic savings provide a "cushion" that might buffer the economy from economic shocks. It is true that Chile, with a very high saving rate, was almost entirely unaffected by the "tequila crisis" of 1995—but so was Colombia, where the saving rate is not high and has in recent years declined dramatically. The few studies of which we are aware fail to find evidence for a "buffering" effect of domestic saving. For example, Tornell and Velasco provide systematic evidence on the determinants of vulnerability to the tequila shock, and they were unable to find any support for the idea that low saving rates contribute to this vulnerability.[8] (They did find, however, a very strong correlation between growth in bank lending and economic vulnerability.) In a systematic investigation of the sources of macroeconomic volatility in roughly 100 countries, Gavin and Hausmann were similarly unable to detect any relationship between saving rates

---

[8] See Tornell and Velasco (1996).

and instability in real GDP or the real exchange rate.[9] But perhaps future research will be more supportive.

What about the unwillingness of domestic savers to place their savings in the domestic financial system, where the savings can be used to finance domestic investment? This reluctance, including occasional episodes of capital flight, was a reaction to the extreme monetary and financial instability that plagued the region. However, since the late 1980s, Mexico and many other countries in the region have reestablished a substantial degree of financial stability, restructured their economies, and liberalized their financial systems. These measures were part of a strategy designed to, among other things, promote domestic savings.

As a result, and particularly in Mexico, domestic bank deposits grew rapidly as the public and the domestic financial system responded to the more stable economic environment. As we discussed above, rapidly expanding bank deposits generated a lending boom that did in fact finance some growth in investment, but the outstanding result of which was a surge of lending to consumers. The strong incentives for domestic financial saving thus had the unintended result of providing the financing for "dissaving" by the private sector, which took place while public saving rates improved dramatically. The decline in saving is thus, ironically, a byproduct of the reforms of the 1990s, which produced financial stability in a more liberalized financial sector, thus producing the bank lending boom that, we shall argue, comprises a more fundamental cause of the crisis.[10]

"SHORT-TERM FINANCE OF CURRENT-ACCOUNT DEFICITS WAS THE CULPRIT"

If it demonstrates anything, the Mexican crisis illustrates the dangers of short-term debt, perhaps in creating and certainly in amplifying the financial crisis. But it is misleading to associate this debt with budgetary and current-account deficits. The Mexican *cetes* (short-term government debt), from which investors began to flee in 1994, were issued not to finance large deficits, but primarily as an instrument to "sterilize" the massive capital inflows that Mexico experienced in 1990-94—to prevent these inflows from generating an inflationary expansion of the domestic money supply. This sterilization would have been necessary even in the absence of fiscal or current-account deficits. The emphasis should therefore be on debt

---

[9] See Gavin and Hausmann (1996b).

[10] The financial liberalization in the United Kingdom was also associated with a sharp decline in private saving. See Bayoumi (1993) and Begg and Griffith-Jones (1996).

structure, not the size of the current account. In this respect, the advice generally given to countries to carry out monetary policy with market-based instruments, as did Mexico, should be amended to include explicit consideration of the resulting debt structure and the required level of international reserves.

"THE TESOBONOS DID IT"

A number of observers have argued that the conversion of (peso-denominated) *cetes* into (dollar-indexed) *tesobonos* was a major contributor to the financial disorder that followed the Mexican devaluation in December 1994. Of course, once the devaluation occurred, Mexico's cost of debt service would have been lower if its debts had not been dollar-indexed. But this would have come at the cost of higher interest payments in the months leading up to the devaluation. With the benefit of hindsight, we now know that the issuance of dollar debt was a bad investment for Mexico, but this was far less obvious with the information available to the authorities in mid-1994. The dollar denomination of the *tesobonos* was far less significant than their short maturity, which exposed the country to the danger of a "run" on the public debt.

However, disruptive as the financial panic may have been in the early stages of the crisis, the evolution of the Mexican crisis casts doubt upon whether either the denomination or the maturity structure of the Mexican public debt was a fundamental source of the economic disruption that engulfed the country during 1995. As a theoretical matter, it is well understood that financial panics generated by (perhaps self-fulfilling) fears about the feasibility of rolling over public debt can create financial and economic crises.[11] But what these stories cannot explain is why the Mexican macroeconomic crisis continued and even intensified well after it became clear that the financial support provided by the international community would be sufficient to amortize the entire stock of *tesobonos*, eliminating the fears that might have created the panic. This suggests that the crisis had deeper roots than the structure of the public debt. We now explore some of these.

4. THREE ALTERNATIVE LESSONS

BANK LENDING BOOMS OFTEN END UP IN TEARS . . .

It is well understood that the current-account deficits that led up to the Mexican crisis resulted from a shortfall of private, not govern-

---

[11] See, for example, Calvo (1996).

ment, savings. One casualty of the crisis therefore has been the idea that current-account deficits are not dangerous unless they reflect public-sector spending imbalances. While this idea has been discredited, there is no consensus on what can cause private decisions to go awry in the way that they seem to have done in Mexico, and there is as a result little understanding of when private borrowing is entering a danger zone, and how policy can respond.

In this context, we would point to the commercial bank lending boom that accompanied the inflation stabilization and capital inflows of the late 1980s and early 1990s in Mexico. As we have noted, bank lending to the private sector exploded between 1989 and 1994 because lower inflation raised the demand for domestic bank deposits, and capital inflows were partly intermediated through the banking system, thus providing banks with funds to lend, while at the same time the government was sharply reducing its reliance upon domestic bank debt. All of these were beneficial developments in themselves, but the magnitude of the resulting lending boom was a sign of trouble—and was almost certainly a key factor behind the private-sector overspending that led to the crisis. The well-understood information and incentive problems associated with financial intermediation help explain why privately optimal decisions could lead to socially suboptimal outcomes. And, as we have noted, the financial vulnerability generated by the lending boom made it more difficult for authorities to respond promptly to the decline in capital inflows during 1994 because of fear that the required increase in domestic interest rates would create additional stress for the banking system.

This suggests that macroeconomic policy-makers need to keep a vigilant eye on the banking system. In particular, they should "lean against the wind" of lending booms to ensure that bank lending does not grow too rapidly, and they should ensure that banks are robust enough to weather the shocks to which they will inevitably be exposed.

In this context, we raise two questions about the Mexican policy framework in the years leading up to the crisis. First, with the benefit of hindsight, it now seems probable that the Mexican policy of zero reserve requirements against commercial bank deposits amplified the lending boom and thus contributed to the development of financial fragility. While increased lending to the private sector is a highly desirable long-run outcome, it would have been better to promote a more gradual increase in financial intermediation, both to reduce the inefficiencies associated with rapid lending booms and to provide the regulatory and supervisory authorities

289

with time to grow into their new and more complex responsibilities. This could have been accomplished by setting high liquidity requirements for banks during the early phase of the adjustment to reform that could then have been reduced gradually to the lower levels that would be required in the steady state for prudential purposes.

A second and related question surrounds the use of privatization revenue. Again, with the benefit of hindsight, it seems clear that the use of these revenues to retire public debt held by the domestic banks contributed to those banks' capacity to lend and may therefore have had counterproductive macroeconomic consequences. This suggests that in deciding whether to use privatization to retire domestic debt, or to retire external debt, or to accumulate international reserves, attention should be paid to the impact on the lending capacity of the domestic financial system.

. . . ESPECIALLY WHEN THEY ARE INTERMEDIATING SHORT-TERM CAPITAL INFLOWS

There is a special danger in permitting easily reversed, short-term capital inflows to be intermediated through the banking system. If they are, they will finance relatively illiquid loans that cannot be liquidated, except at prohibitive cost, in the event that the inflows are suddenly reversed. This transformation of term, in which banks emit short-term liabilities to fund longer-term assets, creates severe liquidity risks for the domestic financial system. To protect the system against these risks, banks need to be induced to hold sufficient amounts of liquid assets to permit them to weather sudden shocks to their funding, such as might be created by a reversal of short-term capital inflows. This suggests that banks should be required to hold very substantial reserves of liquid assets against their short-term international liabilities.

FISCAL EQUILIBRIUM IS ELUSIVE—BALANCED BUDGETS MAY NOT BE ENOUGH

An insidious fiscal "optical illusion" contributes to the difficulty of securing an appropriate response to capital-account shocks such as the one that hit Mexico in 1994. During capital-inflows episodes, the fiscal accounts typically appear healthy, but this is often partly illusory, and fiscal accounts often deteriorate automatically when the capital flows vanish. This is because capital inflows are typically associated with private spending and production booms that temporarily boost fiscal revenues.[12] But when the inflows cease and the spending

---

[12] This argument is developed in Talvi (1996).

boom ends, as eventually it must, an underlying fiscal deficit emerges just at the moment when the country has lost its ability to finance it. This creates the need for sharp and pro-cyclical fiscal adjustments like those required in both Mexico and Argentina after the crisis.

To avoid these costly adjustments, authorities should set fiscal targets to account for such cyclical phenomena and aim for a large enough surplus during good times so that the fiscal accounts will remain viable when things get bad, without the need for a sharp, pro-cyclical fiscal response. The fiscal target should account for the government's tax capacity (governments with weak tax capacities can afford to run much smaller deficits than can governments with stronger tax capacities); it should also account for the depth of the domestic financial market that must finance the imbalance. On both grounds, prudent deficit levels are likely to be smaller in most countries of Latin America than they might be in the industrial economies. The deficit target should also take into account the size and structure of the government's outstanding debt; countries with large, short-term debt are more vulnerable to a confidence crisis and should therefore maintain a more conservative fiscal stance until the debt structure is improved.

In addition to reducing the probability of a crisis of confidence in the public finances, such a policy will also limit the current-account deficits and appreciation of the real exchange rate that accompany inflows, reducing the risk of a subsequent, disruptive outflow.

5. REFLECTIONS ON THE ROLE OF THE IDB

The Inter-American Development Bank (IDB) was no more prescient than other participants in the drama of reform, recovery, and crisis that was played out in Mexico and, in somewhat modified form, other countries of the region. The IDB was largely unaware of the risks posed by bank lending booms and the likelihood that such booms would follow successful stabilization and reform episodes. We therefore failed to monitor financial sector activities during the 1990s in ways that we might have done, and we never questioned the government's management of reserves and public debt. Since the crisis, we, along with the other multilaterals, have stepped up considerably our analysis of banking crises and are now much more active in supporting the design and implementation of improvements in prudential and regulatory structures.

While always ready to applaud fiscal discipline, we tended to view fiscal policy in a somewhat static context, where the aim was budgetary balance, or perhaps a fiscal balance that could be sustained indefinitely. We were not sufficiently aware of the need to push for substantially higher fiscal surpluses when times are temporarily good in order to prevent the need for a fiscal contraction when the good times vanish. We are now helping member-country governments to strengthen their budgetary institutions, with the aim of providing decision-making structures conducive to the conduct of a more stabilizing fiscal policy.

We also were not pushing for the development of social insurance programs that would reduce the social costs of necessary fiscal contractions. In this area there remains progress for us to make. Our support for social safety net programs has been oriented toward the poor—itself a good thing—but has fallen short of helping to create permanent social insurance programs for temporary unemployment that are universal and fiscally sustainable.

6. CONCLUSION

The Mexican case provides in particularly vivid relief lessons about the management of reform that also emerge from a number of recent Latin American experiences. It illustrates, first, that successful stabilization and reform programs generate powerful short-term macroeconomic dynamics. These dynamics reflect fundamentally positive forces, including notably the re-monetization of the economy and an associated increase in the financing of private activity, and a reactivation of domestic demand. But, however positive these developments may be over the longer term, they tend to generate economic and financial vulnerabilities in the short term. If the adjustment process is not carefully managed with an eye toward limiting these vulnerabilities, the boom can give way to crisis. This is what happened in Mexico.

Doing so is neither easy nor automatic. To prevent a potentially destabilizing lending boom, monetary authorities have to "lean against the wind" of the market well in advance of any obvious signals of an impending crisis—just when financial market participants are having the most fun. To prevent the emergence of fiscal vulnerabilities, authorities will have to find some way of inducing the political system to run fiscal surpluses during transitory revenue booms despite the political appeal of using them to expand hard-to-reverse public spending commitments. And they will have to have the foresight to adopt a prudent debt-management policy that reduces the likelihood of a panic by holders of government debt despite the apparently higher costs of issuing longer-term debt.

Given these difficulties, it is not surprising that countries have fallen into crisis in the past, and it is not unlikely that they will do so in the future. Here too, the Mexican experience provides some lessons. First, despite the short-term pain that it may cause, a fiscal contraction will probably be necessary to reestablish confidence in the currency and the public debt. It is essential that the fiscal adjustment be timely and credible. The probable need for fiscal adjustment highlights the need to design targeted extensions of the social safety net: In the short run to protect the most vulnerable, and in the medium run to act as automatic stabilizers, not only minimizing the social costs of recessions, but also dampening the effect of booms. Second, if the crisis requires a revision in the policy framework, it should be comprehensive, credible, and effectively communicated. Here the sharp contrast between the positive reaction to the comprehensive policy response announced by the Mexican authorities in mid-March 1995 and the negative reaction to the rather less comprehensive policy actions that preceded it is instructive. If a banking crisis erupts, prompt action is required to prevent problem banks from "gambling for resurrection," thus compounding the macroeconomic and fiscal costs of the financial crisis.

REFERENCES AND BIBLIOGRAPHY

Aspe, Pedro (1993). *Economic Transformation the Mexican Way*. Cambridge, Mass.: MIT Press.

Bayoumi, Tamin (1993). "Financial Deregulation and Household Saving," *The Economic Journal* 103. November.

Begg, David, and Stephany Griffith-Jones (1996). "Swinging Since the 60s: Fluctuations in UK Savings and Lessons for Latin America." Manuscript prepared for Inter-American Development Bank research project on savings in Latin America. Washington, D.C.: IDB.

Calvo, Guillermo (1996). "Varieties of Financial Crisis." Unpublished manuscript. College Park, Md.: University of Maryland.

Gavin, Michael, and Ricardo Hausmann (1996a). "The Roots of Banking Crises: The Macro-economic Context," in Ricardo Hausmann and Liliana Rojas-Suárez, eds., *Banking Crises in Latin America*. Washington, D.C.: Inter-American Development Bank.

Gavin, Michael, and Ricardo Hausmann (1996b). "Sources of Macro-economic Volatility in Developing Economies." Washington, D.C.: Office of the Chief Economist, Inter-American Development Bank. Mimeograph.

Gavin, Michael, Leonardo Leiderman, and Ricardo Hausmann (1996). "The Macro-economics of Capital Flows to Latin America: Experience and Policy Issues," in Ricardo Hausmann and Liliana Rojas-Suárez, eds., *Volatile Capital Flows: How to Tame their Impact on Latin America*. Washington, D.C.: Inter-American Development Bank.

Gavin, Michael, Ricardo Hausmann, Roberto Perotti, and Ernesto Talvi (1996). "Managing Fiscal Policy in Latin America: Volatility, Procyclicality and Limited Creditworthiness." OCE Working Paper no. 326. Washington, D.C.: Inter-American Development Bank.

Inter-American Development Bank (1996). *Report on Economic and Social Progress in Latin America: 1996*. Washington, D.C.: IDB.

Inter-American Development Bank (1995a). Statement by Enrique Iglesias at the Inaugural Session of the Annual Meeting of the Board of Governors of the Inter-American Development Bank and the Inter-American Investment Corporation. Jerusalem, Israel.

Inter-American Development Bank (1995b). "The Tequila Effect is Over: Evidence, Implications, Lessons." Washington, D.C.: Office of the Chief Economist, IDB.

Naím, Moisés (1995). "Latin America the Morning After," *Foreign Affairs* July/August.

Talvi, Ernesto (1996). "Exchange Rate-Based Stabilization with Endogenous Fiscal Response." Inter-American Development Bank Working Paper. Washington, D.C.: IDB, Office of the Chief Economist. March.

Tornell, Aarón, and Andrés Velasco (1996). "Financial Crises in Emerging Markets: The Lessons of 1995." Brookings Papers on Economic Activity no. 1. Washington, D.C.: Brookings Institution.

12. MEXICO'S LARGER STORY*

MOISÉS NAÍM

arthquakes provide precious data about fault lines, stress points, and cracks buried deep within the Earth. Similarly, Mexico's December 1994 financial earthquake offered a wealth of new information about the fault lines underlying current trends in global economics and politics.

The Mexican crash exposed disturbing traits of the emerging international financial system and offered new insights into the limits and possibilities of the market reforms now common around the world. In particular, it exposed tensions between a drastically changed international financial system and countries beginning to experiment with deeper integration into the global economy.

All governments face political constraints on their capacity to adapt their economic policies to rapid changes in the external economic environment. But, as Mexico has shown, the combination of market reforms and changes in the way the international financial system now operates presents governments with unprecedented challenges. Although the Mexican crisis undoubtedly had Mexican origins, it was not simply the result of government mistakes, corruption, and electoral politicking. All of these elements were present, but Mexico's crisis was as much a story about the new international financial system as it was a story about Mexico. At each of the situation's crucial turning points, external factors helped to shape the outcome.

The Mexican economic reforms followed the script of what is known as the "Washington consensus"—the policy goals of fiscal discipline, tax reform, financial liberalization, a single competitive exchange rate, liberalization of trade and foreign investment, privatization, and deregulation. The boom in foreign portfolio investment initially helped but eventually undermined these reforms. The boom was induced more by transient financial conditions abroad than by permanent reforms in Mexico. Portfolio flows—investments

* Reprinted, with minor revisions and permission, from *Foreign Policy* 99, Summer 1995.

in Mexican stocks and bonds—first masked the gravity of Mexico's current-account deficit. Then, when it should have been evident that the country was importing more than was prudent and that its currency was overvalued, foreign investors—attracted by higher relative earnings—continued to pump dollars into the economy, exacerbating the Mexican peso's overvaluation, stimulating imports, and constraining the government's policy options.

Mexico's participation in the North American Free Trade Agreement (NAFTA) was seen as a panacea for its troubles. Unfortunately, the debate in the United States, instead of highlighting the consequences of Mexico's financial integration into volatile world capital markets, centered on hypothetical U.S. job losses and real environmental problems that in practice had little to do with NAFTA.

It is true that Subcomandante Marcos, the hooded leader of the Zapatista uprising in Chiapas state, wrought havoc in the Mexican stock exchange, the Bolsa. But the impact of his actions was nothing compared with that of U.S. Federal Reserve Chairman Alan Greenspan's decisions. The hike in U.S. interest rates to curb inflationary pressures in the United States caused the Mexican markets to drop much more than did the news of a revolt by indigenous people in the south.

Even when the situation started to deteriorate, foreign actions were as important as domestic factors. In fact, after the initial news of Chiapas, the stock market rapidly recovered, gaining more than 20 percent until it was brought down in reaction to the rise in U.S. interest rates. Foreign mutual funds mattered as much as the most powerful domestic institutions in determining Mexican economic policy. After the devaluation, again, investment decisions made in the world's financial centers and political decisions made in Washington and other capitals determined the nature of the crisis, its ramifications, and the response to it as much as or more than did any action by the Mexican government.

The point is not that the Mexican government was a passive spectator of the unfolding drama. Rather, it was the central actor performing a tightly scripted role that greatly constrained its flexibility. The government needed to rid the economy of its legacy of instability and inefficiency; domestic political restrictions made the task more difficult, while powerful and volatile external forces clouded the government's vision and compromised its policies.

During the early 1990s, Mexico was the model of economic reform that others sought to emulate. Soon thereafter, however,

Mexico surprisingly began to go down policy paths that—as international experience has repeatedly shown—can lead an economy to the precipice. By now, several lessons of macroeconomic management are well established. Governments ignore them at their peril. Still, they often do, and they repeatedly pay the price.

If funding long-term projects with short-term loans is a bad idea, then funding growing, multi-year trade deficits with volatile, short-term foreign capital inflows is not a much better one. Fixing the exchange rate may be a valid alternative at the beginning of a comprehensive anti-inflationary strategy, but fixing it for too long often leads to its appreciation vis-à-vis the currencies of trading partners. All too soon, imports soar, exports lag, the current-account deficit grows out of control, and foreign reserves dry up. A painful devaluation then becomes unavoidable. Perhaps not surprisingly, governments try to postpone this final step as long as possible, often until it is too late. In the process they reconfirm a central lesson: It is far less traumatic to adopt the needed policy corrections proactively instead of reactively; a country should not wait for a run on its currency and for its foreign reserves to dry up before it adjusts the exchange rate.

Another often-ignored lesson is that high interest rates alone cannot compensate for the effects of large and protracted trade or fiscal deficits. Further, even if the fiscal accounts of the federal government seem to be in balance, the spending patterns of other public or quasi-public agencies frequently are not. Such expenditures often grow to the point of undermining the government's fiscal efforts. In Mexico, these off-budget outlays mainly took the form of lending by public regional development banks, which rose from 1 percent of gross domestic product in 1990 to more than 4 percent in 1994.

Last but not least, the political cycle should not be allowed to overwhelm prudent monetary policy. In 1994, which was a difficult election year for the ruling Partido Revolucionario Institucional (PRI), the decisions of the "independent" Mexican central bank were not sufficiently independent of political calculations. During that year, monetary expansion of more than 20 percent and lax credit policies added to the economic instability created by the decline in foreign investment. This demonstrates that in countries where personalities count more than institutions, laws are not enough. In 1993, Mexico adopted legislation to ensure the autonomy of the central bank, yet short-term electoral calculations continued to have an inordinate influence on its policies.

No country, much less a developing country, can afford to ignore these and other economic imperatives. Not even Mexico—a "star" developing country newly admitted to the Organisation for Economic Co-operation and Development (OECD); with a free trade agreement with the United States and Canada; and with economic promise that made it, according to a respected Swiss bank, as quoted in the *Wall Street Journal* just before the crash, "a candidate for investment grade [and]. . . for membership in the European Monetary Union"—can disregard these principles.

What is striking about the economic lessons of the Mexican catastrophe is how little they add to what was already known about the mistakes governments commonly make in the course of implementing economic reforms. In fact, a central lesson of the Mexican experience is how unlearnable some lessons of economic management seem to be, not because they are technically difficult to grasp, but because they are politically difficult to apply.

HOW CAN SUCH SMART GUYS MAKE SUCH DUMB MISTAKES?

In all manmade catastrophes, incompetence and irresponsibility play some role. But blaming them for the Mexican crisis blurs the role of important factors that are also present in other reforming countries. In Mexico, mistakes were made and political expediency often got in the way of economic reason. But the mistakes were not easy to avoid, and the political constraints would have haunted even the most responsible of governments.

President Carlos Salinas de Gortari had the academic training and professional experience to understand the need to maintain fundamental economic equilibria. He also showed both a clear commitment to making economic stability his top political priority and the willingness to incur the unavoidable political costs. His economic team of modern-day philosopher-kings, comprised of experienced, U.S.–trained Ph.D.s, was regarded as one of the best in the world.

In addition, the ravages of high inflation and stagnation had made the Mexican population tolerant of the bitter economic medicines that were prescribed to halt spiraling prices. Another advantage was a political system that at the time still allowed the government to hold dissent within narrowly defined limits.

Salinas's team moved early in his administration to renegotiate the country's gigantic foreign debt, to undertake market reforms that boosted its international prestige, and to join NAFTA, which signaled Mexico's new standing in the world. Mexico soon became a main beneficiary of the unprecedented surge in private capital flow, a favorite son among the "emerging markets." Between 1990 and 1994, Mexico became the world's second-largest recipient of foreign private investment, after China.

Yet all of these favorable factors did not enable the Mexican government to avoid the mistakes that eventually engendered a monumental economic crisis. Why? The answer is that the intersection of market reforms, domestic politics, and international conditions did not leave the government much room to maneuver. Within such narrow margins, the probability of making the wrong calls became too high. In Mexico, the opportunities, risks, and dilemmas faced by most reforming countries appeared with unusual intensity.

Salinas began his term in 1988 with the Mexican economy debilitated by macroeconomic instability, protectionism, and low international competitiveness. His government quickly took all the unpopular fiscal and monetary steps needed to curb inflationary pressures. But the environment was inflation prone, so the initial reforms were not enough. The propensity of the currency to slide had to be stopped. Hence, Salinas's government adopted a foreign exchange regime that pegged the peso to the U.S. dollar. In addition, to spur competitiveness, the government privatized companies, unilaterally liberalized trade, promoted foreign investment, and opened the stock market to foreigners. Foreign money, goods, and machinery began to flow in much faster than exports flowed out. The reforms coincided with a surge in foreign investment, which helped to cover the trade imbalance and eventually allowed the government to run abnormally high current-account deficits. These inflows soon created such an "abundance" of foreign exchange that the local currency became overvalued. Overvaluation in turn stimulated imports to the point that the trade deficit became a critical destabilizing factor. Even more critical was the fact that the bulk of foreign investment was in liquid financial instruments that foreign investors could take out of Mexico as quickly as they had put them in.

The government, in spite of its aura of technical acumen, came to rely on several hopes. First, it hoped that the country's continuing attractiveness to foreign investors would prevent capital flight. A second hope was that dependence on foreign capital would subside as the large gap between imports and exports gradually closed. The government expected Mexican exports to soar as the country's competitiveness improved and international treaties eased access to the markets of industrialized countries. In turn, these treaties were supposed to lower the political risk perceived by foreign investors and to further increase Mexico's attractiveness to international capital. Joining NAFTA thus became a priority; the possibility of its being stillborn became the biggest threat to Mexico's stability.

Meanwhile, both the peso's overvaluation and the political difficulties of doing something about it were increasing rapidly. In 1993, as the debate in the U.S. Congress over the ratification of NAFTA became more bitter, the Mexican government concluded that a devaluation would kill its chances of ratification.

But NAFTA was not the only factor constraining the Salinas administration. Just as the winds of international finance were turning against Mexico, electoral politics erupted with an intensity not seen in over six decades. Devaluation became even less of an option in light of the possibility that the PRI's candidate would lose an election for the first time in 65 years. While in 1993 it was NAFTA that delayed devaluation, in 1994 it was the presidential election. Then the United States raised interest rates, and Mexico suffered the consequences of the lower investment flows induced by these higher foreign rates. The uprising in Chiapas; the assassinations of the PRI's presidential candidate, of a Roman Catholic cardinal, and of a leading PRI official; as well as a string of highly publicized kidnappings of some of Mexico's wealthiest businessmen, all greatly heightened anxiety. Suddenly the country faced both political uncertainty and economic fragility.

In 1993 and 1994, a significant correction of the exchange rate, the reform of the foreign exchange regime, and a tighter monetary policy might have laid the foundation for future stability. But it is also easy to see how, under the circumstances, securing the future became less of a priority than stabilizing the present.

The government initially believed that the main problem was that domestic political shocks were scaring away investors. It failed to react adequately to the rising interest rates in the United States, which were pulling foreign money away from emerging markets in general, not just from Mexico. Calming the political turbulence at home took precedence over reacting to the fundamental economic changes abroad. Instead of adjusting monetary, fiscal, and foreign exchange policies to the new financial realities abroad, the government concentrated on stabilizing the political situation. It found itself unable to devalue, to hike interest rates, to tighten the money supply, or to stop state-owned regional banks from eroding the fiscal balance. Once the government concluded that the problem was more domestic and political than international and economic, political calculations overrode economic ones, and the door to the ensuing debacle was opened. Within two weeks of the initial devaluation, the peso lost more than 30 percent of its value, and the Bolsa dropped almost 50 percent in dollar terms. By March, a quarter of a million Mexicans had joined the ranks of the unemployed.

For most Americans, Mexico's crisis came as a surprise. The NAFTA debate had left them expecting Mexico to take away American jobs, not to require an American bailout. What was startling was how many well-informed actors were also surprised by the crash. Most of the academic analysis and media coverage of the Mexican economy had been laudatory. Warnings about the unsustainability of the situation were uncommon, although there were a few. Writing in an April 1994 Brookings Institution paper, economists Rudiger Dornbusch and Alejandro Werner noted that a significant departure from the present exchange rate was needed and recommended a currency devaluation. I myself wrote in *Foreign Policy* in the fall of 1993 that in both Argentina and Mexico:

> Misaligned exchange rates and other conditions had greatly stimulated imports, thus nurturing large, growing, and potentially destabilizing trade deficits. . . .
>
> The precariousness of the situation is evident. Sooner or later, Argentina and Mexico will be forced to make complex adjustments. Their inflation continues to exceed the U.S. rate, thus eroding their current exchange rate policies. Without broader reforms, high interest rates cannot maintain stability forever. The flow of foreign capital into Latin America is also likely to dwindle—at least temporarily—as investors see heightened devaluation risks and find fewer companies to buy.[1]

Some researchers at universities and think tanks warned that heavy reliance on portfolio capital was dangerous. But, overall, the warnings were too few and too low-key to be heard above the chorus of praise for Mexico coming from Wall Street, Washington, and Mexico City itself.

A unique convergence of interests inhibited important actors from scrutinizing Mexico's economic situation more rigorously. In Washington, Russia's economic reforms and the passage of NAFTA, the Uruguay Round of the General Agreement on Tariffs and Trade, and other priorities monopolized the attention of Congress and the relevant agencies, including the International Monetary Fund (IMF). The Mexican government mounted a well-financed and

---

[1] Naím (1993), pp. 142-143.

effective propaganda campaign to support its bid to enter NAFTA and to attract foreign investment. The U.S. private sector saw Mexico and NAFTA as great business opportunities and lobbied heavily in Mexico's favor, boosting its virtues and obscuring its problems. On Wall Street, salesmen of Mexican stocks and bonds emphasized short-term profit opportunities and paid little attention to underlying trends. This oversight was partly induced by the fact that, in recent years, many economists and market analysts in securities firms have become part of the marketing effort. Their year-end bonuses depend more on their support of sales than on the rigor of their analyses.

In Europe and Asia, worries about NAFTA becoming "Fortress America" blurred the fact that one of the walls of the fortress had shaky foundations. Another important factor was that Mexico's authoritarian traditions rendered the opposition unable to probe the claims of the government effectively. The government treated the production and dissemination of official statistics more like a secret prerogative than a fundamental part of its accountability to society. When the situation started to unravel, economic statistics became scarcer and their scope narrower. For months before the crisis erupted, no official information was available about the level of international reserves, monetary aggregates, capital flows, or outstanding short-term debt.

Few journalists broke the herd instinct to sound a warning. Listening to the Mexican government propaganda, checking it with "objective" economists on Wall Street, and discovering that no one at the U.S. Treasury Department or the IMF seemed worried about Mexico, reporters generally filed favorable articles. The positive stories on Mexico reassured investors and may have postponed the crisis. But deferring the crisis only increased the severity of its backlash as investors, shocked by the unexpected dimensions of the problem, panicked and scrambled to sell their Mexican holdings.

In hindsight, it is clear that better surveillance and more rigorous scrutiny of the Mexican economy would have lessened the severity of the crisis. The IMF, the World Bank, international credit-rating agencies, and investment advisors have probably learned from this crisis that lax scrutiny can have dire consequences and that the availability of timely and reliable data should be a non-negotiable condition for continuous international support. Investors in the stocks of publicly listed companies in developed countries learned long ago not to base their decisions on glossy annual reports or on the recommendations of brokers working on commission. In these countries, the regulatory authorities have also learned the crucial importance of ensuring the reliability of the data that companies provide. Analysts know that their careers depend on their objectivity. The Mexican crisis shows that these principles should hold in the new world of portfolio investments in emerging markets as well, and that government propaganda cannot replace prudent economic policies.

WHAT DO MEXICO, ORANGE COUNTY, AND BARINGS P.L.C. ALL HAVE IN COMMON?

In 1995 a seemingly viable country (Mexico) was brought to its knees, a rich American county (Orange, in California) filed for bankruptcy protection, and a proud British bank (Barings P.L.C.) melted away because of imprudent financial decisions. Do they have common characteristics?

In all three cases, mismanagement and speculation played important roles. More important, however, is that all three entities fell victim to an international financial system that offers sweeping new opportunities but also inflicts immediate, lethal punishments on those who make the wrong calls. Mexico relied on unprecedented volumes of portfolio investment to finance its trade deficits. When these flows stopped, a major crisis erupted. Orange County relied on new financial instruments that could yield enormous profits if interest rates did not move up. When they did, the county went broke. Nicholas Leeson, the now infamous trader at Barings P.L.C. in Singapore, made incredible profits using instruments that did not exist just a few years ago and that depended on the Japanese stock market not moving too much. When it did move down following the Kobe earthquake, a firm that had existed for more than two centuries went on the auction block. In these three cases, very new and poorly understood financial instruments and institutional arrangements opened unprecedented possibilities, but the new instruments and arrangements also amplified the risks to unprecedented levels.

That imprudent economic policies lead to painful economic and social consequences is nothing new. What is new and was dramatically illustrated by the Mexican crisis is how unforgiving the international financial system has become to unsound economic policies and how quickly, how deeply, and how far the shock waves of a crash can be felt. This has more to do with the profound transformations in the international financial system in the past two decades than with Mexico's policy mistakes.

Mexico is not the first country to have a financial crisis with significant international repercussions, and it will not be the last. But the nature of Mexico's disaster clearly indicates that national finan-cial crises are no longer what they used to be. The actors, the vol-umes of money involved, the nature of the crisis, and the dizzying speed of the financial markets' reaction were unprecedented.

In the past, the main international actors in the unfolding of a country's economic collapse were international commercial banks, the IMF, and the World Bank. Now, the priority of the finance minis-ter of any troubled country is to persuade money managers and other private institutional actors not to take their money out—and for good reasons. Between 1977 and 1981, 67 percent of Latin America's external financing came from commercial banks. Between 1989 and 1992, this share plummeted to 14 percent. Meanwhile, money from mutual funds and other stock and bond investors grew to 40 percent of foreign investment in the region, up from a paltry 15 percent in the late 1970s. Between 1990 and 1994, the World Bank disbursed $84 billion to all developing countries. In the same period, private investors poured a net $660 billion into these countries.

When the Mexican crisis erupted—and before the IMF decid-ed to bend its old rules and join the United States in the largest international rescue package until then—the most the Mexican gov-ernment could expect to get from the IMF was less than $2.5 billion in credits. That figure paled in comparison with the amount needed to deal with the crisis.

By the end of 1994, the Mexican government had about $30 billion in short-term, dollar-indexed bonds (*tesobonos*), largely in the hands of foreign investors. In the previous months, these *tesobonos* were being rolled over at the rate of $2 billion per week with the happy acquiescence of private money managers lured by the bonds' high yields.

Today, the magnitude of the funds controlled by private invest-ment managers makes the volumes typically supplied by the IMF and the World Bank almost irrelevant. In the Mexican situation, these institutions were increasingly relegated to the role of external auditors, consultants, and credit-rating agencies, certifying the government's figures, providing advice, and reassuring the investment community of the soundness of economic reforms. Unfortunately, in the Mexican case, the Bretton Woods institutions were not able to perform these functions adequately. As other chapters in this book argue, early warn-ing alarms about the unsustainability of the Mexican policies did sound inside the IMF and the World Bank. But in public, either out of precipitous myopia or out of well-meaning solidarity with Mexico, these institutions did little to modulate the cheerleading coming from

Wall Street. Mutual funds have not only displaced the Bretton Woods institutions as the main providers of money to developing countries, but they are also offering "advice" to officials of the very countries in which they are often the largest foreign investors.

The Mexican crisis offered interesting insights into the new role of international money managers and the conditions they impose on the countries in which they become major investors. Developing countries often chastise the IMF and the World Bank for the conditions these institutions impose on their loans, such as policy reforms or budget cuts. But now that mutual fund managers and credit-rating agencies exert an unprecedented influence on the behavior of governments, the conditionalities of the IMF and the World Bank look enlightened and flexible—even benevolent—by comparison.

In mid-1994, when Mexican instability became more visible, a group of international fund managers active in the Mexican financial markets decided to "advise" Mexico's government. According to the June 14, 1994, *Wall Street Journal*:

> Mexico was asked to curb the speed of the peso's daily devaluation permitted by the country's basic economic pact with labor and business. Secondly, Mexico's government was asked to insure investors against currency-exchange losses on $5 billion of peso-denominated securities if the peso dropped below the prescribed range. The investors also asked that Mexican banks be allowed to increase their foreign-currency liabilities to 25% of total assets from 20%. This could boost the banks' peso buying, but then leave them at greater risk if the peso fell.

> The investor group also suggested the government issue long-term tesobonos, government bonds with built-in devaluation insurance; increase its swap lines with foreign central banks; and, perhaps most important, back all these measures with central-bank peso purchases to push the currency up.[2]

These "suggestions" were delivered with not-so-subtle hints of the consequences of disregarding the advice. The day before the fund managers met with the Mexican authorities, some of the funds represented in the group of self-proclaimed "advisors" refused to buy short-term Mexican treasury certificates in sufficient quantity to replace existing ones. Short-term interest rates soared, and the Bolsa plunged. It was not a bad way to get the attention of embattled government officials.

---

[2] Torres and Vogel Jr. (1994), p. A1.

Even after the crash, as it became evident that Mexico's reserves were almost depleted, that no interest rate seemed high enough to lure foreign money back, and that it would take years to restore investor confidence in Mexico, securities salesmen masquerading as "chief economists" from investment houses mounted a strident campaign aimed at pressing the Mexican government into revaluing the peso to its pre-crisis exchange rate. While these economists gave highly convoluted explanations to justify their prescription, reducing the huge losses they and their gullible clients were facing was probably as much on their minds as "reducing the plight of the Mexican poor," as one of the trader-pundits wrote.

Of course, developing countries have always depended on foreign investors for capital, technology, and access to foreign markets. But the immediate macroeconomic balance of a host country has never been as dependent on the decisions of a few foreign managers as it is today for countries financing trade deficits with portfolio capital.

In the past, a large multinational corporation might wield enormous clout over a host-country government. But its direct investments in factories, mines, or plantations also gave the government some leverage. After all, the corporation could not easily sell and leave. Now portfolio investors in London or New York can leave a country just by striking a key on their computers. This gives them enormous influence. It also creates a new form of international interdependence among countries that have little in common in terms of geography or trade.

THE NEIGHBORHOOD EFFECT

In 1994, the initial reaction of investors to the news of Mexico's debacle seemed to suggest that, as in 1982, a Mexican financial crisis was going to compromise the entire region. Immediately after the Mexican crash of 1994, stock prices in Latin American markets plunged, currencies weakened, and foreign investment flows all but disappeared.

But forces very different from those at work during the 1982 crisis surfaced in 1994. In the aftermath of the latest Mexican crisis, financial markets moved in to attack currencies in Thailand, Spain, Hong Kong, Sweden, Italy, and Russia, substantially weakening them. The Canadian dollar hit an eight-year low against the U.S. dollar, and financial markets in Poland, South Korea, Turkey, Nigeria, Bulgaria, India, Malaysia, Hungary, Pakistan, and the Philippines all experienced sharp drops.

Each of these countries had specific and unique circumstances that explain why investors scrambled away from their markets. The Mexican experience, however, heightened the aversion of international investors to risk and lowered their willingness to park their holdings in potentially unstable countries, even for higher returns. It is true that the Canadian fiscal imbalance has been there for years, Italy's political woes are not new, and Turkey's combination of political and macroeconomic disarray is chronic; but it took the Mexican crisis to make investors unwilling to live with the potential of large swings in the value of their portfolios.

The Mexican crises of 1982 and 1994 show that, increasingly, financial markets tend to cluster those countries perceived to be in the same "neighborhood" and to treat them roughly along the same lines. This time, however, the neighborhood is no longer defined solely in terms of geography. The main defining criterion is the potential volatility of the countries; the contagion spreads inside risk-clusters, or volatility neighborhoods. In the words of one banker, Wolfhard Graetz, quoted in the January 12, 1995, *Wall Street Journal*, "Investors are demanding a higher risk premium, and we have a crowding out . . . . If you have an epidemic, the weakest will be affected first. I won't say they will die, but they will suffer while the strong organisms will get through it much better."

The Mexican crisis sheds light on the motivations underlying the internationalization of investment portfolios. The voracious appetite in the United States and other industrialized countries for investments in emerging markets was initially interpreted as a reaction to opportunities created by economic reforms. The explanation was that investors had realized the benefits of diversifying the risk in their portfolios by spreading them internationally, and emerging markets provided the opportunity to do so.

The Mexican crisis showed that the prospect of high yields rather than prudence motivated this internationalization. Investors were looking abroad for the high returns that they were not getting at home, given the bearishness of financial markets in the United States, Japan, and Europe at the time. All it took to reduce the interest of investors in the benefits of international diversification was for the U.S. Federal Reserve Board to raise interest rates or for the Mexicans to devalue their peso.

In the aftermath of the Mexican crisis, portfolio investors did not cease to invest abroad, nor did they cease to be major players in "emerging markets." But countries with the potential for sudden instability in their economic policies will now have to offer strong enticements to attract foreign funds. Yet given the new realities of the world economy, no country will be able to afford to renounce portfolio investment. The challenge for all developing countries will be to learn to live with portfolio investment and to manage the risks it entails. The Mexican crisis also showed that existing mechanisms of global monetary governance are no longer adequate to deal with a world of integrated, securitized, electronically linked capital markets.

As damage from the peso debacle swiftly traveled around the globe, the urgency of stopping Mexico from defaulting on its short-term debt became apparent. It was also apparent that the United States was the only country with both the interest and the capacity to lead the rescue. The Clinton administration sought approval from Congress for a $40 billion package of loan guarantees aimed at calming investors and minimizing the risk that the Mexican crisis would spread to other countries. This aid package, which in principle did not imply any disbursement on the part of the U.S Treasury, was collateralized with the receipts of Mexican oil exports and was contingent on Mexico's adoption of harsh reforms. Furthermore, the assistance was bound to make money for the U.S government, as the Mexicans had to pay steep fees for using the loan guarantees. A refusal to extend this financial support, President Bill Clinton suggested, would throw Mexico into a major political and economic upheaval, which would hurt the United States. Obviously, other emerging economies would suffer too, and with them the prospects for U.S. exporters and investors.

Upon receiving the request from the administration, Speaker of the House Newt Gingrich (R-Georgia) told reporters that Republicans in Congress literally had "zero choice" but to approve it. Then Senate Majority Leader Bob Dole (R-Kansas) also supported the initiative, as did Greenspan and a bipartisan assemblage of former presidents and secretaries of the treasury, state, and commerce, who lobbied Congress to pass the Mexican package. It was not enough.

When it became clear that lawmakers were impervious to exhortations long on global implications and short on local considerations and that Congress was not going to support the initiative, Clinton acted on his own. He assembled an alternative rescue package that did not require congressional approval and that relied heavily on funds supplied by the U.S. Exchange Stabilization Fund and the IMF. While this decision calmed markets and briefly gave Mexico a second wind, European governments felt bulldozed into a bailout on which they were not adequately consulted and for which some saw little justification. Moreover, the bailout forced the IMF to extend an assistance package seven times bigger than the normal limit and to shell out a fifth of its liquid resources. Were Russia, for example, to get comparable conditions, it would be entitled to receive in excess of $40 billion from the IMF alone.

The Mexican bailout sent the wrong signal to governments and investors. It indicated that the potential losses of private investors eventually could be absorbed by governments and multilateral financial institutions, thus blurring the principle that both governments and investors should enter the game of portfolio investment at their own risk.

Experts disagree on what can be done to reduce the periodic bouts of hypervolatility in global financial markets. It seems unlikely that governments will allow currency traders and mutual fund managers to determine the world's financial stability. Why should a country like Chile, which has all its economic fundamentals in order, see its development prospects impaired by a crisis on the far side of the hemisphere? One of the consequences of the Mexican crisis was to highlight the need to modernize the way the international financial system is governed. It will take time, and the difficulties are enormous, but failure to revamp the mechanisms and institutions of global financial governance will ensure many unhappy surprises in the future.

NO ROOM FOR MISTAKES

In many ways, Mexico's travails resulted from its pioneering stance. Mexico was the first developing country to succeed in entering into a free trade agreement with two of the world's largest and most advanced economies. Portfolio investors with little experience abroad used Mexico as their first entrée to exotic emerging markets. Mutual fund investors discovered in Mexico their new clout. The IMF and the World Bank had little experience with the kinds of challenges coming from Mexico. Mainstream economists exhibited an appalling confusion about the measures needed to deal with a crisis that had many novel elements and that could not be calmed even by an unprecedented package of foreign financial assistance.

The situation in Mexico also showed that while economic fundamentals eventually force governments to adopt painful corrections, political calculations make their imprudent postponement all too frequent. Governments everywhere exhibit politically induced learning disabilities. In Mexico, not even a technocratic, politically shielded government could resist the temptation to bet against the hard lessons of policy experience.

The Mexican government was not alone in ignoring the lessons of sound policy-making. Nor was it alone in underestimating the impact of changing global financial conditions or in believing that a crash could be avoided without radical policy changes. Most journalists, investors, and international agencies echoed the Mexicans' contention that the country's economic fundamentals were sound.

But certain realities are now clear. Some reforming countries cite Mexico's example as the justification for measures designed to decouple their economies from the international economy in general and from the international financial system in particular. In contrast, countries with lower protectionist propensities and a firmer commitment to market reforms use Mexico's example to deepen these reforms. Strengthening economic fundamentals in ways that reduce their vulnerability to volatile international factors will become the first priority for countries bent on benefiting from international trade and investment. One major question confronting these countries will be the extent to which they should limit portfolio investment from abroad. Some, like Chile, will be able to institute a regime that will curb the more speculative flows while still attracting sizable portfolio investments. Others, lacking Chile's institutional capabilities and strong economic fundamentals, may end up with foreign investment regimes that reduce even more the slight appetite for emerging market securities remaining among international investors in the wake of the Mexican crisis. The risk for these countries is that, given the magnitudes of portfolio investment today, they may be unable to achieve adequate economic growth if they cannot tap into this pool of global financial resources. Those resources are ready to move into countries offering attractive rates of return at competitive risk. The challenge will be to develop the economic and institutional conditions that reduce the risks of living with inherently volatile foreign investment flows.

In some developed countries, the Mexican crisis will stimulate a vigorous search for new ways to stabilize the international economy and reduce the risk of systemic instability. Others will simply conclude that frail economies should be left to fend for themselves.

The Mexican example showed that while identifying lessons is important, enhancing the capacity of governments to put them into practice is even more so. Understanding the political factors that underlie the learning disabilities of governments should be accorded as much attention as identifying the correct economic lessons. The need to eliminate the political barriers to adoption of sound economic policies has become crucial, because the chances that a government can coexist with shaky economic fundamentals have all but disappeared. The margin for misguided economic policies has become exceedingly narrow, and the catastrophic consequences of policy mistakes appear with an immediacy and intensity not seen before. That is Mexico's real lesson for the world.

REFERENCES

Naím, Moisés (1993). "Latin America: Post-Adjustment Blues," *Foreign Policy* 92, Fall.

Torres, Craig, and Thomas T. Vogel Jr. (1994). "Some Mutual Funds Wield Growing Clout in Developing Nations," *Wall Street Journal*, June 14.

APPENDIX

MEXICO: A CHRONOLOGY OF FINANCIAL, ECONOMIC, AND POLITICAL EVENTS

Note: Adapted from separate chronologies prepared by Peter H. Smith and Robert L. Bartley.

1946   President Miguel Alemán elected and inaugurated; presides over devaluations in 1948 and 1952.

1954   **April:** Devaluation, 12.5 peso/dollar rate set; "Mexican Miracle" recovery.

1954   Policy of "Stabilizing Development"—under presidents Adolfo Ruíz Cortines (1952-1958), Adolfo López Mateos (1958-1964), and Gustavo Díaz Ordaz (1964-1970).

1968   Tlatelolco massacre—troops open fire on student protesters.

1970   President Luis Echeverría inaugurated (12.5 pesos/dollar).

1971-73 U.S./international economic developments: President Nixon closes gold window, August 15, 1971; OPEC conference pledges measures to ensure real purchasing power of oil, September 21, 1971; final breakdown of Bretton Woods; OPEC oil embargo and price surge, 1973.

1976   **August 31:** 12.5 rate abandoned, peso float to 20 pesos/dollar.

             December 1: President Luis López Portillo inaugurated (24 pesos/dollar).

1979-82 U.S./international developments: After Belgrade IMF meeting, Paul Volcker institutes new monetary measures intended to tighten U.S. monetary policy, tightens again before and after Reagan inauguration. Oil price breaks, March 1981.

1982   **February 5:** López Portillo *"como un perro"* speech, pledging to defend peso.

             February 18: Peso float.

             April-September: Alfa defaults (April), further devaluation to 60-120 pesos/dollar (August), debt moratorium (August 15), bank nationalization and exchange controls (September 1).

             December 1: President Miguel de la Madrid inaugurated (150 pesos/dollar).

313

1983   **February:** Stabilization measures include start of "sliding parities," with daily devaluation of peso by amounts adjusted from time to time with economic conditions over next 14 years.

1985-86   Debt crisis, negotiation and extension. Oil price falling, Mexico out of compliance with IMF agreement, earthquake strikes (September 1985). New IMF agreement sought (October 1985), signed (July 1986), announcement of agreement in principle with creditor banks (October 1986), signed (March 1987).

1986   **August 24:** Mexico joins GATT.

1987   **October 19:** Dow Jones Industrial Average falls 508 points.

November 18: Bank of Mexico, losing reserves as Mexican stocks collapse, withdraws support from free-market peso. Opening trading at 1,715 against the controlled rate of 1,723, the free peso plunges to range of 2,200 to 2,500.

December 14: Bank of Mexico devalues official rate of peso 18 percent to 2,200.

1988   **December 1:** President Carlos Salinas inaugurated (2,250 pesos/dollar).

1989   **January 10:** Joaquín Hernández Galicia (*La Quina*) and other leaders of petroleum workers' union arrested and jailed.

April 10: Arrest of Miguel Angel Félix Gallardo, one of Mexico's most powerful drug traffickers.

June 12: Aeroméxico is privatized.

July 3: For first time ever, PRI (Partido Revolucionario Institucional) loses a state governorship (in Baja California).

July 23: Completion of renegotiation of foreign debt.

August 22: Privatization of Compañía Mexicana de Aviación.

November 10: Approval of Pact for Stability and Economic Growth (*Pacto para la Estabilidad y Crecimiento Económico*).

1990   **April 19:** Inauguration of Centro Bursátil 2000.

May 21: Assassination of Norma Corona, president of local Human Rights Commission in the state of Sinaloa.

September 28: Privatization of Compañía Minera de Cananea.

December 13: Privatization of Teléfonos de México.

1991   **June-November:** Privatization of banks.

August 18: Federal elections: PRI wins 290 out of 300 districts and 31 out of 32 Senate seats.

December 5: Reform of Article 27 of Constitution (on land reform); passage of Nueva Ley Agraria.

December 20: Privatization of Altos Hornos de México.

1992   **January 1:** Implementation of free trade agreement with Chile.

January-April, June-July: Bank privatizations continue.

May 13: Kidnapping of Joaquín Vargas, prominent businessman.

July 25: Modification of Article 130 of Constitution, granting legal status to Roman Catholic Church.

October 7: Conclusion of NAFTA negotiations.

December 17: Presidents of Mexico, United States, and Canada sign NAFTA.

1993   **January 1:** New peso, at rate of 1000/1 to old peso and 3.1/dollar; daily devaluations continue with band for peso/dollar relationship.

May 23: Assassination of Cardinal Juan Jesús Posadas Ocampo at Guadalajara airport.

June 30: Recording of single-digit inflation—lowest rate in 20 years.

July 30: Privatization of television *Canal 13*.

August 20: Mexican Constitution amended to provide for independence of Bank of Mexico. Enabling legislation published December 23, effective April 1, 1994. The acts provided that the central bank would conduct monetary policy without direction from the Executive. However, as is the case in many countries, the Treasury retained formal control of exchange rate policy.

September 2: Approval of electoral reform, establishing autonomy of Tribunal Federal Electoral.

September 14: Approval of parallel agreements on labor and environment for NAFTA.

October 3: Approval of Pact for Stability, Competitiveness, and Employment (*Pacto para la Estabilidad, la Competitividad y el Empleo*).

November 18: Mexico admitted to forum for Asia-Pacific Economic Cooperation (APEC).

November 28: PRI selects Luis Donaldo Colosio as candidate for presidential campaign.

1994   **January 1:** NAFTA goes into effect; uprising of EZLN (Zapatista National Liberation Army) in Chiapas.

February 4: U.S. Federal Reserve starts series of interest-rate increases, with Fed Funds rate at 3.0 percent in February 1994 and 6.0 percent in March 1995.

February 28: Mexican foreign exchange position at $29.2 billion.

March 14: Kidnapping of Alfredo Harp Helú, banker and businessman.

March 23: Assassination of PRI presidential candidate Luis Donaldo Colosio in Tijuana.

March 24: Peso devalued 11 percent within previous band.

March 25: Swap line of credit ($6.7 billion) set up by U.S. government to support peso.

March 29: Nomination of Ernesto Zedillo Ponce de León as new PRI candidate for presidency.

April: Mexican government begins issuing *tesobonos* (dollar-linked debt instruments).

April 14: Mexico accepted into Organisation for Economic Co-operation and Development (OECD).

May 12: Congress approves yet another electoral reform, which provides for citizen-councillors on the Federal Election Commission (IFE).

June 13: Signing of free trade agreement with Colombia and Venezuela.

August 21: Ernesto Zedillo wins election.

September 5: Eruption of Grupo Financiero Cremi-Unión business scandal.

September 24: Government announces Pact for Welfare, Stability, and Growth (*Pacto para el Bienestar, la Estabilidad, y el Crecimiento, PABEC*) in hopes of reassuring investment community.

September 28: Assassination of José Francisco Ruíz Massieu, Secretary General of PRI.

October 15: Mexican foreign exchange reserves down to $17 billion.

November 14: Deputy Attorney General Mario Ruíz Massieu charges that PRI officials obstructed his investigation of his brother's murder.

November 15: Federal Reserve boosts Fed Funds rate 75 basis points—largest increase to date.

November 18: Mexican foreign-exchange reserves fall to $13 billion.

November 20: Meeting at presidential residence on possible devaluation of peso; in presence of Zedillo's team, government announces that flotation band of peso against dollar will remain unchanged.

November 20: PRI wins governor's election in Tabasco; PRD claims fraud.

November 23: Mario Ruíz Massieu resigns as Deputy Attorney General, charging high-level participation in cover-up of brother's assassination.

November 30: Zedillo cabinet is announced. Secretary of Finance Pedro Aspe leaves government, replaced by Jamie Serra Puche, who, as Secretary of Commerce, had led the NAFTA negotiation. *Bolsa* drops 50 points.

December 1: President Zedillo inaugurated (3.4 pesos/dollar). Foreign exchange reserves at $12.5 billion.

December 8: Zedillo attends inauguration of Eduardo Robledo Rincón, *priista* governor of Chiapas.

December 18: Renewal of armed hostilities in Chiapas.

December 19: Mexican foreign exchange reserves decline to $6 billion.

December 20: After a hastily called meeting of the *Pacto*, government announces that upper margin of flotation band for peso will be widened by 15.26 percent.

December 21: After widening of band fails to quell attack against peso, government decides to let market freely set the exchange rate.

December 22: Serra Puche travels to New York, fails to convince investors. Peso continues to slide.

December 27: Peso falls to 5.10 per dollar.

317

December 28: Interest rate on 28-day *cetes* increases 15 points, to 31 percent.

December 29: Zedillo announces that government will implement an emergency economic plan, to be revealed by January 2. Serra Puche resigns as Finance Minister and is replaced by Guillermo Ortiz Martínez.

December 31: U.S. President Clinton proposes $40 billion in U.S. loan guarantees for Mexico; foreign exchange position of Mexico $6.2 billion.

1995

January 3: After one-day delay, Zedillo announces Unity Accord to Overcome the Economic Emergency (*Acuerdo de Unidad para Superar la Emergencia Económica, AUSEE*), attributing crisis to unsustainable current-account deficit.

January 17: Through *Pacto de los Pinos*, political parties reach agreement on electoral reform; PRD conditions approval on resolution of disputes over Chiapas and Tabasco.

January 31: Peso falls to 6.50/dollar; President Clinton unveils $50 billion rescue plan with international support.

February 10: PRD withdraws from *Pacto de los Pinos*.

February 12: PRI suffers major loss in gubernatorial election in Jalisco (and mayoral election in Guadalajara).

February 14: Robledo Rincón takes leave of absence as Governor of Chiapas.

February 24: Fausto Alzati resigns as Secretary of Education, suggesting disarray within Zedillo administration.

February 25: Mexico–U.S. loan agreement.

February 28: Raúl Salinas de Gortari is arrested in connection with assassination of Ruíz Massieu.

March 1: Deputy Attorney General Pablo Chapa Bezanilla accuses Mario Ruíz Massieu of obstruction of justice (while heading investigation into death of his brother); Carlos Salinas withdraws candidacy for directorship of World Trade Organization.

March 2: Carlos Salinas initiates hunger strike in order to clear reputation; Mario Ruíz Massieu leaves Mexico.

March 3: Government issues statement exonerating Carlos Salinas of obstruction of investigations of Colosio assassination; while boarding a plane to Madrid, Mario Ruíz Massieu is arrested in Newark, New Jersey, for falsely reporting possession of $8,000 (while actually carrying $40,000).

318

March 4: Carlos Salinas ends fast.

March 9: In yet another effort to stabilize markets, Secretary of Finance Guillermo Ortiz presents the Action Program for Reinforcement of the Unity Accord to Overcome the Economic Emergency (*PARAUSEE*).

March 10: Peso falls to 7.59/dollar.

April 21: Peso appears to stabilize around 6.0/dollar.

April 24: International Monetary Fund declares that "tequila effect" has been contained.

April: Monthly inflation reaches 8 percent.

May 1: Official Labor Day parade is canceled.

May 23: Authorities arrest son of prominent politician (and *salinista* cabinet minister) Carlos Hank González on charges of smuggling and tax evasion, but he is soon released.

May 28: PAN (*Partido de Acción Nacional*) candidate Vicente Fox wins governorship of Guanajuato.

June 9: Government and EZLN initiate third round of negotiations in Chiapas.

June 22: U.S. judge rejects Mexican government request for extradition of Mario Ruíz Massieu.

June 28: Close Zedillo associate Esteban Moctezuma steps down as Secretary of the Interior, to be replaced by Emilio Chuayffet (with strong links to traditional political forces).

June: Open unemployment rate climbs to 6.6 percent (compared with 3.2 percent in December 1994).

July 19: U.S. House of Representatives votes against new disbursements of economic support to Mexico.

August 11: PAN wins governorship of Baja California for second consecutive time.

August 19: María de los Angeles Moreno resigns as president of the PRI; is replaced by Santiago Oñate Laborde.

September 1: Ernesto Zedillo delivers state of the nation address.

September 20: Ex-President Luis Echeverría charges that Salinas had in 1993 been making plans for his own re-election as president.

October 10: Peso slides to 6.82/dollar.

November 1: Peso drops to 7.30/dollar.

November 4: Amid rumors of a possible military coup in Mexico, peso drops to 7.90/dollar.

November 8: Peso falls to 8.20-8.30/dollar.

November 24: Patricia Paulina Castañón, spouse of Raúl Salinas de Gortari, is arrested in Switzerland while attempting to withdraw $84 million from six different bank accounts.

December 1: Ernesto Zedillo completes first year in office.

ABOUT THE AUTHORS

ROBERT L. BARTLEY is Editor and Vice President of *The Wall Street Journal*, where he has guided editorial opinion for over 25 years. He is responsible for the editorials, op-ed articles, and leisure and arts criticism, and he also directs *The Asian Wall Street Journal, The Wall Street Journal Europe,* and *The Wall Street Journal Interactive Edition.* He won a Pulitzer Prize for editorial writing in 1980 and published a book on the Reagan Administration's economic policy, *The Seven Fat Years and How To Do It Again.* Mr. Bartley has written extensively on Mexico since 1981.

NANCY BIRDSALL is the Executive Vice-President of the Inter-American Development Bank. Prior to joining the Bank, she held various policy and management positions at the World Bank. She has been a senior advisor to the Rockefeller Foundation and a member of various study committees of the National Academy of Sciences. She has written extensively on development issues, most recently on income distribution in Asia and Latin America, and is a co-editor of *Beyond Trade-Offs: Market Reforms and Equitable Growth in Latin America* (1998).

SHAHID JAVED BURKI has been Regional Vice President for Latin America and the Caribbean at the World Bank since January 1994. From 1987 to 1994, he was the Bank's Country Director for China. Prior to joining the Bank in 1974, Mr. Burki, a citizen of Pakistan, served in senior positions in the Pakistan government and was a Senior Fellow of Harvard University's Development Advisory Service. His many publications include (with Guillermo Perry) *The Long March: A Reform Agenda for Latin America and the Caribbean in the Next Decade* (1997). Mr. Burki was a Rhodes Scholar at Oxford University and a Masons Fellow at Harvard.

AGUSTÍN CARSTENS is Director General for Economic Research at the Bank of Mexico. Previous positions he has held at the Bank of Mexico have been: Chief of Staff of the Governor, and Treasurer. He holds a doctorate in economics from the University of Chicago.

RUDI DORNBUSCH is Ford Professor of Economics and International Management at the Massachusetts Institute of Technology, where he has taught since 1975. He was born in Germany, studied in Switzerland, and received his doctorate from the University of Chicago in 1971. He is a fellow of the Econometric Society and the American Academy of Science, Honorary Professor of the University of the Pacific in Lima (Peru), and holds an honorary doctorate from the University of Basle.

DENISE DRESSER is a Professor of Political Science at the Instituto Tecnológico Autónomo de México (ITAM). She has been a Visiting Fellow at the Center for U.S.-Mexican Studies, University of California, San Diego, and at the Inter-American Dialogue in Washington. Dr. Dresser is the author of

Neopopulist Solutions to Neoliberal Problems: Mexico's National Solidarity Program and numerous articles on Mexican politics and U.S.–Mexico relations; writes a column for the newspaper *Reforma*; hosts a political talk show on Mexican television; and is a regular contributor to the editorial pages of the *Los Angeles Times* and the *Globe and Mail*. She received her Ph.D. from Princeton University.

SEBASTIAN EDWARDS is the Henry Ford II Professor of International Business Economics at UCLA's Anderson Graduate School of Management. He was previously Chief Economist for the Latin America and Caribbean Region at the World Bank and has been a consultant to other multilateral institutions, including the Inter-American Development Bank, the IMF, and the OECD. He has published widely on international economics, macroeconomics, and economic development. His latest book is *Labor Markets in Latin America: Combining Social Protection with Market Flexibility* (1997). Born and educated in Chile, he holds a Ph.D. from the University of Chicago.

JEFFRY A. FRIEDEN is a Professor of Government at Harvard University. He specializes in the politics of international monetary and financial relations. He is the author of *Banking on the World: The Politics of American International Finance* (1987), and *Debt, Development, and Democracy: Modern Political Economy and Latin America, 1965-1985* (1991). His co-edited works include (with Barry Eichengreen) *Forging an Integrated Europe* (1998); (with Barry Eichengreen and Jürgen von Hagen) *Monetary and Fiscal Policy in an Integrated Europe* (1995); and (with David Lake) *International Political Economy: Perspectives on Global Power and Wealth*, third edition (1995).

MICHAEL GAVIN is Lead Research Economist at the Inter-American Development Bank. Prior to joining the IDB, he was an Associate Professor of Economics at Columbia University. He has also worked in the International Finance Division of the U.S. Federal Reserve Board, and has been visiting scholar with or consultant to the IMF, the Federal Reserve Board, the World Bank, and the Bank of Jamaica. His research interests include determinants and consequences of macroeconomic volatility, fiscal policy in Latin America, and the implications of financial fragility for monetary and exchange rate policy.

FRANCISCO GIL-DÍAZ was recently named Director General of the Mexican telecommunications company Avantel, S.A. From 1994 to 1997, he served as Vice Governor of the Bank of Mexico. He previously served as Under Secretary in the Mexican Department of Finance and Public Credit. Dr. Gil-Díaz received his doctorate in economics from the University of Chicago.

DAVID D. HALE is the Global Chief Economist for the Zurich Group, which he joined following its acquisition of the Kemper Corporation, where he was Chief Economist for many years. Mr. Hale writes on a broad range of economic subjects and frequently testifies before U.S. Congressional committees and briefs senior government officials on economic policy issues. He is a member of the Financial Instruments Steering Committee of the Chicago Mercantile Exchange, the Academic Advisory Board of the Federal Reserve Bank of Chicago, and a variety of government and private economic policy research groups in Washington, Tokyo, and Bonn.

RICARDO HAUSMANN is the Chief Economist of the Inter-American Development Bank. He previously served as the Minister of Coordination and Planning of Venezuela, as the Chairman of the Joint Development Committee of the International Monetary Fund and the World Bank, and as Director of the Board of the Central Bank of Venezuela. He founded the Center of Public Policy at the Instituto de Estudios Superiores de Administración in Venezuela, where he is a Professor of Economics (currently on leave). His recent publications deal with macroeconomic volatility, banking crises, budgetary institutions, and the organization of social services.

CLAUDIO M. LOSER, an Argentine national, has had an extensive career in the International Monetary Fund and since December 1994 has been Director of the Western Hemisphere Department. He holds a Ph.D. in economics from the University of Chicago and an economics degree from the Universidad Nacional de Cuyo in Argentina.

MOISÉS NAÍM is the Editor of *Foreign Policy* magazine. Between 1992 and 1996, he was a Senior Associate at the Carnegie Endowment for International Peace, directing the programs on Economic Reforms and on Latin America. Dr. Naím has served as Venezuela's Minister of Trade and Industry, Executive Director and Senior Adviser to the President of the World Bank, and Professor and Dean of IESA in Caracas. He has written extensively on economic reforms, the politics and economics of international trade and investment, and the many facets of globalization. He holds a doctorate from the Massachusetts Institute of Technology.

PETER H. SMITH is a Professor of Political Science, the Simón Bolivar Professor of Latin American Studies, and Director of Latin American Studies at the University of California, San Diego. His published work includes *Labyrinths of Power: Political Recruitment in Twentieth-Century Mexico* and numerous articles on Mexican politics. His latest book is *Talons of the Eagle: Dynamics of U.S.–Latin American Relations* (Oxford University Press, 1996).

EWART S. WILLIAMS has had a long career in the International Monetary Fund and since May 1993 has been Assistant Director, in charge of the Mexico/Latin Caribbean Division of the Western Hemisphere Department. A national of Trinidad and Tobago, he holds an M.Sc. in economics from the University of the West Indies, Trinidad and Tobago.

THE CARNEGIE ENDOWMENT FOR INTERNATIONAL PEACE

The Carnegie Endowment for International Peace was established in 1910 in Washington, D.C., with a gift from Andrew Carnegie. As a tax-exempt operating (not grant-making) foundation, the Endowment conducts programs of research, discussion, publication, and education in international affairs and U.S. foreign policy. The Endowment publishes the quarterly magazine, *Foreign Policy*.

Carnegie's senior associates—whose backgrounds include government, journalism, law, academia, and public affairs—bring to their work substantial first-hand experience in foreign policy. Through writing, public and media appearances, study groups, and conferences, Carnegie associates seek to invigorate and extend both expert and public discussion on a wide range of international issues, including worldwide migration, nuclear nonproliferation, regional conflicts, multilateralism, democracy-building, and the use of force. The Endowment also engages in and encourages projects designed to foster innovative contributions in international affairs.

In 1993, the Carnegie Endowment committed its resources to the establishment of a public policy research center in Moscow designed to promote intellectual collaboration among scholars and specialists in the United States, Russia, and other post-Soviet states. Together with the Endowment's associates in Washington, the center's staff of Russian and American specialists conduct programs on a broad range of major policy issues ranging from economic reform to civil-military relations. The Carnegie Moscow Center holds seminars, workshops, and study groups at which international participants from academia, government, journalism, the private sector, and nongovernmental institutions gather to exchange views. It also provides a forum for prominent international figures to present their views to informed Moscow audiences. Associates of the center also host seminars in Kiev on an equally broad set of topics.

The Endowment normally does not take institutional positions on public policy issues. It supports its activities primarily from its own resources, supplemented by nongovernmental, philanthropic grants.

Carnegie Endowment for International Peace
1779 Massachusetts Ave., N.W.
Washington, D.C. 20036
Tel: 202-483-7600
Fax: 202-483-1840
e-mail: carnegie@ceip.org
Web Page: www.ceip.org

Carnegie Moscow Center
Ul. Tverskaya 16/2
7th Floor
Moscow 103009
Tel: 7-095-935-8904
Fax: 7-095-935-8906
e-mail: info@carnegie.ru
Web Page: www.carnegie.ru